New Inside Out

Sue Kay, Vaughan Jones,

Helena Gomm, Peter Maggs

& Chris Dawson

Pre-intermediate

Teacher's Book

MACMILLAN

Macmillan Education
Between Towns Road, Oxford OX4 3PP
A division of Macmillan Publishers Limited
Companies and representatives throughout the world

ISBN 978-1-4050-9965-3

Text © Sue Kay and Vaughan Jones 2008
Text by Helena Gomm
Language and cultural notes by Peter Maggs
Photocopiable resource materials by Peter Maggs, with Carmen Santos Maldonado,
Katherine Stannett, Jon Hird, Simone Foster, Matthew Jones and David Seymour
Design and illustration © Macmillan Publishers Limited 2008

First published 2008

Designed by 320 Design Limited
Page layout by Carolyn Gibson
Illustrated by Kathy Baxendale, Beach, Neil Chapman, Ivan Gillet, Rebecca Halls,
Peter Harper, Ben Hasler, Katie Mac, Ed McLachlan, Bill Piggins and Mark Ruffle
Cover design by Andrew Oliver

The authors and publishers would like to thank the following for permission to reproduce
their material:
Quotation from *Language and Problems of Knowledge* by Noam Chomsky copyright © Noam
Chomsky 1988 Massachusetts Institute of Technology, reprinted by permission of The
MIT Press, Cambridge, Massachusetts. Quotation from *Understanding Second Language
Acquisition* by Rod Ellis copyright © Rod Ellis 1985, reproduced by permission of
Oxford University Press.

The authors and publisher are grateful for permission to reprint the following copyright
material:

Stand By Me composed by Jerry Leiber, Mike Stoller, Ben E King, reprinted by permission
of Hornall Brothers Music Ltd.
Suspicious Minds Words by Francis Zambon, copyright © Sony/ATV Music Publishing
Limited, reprinted by permission of the publishers. All Rights Reserved.
Money (That's What I Want) Words and Music by Berry Gordy Jr and Janie Bradford
copyright © Jobete Music Co Inc/Jobec Music/EMI Music Publishing Limited 1959,
reprinted by permission of EMI Music Publishing Ltd, London, WC2H 0QY and
International Music Publications Ltd (a trading name of Faber Music Ltd). All Rights
Reserved.
I Have a Dream Words and Music by B Andersson/B Ulvaeus, reprinted by permission of
Bocu Music Ltd.

These materials may contain links for third party websites. We have no control over, and
are not responsible for, the contents of such third party websites. Please use care when
accessing them.

Although we have tried to trace and contact copyright holders before publication, in some
cases this has not been possible. If contacted, we will be pleased to rectify any errors or
omissions at the earliest opportunity.

Printed in Thailand

2012   2011   2010   2009
10 9 8 7 6 5 4 3 2

Contents

Student's Book contents map

(WB) = **Workbook**. Each unit of the Workbook contains a one-page section which develops practical writing skills.

Introduction

Welcome to *New Inside Out!*

New Inside Out is the fruit of many years teaching, writing and developing material. Everything we write is informed by the reactions we get from our students. Our aim is simply to produce a set of materials that will help you create optimum conditions in your classroom for learning to take place.

Sue Kay *Vaughan Jones*

Engaging content

The American linguist and philosopher Noam Chomsky once said:

'The truth of the matter is that about 99% of teaching is making the students feel interested in the material. Then the other 1% has to do with your methods'.

While we might want to quibble with the percentages, we would nevertheless agree whole-heartedly with the central message in Professor Chomsky's assertion: namely, students learn best when they're interested in the material. It's as simple as that. A text might contain six beautifully-crafted examples of the past simple, a good spread of high frequency lexical items and exemplify some useful functional language, but if it doesn't engage the students, if they can't relate to it, if it feels alien to them, then the most important ingredient for successful learning is missing.

In *New Inside Out*, we've drawn on our own classroom experience, and that of our colleagues around the world, to select topics, texts and tasks that engage students both emotionally and intellectually. Students are our richest resource. They come to class with their own knowledge of the world, their own tastes, feelings and opinions. It's up to us to exploit this rich resource by organising learning around topics that they can relate to – topics that are part of their life experience.

Structured support

We all know that learning a language is a messy, non-linear business. We're dismayed when there seems to be little correlation between what is taught and what is learned! However, there is plenty of evidence to suggest that 'instructed' learners (those who attend classes or follow a course of study) learn faster, and ultimately attain a higher level of proficiency than 'non-instructed' learners.

In *New Inside Out*, new language input is carefully controlled: we aim to maximise exposure to high frequency language appropriate to this level. Students are encouraged to notice new grammar and new vocabulary in contexts where the meaning is clear. They are then given opportunities to manipulate the new language and try it out in different situations. They discover why using one particular form rather than another one actually matters: not just because it's right or wrong, but because it does or doesn't communicate a meaning successfully. The emphasis is always on what students can do with the language rather than what they know about the language. The new language is systematically reviewed and recycled until finally the students feel confident enough to use it to make their own meanings. It becomes part of their available repertoire. It has been 'learned'.

Real world tasks

We're strong believers in the old adage: 'practice makes perfect'. *New Inside Out* emphasises output, particularly speaking, and there are a huge number of tasks that are designed to develop fluency. Students practise functional language in sections entitled *Useful phrases*. But for the most part, the speaking tasks simply encourage the students to talk about things that actually matter to them, rather than playing roles or exchanging invented information. One of our main objectives is to ensure that the language our students spend time rehearsing in the classroom is transferable to the real world. By orchestrating tasks that require the students to use grammar and vocabulary to make meaningful utterances, this objective becomes obtainable. As the linguist and academic Rod Ellis reminds us:

'It is the need to get meanings across and the pleasure experienced when this is achieved that motivates second language acquisition.'

www.insideout.net
'the art of communication'

Components of the course

Student's materials

- Student's Book *see page viii–x*
- CD-ROM *see page xi*
- Workbook and Audio CD *see page xi*

Teacher's materials

- Teacher's Book
  see page xii
- Class Audio CDs
  see page xii
- Test CD *see page xii*
- DVD *see page xiii*
- DVD Teacher's Book
  see page xiii
- Website *see page xiii*

Student's Book page 68

A language menu at the beginning of each unit summarises the main teaching points.

Headings throughout the units provide clear information about what the students are studying.

Motivating reading texts have been adapted and graded to suit the Pre-intermediate level student. They have been selected not only for their language content, but also for their interest and appropriacy.

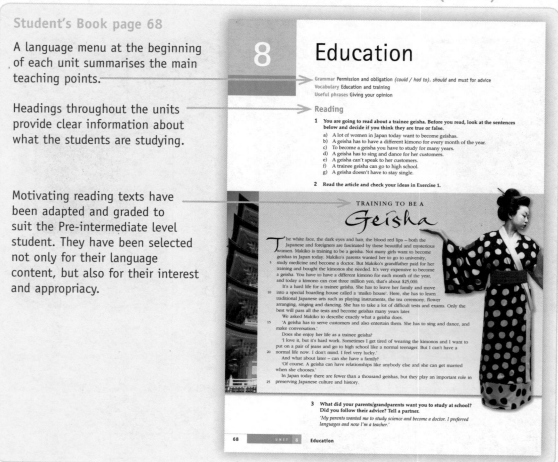

8 Education

Grammar Permission and obligation (could / had to). should and must for advice
Vocabulary Education and training
Useful phrases Giving your opinion

Reading

1 You are going to read about a trainee geisha. Before you read, look at the sentences below and decide if you think they are true or false.
   a) A lot of women in Japan today want to become geishas.
   b) A geisha has to have a different kimono for every month of the year.
   c) To become a geisha you have to study for many years.
   d) A geisha has to sing and dance for her customers.
   e) A geisha can't speak to her customers.
   f) A trainee geisha can go to high school.
   g) A geisha doesn't have to stay single.

2 Read the article and check your ideas in Exercise 1.

TRAINING TO BE A Geisha

The white face, the dark eyes and hair, the blood red lips – both the Japanese and foreigners are fascinated by these beautiful and mysterious women. Makiko is training to be a geisha. Not many girls want to become geishas in Japan today. Makiko's parents wanted her to go to university, study medicine and become a doctor. But Makiko's grandfather paid for her training and bought the kimonos she needed. It's very expensive to become a geisha. You have to have a different kimono for each month of the year, and today a kimono can cost three million yen, that's about $25,000.

It's a hard life for a trainee geisha. She has to leave her family and move into a special boarding house called a 'maiko house'. Here, she has to learn traditional Japanese arts such as playing instruments, the tea ceremony, flower arranging, singing and dancing. She has to take a lot of difficult tests and exams. Only the best will pass all the tests and become geishas many years later.

We asked Makiko to describe exactly what a geisha does.
'A geisha has to serve customers and also entertain them. She has to sing and dance, and make conversation.'

Does she enjoy her life as a trainee geisha?
'I love it, but it's hard work. Sometimes I get tired of wearing the kimonos and I want to put on a pair of jeans and go to high school like a normal teenager. But I can't have a normal life now. I don't mind. I feel very lucky.'

And what about later – can she have a family?
'Of course. A geisha can have relationships like anybody else and she can get married when she chooses.'

In Japan today there are fewer than a thousand geishas, but they play an important role in preserving Japanese culture and history.

3 What did your parents/grandparents want you to study at school? Did you follow their advice? Tell a partner.
   'My parents wanted me to study science and become a doctor. I preferred languages and now I'm a teacher.'

68 UNIT 8 Education

Student's Book page 69

Vocabulary is presented in context and is related to the themes and topics in the unit.

Pronunciation work on particular areas of sound, stress and intonation is integrated into every unit.

Anecdotes give students a chance to tackle a longer piece of discourse.

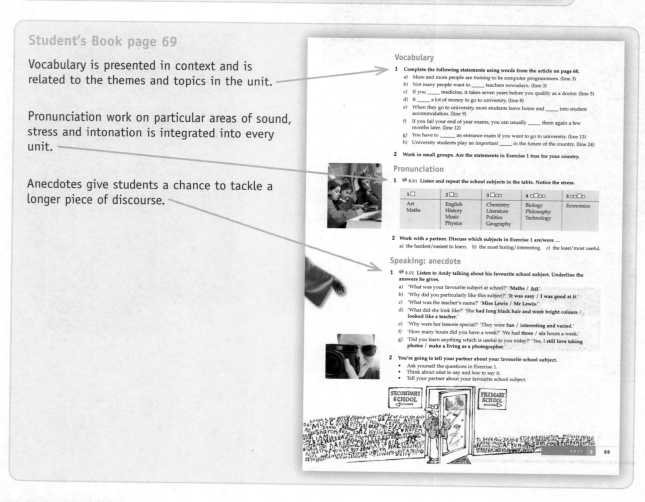

Vocabulary

1 Complete the following statements using words from the article on page 68.
   a) More and more people are *training* to be computer programmers. (line 3)
   b) Not many people want to _____ teachers nowadays. (line 3)
   c) If you _____ medicine, it takes seven years before you qualify as a doctor. (line 5)
   d) It _____ a lot of money to go to university. (line 8)
   e) When they go to university, most students leave home and _____ into student accommodation. (line 9)
   f) If you fail your end of year exams, you can usually _____ them again a few months later. (line 12)
   g) You have to _____ an entrance exam if you want to go to university. (line 13)
   h) University students play an important _____ in the future of the country. (line 24)

2 Work in small groups. Are the statements in Exercise 1 true for your country?

Pronunciation

1 8.01 Listen and repeat the school subjects in the table. Notice the stress.

1 □	2 □□	3 □□□	4 □□□□	5 □□□□
Art	English	Chemistry	Biology	Economics
Maths	History	Literature	Philosophy	
	Music	Politics	Technology	
	Physics	Geography		

2 Work with a partner. Discuss which subjects in Exercise 1 are/were …
   a) the hardest/easiest to learn. b) the most boring/interesting. c) the least/most useful.

Speaking: anecdote

1 8.02 Listen to Andy talking about his favourite school subject. Underline the answers he gives.
   a) 'What was your favourite subject at school?' 'Maths / Art.'
   b) 'Why did you particularly like this subject?' 'It was easy / I was good at it.'
   c) 'What was the teacher's name?' 'Miss Lewis / Mr Lewis.'
   d) 'What did she look like?' 'She had long black hair and wore bright colours / looked like a teacher.'
   e) 'Why were her lessons special?' 'They were fun / interesting and varied.'
   f) 'How many hours did you have a week?' 'We had three / six hours a week.'
   g) 'Did you learn anything which is useful to you today?' 'Yes, I still love taking photos / make a living as a photographer.'

2 You're going to tell your partner about your favourite school subject.
   • Ask yourself the questions in Exercise 1.
   • Think about *what* to say and *how* to say it.
   • Tell your partner about your favourite school subject.

UNIT 8 69

Student's Book page 71

New Inside Out Pre-intermediate includes an average of two grammar sections in every unit. Typically, these follow a five-stage approach.

1 Students explore new grammatical structures.

2 Students focus on the way the new language works.

3 Students listen to the sentences and do choral repetition of the new language.

4 The practice stage is designed to be realistic and meaningful.

5 Students use the target sentences for controlled, personalised practice.

Additional support is provided in the margin.

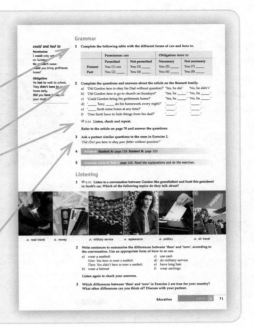

Student's Book page 71

There is one pairwork for every unit which offers further speaking practice. These are clearly labelled for the student.

The listenings include texts specially written for language learning. There are dialogues, conversations and monologues. There is a variety of English accents and the tasks are designed to develop real-life listening skills.

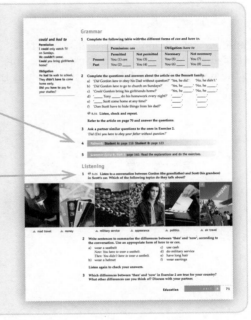

Student's Book page 73

Here is another example of a typical grammar section.

Additional support is provided in the margin.

In addition, students are referred to the *Grammar Extra* pages at the back of the Student's Book for extended explanations and further practice.

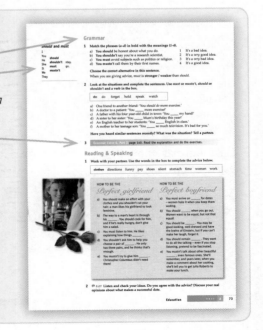

Student's Book page 74

Useful phrases gives students a portable toolkit of functional language. These sections are designed to be fun and engaging and the phrases are recorded on the Audio CD.

Student's Book page 75

The *Vocabulary Extra* pages at the end of every unit recycle the key vocabulary items taught in the unit. This provides students with an activated wordlist and a useful bank of vocabulary.

The *Focus on* section singles out a specific area of high frequency vocabulary and provides extra practice.

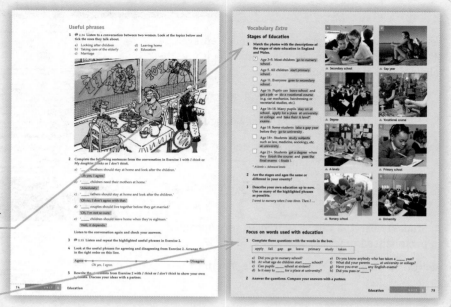

Student's Book page 84

There are four Review units in *New Inside Out* Pre-intermediate Student's Book. Each Review unit revises the new structures taught in the previous three teaching units.

Student's Book pages 140 and 141

The *Grammar Extra* pages at the back of the Student's Book provide a summary of the new grammatical structures as well as extra practice.

Each unit has one full page of explanations and exercises.

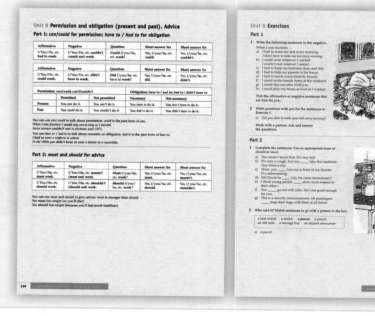

CD-ROM

The CD-ROM in the back of every Student's Book provides a wealth of interactive practice activities along with integrated listening material and video clips contextualising the *Useful phrases*.

Workbook pages 46 and 47

The Workbook provides revision of all the main points in the Student's Book, plus extra listening practice, pronunciation work and a complete self-contained writing course. There are *with* and *without key* versions, and an extract from the *The Dancing Men* (Macmillan Graded Reader) is included in the back of the Workbook.

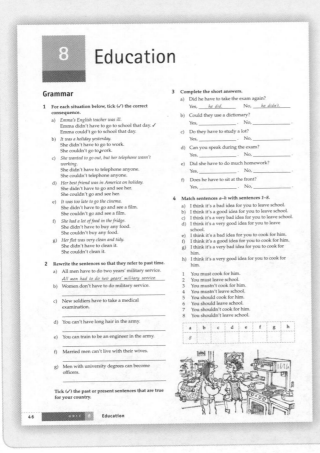

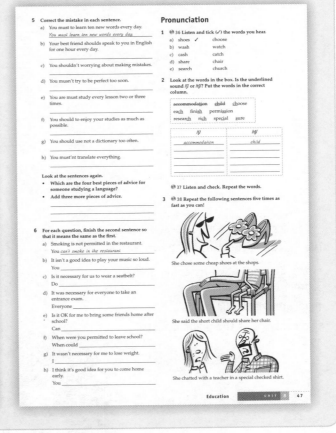

Teacher's materials

The 6-in-1 Teacher's Book contains:

- an Introduction
- Practical methodology
- Council of Europe (CEF) checklists
- complete teaching notes with answer keys
- a bank of extra photocopiable grammar, vocabulary and communicative activities
- a Test CD with word files that you can edit and the recordings of the listening test activities

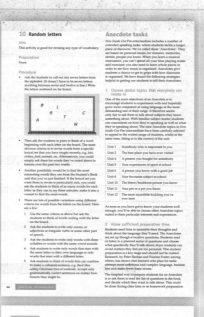

Class CD set

The Class CDs contain:

- the dialogues and listening activities from the Student's Book
- recordings of the songs
- recordings of the reading texts

DVD and DVD Teacher's Book

The DVD contains programmes which complement the topics in the Student's Book. There is a wide variety of formats including interviews, profiles, documentaries and video diaries. The DVD Teacher's Book contains related teaching notes and photocopiable worksheets.

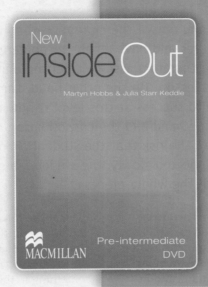

Website

www.insideout.net

Visit www.insideout.net to find out more details about the course and its authors. The new magazine-style website provides downloadable resources and more information about *New Inside Out*.

Practical methodology

Teaching pre-intermediate students

In many ways, pre-intermediate is the one of the more rewarding levels to teach. Students have seen most of the basic structures and have a core vocabulary enabling them to 'get by' in most situations. The teacher can therefore assume a certain amount of knowledge and this helps the pace and flow of the lesson. On the other hand, there are still plenty of new language areas to explore. The key to success at this level is how to strike the right balance between forward progress on the one hand and the consolidation of 'learned' language on the other. If you go too fast, there's the risk that the students' more basic errors become permanent 'fossilised' errors. If you go too slowly, the students are likely to become bored, demotivated and disenchanted with the whole process.

In *New Inside Out* Pre-intermediate we've tried to get this balance right. Students are challenged to explore new grammar and vocabulary, but they mix this with important recycling and consolidation work in more familiar areas. A relentless focus on meaning, and in particular how students can make their own meanings with the language, is built into every stage of the learning process. It's this core feature of *Inside Out* which helps students maintain their enthusiasm and motivation.

Right from the start

Every teacher has their own way of setting up their classroom, interacting with their students and conducting their lessons. Here are a few things that we have found useful to bear in mind.

The right atmosphere

It's important to do everything you can to create a supportive learning environment. Start by memorising every student's name and learn as much information as you can about them. Make sure students learn each other's names too and that they all get to know things about each other early on in the course. Think of appropriate ways you could help foster good classroom dynamics. For example, you could nominate a 'homework partner' for each student. They'd then be responsible for collecting handouts or passing on lesson notes or homework instructions when their partner is absent.

Pay attention to how you respond to students both individually and collectively. Make sure you find time to chat to individual students or small informal groups of students before or after class. More formally, it's a good idea to devote at least one lesson per term to counsel your students individually and discuss their progress.

Even at pre-intermediate level students are often shy and under-confident about speaking in class. As anyone who has learnt a foreign language will know, it takes a great deal of courage to open your mouth and say something in the very early stages of a course. Yet we know that the sooner you start, the more practice you get, the more confident you feel and the easier it becomes. For this reason, students are encouraged to work in pairs and groups so they can rehearse the language in private rather than be immediately required to speak in the more intimidating arena of the class.

Always give your students time to think. It's perfectly normal to have moments of silence while students absorb and process new information, write down new vocabulary from the board, or think about their answers. Don't be afraid of the pregnant pause!

The right environment

Your classroom might be the only exposure to English that students get. Make that exposure as rich as you can by decorating the walls with maps and posters. Here are some further ideas:

- Stick up useful formulaic phrases. For example, *Can you spell that please?*, *Can you repeat that please?*, or *What does XXX mean?*, etc.

- Keep a 'wordbox' on your table where words or phrases that come up in the lesson are recorded on strips of paper and put in the box. Invite the students to record the words for you. They can then be used in a variety of quick revision games in subsequent lessons. Alternatively, you could institute the 'class scribe' idea. One student in the class is given the role of recording any new language that comes up during the lesson that isn't necessarily the target language of that lesson. This record is then photocopied for everyone in the class, including the teacher, who can use the data for revision activities. The role of class scribe is rotated.

- Introduce your students to simplified graded readers. Many of them now come as 'talking books' with CDs. This is invaluable input. Get your students hooked on books!

- Use English in the classroom. It's very tempting to slip into the students' language – particularly if you are teaching in a monolingual situation. Try only to use L1 as an absolute last resort: an occasional quick translation or brief explanation.

The right learning skills

Students will always benefit from help with learning strategies. Here are some thoughts:

- Spend time encouraging students to experiment with how they record words and phrases from the lesson. Get them to draw the word rather than translate it. They're then associating the word with the concept rather than with another word. Make sure they note the part of speech – verb, noun, adjective, etc. Tell them to find a way of noting the pronunciation of the word, either using phonemic script (in the back of the Student's Book) or by developing their own system. Ask them to write complete personalised sentences putting the new word or phrase in a real context and thereby making it more memorable.

- A dictionary is a very important language learning tool and most students will buy one. Usually students prefer a bilingual dictionary as this provides them with a quick translation of the word they need. Spend time showing them all the other information that a dictionary can give them, in particular the phonetic symbols. Work with monolingual dictionaries in the classroom.

The right amount of practice

In our experience, the most successful lessons consist of a manageable amount of new input, and then a lot of meaningful practice. For this reason, we've tried to provide maximum practice activities in *New Inside Out*, both in the Student's Book and in the other supporting components. But there is never enough time in the lessons alone. Always set homework, even if it's just reading a chapter from a reader, and make homework feedback or correction an integral part of the lesson.

The top 10 activities for pre-intermediate students

These tried and trusted activities can be used as lead-ins, warmers, fillers, pair-forming activities, or for revision and recycling. Most of them require very little or no preparation and can be adapted to cover a wide variety of different language points. You may be familiar with some of the ideas and others may be new. In any event, we hope they provide a useful extension to your teaching repertoire. They certainly get used and re-used in our own classrooms!

It's always useful to have a stock of small white cards and access to a stock of pictures. Magazine pictures are ideal, and can be filed in alphabetical order according to topics.

1 Board bingo

Aim

This activity is good for revising any type of vocabulary.

Preparation

Write down twelve to fifteen words you want to revise on the board.

Procedure

- Ask the students to choose five of the words and write them down. When they've done that, tell the students that you're going to read out dictionary definitions of the words in random order and that they should cross out their words if they think they hear the definition. When they've crossed out all five words, they shout *Bingo!* Make sure you keep a record of the word definitions you call out so that you can check the students' answers.

- If you teach a monolingual class, you could read out a translation of each word rather than an English definition. Alternatively, you could turn it into a pronunciation exercise by working on the recognition of phonetic script. Hold up cards with phonetic transcriptions of the words in random order. Students cross out their words if they think they've seen the corresponding phonetic transcription.

2 Standing in line

Aim

This is a great way to review names after Unit 1.

Preparation

None.

Procedure

Ask all the students to stand up and then line up in alphabetical order according to the first letter of their first name. Show the class where the line should begin. Once they've lined up, check that they're in the correct order by asking them to take it in turns down the line to say *My name's …*

- Here are some more criteria for different line-ups.

  1 Alphabetical order according to their surnames or their mother's or father's first name, or a random selection of words that you want to revise written on cards (they say the words out aloud and line up according to the first letter).

  2 Numerical order according to age or age of mother, or age of youngest member of their family, or number of cousins they have (most/fewest), or number of times they've been to London, etc.

  3 Distance order (furthest/nearest) according to distance they live from the school, or distance they were born from the school, or longest distance they have ever walked, cycled or driven, etc.

  4 Time order according to the time they got up this morning, or the time they went to bed last night, or the time they started work, or their favourite time of the day, etc.

  5 Spelling order according to long words they know. Give each student a letter of the word you want to revise and ask them to sort themselves out into the correct order to spell the word. Here's a selection of words you might want to revise from Unit 1: *colleague, exercise, fashionable, neighbour, signature, technique,* etc.

  6 Word order according to a sentence with at least eight words in it. Give each student a word and ask them to sort themselves out so that the sentence makes sense.

3 Battleships

Aim

To revise vocabulary.

Preparation

Each student will need two grids of 10 squares across and down (see below). Graph paper is ideal for this activity.

Procedure

- Demonstrate the activity by drawing a blank grid on the board. Think of a word or words you want to revise and write them onto a different grid on a piece of paper, but do not tell the students what they are yet. You should write the words horizontally, one letter per square, as shown below.

	1	2	3	4	5	6	7	8	9	10
A	p	y	j	a	m	a	s			
B								t	i	e
C		g	l	o	v	e	s			
D										
E			e	a	r	r	i	n	g	s
F										
G										
H		s	u	i	t					
I										
J					t	i	g	h	t	s

- Now tell the students that there are some words hidden in the grid. Explain that they need to find the squares with letters in them. Tell them to guess squares by giving letter and number references. For example, C–2, F–10, J–4, etc. When a student guesses a square with a letter in, write the letter in the square. They can guess a word when they think they know what it is. Continue like this until they've found all the words.

- Now ask the students to work in pairs. First, they should draw two grids. One of them should remain blank, and on the other they need to write down six words, but without showing their partner. Either you can let the students choose their own words from the ones they've learnt recently, or else you can give them a topic. For example, write six nationalities / jobs / classroom objects / weather conditions / animals.

- When they've written their words, tell the students to take it in turns to name a square on their partner's grid. If there's a letter in the square, their partner should say what the letter is and they should write it in the blank grid.

- As soon as they think they know their partner's word, they can guess. If it's wrong, they miss a turn.

4 Category dictation

Aim

This activity can be adapted to review almost any vocabulary. It can also be used to review certain pronunciation and grammar points.

Preparation

Choose the language you want to review and devise a way of categorising it into two or more categories.

Procedure

- Write the category headings on the board and ask the students to copy them onto a piece of paper. Two simple categories is usually best. More than three can get complicated. Then dictate the words (10–12 maximum) slowly and clearly, and ask the students to write them down in the correct category.

  For example, you want to revise jobs from Unit 6, your categories might be jobs you do inside and jobs you do outside. So, write the following on the board and ask the students to copy it down.

Inside	Outside

- Then dictate the words: e.g. *a farmer, an archaeologist, a surgeon, an au pair, a vet*, etc. The students write down the words in the correct category. When you've dictated 10 or 12 words, ask students to compare their lists. When they've done this, ask them to call out their answers and write them on the board in the correct category, so that they can check the spelling. Alternatively, you could ask the students to take it in turns to write the answers on the board.

- Here are some more ideas for categories:

  1 Revise family words. (Unit 1)
    Suggested categories: *Male* or *Female, Have* or *Don't have* (this will obviously lead to different answers for each student).

  2 Revise adjectives to describe places. (Unit 2)
    Suggested categories: *Positive* or *Negative, Can describe where we are now* or *Can't describe where we are now*.

  3 Revise past tense forms. (Unit 3)
    Suggested categories: *Regular* or *Irregular, Past form the same as the infinitive* (e.g. *beat / beat, hit / hit, set / set*, etc.) or *Past form different from the infinitive* (e.g. *choose / chose, forget / forgot, ride / rode*, etc.)

  4 Revise sports. (Unit 5)
    Suggested categories: *Sports with a ball* and *Sports without a ball; Sports you play in teams* and *Sports you play individually; Sports you use 'go' with* or *Sports you use 'play' with*.

  5 Revise parts of the body (Unit 9)
    Suggested categories: *Above the waist* and *Below the waist*, or *You have one of these* and *You have two of these*.

5 Mill drills

Aim

To provide controlled practice of new language in a drill-like way and to give students the opportunity to repeat the same language with several different partners.

Preparation

Organise your classroom so that the students can move around and speak to one another. Prepare one prompt card for each student in the class. The prompts will depend on the language you want to practise. (See below for examples of cue cards.)

Procedure

- Tell the students that they're going to spend 10 to 15 minutes practising the new language, and that you're going to demonstrate this.

- Give one card to each student in the class, and keep one for yourself. Write a sample dialogue on the board. Point to the part of the dialogue to be supplied by the picture or word prompts on the card. For example:

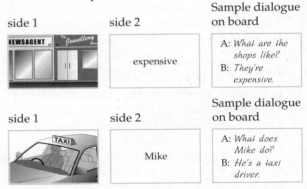

- Explain that the language will change according to the prompt on the card. Show the students how to hold their cards. This is important because cards must be held in such a way that when the students are talking to a partner, they're both able to see each other's cards.

- Choose a confident student to demonstrate the activity with you. Then ask two or three pairs of students to demonstrate the dialogue.

- Ask all the students to stand up and to go round the class or group, repeating the dialogue with as many different partners as possible, and using their cards as prompts.

- Stop the activity after a few moments and ask the students to either exchange cards with another student, or turn their card around so that students get the opportunity to make new responses.

6 Five favourites

Aim

This activity is good for revising any words learnt recently.

Preparation

None

Procedure

- Students look back through their lesson notes for the last two weeks and select from the words they've recorded five words that they think are particularly useful. They compare their list with a partner and together they produce a common list of five words from the combined list of ten. To do this they'll have to argue for and against words on the combined list until they are both satisfied that they have the most useful five. If you wanted to continue the activity, you could then have each pair join up with another pair as a group of four and repeat the procedure. Depending on the size of your class, you might continue until you had established a list of 'five favourites' for the whole class.

- The value of this activity lies in the students looking back through their notes, choosing the words and then arguing for them to be part of the combined list. The whole procedure gives them valuable repeat exposure to words recently learned.

- A possible extension activity after each pair has formed their common list of five words is to collect the lists and redistribute them so that each pair has a different list. The pairs then write a dialogue or short story incorporating the five words they have on the list they've just received. You could then ask them to read out their dialogues or stories and the other students guess what the five listed words were.

7 Crosswords

Aim

This activity is good for revising lexical sets and can help with spelling.

Preparation

Choose a lexical set you want to revise. For example, *places in a city* (Unit 2), *office equipment* (Unit 6), *school subjects* (Unit 8), *food* (Unit 10), *animals* (Unit 11), etc.

Procedure

- Students work in pairs. They'll need a piece of paper, preferably graph paper with squares on.

- Choose a topic, for example, *school subjects*.

- Student A writes 'Across' words, and Student B writes 'Down' words.

- It's a good idea to provide the first word across, and make sure that it's a long one. Student B then adds another school subject down the paper from top to bottom. This word must intersect with the school subject written across the page.

- Student A then writes another school subject across that intersects with the school subject Student B has written down. Students continue taking it in turns to write in their words.

- Students build up a crossword until they can't think of any more school subjects. (You could make it into a game by saying that the last person to write a school subject is a winner.) Note that students must leave a one square between each word – this is why it's better and clearer to use squared paper.

8 Odd one out

Aim

This activity can be used to revise almost any language.

Preparation

Think of the vocabulary, pronunciation or grammar point you want to revise.

Procedure

- Write five words on the board and ask students which one is the odd one out. The students then explain why. This is usually relates to the meaning of the word.

pink	red	dog	blue	yellow

- Here *dog* is the odd one out because it's an animal. The other words are colours.

- Note that it doesn't matter if the students can't explain in perfect English why *dog* is the odd one out. The important thing is that they're looking at and thinking about the words you want them to revise.

- You can use this format to practise and revise all sorts of things. Here are some examples:

  1 For meaning:
     sister / nephew / daughter / wife / mother
     nephew is the odd one out because he's a man. The other words describe women.

  2 For spelling:
     pen / book / bag / phone / diary
     diary is the odd one out because you spell the plural *ies*. The other words you just add *s*.

  3 For pronunciation: sounds
     A / I / H / J / K
     I is the odd one out because the vowel sound is different.

  4 For pronunciation: stress
     hospital / banana / potato / Italian / computer
     hospital is the odd one out because the stress is on the first syllable. The other words have the stress on the second syllable.

  5 For collocation: *do* or *make*
     your homework / the washing / an appointment / a training course / the shopping
     an appointment is the odd one out because you use *make*. For the others you use *do*.

  6 For grammar:
     cash / credit card / cheque / coin / note
     cash is the odd one out because it is uncountable – you can't say *a cash*. All the other words are countable.

- You should tell the students what the criteria is, for example 'think about meaning' or 'think about the sounds'. To make the activity a little more challenging, instead of writing the words on the board, you can dictate them. As a follow-up, ask the students to write their own odd ones out.

9 Making sentences

Aim

This activity is good for revising any type of vocabulary. It works best if the words are a fairly random selection and not part of a tight lexical set.

Preparation

Choose 12 words you want to revise and write them in a circle (like a clockface) on the board.

Procedure

- Students work in pairs. They choose two or more of the words and try to make a sentence with them.

  Example sentences:

  My brother is doing yoga in the park.

  The snowboarder eats organic vegetables on Friday.

  I saw an ambitious puppy in the canal with a blue neck.

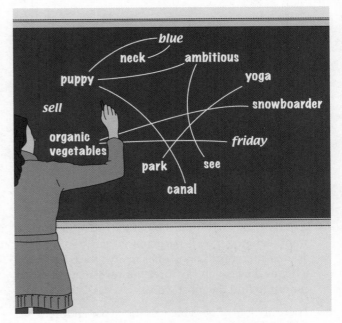

- The students then read out their sentences and you connect the words they have used on the board. You can correct the grammar as necessary (or you can make it more difficult for the students by only accepting grammatically correct sentences). It doesn't matter how bizarre the sentences are, the important thing is that students spend time looking at and remembering the vocabulary.

- If you write the words and draw the connecting lines on an OHP transparency, you can show it to the students a few weeks later and see if they remember the sentences they wrote.

10 Random letters

Aim

This activity is good for revising any type of vocabulary.

Preparation

None

Procedure

- Ask the students to call out any seven letters from the alphabet. (It doesn't have to be seven letters: anything between seven and twelve is fine.) Write the letters scattered on the board.

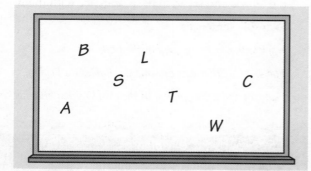

- Then ask the students in pairs to think of a word beginning with each letter on the board. The most obvious criteria is to revise words from a specific lexical set that you have taught recently, e.g. *jobs*, *clothes*, *food*, *animals*, etc. Alternatively, you could simply ask them for words they've noted down in lessons over the past two weeks.

- Another possibility would be to find the most interesting words they can from the Student's Book unit that you've just finished. If the lexical set you want them to revise is particularly rich, you could ask the students to think of as many words for each letter as they can in say three minutes: make it into a contest to find the most words.

- There are lots of possible variations using different criteria for words from the letters on the board. Here are a few:

  1 Use the same criteria as above but ask the students to think of words ending with the letter on the board.

  2 Ask the students to write only nouns, or adjectives or irregular verbs or some other part of speech.

  3 Ask the students to write only words with three syllables or words with the same vowel sounds.

  4 Ask students to write only words that start with the same letter in their own language or only words that start with a different letter.

  5 Ask students to think of words that can combine to make a coherent sentence, e.g. *Basil likes selling Christmas trees at weekends*. Accept only grammatically correct sentences no matter how bizarre they might be.

Anecdote tasks

New Inside Out Pre-intermediate includes a number of extended speaking tasks, where students tackle a longer piece of discourse. We've called these 'Anecdotes'. They are based on personal issues, for instance, memories, stories, people you know. When you learn a musical instrument, you can't spend all your time playing scales and exercises: you also need to learn whole pieces in order to see how music is organised. Anecdotes give students a chance to get to grips with how discourse is organised. We have found the following strategies helpful in getting our students to tell their Anecdotes.

1 Choose global topics that everybody can relate to

One of the main objectives of an Anecdote is to encourage students to experiment with and hopefully grow more competent at using language at the more demanding end of their range. It therefore seems only fair to ask them to talk about subjects they know something about. With familiar subject matter students can concentrate on how they're speaking as well as what they're speaking about. The nine Anecdote topics in *New Inside Out* Pre-intermediate have been carefully selected to appeal to the widest range of students, whilst at the same time, fitting in to the context of the unit.

Unit 1	Somebody who is important to you
Unit 2	The best place you have ever visited
Unit 4	A present you bought for somebody
Unit 5	Your experiences of sport at school
Unit 6	A person you know with a good job
Unit 8	Your favourite subject at school
Unit 10	The fittest/healthiest person you know
Unit 11	Your pet or a pet you know
Unit 12	The most incredible building you've ever seen

As soon as you have got to know your students well enough, you'll be able to choose other Anecdote topics suited to their particular interests and experiences.

2 Allow sufficient preparation time

Students need time to assemble their thoughts and think about the language they'll need. The Anecdotes are set up through evocative questions. Students read or listen to a planned series of questions and choose what specifically they'll talk about; shyer students can avoid matters they feel are too personal. This student preparation is a key stage and should not be rushed. Research, by Peter Skehan and Pauline Foster among others, has shown that learners who plan for tasks attempt more ambitious and complex language, hesitate less and make fewer basic errors.

The simplest way to prepare students for an Anecdote is to ask them to read the list of questions in the book and decide which they want to talk about. This could be done during class time or as homework preparation for the following lesson. Ask them to think about the language they'll need. Sentence beginnings are provided in the Student's Book to give the students some extra help. Encourage them to use dictionaries and make notes – but not to write out what they'll actually say. Finally, put them into pairs to exchange Anecdotes.

A variation is to ask the students to read the questions in the book while, at the same time, listening to you read them aloud. Then ask them to prepare in detail for the task, as above.

Alternatively, ask the students to close their books – and then to close their eyes. Ask them to listen to the questions as you read them aloud and think about what they evoke. Some classes will find this a more involving process. It also allows you to adapt the questions to your class: adding new ones or missing out ones you think inappropriate. After the reading, give them enough time to finalise their preparation before starting the speaking task.

3 Monitor students and give feedback

It's important for students to feel that their efforts are being monitored by the teacher. Realistically, it's probably only possible for a teacher to monitor and give feedback to one or two pairs of students during each Anecdote activity. It's therefore vital that the teacher adopts a strict rota system, and makes sure that everyone in the class is monitored over the course of a term. Constructive feedback helps students improve their delivery.

4 Provide a 'model anecdote'

It's always useful for the students to hear a model Anecdote at some stage during the Anecdote task cycle. The most obvious model is you, the teacher. Alternatively, you might ask a teaching colleague or friend to talk to the students. For every Anecdote activity in *New Inside Out* Pre-intermediate there's a model listening on the CD with an accompanying task in the student's book.

5 Repeat the same anecdote with a new partner at regular intervals

Consider going back to Anecdotes and repeating them in later classes. Let the students know that you're going to do this. This will reassure them that you're doing it on purpose, but more importantly, it will mean that they'll be more motivated to dedicate some time and thought to preparation. When you repeat the task, mix the class so that each student works with a new partner, i.e. one who has not previously heard the Anecdote.

In our experience, most students are happy to listen to their partner's Anecdotes. If, however, any of your students are reluctant listeners, you might think about giving them some sort of 'listening task'. Here are three examples:

- Ask the listener to tick the prompt questions that the 'Anecdote teller' answers while telling the Anecdote.

- Ask the listener to time the 'Anecdote teller'. In *Teaching Collocations* (page 91) Michael Lewis suggests reducing the time allowed to deliver the Anecdote each time it's repeated: for example, in the first instance the student has five minutes; for the second telling they have four minutes; and the third three minutes.

- Ask the listener to take brief notes about the Anecdote and write them up as a summary for homework. Then give the summary to the 'Anecdote teller' to check.

The pedagogic value of getting students to re-tell Anecdotes – repeat a 'big chunk' of spoken discourse – cannot be over-stated. Repeating complex tasks reflects real interactions. We all have our set pieces: jokes, stories, and we tend to refine and improve them as we retell them. Many students will appreciate the opportunity to do the same thing in their second language. Research by Martin Bygate among others has shown that given this opportunity students become more adventurous and at the same time more precise in the language they use.

You can also use the Anecdotes to test oral proficiency and thereby add a speaking component to accompany the tests in the Teacher's Book.

Key concepts in *New Inside Out*

The following excerpts are from *An A–Z of ELT* by Scott Thornbury (Macmillan Books for Teachers, 2006). They give clear authoritive definitions and explanations of some of the most important concepts in *New Inside Out*.

Scott Thornbury

Contents

Note: SLA = Second Language Acquisition

classroom interaction METHODOLOGY

Classroom interaction is the general term for what goes on between the people in the classroom, particularly when it involves language. In traditional classrooms, most interaction is initiated by the teacher, and learners either respond individually, or in unison. Teacher-centred interaction of this kind is associated with *transmissive* teaching, such as a lecture or presentation, where the teacher *transmits* the content of the lesson to the learners. In order to increase the amount of student involvement and interaction, teacher–learner interaction is often combined with **pairwork** and **groupwork**, where learners interact among themselves in pairs or small groups. Other kinds of interaction include *mingling* or *milling*. Pairwork and groupwork are associated with a more **learner-centred** approach. Rather than passively receiving the lesson content, the learners are actively engaged in using language and discovering things for themselves. The value of pairwork and groupwork has been reinforced by the belief that **interaction** facilitates language learning. Some would go as far as to say that it is *all* that is required.

The potential for classroom interaction is obviously constrained by such factors as the number of students, the size of the room, the furniture, and the purpose or type of activity. Not all activities lend themselves to pairwork or groupwork. Some activities, such as reading, are best done as *individual work*. On the other hand, listening activities (such as listening to an audio recording, or to the teacher) favour a *whole class* format, as do grammar presentations. The whole class is also an appropriate form of organization when reviewing the results of an activity, as, for example, when spokespersons from each group are reporting on the results of a discussion or survey.

The success of any classroom interaction will also depend on the extent to which the learners know what they are meant to be doing and why, which in turn depends on how clearly and efficiently the interaction has been set up. Pair- and groupwork can be a complete waste of time if learners are neither properly prepared for it, nor sure of its purpose or outcome.

Finally, the success of pair- and groupwork will depend on the kind of group **dynamics** that have been established. Do the students know one another? Are they happy working together? Do they mind working without constant teacher supervision? Establishing a productive classroom dynamic may involve making decisions as to who works with whom. It may also mean deliberately staging the introduction of different kinds of interactions, starting off with the more controlled, teacher-led interactions before, over time, allowing learners to work in pairs and finally in groups.

collocation VOCABULARY

If two words *collocate*, they frequently occur together. The relation between the words may be grammatical, as when certain verbs collocate with particular prepositions, such as *depend on*, *account for*, *abstain from*, or when a verb, like *make*, *take*, or *do*, collocates with a noun, as in *make an arrangement*, *take advantage*, *do the shopping*. The collocation may also be lexical, as when two **content words** regularly co-occur, as in *a broad hint*, *a narrow escape* (but not *a wide hint* or *a tight escape*). The strength of the collocation can vary: *a broad street* or *a narrow path* are weak collocations, since both elements can co-occur with lots of other words: *a broad river*, *a busy street*, etc. *Broad hint* and *narrow escape* are stronger. Stronger still are combinations where one element rarely occurs without the other, as in *moot point*, *slim pickings* and *scot free*. Strongest of all are those where both elements never or rarely occur without the other, such as *dire straits* and *spick and span*. These have acquired the frozen status of *fixed expressions*.

Unsurprisingly, learners lack intuitions as to which words go with which, and this accounts for many errors, such as *You can <u>completely</u> enjoy it* (instead of *thoroughly*), *On Saturday we <u>made</u> shopping* (instead of *went*), and *We went the <u>incorrect</u> way* (for *wrong*). Using texts to highlight particular collocations, and teaching new words in association with their most frequent collocations are two ways of approaching the problem. Nowadays learners' dictionaries, such as the Macmillan English Dictionary for Advanced Learners, also include useful collocational information.

communicative activity METHODOLOGY

A communicative activity is one in which real communication occurs. Communicative activities belong to that generation of classroom **activities** that emerged in response to the need for a more **communicative approach** in the teaching of second languages. (In their more evolved form as **tasks**, communicative activities are central to **task-based learning**). They attempt to import into a practice activity the key features of 'real-life' communication. These are

- *purposefulness*: speakers are motivated by a communicative goal (such as getting information, making a request, giving instructions) and not simply by the need to display the correct use of language for its own sake
- *reciprocity*: to achieve a purpose, speakers need to interact, and there is as much need to listen as to speak

- *negotiation*: following from the above, they may need to check and **repair** the communication in order to be understood by each other
- *unpredictability*: neither the process, nor the outcome, nor the language used in the exchange, is entirely predictable
- *heterogeneity*: participants can use any communicative means at their disposal; in other words, they are not restricted to the use of a pre-specified grammar item.

And, in the case of spoken language in particular:

- *synchronicity*: the exchange takes place in real time

The best known communicative activity is the *information gap* activity. Here, the information necessary to complete the task is either in the possession of just one of the participants, or distributed among them. In order to achieve the goal of the task, therefore, the learners have to share the information that they have. For example, in a *describe-and-draw* activity, one student has a picture which is hidden from his or her partner. The task is for that student to describe the picture so that the partner can accurately draw it. In a *spot-the-difference* task, both students of a pair have pictures (or texts) that are the same apart from some minor details. The goal is to identify these differences. In a *jigsaw activity*, each member of a group has different information. One might have a bus timetable, another a map, and another a list of hotels. They have to share this information in order to plan a weekend break together.

Information gap activities have been criticized on the grounds that they lack **authenticity**. Nor are information gap activities always as productive as might be wished: unsupervised, learners may resort to **communication strategies** in order to simplify the task. A more exploitable information gap, arguably, is the one that exists between the learners themselves, ie, what they don't know – but might like to know – about one another (→ **personalization**).

context LINGUISTICS

The context of a language item is its adjacent language items. In the absence of context, it is often impossible to assign exact meaning to an item. A sentence like *Ben takes the bus to work*, for example, could have past, present, or future reference, depending on the context:

> I know this chap called Ben. One day *Ben takes the bus to work*, and just as …
> Most days *Ben takes the bus to work*, but sometimes he rides his bike …
> If *Ben takes the bus to work* tomorrow, he'll be late, because there's a strike …

Likewise, a sentence like *You use it like this* is meaningless in the absence of a context. By the same token, a word or sentence in one context can have a very different meaning in another. The sign *NO BICYCLES* in a public park means something different to *NO BICYCLES* outside a bicycle rental shop. It is sometimes necessary to distinguish between different kinds of context. On the one hand, there is the context of the accompanying **text**, sometimes called the *co-text*. The co-text of this sentence, for example, includes the sentences that precede and follow it, as well as the paragraph of which it forms a part. It is the co-text that offers clues as to the meaning of unfamiliar vocabulary in a text. The *situational* context (also *context of situation, context of use*), on the other hand, is the physical and temporal setting in which an instance of language use occurs. The typical context for the spoken question *Are you being served?* is in a shop, for example. Both co-text and context influence the production and interpretation of language. **Discourse analysis** studies the relationship between language and co-text, including the way that sentences or utterances are connected. **Pragmatics** studies the relationship between language and its contexts of use, including the way meaning can be inferred by reference to context factors.

Various theories have been proposed in order to account for the ways that language choices are determined by contextual factors. One of the best known of these is Michael Halliday's **systemic functional linguistics**. Halliday distinguishes three variables in any context that systematically impact on language choices and which, together, determine a text's **register**:

- the *field*: what the language is being used to talk about, and for what purposes
- the *tenor*: the participants in the language event, and their relationship
- the *mode*: how language is being used in the exchange, eg is it written or spoken?

For example, this short text shows the influence of all three factors:

> Do u fancy film either 2nite or 2moro? Call me.

The field is 'making arrangements about leisure activities', hence the use of words like *film, 2nite* (*tonight*), *2moro* (*tomorrow*). The tenor is one of familiarity and equality (accounting for the informal *fancy* and the imperative: *call me*); and the mode is that of a written text message, which explains its brevity, its use of abbreviated forms (*u, 2nite*) and the absence of salutations. A change in any of these contextual factors is likely to have a significant effect on the text.

Language learners, it is argued, need to know how these contextual factors correlate with language choices in order to produce language that is appropriate to the context. One way of doing this is to ask them to make changes to a text (such as the text message above) that take into account adjustments to the field, tenor, or mode.

drill METHODOLOGY

A drill is repetitive oral practice of a language item, whether a sound, a word, a phrase or a sentence structure. Drills that are targeted at sentence structures are sometimes called *pattern practice drills*.

Drills follow a prompt–response sequence, where the prompt usually comes from the teacher, and the students respond, either in chorus (a *choral drill*) or individually. An *imitation drill* simply involves repeating the prompt, as in:

| **Teacher** | They have been watching TV. |
| **Student** | They have been watching TV. |

A *substitution drill* requires the students to substitute one element of the pattern with the prompt, making any necessary adjustments:

Teacher	They have been watching TV.
Student	They have been watching TV.
Teacher	She
Student	She has been watching TV.
Teacher	I
Student	I have been watching TV.

etc.

A *variable substitution drill* is the same, but the prompts are not restricted to one element of the pattern:

Teacher	They have been watching TV.
Student	They have been watching TV.
Teacher	She
Student	She has been watching TV.
Teacher	radio
Student	She has been listening to the radio.
Teacher	We
Student	We have been listening to the radio.

etc.

Drills were a defining feature of the **audiolingual** method, and were designed to reinforce good language 'habits'. The invention of language laboratories allowed sustained drilling without the need for a teacher to supply the prompts. With the demise of audiolingualism, drilling fell from favour. However, many teachers – even those who subscribe to a **communicative approach** – feel the need for some form of repetition practice of the kind that drills provide. This may be for the purpose of developing **accuracy**, or as a form of **fluency** training, ie, in order to develop **automaticity**. Hence, communicative drills were developed. A communicative drill is still essentially repetitive, and focuses on a particular structure or pattern, but it has an *information gap* element built in. Learners can perform the drill in pairs, or as a *milling activity* (→ **classroom interaction**) and they are required to attend to what they hear as much as what they say. The milling activity popularly known as *Find someone who ...* is one such activity. Students are set the task of finding other students in the class who, for example, can ride a horse, can speak French, can play the guitar, etc. They mill around, asking questions of the type *Can you ...?* until they have asked all the other students their questions, and then they report their findings.

dynamics: group, classroom METHODOLOGY

Dynamics are the actions and interactions, both conscious and unconscious, that take place between members of a group, whether the whole class or sub-groups. Group dynamics are instrumental in forging a productive and motivating classroom environment. They are determined by such factors as: the composition of the group (including the age, sex, and relative status of the members, as well as their different attitudes, beliefs, learning styles and abilities); the patterns of relationships between members of the group, including how well they know each other, and the roles they each assume, such as group leader, spokesperson, etc; physical factors such as the size of the group and the way it is seated; and the tasks that the group are set, eg: Does the task require everyone to contribute? Does it encourage co-operation or competition? Are the goals of the task clear to the group members?

Ways that the teacher can promote a positive group (and class) dynamic include:

- ensuring all class or group members can see and hear one another, and that they know (and use) each other's names
- keeping groups from getting too big – three to six members is optimal
- setting – or negotiating – clear rules for groupwork, such as using only the target language, giving everyone a turn to speak, allowing individuals to 'pass' if they don't want to say anything too personal
- using 'ice-breaking' activities to encourage interaction, laughter, and relaxation
- ensuring that group tasks are purposeful, interactive, and collaborative
- personalizing tasks, ie, setting tasks that involve the sharing of personal experiences and opinions
- defining the roles and responsibilities within the group, and varying these regularly, eg by appointing a different spokesperson each time
- monitoring groupwork in progress, and being alert to any possible conflicts or tensions between members, and reconstituting groups, if necessary
- discussing the importance of groupwork with learners, and getting feedback on group processes

fluency SLA

If someone is said to be fluent in a language, or to speak a language fluently, it is generally understood that they are able to speak the language idiomatically and accurately, without undue pausing, without an intrusive accent, and in a manner appropriate to the context. In fact, research into listeners' perceptions of fluency suggests that fluency is primarily the ability to produce and maintain speech in *real time*. To do this, fluent speakers are capable of:

- appropriate pausing, ie:
  - their pauses may be long but are not frequent
  - their pauses are usually filled, eg with **pause fillers** like *erm, you know, sort of*
  - their pauses occur at meaningful transition points, eg at the intersections of clauses or phrases, rather than midway in a phrase
- long runs, ie, there are many syllables and words between pauses

All of the above factors depend on the speaker having a well-developed grammar, an extensive vocabulary, and, crucially, a store of memorized *chunks*. Being able to draw on this store of chunks means not having to depend on grammar to construct each utterance from scratch. This allows the speaker to devote **attention** to other aspects of the interaction, such as planning ahead. Speakers also use a number of 'tricks' or *production strategies* to convey the illusion of fluency. One such strategy is disguising pauses by filling them, or by repeating a word or phrase.

Some proponents of the **communicative approach** re-defined fluency so as to distinguish it from **accuracy**. Fluency came to mean 'communicative effectiveness', regardless of formal accuracy or speed of delivery. Activities that are communicative, such as information-gap activities, are said to be *fluency-focused*. This is the case even for activities that produce short, halting utterances. Separating accuracy and fluency, and defining the latter as *communicative* language use, is misleading, though. There are many speech events whose communicativeness depends on their accuracy. Air traffic control talk is just one. Moreover, many learners aspire to being more than merely communicative.

Classroom activities that target fluency need to prepare the learner for real-time speech production. Learning and memorizing lexical chunks, including useful conversational gambits, is one approach. **Drills** may help here, as will some types of **communicative activity** that involve repetition. Research has also shown that fluency improves the more times a **task** is repeated. Fluency may also benefit from activities that manage to distract learners' attention away from formal accuracy so that they are not tempted to slow down. (This has been called 'parking their attention'). Some interactive and competitive language **games** have this effect. **Drama** activities, such as roleplays, recreate conditions of real-time language use, and are therefore good for developing fluency. Finally, learners can achieve greater fluency from learning a repertoire of **communication strategies**, ie, techniques for getting around potential problems caused by a lack of the relevant words or structures.

focus on form SLA

When learners focus on form, they direct conscious attention to some formal feature of the language **input**. The feature may be the fact that the past of *has* is *had*, or that *enjoy* is followed by verb forms ending in *-ing*, or that adjectives do not have plural forms in English. The learners' attention may be self-directed, or it may be directed by the teacher or by another learner. Either way, it has been argued that a focus on **form** is a necessary condition for language learning. Simply focusing on the **meaning** of the input is not enough. Focusing on form is, of course, not a new idea: most teaching methods devote a great deal of time to the forms of the language, eg when new grammar items are presented. But the term *focus on form* captures the fact that this focus can, theoretically, occur at any stage in classroom instruction. Thus, **correction**, especially in the form of negative **feedback**, is a kind of focus on form. In fact, some researchers argue that the most effective form focus is that which arises incidentally, in the context of communication, as when the teacher quickly elicits a correction during a classroom discussion. This incidental approach contrasts with the more traditional and deliberate approach, where teaching is based on a **syllabus** of graded structures (or *forms*), and these are pre-taught in advance of activities designed to practise them. This traditional approach is called – by some researchers – a *focus on formS*.

function LINGUISTICS

The function of a language item is its communicative purpose. Language is more than simply **forms** and their associated meanings (ie, **usage**). It is also the communicative **uses** to which these forms and meanings are put. These two sentences, for example, share the same forms, but function quite differently:

> [in an email] *Thank you for sending me the disk.*
> [a notice in a taxi] *Thank you for not smoking.*

The function of the first is *expressing thanks*, while the second is more like a *prohibition*. Likewise, the same function can be expressed by different forms:

> [a notice in a taxi] *Thank you for not smoking.*
> [a sign in a classroom] *No smoking.*

Thus, there is no one-to-one match between form and function. Assigning a function to a text or an utterance usually requires knowledge of the **context** in which the text is used. The study of how context and function are interrelated is called **pragmatics**.

Communicative functions can be categorized very broadly and also at increasing levels of detail. The 'big' functions, or macrofunctions, describe the way language is used in very general terms. These include the use of language for *expressive* purposes (eg poetry), for *regulatory* purposes (eg for getting people to do things), for *interpersonal* purposes (eg for socializing), and for *representational* purposes (eg to inform). More useful, from the point of view of designing language syllabuses, are microfunctions. These are usually expressed as **speech acts**, such as *agreeing and disagreeing, reporting, warning, apologizing, thanking, greeting*, etc. Such categories form the basis of **functional syllabuses**, a development associated with the **communicative approach**. They often appear as one strand of a coursebook **syllabus**. Functions differ from notions in that the latter describe areas of meaning – such as *ability, duration, quantity, frequency*, etc – rather than the uses to which these meanings are put.

One way to teach functions is to adopt a 'phrasebook' approach, and teach useful ways of expressing common functions (what are called *functional exponents*), such as *Would you like …?* (*inviting*) and *Could you …, please?* (*requesting*). More memorable, though, is to teach these expressions in the contexts of **dialogues**, so that the functional exponents are associated not only with common situations in which they are used, but with related functions (such as *accepting* and *refusing*). The term *function*, in contrast to **form**, is also used in linguistics, specifically with regard to the functions of the different elements of a **clause** (such as subject and object).

grammar teaching METHODOLOGY

Like the word **grammar** itself, the topic of grammar teaching is a controversial one, and teachers often take opposing views. Historically, language teaching methods have positioned themselves along a scale from 'zero grammar' to 'total grammar', according to their approach to grammar teaching. Proponents of *natural methods*, who model their approach to teaching second languages on the way that first languages are acquired, reject any explicit teaching of grammar at all. (They may, however, teach according to a grammar **syllabus**, even if no mention of grammar as such is made in the classroom). This implicit approach is common both to the **direct method** and to **audiolingualism**. Through exposure to demonstrations, situations or examples, learners are expected to pick up the rules of grammar by **inductive learning**. At the other end of the spectrum, there are approaches, such as **grammar-translation**, that adopt an explicit and **deductive learning** approach. From the outset, learners are presented with rules which they study and then practise. Occupying a midway point between zero grammar and total grammar is the approach called **consciousness-raising**. Instead of being given rules, learners are presented with language data which challenge them to re-think (and *restructure*) their existing mental grammar. This data might take the form of **input** that has been manipulated in some way. For example, pairs of sentences, such as the following, have to be matched to pictures, forcing learners to discriminate between them, and, in theory, **notice** the difference (→ **noticing**):

> The Queen drove to the airport.
> The Queen was driven to the airport.

(This is sometimes called a *grammar interpretation task*, or *structured input*.) In order to do the task, learners have to process not just the individual words, but also their grammatical form. That is why this approach to teaching grammar is sometimes called *processing instruction*. There are other researchers who argue that it is by means of manipulating the learner's output, eg through productive practice, that mental restructuring is best effected.

The **communicative approach** accommodates different approaches to grammar teaching. Proponents of **task-based learning**, for example, argue that, if the learner is engaged in solving problems using language, then the mental grammar will develop of its own accord. However, advocates of the weaker version of the communicative approach (and the version that is most widespread) justify a role for the pre-teaching of grammar in advance of production. This view finds support in **cognitive learning theory**, which suggests that conscious attention to grammatical form (called **focus on form**) speeds up language learning, and is a necessary corrective against premature **fossilization**. There is some debate, though, as to whether this form focus should be planned or incidental. Incidental grammar teaching occurs when the teacher deals with grammar issues as and when they come up, eg in the form of **correction**, or task **feedback**. In this way (it is argued) grammar teaching follows the learners' own 'syllabus'. Such an approach attempts to address one of the dilemmas of grammar teaching: the fact that the learner's mental grammar, and the way it develops, bears only an accidental relation to a formal grammar syllabus.

Nevertheless, the research into these different choices is still inconclusive. It may be the case that some items of grammar respond better to explicit teaching, while others are more easily picked up through exposure. There are also different learner types: some prefer learning and applying rules, while others are happier with a more 'deep-end' approach (→ **learning style**). Most current teaching materials hedge their bets on these issues. They offer both deductive and inductive grammar presentations, and opportunities for incidental as well as for planned learning.

learner-centred instruction, learner-centredness
METHODOLOGY

Learner-centred instruction aims to give learners more say in areas that are traditionally considered the domain of the teacher or of the institution. Learner-centred instruction is true to the spirit of progressive education, including the movement towards providing learners with greater **autonomy**. For example, a learner-centred **curriculum** would involve learners in negotiating decisions relating to the choice of syllabus content, of materials, of activity-types, and of assessment procedures. Learner-centredness also describes ways of organizing **classroom interaction** so that the focus is directed away from the teacher, and on to the learners, who perform tasks in pairs or small groups. This contrasts with traditional, teacher-centred, classroom interaction. Some writers believe that the dichotomy between learner-centred (= good) and teacher-centred (= bad) is a false one. It might be more useful to talk about *learning-centred instruction*, ie, instruction which prioritizes sound learning principles. In a learning-centred approach there would be room for both learner-centred *and* teacher-centred interactions.

learning style PSYCHOLOGY

Your learning style is your preferred way of learning. This style may be influenced by biographical factors (such as how you were taught as a child) or by innately endowed factors (such as whether you have a 'good ear' for different sounds). Types of learning style are often presented in the form of polarities (some of which may overlap), such as:

- analytic versus global (or holistic) thinkers, ie, learners who tend to focus on the details, versus learners who tend to see 'the big picture'

- rule-users versus data-gatherers, ie, learners who learn and apply rules, versus those who prefer exposure to lots of examples
- reflective versus impulsive learners
- group-oriented versus solitary learners
- extrovert versus introverted learners
- verbal versus visual learners
- passive versus active learners

Attempts have been made to group these polarities and relate them to brain lateralization. So, a bias towards left-brain processing correlates with analytic, rule-forming and verbal learners, while a bias towards right-brain processing correlates with their opposite. A less binary view of learning style is that proposed by the psychologist Howard Gardner. He identified at least seven distinct intelligences that all individuals possess but to different degrees. These include the *logical/mathematical*, the *verbal/linguistic*, and the *visual/spatial*. Similarly, proponents of **neuro-linguistic programming** distinguish between different sensory orientations, including the *visual*, *aural* and *kinesthetic* (ie, related to movement, touch). So far, though, there is no convincing evidence that any of these dispositions correlates with specific learning behaviours. Nor has it been shown that a preference in one area predicts success in language learning. In fact, it is very difficult to separate learning style from other potentially influential factors, such as personality, intelligence, and previous learning experience. Nor is it clear to what extent learning style can be manipulated, eg through **learner training**. The best that can be said is that, if the learner's preferred learning style is out of synch with the type of instruction on offer, then success is much less likely than if the two are well matched. This supports the case for an **eclectic** approach, on the one hand, and the individualization of learning, on the other.

listening METHODOLOGY

Listening is the skill of understanding spoken language. It is also the name given to classroom activities that are designed to develop this skill – what are also called *listening comprehension* activities – as in 'today we're going to do a listening'. Listening is one of the four language **skills**, and, along with **reading**, was once thought of as being a 'passive' skill. In fact, although receptive, listening is anything but passive. It is a goal-oriented activity, involving not only processing of the incoming speech signals (called *bottom-up processing*) but also the use of prior knowledge, contextual clues, and expectations (*top-down processing*) in order to create meaning. Among the sub-skills of listening are:

- perceiving and discriminating individual sounds
- segmenting the stream of speech into recognizable units such as words and phrases
- using **stress** and **intonation** cues to distinguish given information from new information
- attending to **discourse markers** and using these to predict changes in the direction of the talk

- guessing the meaning of unfamiliar words
- using clues in the text (such as vocabulary) and context clues to predict what is coming
- making inferences about what is not stated
- selecting key information relevant to the purpose for listening
- integrating incoming information into the mental 'picture' (or **schema**) of the speech event so far

Also, since listening is normally interactive, listeners need to be capable of:

- recognizing when speakers have finished their turns, or when it is appropriate to interrupt
- providing ongoing signals of understanding, interest, etc. (*backchannelling*)
- asking for clarification, asking someone to repeat what they have just said, and repairing misunderstandings

These sub-skills exist across languages, so, in theory, learners should be able to transfer them from their first language into their second. In fact, there are a number of reasons why this does not always happen. One is that speakers of different languages process speech signals differently, depending on the phonetic characteristics of the language they are used to. This means that speakers of some languages will find it harder than others to match the spoken word to the way that the word is represented in their mind. They simply do not recognize the word. Another problem is lack of sufficient L2 knowledge, such as vocabulary or grammar. A third problem is that learners may lack the means (and the confidence) to negotiate breakdowns in understanding. Finally, many learners simply lack exposure to spoken language, and therefore have not had sufficient opportunities to experience listening. These problems can be compounded in classrooms because:

- Listening to audio recordings deprives the learners of useful visual information, and allows the learners no opportunity to interact and repair misunderstandings.
- Classroom acoustics are seldom ideal.
- If learners do not know what they are listening for (in the absence, for example, of some pre-set listening task) they may try to process as much information as possible, rather than being selective in their listening. This can lead to listening overload, which in turn can cause inhibiting anxiety.
- Listening texts that have been specially written for classroom use are often simplified. But if this simplification means eliminating a lot of redundant language, such as speaker repetitions, pause fillers and vague language, the density of information that results may make it harder – not easier – to process.

For this reason, the use of audio recordings to develop listening skills needs to be balanced against the advantages of using other media, such as video, and face-to-face interaction with the teacher or another speaker.

Nevertheless, the use of audio recordings is an established part of classroom practice, so it is important to know how to use them to best advantage. The following approach is one that is often recommended:

- Provide some minimum contextual information, eg who is talking to whom about what, and why. This helps to compensate for lack of visual information, and allows learners to activate the relevant mental **schema**, which in turn helps top-down processing, including the sub-skill of prediction.
- Pre-teach key vocabulary: this helps with bottom-up processing, although too much help may mean that learners don't get sufficient practice in guessing from context.
- Set some 'while-listening' questions. Initially, these should focus on the overall *gist* of the text. For example: true/false questions, selecting, ordering or matching pictures, ticking items on a list, following a map.
- Play a small section of the recording first, to give learners an opportunity to familiarize themselves with the different voices, and to trigger accurate expectations as to what they will hear.
- Play the recording right through, and then allow learners to consult on the answers to the pre-set task. Check these answers. If necessary, re-play the recording until satisfied that learners have 'got the gist'.
- Set a more demanding task, requiring more intensive listening, such as listening for detail, or inferring speakers' attitudes, intentions, etc. If the recording is a long one, it may pay to stage the intensive listening in sections. Again, allow learners to consult in pairs, before checking the task in open class.
- On the basis of the learners' success with these tasks, identify problem sections of the recording and return to these, playing and re-playing them, and perhaps eliciting a word-by-word transcription and writing this on the board.
- Distribute copies of the transcript of the recording (if available) and re-play the recording while learners read the transcript. This allows the learners to clear up any remaining problems, and also to match what they hear to what they see.

The above approach can be adapted to suit different kinds of recorded texts and different classroom needs. For higher level learners, for example, it may be counter-productive to make listening *too* easy. The approach can also be adapted to the use of video, and even to *live listenings*, such as listening to the teacher or a guest.

motivation PSYCHOLOGY

Motivation is what drives learners to achieve a goal, and is a key factor determining success or failure in language learning. The learner's goal may be a short-term one, such as successfully performing a classroom task, or a long-term one, such as achieving native-like proficiency in the language. With regard to long-term goals, a distinction is often made between *instrumental motivation* and *integrative motivation*. Instrumental motivation is when the learner has a functional objective, such as passing an exam or getting a job. Integrative motivation, on the other hand, is when the learner wants to be identified with the target language community. Intersecting with these two motivational *orientations* are two different *sources* of motivation: *intrinsic* (eg the pleasure of doing a task for its own sake) and *extrinsic* (eg the 'carrot and stick' approach). Another motivational source that has been identified is success: experience of succeeding can result in increased motivation (called *resultative motivation*), which raises the question as to whether motivation is as much a result as a cause of learning.

Various theories of motivation have been proposed. Most of these identify a variety of factors that, in combination, contribute to overall motivation, such as:

- *attitudes*, eg to the target language and to speakers of the language
- *goals*, both long-term and short-term, and the learners' *orientation* to these goals
- how much *value* the learner attaches to achieving the goals, especially as weighed against *expectancy of success*; expectancy of success may come from the learner's assessment of their own abilities, and how they account for previous successes or failures
- *self-esteem*, and the need to achieve and maintain it
- *intrinsic interest*, *pleasure*, *relevance* or *challenge* of the task
- *group dynamic*: is it competitive, collaborative, or individualistic?
- *teacher's attitudes*, eg what expectations does the teacher project about the learners' likelihood of success?

As the last point suggests, teachers can play a key role in motivating learners, not just in terms of choosing activities that are intrinsically motivating, but in the attitudes they project. Two researchers on motivation offer the following advice for teachers:

Ten commandments for motivating language learners

1   Set a personal example with your own behaviour.
2   Create a pleasant, relaxed atmosphere in the classroom.
3   Present the tasks properly.
4   Develop a good relationship with the learners.
5   Increase the learner's linguistic self-confidence.
6   Make the language classes interesting.
7   Promote learner autonomy.
8   Personalise the learning process.
9   Increase the learners' goal-orientedness.
10 Familiarise learners with the target language culture.

noticing SLA

If you notice a feature of the language that you are exposed to, it attracts your attention and you make a mental note of it. For example, a learner might notice (without necessarily understanding) the sign *Mind the gap*, repeated several times on a railway station platform. That same day, the learner hears the teacher say *would you mind* in the context of making a request in class. A day or two later, the same learner hears someone else say *I don't mind*. Each successive 'noticing' both primes the learner to notice new occurrences of *mind*, and at the same time contributes to a growing understanding of the use and meaning of *mind*. Proponents of **cognitive learning theory** believe that noticing is a prerequisite for learning: without it input would remain as mere 'noise'. The *noticing hypothesis*, then, claims that noticing is a necessary condition for acquisition, although not the only one. Some kind of mental processing of what has been noticed is also necessary before the **input** becomes *intake*, ie before it is moved into long-term **memory**.

Teachers obviously play an important role in helping learners to notice features of the language. They do this when they repeat words or structures, write them on the board, or even drill them. One way of increasing the chance of learners' noticing an item is to include it lots of times in a text, a technique called *input flood*. For example, learners read a text with the word *mind* included several times. They then categorize these examples according to their meaning. A set of **concordance** lines for a particular word can be used in the same way.

There is another type of noticing, called *noticing the gap*. This is when learners are made aware of a gap in their language knowledge. This might happen when they do a **dictation**, for example. When they compare their version with the correct version, they may notice certain differences, such as the lack of past tense endings, that represent a gap in their **interlanguage**. It has been argued that noticing the gap can trigger the **restructuring** of interlanguage. That is, 'minding the gap' leads learners to 'fill the gap'.

personalization METHODOLOGY

When you personalize language you use it to talk about your knowledge, experience and feelings. Personalization of the type *Now write five true sentences about yourself using 'used to'* is often motivated by the need to provide further practice of pre-taught grammar structures. But it is also good preparation for the kinds of situations of genuine language use that learners might encounter outside the classroom. These advantages are lost, though, if the teacher's response is to treat the exercise as *only* an exercise, and correct the learners' errors without responding to the content. The influence of **humanistic approaches** has given a fresh impetus to personalization, both in terms of providing a more coherent rationale and suggesting a broader range of activity types. For a start (it is argued), personalization creates better classroom **dynamics**. This is because groups are more likely to form and bond if the individuals in them know more about one another. And the mental and emotional effort that is involved in finding personal associations with a language item is likely to make that item more memorable. This quality is called cognitive and affective *depth*. Finally, lessons are likely to be more interesting, and hence more motivating, if at least some of the content concerns the people in the room, rather than the characters in coursebooks. On these grounds, some writers have suggested that personalization should not be considered simply as an 'add-on', but should be the principle on which most, if not all, classroom content should be based. One teaching approach that is committed to this view is **community language learning**. In this approach, all the content of the lesson comes from the learners themselves. Personalization is not without risks, though. Teachers need to be sensitive to learner resistance: learners should have the right to 'pass' on questions that they consider too intrusive. And teachers should be authentic in the way that they respond to learners' personalizations. This means that they should respond to *what* their learners are saying, not just how they say it.

practice METHODOLOGY

If you practise a skill, you experience doing it a number of times in order to gain control of it. The idea that 'practice makes perfect' is fundamental to **cognitive learning theory**. It is through practice that the skill becomes automatic. **Sociocultural learning theory** finds room for practice too. Performing a skill with the assistance of someone who is good at it can help in the **appropriation** of the skill. At issue, then, is not so much whether practice is beneficial, but what form it should take, when, and how much of it is necessary. In addressing these questions, it is customary to distinguish between different kinds of practice, such as *controlled practice* vs *free practice*, *mechanical practice* vs *meaningful/communicative practice*, and *receptive practice* vs *productive practice*.

Controlled practice is associated with the second P of the **PPP** instructional model. Practice can be controlled in at least two senses: *language control* and *interactional control*. In the first, the language that is being practised is restricted to what has just been presented (hence it is also called *restricted practice*). For example, if the first **conditional** has been presented, learners practise this, and only this, structure, and in a repetitive way, eg through a sequence of **drills**. Practice is also said to be controlled if the learners' participation is overtly managed and monitored by the teacher, such as in open-class work, as opposed to closed **pairwork** or **groupwork**. One reason for

this degree of control is that it maintains a focus on accuracy, and pre-empts or corrects errors. *Free practice*, on the other hand, allows learners a measure of creativity, and the opportunity to integrate the new item into their existing language 'pool'. It is also less controlled in terms of the interactions, with pairwork and groupwork being favoured. Typical free practice activities might be **games**, **discussions** or **drama**-based activities.

Mechanical practice is a form of controlled practice, where the focus is less on the meaning of an item than on manipulating its component parts. Mechanical practice can be either oral or written: many traditional **exercises** are mechanical in this sense, such as when learners transform sentences from active into passive, or from direct speech into reported speech. The arguments in favour of controlled and mechanical practice have lost their force since the decline of **behaviourism** and its belief that learning is simply habit-formation.

Meaningful practice requires learners to display some understanding of what the item that they are practising actually means. One way of doing this is through **personalization**. *Communicative practice* involves the learners interacting in order to complete some kind of task, such as in an *information gap* activity ($\rightarrow$ **communicative activity**). Proponents of a communicative approach argue that it is only this kind of practice that is truly effective. This is because learners are not simply practising language, but are practising the behaviours associated with the language, and this is a pre-condition for long-term behavioural change.

Finally, some practice activities are purely *receptive*. They involve the learners in identifying, selecting, or discriminating between language items, but not actually producing them. Many **consciousness-raising** activities are receptive, on the grounds that learners first need to understand a new structure before they can properly internalize it. Receptive practice is also associated with comprehension-based approaches to teaching. *Productive practice*, on the other hand, requires learners to produce the targeted items (either orally or in writing), and is associated with output-based models of learning.

There is fairly general agreement nowadays that the most effective practice activity combines at least some of the following features:

- It is meaningful, which may mean that is personalized.
- It is communicative, thus it will require learners to interact.
- It involves a degree of repetition – not of the mindless type associated with imitation drills, but of the type associated with many games.
- It is language-rich, ie, learners have to interpret or produce a lot of language.
- Learners can be creative and take risks, but support is at hand if they need it.
- Learners are pushed, at least some of the time, to the limits of their competence.
- Learners get **feedback**.

pronunciation teaching PHONOLOGY

Pronunciation is the general term for that part of language classes and courses that deals with aspects of the **phonology** of English. This includes the individual sounds (**phonemes**) of English, sounds in **connected speech**, word and sentence **stress**, **rhythm** and **intonation**. These components are customarily divided into two groups: the *segmental* features of pronunciation, ie, the individual sounds and the way they combine, and the *suprasegmental* features, ie, stress, rhythm and intonation. **Paralinguistic** features of speech production such as voice quality, tempo and loudness, are also classed as suprasegmental.

Effective pronunciation teaching needs to consider what goals, course design and methodology are most appropriate for the learners in question. The goal of acquiring a native-like **accent** is generally thought to be unachievable for most learners (and perhaps even undesirable). Instead, the goal of **intelligibility** is nowadays considered more realistic, if less easily measurable. It is often claimed that suprasegmental features play a greater role in intelligibility than do segmental ones. Unfortunately, however, some of these suprasegmental features, such as intonation, are considered by many teachers to be unteachable. Moreover, learners intending to interact with native speakers may need to set different goals from those learners whose purpose is to learn **English as an international language (EIL)**. For this latter group, the so-called **phonological core** is a checklist of those pronunciation features considered critical for intelligibility in EIL.

In terms of the design of course content, a basic choice is whether the pronunciation focus is *integrated* or *segregated*. In an integrated approach, pronunciation is dealt with as part of the teaching of grammar and vocabulary, or of speaking and listening. In a segregated approach it is treated in isolation. A classical segregated exercise is the **minimal pairs** task, in which learners are taught to discriminate and produce two contrasted phonemes (as in *hit* and *heat*). There are doubts as to whether this item-by-item approach to pronunciation reflects the way that the features of pronunciation are interconnected. Nor does it reflect the way that they jointly emerge over time ('as a photo emerges in the darkroom'). A related issue is whether pronunciation teaching should be *pre-emptive* or *reactive*. That is to say, should pronunciation teaching be planned around a syllabus of pre-selected items, or should the focus on pronunciation emerge *out of* practice activities, in the form, for example, of **correction**? There is evidence that the latter approach is more effective than the former.

In 1964 the writer (and former language teacher) Anthony Burgess wrote, 'Nothing is more important than to acquire a set of foreign phonemes that shall be entirely acceptable to your hosts.' However, there is generally less emphasis given to pronunciation teaching nowadays. Indeed, some teachers are sceptical as to the value of teaching pronunciation at all. This view is reinforced by research that suggests that the best predictors of intelligible pronunciation are 'having a good ear' and prolonged residence in an English-speaking country. On the other hand, faulty pronunciation is one of the most common causes of misunderstandings. This is an argument for demanding higher standards than the learners can realistically achieve, in the hope that they will meet you 'halfway'.

reading METHODOLOGY

Reading is a receptive **skill**. But the fact that it is receptive does not mean that it is passive: reading is an active, even interactive, process. Readers bring their own questions to the text, which are based on their background knowledge, and they use these to interrogate the text, modifying their questions and coming up with new ones according to the answers they get. In order to do this, they draw on a range of knowledge bases. They need to be able to decode the letters, words and grammatical structures of the individual sentences – what is called *bottom-up processing*. But they also enlist *top-down processes*, such as drawing on **discourse** and schematic knowledge, as well as on immediate contextual information. Discourse knowledge is knowing how different text-types – such as news reports, recipes or academic papers – are organized. Schematic knowledge is the reader's existing knowledge of the topic. Reading involves an interaction between these different 'levels' of knowledge, where knowledge at one 'level' can compensate for lack of knowledge at another.

Readers also bring their own *purposes* to texts, and these in turn determine the way they go about reading a text. The two main purposes for reading are for *information* (such as when consulting a directory), and for *pleasure* (such as when reading a novel), although these purposes may overlap. Different ways of reading include:

- *skimming* (*skim-reading*, *reading for gist*): rapidly reading a text in order to get the *gist*, or the main ideas or sense of a text. For example, a reader might skim a film review in order to see if the reviewer liked the film or not.
- *scanning*: reading a text in search of specific information, and ignoring everything else, such as when consulting a bus timetable for a particular time and destination.
- *detailed reading*: reading a text in order to extract the maximum detail from it, such as when following the instructions for installing a household appliance.
- *reading aloud*: such as when reading a prepared speech or lecture, or reading a story aloud, or an extract from the newspaper.

A reader's purpose usually matches the writer's intentions for the text. Readers seldom read telephone books from cover to cover, for example. Nor do they normally skim through a novel looking for names beginning with *Vron* .... In classrooms, however, texts are frequently used for purposes other than those for which they were originally intended. They are often used not so much as vehicles of information or of pleasure, but as 'linguistic objects', that is, as contexts for the study of features of the language. A distinction needs to be made, therefore, between two types of classroom reading: reading as *skills development*, and reading as *language study*. There is no reason why the same text cannot be used for both purposes.

Another distinction that is often made is between *intensive reading* and *extensive reading*. The former applies to the way short texts are subject to close and detailed classroom study. Extensive reading, on the other hand, means the more leisurely reading of longer texts, primarily for pleasure, or in order to accumulate vocabulary, or simply to develop sound habits of reading. This is typically done outside class, using graded **readers**, authentic texts, or literary texts.

A third important distinction is between testing reading and teaching reading. Traditional reading tasks usually involve reading a text and then answering **comprehension questions** about it. This is the testing approach. A teaching approach, on the other hand, aims to help learners to become more effective readers by training them in the *sub-skills* of reading, and by teaching them *reading strategies*. Some of the sub-skills of reading are:

- understanding words and identifying their grammatical function
- recognizing grammar features, such as word endings, and 'unpacking' (or **parsing**) the syntax of sentences
- identifying the topic of the text, and recognizing topic changes
- identifying text-type, text purpose, and text organization, and identifying and understanding **discourse markers** and other cohesive devices
- distinguishing key information from less important information
- identifying and understanding the gist
- inferring the writer's attitude
- following the development of an argument
- following the sequence of a narrative
- paraphrasing the text

Activities designed to develop these sub-skills include: underlining topic-related words; contrasting different text-types; comparing different examples of the same text type and identifying *generic* features; circling and categorizing discourse markers; identifying what the pronouns refer to; predicting the direction the text will take at each discourse marker; choosing the best summary of a text; putting a set of pictures in order; extracting key information on to a grid, writing a summary of the text, etc. *Strategy training* involves training learners in ways of overcoming problems when they are reading. Some useful strategies include:

- using contextual and extra-linguistic information (such as pictures, layout, headlines) to make predictions regarding what the text is about

- brainstorming background (or schematic) knowledge in advance of reading
- skimming a text in advance of a more detailed reading
- keeping the purpose of the text in mind
- guessing the meaning of words from context
- **dictionary** use

There is some argument, however, as to the value of a 'skills and strategies' approach to teaching reading. Most adult learners of English come to English texts with already well-developed reading skills in their own language. They already know how to skim, scan, use context clues, enlist background knowledge, and so on. Theoretically, at least, these skills are transferable. What makes reading difficult is not so much lack of reading skills as lack of *language knowledge*. That is, learners lack sufficient vocabulary and grammar to unpack sentences, and they cannot easily identify the ways that sentences are connected. This can result in 'tunnel vision', with readers becoming distracted by unfamiliar words, at the expense of working out meaning from context. On the other hand, it can also result in an over-reliance on guesswork, and on superficial 'text attack' strategies such as skimming. This suggests that texts needs to be chosen that do not over-stretch learners' ability to read them fluently. At the same time, texts should not be so easy that learners can process them simply by skimming. It also means that tasks need to be chosen that both match the original purpose of the text, and that encourage learners to transfer their first language reading skills. Such tasks are likely to be those that motivate learners to *want* to read the text. This might mean activating interest in the topic of the text, through, for example, a pre-reading quiz. At the same time, classroom reading texts should be exploited, not just for their potential in developing reading skills, but as sources of language input. This will involve, at some point, detailed study of the text's formal features, such as its linking devices, its collocations or its grammar.

speaking METHODOLOGY

Speaking is generally thought to be the most important of the four **skills**. The ability to speak a second language is often equated with proficiency in the language, as in *She speaks excellent French*. Indeed, one frustration commonly voiced by learners is that they have spent years studying English, but still can't speak it. One of the main difficulties, of course, is that speaking usually takes place spontaneously and in real time, which means that planning and production overlap. If too much **attention** is paid to planning, production suffers, and the effect is a loss of **fluency**. On the other hand, if the speaker's attention is directed solely on production, it is likely that **accuracy** will suffer, which could prejudice **intelligibility**. In order to free up attention, therefore, the speaker needs to have achieved a degree of **automaticity** in both planning and production. One way of doing this is to use memorized routines, such as **formulaic language**. Another is to use *production strategies*, such as the use of **pause fillers**, in order to 'buy' planning time. The situation is complicated by the fact that most speaking is interactive. Speakers are jointly having to manage the flow of talk. The management of interaction involves *turn-taking skills*, such as knowing how and when to take, keep, and relinquish speaker turns, and also knowing how to repair misunderstandings.

For language learners these processing demands are magnified through lack of basic knowledge of grammar and vocabulary. For the purposes of most day-to-day talk, however, the grammar that is required is not as complex nor need be as accurate as the grammar that is required for writing. Nor do speakers need an enormous vocabulary, especially if they have developed some **communication strategies** for getting round gaps in their knowledge. A core vocabulary of 1000–1500 high-frequency words and expressions will provide most learners with a solid basis for speaking.

Activating this knowledge, though, requires **practice**. This in turn suggests that the more speaking practice opportunities that learners are given, and the sooner, the easier speaking will become. Speaking practice means more than simply answering the teacher's questions, or repeating sentences, as in grammar practice activities. It means interacting with other speakers, sustaining long turns of talk, speaking spontaneously, and speaking about topics of the learners' choice.

Approaches to teaching speaking vary. Traditionally, speaking was considered to be a by-product of teaching grammar and vocabulary, reinforced with work on **pronunciation**. This view has been replaced by approaches that treat speaking as a skill in its own right. One such approach is to break down the speaking skill into a number of discrete sub-skills, such as *opening and closing conversations, turn-taking, repairing, paraphrasing, interrupting*, etc. Another approach is to focus on the different *purposes* of speaking and their associated **genres**, such as *narrating, obtaining service, giving a presentation, making small talk*, etc. This approach is particularly well suited to learners who have a specific purpose for learning English. A third is to adopt a topic-based approach, where learners are encouraged to speak freely on a range of topics, at least some of which they have chosen themselves. This is the format used in many conversation classes. Typical activity types for the teaching of speaking include: **dialogues**, **drama** activities (including *roleplays* and *simulations*), many **games**, **discussions** and debates, as well as informal classroom chat.

task METHODOLOGY

A task is a classroom activity whose focus is on communicating meaning. The objective of a task may be to reach some consensus on an issue, to solve a problem, to draft a plan, to design something, or to persuade someone to do something. In contrast, practising a pre-selected item of language (such as the present perfect) for its own sake would not be a valid task objective. In the performance of the task, learners are expected to make use of their own language resources. In theory, tasks may be receptive or productive, and may be done individually or in pairs or small groups. However, in practice, most activities that are labelled 'tasks' in coursebooks involve production (either speaking or writing, or both) and require learners to interact with one another.

Tasks are the organizing principle in **task-based learning**. In order to devise a syllabus of tasks it is necessary both to classify tasks, and to identify the factors that make one task more difficult than another. Different criteria for classifying tasks have been suggested. For example, tasks can be *open-ended* or *closed*. An open-ended task is one in which learners know there is no predetermined solution. It might be planning an excursion, or debating a topical issue. A closed task, on the other hand, requires learners to discover the solution to a problem, such as identifying the differences in a *spot-the-difference* task (→ **communicative activity**). Tasks can also be classified according to the kinds of operations they involve, such as *ranking, selecting, sorting, comparing, surveying* and *problem-solving*.

Factors which influence the degree of difficulty of the task, and hence which affect the grading of tasks, include:

- *linguistic factors*: How complex is the language that learners will need to draw on, in order to do the task? How much help, either before, or during the task, will they get with their language needs?
- *cognitive factors*: Does the task require the processing of complex data? Is the task type familiar to learners?
- *performance factors*: Do the learners have to interact in real time in order to do the task? Do they have time to rehearse? Do they have to 'go public'?

The term *task* is now widely accepted as a useful way of labelling certain types of classroom activity, including many which have a thinly disguised grammar agenda. But the concept of task is not without its critics. Some writers feel that the associations of task with 'work' undervalues the more playful – and possibly less authentic or communicative – types of classroom activity, such as games, songs and drama.

vocabulary teaching METHODOLOGY

Vocabulary describes that area of language learning that is concerned with word knowledge. Vocabulary learning is a major goal in most teaching programmes. It hasn't always been so. In methods such as **audiolingualism**, vocabulary was subordinated to the teaching of grammar structures. Words were simply there to fill the slots in the sentence patterns. The move towards *semantic* (ie, meaning-based) **syllabuses** in the 1970s, along with the use of **authentic** materials, saw a revival of interest in vocabulary teaching. Subsequently, developments in **corpus** linguistics and **discourse analysis** started to blur the distinction between vocabulary and grammar. In the 1990s the **lexical approach** ushered in a major re-think regarding the role of vocabulary. This concerned both the *selection* of items (**frequency** being a deciding factor) and the *type* of items: **formulaic language** (or lexical chunks) were recognized as being essential for both **fluency** and **idiomaticity**. These developments have influenced the design of teaching materials. Most contemporary coursebooks incorporate a lexical syllabus alongside the grammar one. Recent developments in lexicography have complemented this trend. There is now a wide range of **dictionaries** available for learners, many of which come with sophisticated software for accessing databases of examples and collocations.

It is now generally agreed that, in terms of goals, learners need a receptive vocabulary of around 3000 high-frequency words (or, better, **word families**) in order to achieve independent user status. This will give them around ninety per cent coverage of normal text. For a productive vocabulary, especially for speaking, they may only need half this number.

Classroom approaches to achieving these goals include dedicated vocabulary lessons. Typically these take the form of teaching *lexical sets* of words (ie, groups of thematically linked words) using a variety of means, including visual **aids**, demonstration, situations, texts and dictionary work. As well as the **meaning** of the items, the **form**, both spoken (ie, **pronunciation**) and written (ie, **spelling**), needs to be dealt with, especially if the words are being taught for productive use. Other aspects of word knowledge that may need to be highlighted include **connotation** and **style**, **collocation**, derived forms, and grammatical features, such as the word's **word class**. Vocabulary is also taught as preparation for listening or reading (*pre-teaching vocabulary*) or as a by-product of these skills.

It would be impossible, in class, to teach all the words that learners need. Learners therefore need opportunities for *incidental* learning, eg through *extensive reading*. They may also benefit from training in how to make the most of these opportunities, eg by means of dictionary use, note-keeping, etc. Some strategies for deducing the meaning of unfamiliar words will also help.

Amassing a fully-functioning vocabulary is essentially a **memory** task, and techniques to help in the memorizing of words can be usefully taught, too. It also helps to provide learners with repeated encounters with new words, eg through the re-reading of texts, or by reading several texts about the same topic. Constant recycling of newly learned words is essential. One simple way of doing this is to have a *word box* (or word bag) in the classroom. New words are written on to small cards and added to the word box. At the beginning of the next lesson, these words can be used as the basis for a review activity. For example, the teacher can take words out of the box and ask learners to define them, provide a translation or put them into a sentence. The words can also form the basis for peer-testing activities, in which learners take a number of word cards and test each other in pairs or small groups.

writing METHODOLOGY

Like speaking, writing is a productive **skill**, and, like other skills, writing involves a hierarchy of *sub-skills*. These range from the most mechanical (such as handwriting or typing legibly) through to the ability to organize the written text and lay it out according to the conventions of the particular text type. Along the way, writers also need to be able to:

- produce grammatically accurate sentences
- connect and punctuate these sentences
- select and maintain an appropriate style
- signal the direction that the message is taking
- anticipate the reader's likely questions so as to be able to structure the message accordingly

In order to enable these skills, writers need an extensive knowledge base, not only at the level of vocabulary and grammar, but at the level of connected discourse. This includes familiarity with a range of different text types, such as *informal letters*, *instructions*, *product descriptions*, etc. It follows that if classroom writing is mainly spelling- or grammar-focused, many of the sub-skills of writing will be neglected.

Nevertheless, the teaching of writing has tended to focus on the 'lower-level' features of the skill, such as being able to write sentences that are both accurate and complex, that demonstrate internal cohesion, and that are connected to the sentences next to them. This language-based approach is justified on the grounds that stricter standards of accuracy are usually required in writing than in speaking. Also, writing demands a greater degree of explicitness than speaking, since writers and their readers are separated in time and space. They therefore can't rely on immediate feedback in order to clear up mis-understandings.

By contrast, a text-based approach to teaching writing takes a more 'top-down' view. This approach finds support in **discourse analysis**, which shows that a **text** is more than a series of sentences, however neatly linked. Instead, texts are organized according to larger *macrostructures*, such as problem-solution, or definition-examples. Hence, learners need explicit guidance in how texts are structured. This typically involves analysing and imitating models of particular text types. For example, a business letter might be analysed in terms of its overall layout, the purpose of each of its paragraphs, the grammatical and lexical choices within each paragraph, and the punctuation. Each of these features is then practised in isolation. They are then recombined in tasks aimed first at reproducing the original text and then at producing similar texts incorporating different content.

This approach is called a *product approach* to the teaching of writing, since the focus is exclusively on producing a text (the product) that reproduces the model. By contrast, a *process approach* argues that writers do not in fact start with a clear idea of the finished product. Rather, the text emerges out of a creative process. This process includes:

planning (*generating ideas*, *goal setting* and *organizing*), *drafting* and *re-drafting*; *reviewing*, including *editing* and *proofreading*, and, finally, '*publishing*'. Advocates of a process approach argue for a more organic sequence of classroom activities, beginning with the brainstorming of ideas, writing preliminary drafts, comparing drafts, re-drafting, and *conferencing*, that is, talking through their draft with the teacher, in order to fine-tune their ideas.

The process approach to writing has a lot in common with the **communicative approach** to language teaching, and each has drawn support from the other. The communicative approach views writing as an act of communication in which the writer interacts with a reader or readers for a particular purpose. The purpose might be to ask for information about a language course, to relay personal news, to complain about being overcharged at a hotel, or simply to entertain and amuse. Thus, advocates of a communicative approach argue that classroom writing tasks should be motivated by a clear purpose and that writers should have their reader(s) in mind at all stages of the writing process. Such principles are now reflected in the design of writing tasks in public examinations, such as this one, from the Cambridge ESOL First Certificate in English (FCE) paper:

> The school where you learn English has decided to buy some videos in English. You have been asked to write a report to the Principal, suggesting what kinds of videos the school should buy. In your report you should also explain why students at the school will like these videos.
>
> Write your report.

The social purposes of writing are also foregrounded by proponents of a *genre-based approach*. **Genre** analysis attempts to show how the structure of particular text-types are shaped by the purposes they serve in specific social and cultural contexts. Put simply, a business letter is the way it is because of what it does. Advocates of genre-based teaching reject a process approach to teaching writing. They argue that to emphasize self-expression at the expense of teaching the generic structures of texts may in fact disempower learners. Many learners, especially those who are learning English as a *second* language, need a command of those genres – such as writing a CV, or requesting a bank loan – that permit access to the host community. A genre approach to teaching writing is not unlike a product approach, therefore. It starts with model texts that are subjected to analysis and replication. The difference is that these models are closely associated with their contexts of use, and they are analysed in functional terms as much as in linguistic ones. The genre approach has been particularly influential in the teaching of academic writing.

In reality, none of these approaches is entirely incompatible with any other. Resourceful teachers tend to blend elements of each. For example, they may encourage learners to 'discover' what they want to write, using a process approach. They may then give them a model text, both as a source of useful language items, and as a template for the final product. They may also provide exercises in specific sub-skills, such as linking sentences, or using a formal style.

The Common European Framework and *New Inside Out*

The Common European Framework for language learning

Introduction

The Common European Framework (CEF) is a widely used standard created by the Council of Europe. In the classroom, familiarity with the CEF can be of great help to any teacher in identifying students' actual progress and helping them to set their learning priorities.

Students can use the descriptors (description of competences) at any point to get a detailed, articulated, and personal picture of their own individual progress. This is important, as no two language learners progress in the same way, and consequently it's always rather artificial to apply a 'framework level' to a class as a whole, or to a course or coursebook.

The European Language Portfolio is another Council of Europe project, designed to give every learner a structure for keeping a record of their language learning experiences and their progress as described in the CEF. Up-to-date information about developments with the CEF and Portfolio can be found on www.coe.int/portfolio.

The Swiss-based Eurocentres Foundation played a major role in the development of the levels and the descriptors for the CEF and the prototype Portfolio. The CEF descriptors, developed in a Swiss National Research Foundation project, were presented in clearer, simpler, self-assessment form in the prototype (Swiss) Portfolio[1]. There are now dozens of different national versions of the Portfolio for different educational sectors, but the only version for adults is that developed from the Swiss version by EAQUALS (European Association for Quality Language Services) in collaboration with ALTE[2]. The descriptors used in this guide are taken from the EAQUALS/ALTE Portfolio. An electronic version that can be completed on-line can be downloaded in English or French from www.eelp.org. The EAQUALS/ALTE portfolio descriptors have been used in this guide, as they're more concrete and practical than the original CEFR descriptors.

New Inside Out CEF checklists

New Inside Out Pre-intermediate is appropriate for students who have seen most of the basic structures of the language and have enough vocabulary to cope in most situations. By the end of *New Inside Out* Pre-intermediate, if the students have had access to English outside the classroom, and have had the opportunity to practise, they should be able to do the things described at the A2 level quite comfortably, and should sometimes be able to accomplish things described at the B1 level, although these will still be quite challenging.

In order to help the teacher and student assess their progress, we've provided a list of A2 and B1 descriptors for each unit of *New Inside Out* Pre-Intermediate. A basic level of confidence with the A2 descriptors is presupposed at the start of the book. Students will first consolidate their A2 abilities, and as the course proceeds they'll gradually start to work on B1 descriptors. Many of the B1 descriptors talk of greater confidence with the same kinds of ability already described at A2: others only emerge for the first time at B1. The descriptors in these charts allow the teacher to see a typical pattern of language acquisition, but it's important always to remember that every student learns differently, and that the various abilities will be acquired in a different sequence and at a different pace by each individual.

At pre-intermediate level, students might begin to be able to make some sense of the descriptors for purposes of self-assessment, but it will still be more useful to them to work with descriptors in their first language. The descriptors given here will be of more use to the teacher in gauging the students' progress through the course across the whole range of language abilities. This will help clarify for the teacher which students are making quicker or slower progress in the different areas, and will assist them in planning the focus of future lessons.

New Inside Out offers a wide range of teaching materials in its various components, which together give teachers the opportunity to develop all aspects of their students' language ability. The CEF can be used to follow their progress. By checking whether the students' confidence is at an appropriate level across the whole range of language skills at any point in the course, the teacher can decide if there is an area that requires more practice. Suggested targets for the checklist are provided on the website www.insideout.net and on the Test CD at the back of the Teacher's Book.

---

1 Schneider, Günther, & North, Brian (2000): "Fremdsprachen können – was heisst das?" Zürich, Rüegger
North, Brian (2000): "The Development of a Common Framework Scale of Language Proficiency", New York, Peter Lang

2 EAQUALS is a pan-European language school accreditation body with over 100 full members. ALTE is an association dedicated to raising standards in language testing and encompasses the major European examination providers. Eurocentres provides high quality language teaching in countries where the language concerned is spoken. EAQUALS, ALTE and Eurocentres are the three NGOS advisers for language learning to the Council of Europe and all three implement the CEFR.

CEF Student checklists

Unit 1

Complete the checklist.

1 = I can do this with a lot of help from my teacher
2 = I can do this with a little help
3 = I can do this fairly well
4 = I can do this really well
5 = I can do this almost perfectly

Competences	Page	Your score				
I can describe myself, my family and other people.	4, 9	1	2	3	4	5
I can identify important information in news summaries or simple newspaper articles in which numbers and names play an important role and which are clearly structured and illustrated.	5	1	2	3	4	5
I can fill in a questionnaire giving an account of my educational background, my job, my interests and my specific skills.	8	1	2	3	4	5
I can indicate when I am following.	10	1	2	3	4	5
I can express and respond to feelings such as surprise, happiness, sadness, interest and indifference.	10	1	2	3	4	5

Unit 2

Complete the checklist.

1 = I can do this with a lot of help from my teacher
2 = I can do this with a little help
3 = I can do this fairly well
4 = I can do this really well
5 = I can do this almost perfectly

Competences	Page	Your score				
I have a sufficient vocabulary for coping with simple everyday situations.	12, 13, 14, 19	1	2	3	4	5
I can find the most important information on leisure time activities, exhibitions, etc. in information leaflets.	15	1	2	3	4	5
I can write about aspects of my everyday life in simple phrases and sentences (people, places, job, school, family, hobbies).	15	1	2	3	4	5
I can understand a simple personal letter in which the writer tells or asks me about aspects of everyday life.	16	1	2	3	4	5
I can describe past experiences and personal experiences (e.g. the last weekend, my last holiday).	17	1	2	3	4	5

Unit 3

Complete the checklist.

1 = I can do this with a lot of help from my teacher
2 = I can do this with a little help
3 = I can do this fairly well
4 = I can do this really well
5 = I can do this almost perfectly

Competences	Page	Your score				
I can use some simple structures correctly.	21, 23, 25, 27	1	2	3	4	5
I can catch the main points in TV programmes on familiar topics when the delivery is relatively slow and clear.	22	1	2	3	4	5
I can understand short narratives about everyday things dealing with topics which are familiar to me if the text is written in simple language.	23, 24	1	2	3	4	5
I can narrate a story.	25	1	2	3	4	5
I can agree and disagree politely.	26	1	2	3	4	5

Unit 4

Complete the checklist.

1 = I can do this with a lot of help from my teacher
2 = I can do this with a little help
3 = I can do this fairly well
4 = I can do this really well
5 = I can do this almost perfectly

Competences	Page	Your score				
I can read columns or interviews in newspapers and magazines in which someone takes a stand on a current topic or event and understand the overall meaning of the text.	32	1	2	3	4	5
I can give short, basic descriptions of events.	34	1	2	3	4	5
I can express myself reasonably accurately in familiar, predictable situations.	34, 35	1	2	3	4	5
I can say what I like and dislike.	35	1	2	3	4	5
I can make simple transactions in shops, post offices or banks.	38	1	2	3	4	5

 New Inside Out Pre-intermediate Teacher's Book © Macmillan Publishers Limited 2008

Unit 5

Complete the checklist.

1 = I can do this with a lot of help from my teacher
2 = I can do this with a little help
3 = I can do this fairly well
4 = I can do this really well
5 = I can do this almost perfectly

Competences	Page	Your score				
I can narrate a story.	41	1	2	3	4	5
I can follow clearly articulated speech directed at me in everyday conversation, though I sometimes have to ask for repetition of particular words and phrases.	42	1	2	3	4	5
I can use some simple structures correctly.	42, 43, 46	1	2	3	4	5
I have a sufficient vocabulary to express myself with some circumlocutions on most topics pertinent to my everyday life such as family, hobbies and interests, work, travel, and current events.	44, 46	1	2	3	4	5
I can understand the main points of radio news bulletins and simpler recorded material on topics of personal interest delivered relatively slowly and clearly.	45	1	2	3	4	5

Unit 6

Complete the checklist.

1 = I can do this with a lot of help from my teacher
2 = I can do this with a little help
3 = I can do this fairly well
4 = I can do this really well
5 = I can do this almost perfectly

Competences	Page	Your score				
I can skim short texts (for example news summaries) and find relevant facts and information (for example who has done what and where).	50	1	2	3	4	5
I can ask people questions about what they do at work and in their free time, and answer such questions addressed to me.	50, 54	1	2	3	4	5
I can keep a conversation going comprehensibly, but have to pause to plan and correct what I am saying – especially when I talk freely for longer periods.	51	1	2	3	4	5
I can briefly introduce myself in a letter with simple phrases and sentences (family, school, job, hobbies).	53	1	2	3	4	5
I can describe my educational background, my present or most recent job.	53, 54	1	2	3	4	5

Unit 7

Complete the checklist.

1 = I can do this with a lot of help from my teacher
2 = I can do this with a little help
3 = I can do this fairly well
4 = I can do this really well
5 = I can do this almost perfectly

Competences	Page	Your score				
I can understand the main points in short newspaper articles about current and familiar topics.	60	1	2	3	4	5
I can guess the meaning of single unknown words from the context thus deducing the meaning of expressions if the topic is familiar.	60	1	2	3	4	5
I have a sufficient vocabulary to express myself with some circumlocutions on most topics pertinent to my everyday life such as family, hobbies and interests, work, travel, and current events.	60, 61, 67	1	2	3	4	5
I can express myself reasonably accurately in familiar, predictable situations.	61, 62, 65, 67	1	2	3	4	5
I can write simple texts about experiences or events, for example about a trip, for a school newspaper or a club newsletter.	63	1	2	3	4	5

Unit 8

Complete the checklist.

1 = I can do this with a lot of help from my teacher
2 = I can do this with a little help
3 = I can do this fairly well
4 = I can do this really well
5 = I can do this almost perfectly

Competences	Page	Your score				
I can read columns or interviews in newspapers and magazines in which someone takes a stand on a current topic or event and understand the overall meaning of the text.	68, 72, 73	1	2	3	4	5
In private letters I can understand those parts dealing with events, feelings and wishes well enough to correspond regularly with a pen friend.	70	1	2	3	4	5
I can generally follow the main points of extended discussion around me, provided speech is clearly articulated in standard dialect.	71, 72	1	2	3	4	5
I can give or seek personal views and opinions in an informal discussion with friends.	71, 72, 73, 74	1	2	3	4	5
I can listen to a short narrative and form hypotheses about what will happen next.	72	1	2	3	4	5

 New Inside Out Pre-intermediate Teacher's Book © Macmillan Publishers Limited 2008

Unit 9

Complete the checklist.

1 = I can do this with a lot of help from my teacher
2 = I can do this with a little help
3 = I can do this fairly well
4 = I can do this really well
5 = I can do this almost perfectly

Competences	Page	Your score				
I can understand the main points in short newspaper articles about current and familiar topics.	76	1	2	3	4	5
I can understand the most important information in short simple everyday information brochures.	79	1	2	3	4	5
I can understand the main points of radio news bulletins and simpler recorded material on topics of personal interest delivered relatively slowly and clearly.	80	1	2	3	4	5
I can make myself understood using memorised phrases and single expressions.	81, 82	1	2	3	4	5
I can express myself reasonably accurately in familiar, predictable situations.	81, 83	1	2	3	4	5

Unit 10

Complete the checklist.

1 = I can do this with a lot of help from my teacher
2 = I can do this with a little help
3 = I can do this fairly well
4 = I can do this really well
5 = I can do this almost perfectly

Competences	Page	Your score				
I can understand the main points in short newspaper articles about current and familiar topics.	88	1	2	3	4	5
I have a sufficient vocabulary to express myself with some circumlocutions on most topics pertinent to my everyday life such as family, hobbies and interests, work, travel, and current events.	88, 93, 94, 95	1	2	3	4	5
I can generally follow the main points of extended discussion around me, provided speech is clearly articulated in standard dialect.	89	1	2	3	4	5
I can describe myself, my family and other people.	91	1	2	3	4	5
I can describe dreams, hopes and ambitions.	93	1	2	3	4	5

Unit 11

Complete the checklist.

1 = I can do this with a lot of help from my teacher
2 = I can do this with a little help
3 = I can do this fairly well
4 = I can do this really well
5 = I can do this almost perfectly

Competences	Page	Your score				
I can maintain a conversation or discussion but may sometimes be difficult to follow when trying to say exactly what I would like to.	96	1	2	3	4	5
I can generally follow the main points of extended discussion around me, provided speech is clearly articulated in standard dialect.	97	1	2	3	4	5
I can understand short narratives about everyday things dealing with topics which are familiar to me if the text is written in simple language.	98	1	2	3	4	5
I can give detailed accounts of experiences, describing feelings and reactions.	101	1	2	3	4	5
I can deal with most situations likely to arise when making travel arrangements through an agent or when actually travelling.	102	1	2	3	4	5

Unit 12

Complete the checklist.

1 = I can do this with a lot of help from my teacher
2 = I can do this with a little help
3 = I can do this fairly well
4 = I can do this really well
5 = I can do this almost perfectly

Competences	Page	Your score				
I have a sufficient vocabulary to express myself with some circumlocutions on most topics pertinent to my everyday life such as family, hobbies and interests, work, travel, and current events.	105, 111	1	2	3	4	5
I can understand the most important information in short simple everyday information brochures.	106	1	2	3	4	5
I can skim short texts (for example news summaries) and find relevant facts and information (for example who has done what and where).	106	1	2	3	4	5
I can express myself reasonably accurately in familiar, predictable situations.	107, 108, 110	1	2	3	4	5
I can describe dreams, hopes and ambitions.	109	1	2	3	4	5

 New Inside Out Pre-intermediate Teacher's Book © Macmillan Publishers Limited 2008

CEF Student checklists: Answer key

Unit 1

Competences	Page	Your score
I can describe myself, my family and other people.	4, 9	1 2 3 ④ 5
I can identify important information in news summaries or simple newspaper articles in which numbers and names play an important role and which are clearly structured and illustrated.	5	1 2 ③ 4 5
I can fill in a questionnaire giving an account of my educational background, my job, my interests and my specific skills.	8	1 2 ③ 4 5
I can indicate when I am following.	10	1 2 ③ 4 5
I can express and respond to feelings such as surprise, happiness, sadness, interest and indifference.	10	① 2 3 4 5

Unit 2

Competences	Page	Your score
I have a sufficient vocabulary for coping with simple everyday situations.	12, 13, 14, 19	1 2 3 ④ 5
I can find the most important information on leisure time activities, exhibitions, etc. in information leaflets.	15	1 2 ③ 4 5
I can write about aspects of my everyday life in simple phrases and sentences (people, places, job, school, family, hobbies).	15	1 2 ③ 4 5
I can understand a simple personal letter in which the writer tells or asks me about aspects of everyday life.	16	1 2 ③ 4 5
I can describe past experiences and personal experiences (e.g. the last weekend, my last holiday).	17	1 2 3 ④ 5

Unit 3

Competences	Page	Your score
I can use some simple structures correctly.	21, 23, 25, 27	1 2 3 ④ 5
I can catch the main points in TV programmes on familiar topics when the delivery is relatively slow and clear.	22	1 ② 3 4 5
I can understand short narratives about everyday things dealing with topics which are familiar to me if the text is written in simple language.	23, 24	1 2 ③ 4 5
I can narrate a story.	25	① 2 3 4 5
I can agree and disagree politely.	26	1 ② 3 4 5

Unit 4

Competences	Page	Your score
I can read columns or interviews in newspapers and magazines in which someone takes a stand on a current topic or event and understand the overall meaning of the text.	32	① 2 3 4 5
I can give short, basic descriptions of events.	34	1 2 ③ 4 5
I can express myself reasonably accurately in familiar, predictable situations.	34, 35	① 2 3 4 5
I can say what I like and dislike.	35	1 2 3 ④ 5
I can make simple transactions in shops, post offices or banks.	38	1 2 ③ 4 5

Unit 5

Competences	Page	Your score
I can narrate a story.	41	1 ② 3 4 5
I can follow clearly articulated speech directed at me in everyday conversation, though I sometimes have to ask for repetition of particular words and phrases.	42	① 2 3 4 5
I can use some simple structures correctly.	42, 43, 46	1 2 3 4 ⑤
I have a sufficient vocabulary to express myself with some circumlocutions on most topics pertinent to my everyday life such as family, hobbies and interests, work, travel, and current events.	44, 46	① 2 3 4 5
I can understand the main points of radio news bulletins and simpler recorded material on topics of personal interest delivered relatively slowly and clearly.	45	① 2 3 4 5

Unit 6

Competences	Page	Your score
I can skim short texts (for example news summaries) and find relevant facts and information (for example who has done what and where).	50	① 2 3 4 5
I can ask people questions about what they do at work and in free time, and answer such questions addressed to me.	50, 54	1 2 ③ 4 5
I can keep a conversation going comprehensibly, but have to pause to plan and correct what I am saying – especially when I talk freely for longer periods.	51	① 2 3 4 5
I can briefly introduce myself in a letter with simple phrases and sentences (family, school, job, hobbies).	53	1 2 ③ 4 5
I can describe my educational background, my present or most recent job.	53, 54	1 2 ③ 4 5

Unit 7

Competences	Page	Your score
I can understand the main points in short newspaper articles about current and familiar topics.	60	① 2 3 4 5
I can guess the meaning of single unknown words from the context thus deducing the meaning of expressions if the topic is familiar.	60	① 2 3 4 5
I have a sufficient vocabulary to express myself with some circumlocutions on most topics pertinent to my everyday life such as family, hobbies and interests, work, travel, and current events.	60, 61, 67	1 ② 3 4 5
I can express myself reasonably accurately in familiar, predictable situations.	61, 62, 65, 67	1 ② 3 4 5
I can write simple texts about experiences or events, for example about a trip, for a school newspaper or a club newsletter.	63	① 2 3 4 5

Unit 8

Competences	Page	Your score
I can read columns or interviews in newspapers and magazines in which someone takes a stand on a current topic or event and understand the overall meaning of the text.	68, 72, 73	1 **(2)** 3 4 5
In private letters I can understand those parts dealing with events, feelings and wishes well enough to correspond regularly with a pen friend.	70	1 **(2)** 3 4 5
I can generally follow the main points of extended discussion around me, provided speech is clearly articulated in standard dialect.	71, 72	**(1)** 2 3 4 5
I can give or seek personal views and opinions in an informal discussion with friends.	71, 72, 73, 74	**(1)** 2 3 4 5
I can listen to a short narrative and form hypotheses about what will happen next.	72	**(1)** 2 3 4 5

Unit 9

Competences	Page	Your score
I can understand the main points in short newspaper articles about current and familiar topics.	76	1 **(2)** 3 4 5
I can understand the most important information in short simple everyday information brochures.	79	**(1)** 2 3 4 5
I can understand the main points of radio news bulletins and simpler recorded material on topics of personal interest delivered relatively slowly and clearly.	80	1 **(2)** 3 4 5
I can make myself understood using memorised phrases and single expressions.	81, 82	1 2 3 4 **(5)**
I can express myself reasonably accurately in familiar, predictable situations.	81, 83	1 2 **(3)** 4 5

Unit 10

Competences	Page	Your score
I can understand the main points in short newspaper articles about current and familiar topics.	88	1 2 **(3)** 4 5
I have a sufficient vocabulary to express myself with some circumlocutions on most topics pertinent to my everyday life such as family, hobbies and interests, work, travel, and current events.	88, 93, 94, 95	1 2 **(3)** 4 5
I can generally follow the main points of extended discussion around me, provided speech is clearly articulated in standard dialect.	89	1 **(2)** 3 4 5
I can describe myself, my family and other people.	91	1 2 3 4 **(5)**
I can describe dreams, hopes and ambitions.	93	**(1)** 2 3 4 5

Unit 11

Competences	Page	Your score
I can maintain a conversation or discussion but may sometimes be difficult to follow when trying to say exactly what I would like to.	96	**(1)** 2 3 4 5
I can generally follow the main points of extended discussion around me, provided speech is clearly articulated in standard dialect.	97	1 2 **(3)** 4 5
I can understand short narratives about everyday things dealing with topics which are familiar to me if the text is written in simple language.	98	1 2 3 4 **(5)**
I can give detailed accounts of experiences, describing feelings and reactions.	101	**(1)** 2 3 4 5
I can deal with most situations likely to arise when making travel arrangements through an agent or when actually travelling.	102	**(1)** 2 3 4 5

Unit 12

Competences	Page	Your score
I have a sufficient vocabulary to express myself with some circumlocutions on most topics pertinent to my everyday life such as family, hobbies and interests, work, travel, and current events.	105, 111	1 2 3 **(4)** 5
I can understand the most important information in short simple everyday information brochures.	106	1 **(2)** 3 4 5
I can skim short texts (for example news summaries) and find relevant facts and information (for example who has done what and where).	106	1 **(2)** 3 4 5
I can express myself reasonably accurately in familiar, predictable situations.	107, 108, 110	1 2 3 **(4)** 5
I can describe dreams, hopes and ambitions.	109	1 **(2)** 3 4 5

New Inside Out Pre-intermediate Teacher's Book © Macmillan Publishers Limited 2008

Name *Overview*

Section & Aims	What the students are doing
🌐 Listening **SB page 4** Listening for specific information	Listening to people talking about names. Identifying nicknames and matching them to people. Talking about their own names.
🌐 Vocabulary **SB page 4** Family	Listening and repeating words for family members. Identifying male and female family words and completing a table. Talking about names.
Reading **SB page 5** Reading for specific information	Reading an article and finding out the reasons for choosing a name. Talking about choosing names.
Grammar **SB page 5** Tenses and auxiliary verbs	Matching verb phrases with tense names. Writing negative forms of sentences and naming tenses. Turning sentences into questions.
🌐 Pronunciation **SB page 6** Long vowel sounds	Listening and repeating names which contain long vowel sounds.
🌐 Listening **SB page 6** Listening and remembering	Listening to the names of people in photos and remembering them. Discussing techniques for remembering names.
Reading **SB page 7** Reading for gist	Matching headings to sections of a text. Discussing advice in a text on improving your memory.
🌐 Grammar **SB page 7** *look(s) / look(s) like*	Identifying parts of speech and using *look(s)* and *look(s) like* with adjectives and nouns. Writing sentences describing people using *look(s)* and *look(s) like*.
Reading **SB page 8** Reading for specific information	Reading and completing a questionnaire. Matching language learning tips with questions in a questionnaire.
Speaking **SB page 8** Fluency practice	Making changes to questions and asking a partner the questions.
Grammar **SB page 9** Question forms	Matching questions and answers. Rewriting questions and discussing the acceptability of them.
🌐 Speaking: anecdote **SB page 9** Fluency practice	Talking about a person who is important to them.
🌐 Useful phrases **SB page 10** Useful conversational phrases: showing you're interested	Matching conversations with pictures. Listening and repeating useful phrases for showing interest. Completing a conversation and practising it. Writing a new conversation about last weekend.
Vocabulary *Extra* **SB Page 11** Revision of words from the unit: family and relationship words; names	Completing a table with family words. Answering questions about family and relationships. Underlining the correct words in sentences. Completing a form about names.
Writing **WB page 9**	Filling in a form with personal information.

Name *Teacher's notes*

Warm up

- Write on the board a list of the first names of some of the members of your family. Draw an empty family tree with spaces for each of the names. Tell the students that all these people are related to you. Ask them to ask questions to find out how they are related. For example, *Is Mark your brother? Is Jeff Mary's husband?* Students who get a *yes* answer to their questions can come up to the board and write the name in the correct place in the family tree.

- Ask the students to write down the names of three friends and take turns with a partner asking and answering about them:

  'Who's Marina?'

  'She's my best friend. She lives near my house. We do a lot of things together.'

Listening (SB page 4)

1 🌐 1.01

- Focus the students' attention on the photos. Tell the students that they're going to hear a conversation between these two people, who have never met before. Then focus attention on the names. Explain that people are sometimes given *nicknames* by their family and friends. These names are generally given in childhood, but sometimes continue to be used when the people have grown up. They often refer to the person's physical appearance. Point out that *Tree* is likely to be a *nickname* and ask the students to guess what sort of person might get the nickname *Tree* (a very tall person). Explain also the concept of a *middle name* (a second name between the first name and the surname which can act as an alternative first name; it may also have religious or family significance), and the way some names are shortened (e.g. *Mike* is a short form of *Michael*, *Sue* is a short form of *Susan*).

- Play the recording and ask the students to tick the four names they hear for each person. Check answers with the class. Point out, or get the students to identify, that *Tree*, *Big Ben*, *Marie Antoinette* and *Baby* are nicknames. *Ben* is a short form of Benjamin and *Marie* a short form of Anne-Marie.

> The man: Benjamin, Ben, Tree, Big Ben
>
> The woman: Marie, Anne-Marie, Marie Antoinette, Baby

🌐 1.01 (M = Marie; B = Benjamin)

M: *Hi, I'm Marie.*

B: *Hi Marie. My name's Benjamin, but nobody calls me Benjamin. Well, my parents do, but my friends call me Ben.*

M: *Ben – that's nice.*

B: *Thanks. Actually, my old friends call me Tree.*

M: *Tree? Why?*

B: *Well, as you can see, I'm very tall.*

M: *Oh, ha ha. … My friends call me lots of different names.*

B: *Really?*

M: *Yes. My mum's French and my dad's English, so I've got English and French friends, and they call me different things.*

B: *What do your French friends call you?*

M: *They use my full name – Anne-Marie.*

B: *And your English friends?*

M: *They just call me Marie. Some of them call me Marie Antoinette.*

B: *Marie Antoinette! Oh dear.*

M: *Well, it could be worse. My brother calls me Baby, because I'm the youngest in the family.*

B: *That's not so bad – my sisters call me Big Ben.*

M: *Ha ha. Oh no!*

Language notes

Vocabulary: names

- Benjamin and Marie just give their first names when they introduce themselves as the situation is quite informal. In more formal situations, people usually give both their first name and their surname.

- Benjamin got the nicknames *Tree* and *Big Ben* because he's tall. Big Ben is the bell in the clock tower of the Houses of Parliament in London, so again this is a jokey reference to his height. Marie-Antoinette was the wife of Louis XVI and Marie's English friends use this as a nickname for her because she has a similar sounding French name.

2

Ask the students to try to complete the sentences from memory. Allow them to compare and discuss their results in pairs before playing the recording again for them to check. Go through the answers with the class.

a) parents	d) French friends
b) old friends	e) English friends
c) sisters	f) brother

3

Ask the students if they have any special names that their family or friends call them. Then ask them to write down any of the names and the people who use them. If any students say that they don't have any special names, ask them if any members of their family or friends have special names. Then put them in pairs to tell their partners about their names. Remind them to say which names they like best.

Vocabulary (SB page 4)

1 🌐 1.02

- Focus the students' attention on the box. Point out that the underlining indicates the syllable of the word that has the strongest stress. Play the recording for the students to listen and repeat the words. Play it a second time and ask them to pay special attention to the stressed syllables. Allow them to compare results in pairs before checking with the whole class.

- Ask several students to repeat the words individually and check that they're putting the stress on the correct syllables.

2

- Focus the students' attention on the table. Point out that most relationship words describe either male or female family members. Ask the students to complete the table with the words in the box in Exercise 1, adding the names of their own family members where appropriate. (If you wish, you could turn this into a competition, with the winner being the person in the class who can match a name from their family to as many different words as possible.)

- When the students have completed the table, ask them if any of the words could go in both columns (*cousin*). Check answers with the class. Then read out the example and put the students in pairs to tell each other about some of the members of their families.

- Go round, monitoring and giving help. Make sure the students are pronouncing all the words for family members correctly.

Male: boyfriend, brother, brother-in-law, cousin, father, grandfather, half-brother, nephew, son, stepfather, uncle

Female: aunt, cousin, daughter, girlfriend, grandmother, half-sister, mother, niece, sister, sister-in-law, stepmother
(Note that *cousin* can be both male and female.)

Language notes

Vocabulary: *sister-in-law*

Your sister-in-law could be any of the following: the wife of your brother; the sister of your husband; the sister of your wife.

Vocabulary: *stepsister*

If one of your parents marries again, the children of the person they marry become your stepbrothers and/or stepsisters.

Vocabulary: *half-sister*

Your half-sister shares either the same mother or the same father as you, but not both.

3

Pairwork. Focus the students' attention on the table again. Go through the questions with the class and elicit a couple of answers to the first question. You could give some examples from your own country, if appropriate. Ask the students to discuss the questions in pairs. Go round, monitoring and giving help, and encourage some pairs to report back to the class on their discussions.

Reading (SB page 5)

1

Explain to the class how your own parents chose your own name (or give an example of someone you know). Then go through the reasons with the class. Put the students in pairs to discuss how their parents chose their names. Go round, monitoring and giving help if necessary. Take note of any interesting discussions and ask the students to report these back to the class.

2

- Focus the students' attention on the text *What's in a name?* Give them plenty of time to read it, and answer any questions they may have about vocabulary. Ask them which of the reasons listed in Exercise 1 isn't mentioned.

- Ask the students what the writer's first name and middle name are (Enid Blodwen). Ask them if they think she likes these names. (No, she doesn't. She says unfortunately her mother chose to name her after her grandmother.) You may need to explain that the first of these names sounds very old-fashioned to someone from the UK and that the second is an old Welsh name, which would sound a little odd to anyone not from Wales.

Reason *e* isn't mentioned.

Madonna (born 1958)
Madonna is one of the most successful recording artists of all time, with songs such as *Material Girl* and *Into the Groove*. She's also acted in a number of films, including *Desperately Seeking Susan* and *Evita*. In 2000, she married British film director Guy Ritchie. She continues to produce best-selling albums.

Lourdes /lɔːdz/
Small town in southwest France. The spring water found in caves here is believed to have healing properties, and thousands of Roman Catholic pilgrims visit Lourdes every year hoping for a cure. Madonna named her daughter after the town because her mother had wanted to visit Lourdes just before she died.

David Beckham (born 1975)
English footballer. He played for Manchester United (1992–2003) and Real Madrid (2003–2007) before moving to the United States to play for LA Galaxy. He captained the England football team on 99 occasions. He married ex-Spice Girls singer Victoria Adams in 1999.

Victoria Beckham (born 1974)
Also known as 'Posh Spice', Victoria Beckham was a member of the Spice Girls pop group from 1994 to 2000. She married footballer David Beckham in 1999. They have three sons.

Brooklyn
Brooklyn is a borough of New York City. According to Victoria Beckham's autobiography, she and her husband learnt that she was pregnant with their first child in Brooklyn (NY), so they decided to name him after the borough.

Leonardo DiCaprio /lijɒˈnɑːdəʊ dɪˈkæprɪjəʊ/ (born 1974)
Leonardo DiCaprio was named after Leonardo da Vinci. He started acting when he was fourteen, appearing in TV commercials and educational films. He's starred in a number of successful films, such as *Romeo and Juliet* (1995), *Titanic* (1996), *Gangs of New York* (2002) and *The Aviator* (2005). He's also greatly involved in environmental work in the US.

Leonardo da Vinci /lijɒˈnɑːdəʊ dæ ˈvɪntʃiː/ (1452–1519)
Leonardo da Vinci was an Italian Renaissance artist, famous for paintings such as the *Mona Lisa* and *The Last Supper*. He also made designs, some hundreds of years ahead of his time and contributed greatly to the study of anatomy, astronomy, and civil engineering.

Beyoncé Knowles /biˈjɒnseɪ nəʊlz/ (born 1981)
American R&B singer. She was originally in the girl band Destiny's Child, and is now a solo artist, actor and fashion designer. Her first solo album *Dangerously in Love* (2001) became one of the biggest commercial successes of that year. She received five Grammy Awards in 2004 and had a worldwide number one hit with *Irreplaceable* in 2006.

Britney Spears /ˈbrɪtniː ˈspɪəz/ (born 1981)
American pop singer. She started out aged 11 in *The New Mickey Mouse Club* on the Disney Channel. In the late 1990s, she had hits with *Baby One More Time* and *Oops!… I Did It Again*. In 2004, she married dancer Kevin Federline. They had two children but divorced in 2006.

Keanu Reeves /kɪjɑːnuː riːvz/ (born 1964)
Canadian actor. His first hit film *Bill and Ted's Excellent Adventure* (1989) saw him cast in a comedy role. But then, in the 1990s, he made a succession of action blockbusters, including *Point Break* (1991), *Speed* (1994) and *The Matrix* (1999) establishing him as a top name in Hollywood.

Bruce Willis (born 1955)
American actor who found fame in the TV series *Moonlighting* (1985–1989), but is best known for his roles in the *Die Hard* films (1988 and 1989). His other films include *Pulp Fiction* (1994), *The Jackal* (1997), and *The Sixth Sense* (1999). He was married to Demi Moore.

Demi Moore (born 1962)
American actress who started out in teen films in the 1980s and became one of the best known actresses in 1990s. Her films include *Ghost* (1990) and *A Few Good Men* (1992). She was married to actor Bruce Willis from 1987 to 2000. She and Bruce Willis had three daughters. She married actor Ashton Kutcher (born 1978) in 2005.

3
Ask the students to think about the question for a moment or two and then discuss in pairs which names they would choose. Ask them to report back to the class.

Grammar (SB page 5)
Tenses and auxiliary verbs

1

- This exercise offers quick revision of some of the tenses the students should already have encountered. Focus the students' attention on the information in the margin which gives them the names of the tenses they'll need and the auxiliary verbs that these tenses use. Explain that the present simple and past simple only use auxiliary verbs in negatives and questions. (You can use *do* in affirmative sentences for emphasis, but this is not taught at this level.)

- Ask the students to look at the highlighted verb phrases in the article in the previous section and ask them to match them to the tense names. Allow them to work in pairs or small groups. Then check answers with the class.

> *people are changing* – present continuous
> *I've chosen* – present perfect
> *I'm going to call* – (be) going to future
> *I like* – present simple
> *she named* – past simple

Extra activity

To give further practice of the link between auxiliary verbs and tenses, put this matching activity on the board:

Match each tense with its auxiliary verb.

a) Present simple   *am/am not   are/aren't
is/isn't*

b) Present continuous   *has/hasn't   have/haven't*

c) Present perfect   *do/don't   does/doesn't*

d) Past simple   *am/am not   are/aren't
is/isn't*

e) Future *(be) going to*   *did/didn't*

Language notes

Grammar: tense review

- The present simple is used to talk about facts, habits or routines.
  I live in a small house in Oxford.

- The present continuous is used to talk about activities in progress now or around now.
  He's wearing an old pair of jeans.

- The present perfect is used to talk about completed past actions in 'time up to now'. There is no past time marker.
  They've visited fourteen different countries.

- The past simple is used to talk about completed past actions, where a past time marker is mentioned or implied.
  She met him a long time ago.

- The future *(be) going to* is used to talk about future plans and intentions: things you've decided to do.
  I'm going to see him on Thursday.

Grammar: auxiliary verbs

- *Do/does/did* are used with the present simple and past simple to help form questions, negatives and short answers.
  Do you come here every day?
  Yes, I do. I didn't see you yesterday.

- *Am/are/is* are used to form the present continuous: *I'm studying art and design. / She's staying with her friend.* They're usually used in contracted form ('m, 're, 's) except in formal writing. *Am/are/is* are also used to form *going to* sentences for the future and are usually used in contracted form: *I'm going to see two old friends this weekend.* When *am/are/is* are used in questions and short answers, they aren't contracted. *Are you listening to me? Yes, I am* (not *Yes, I'm*).

- *Have/has* are used to form the present perfect: *I've been to Japan. My brother's been to most Asian countries.* They're usually used in contracted form ('ve, 's) except in formal writing. When *have/has* are used in questions and short answers, they aren't contracted. *Have you been to Italy? Yes, I have* (not *Yes, I've*).

2

- Go through the example with the class and then ask the students to write the negative forms of the remaining sentences. Allow them to compare in pairs before checking answers with the class.

- Ask them to go through the negative sentences and tick the ones that are true for them.

> a) I don't like British pop music. (Present simple)
> b) I'm not reading a good book at the moment. (Present continuous)
> c) I'm not going to have a coffee after the lesson. (Future *be going to*)
> d) I didn't go out last night. (Past simple)
> e) I haven't been to Ireland. (Present perfect)
> f) I can't play the piano. (Present simple)

3

Students write the question forms. As they do this, go round checking that they're forming the questions correctly. With weaker classes, check the questions with the class before putting the students into pairs to practise asking and answering them.

> a) Do you like British pop music?
>   Yes, I do. / No, I don't.
> b) Are you reading a good book at the moment?
>   Yes, I am. / No, I'm not.
> c) Are you going to have a coffee after the lesson?
>   Yes, I am. / No, I'm not.
> d) Did you go out last night?
>   Yes, I did. / No, I didn't
> e) Have you been to Ireland?
>   Yes, I have. / No, I haven't.
> f) Can you play the piano?
>   Yes, I can. / No, I can't.

Pronunciation (SB page 6)

1 🔊 1.03

- Focus the students' attention on the long vowel sounds. Play the recording and ask them to repeat the vowel sounds. After they've done this chorally, ask several students to repeat the words individually, and check that everyone is producing the sounds correctly.

- If the students are unfamiliar with phonemic symbols, you may want to do a bit more work on this. Write the symbols on the board and point to them at random, asking the students (at first chorally and then individually) to say the sounds. Choose the names of some of the students in the class whose names exemplify the different sounds and write them on the board next to the appropriate phonemes.

2 🔊 1.04

- Focus the students' attention to the table. Read the names in the first column aloud, exaggerating the vowel sound. Then play the recording and ask the students to listen and repeat.

- Give the students a minute or two to write in the correct phonemic symbols. Remind them that they are all listed in Exercise 1. Encourage them to say the sounds as they write them to reinforce the link between the sounds and the symbols. Check answers with the class. Then ask different students to read out the different columns of names.

> 1 /uː/ 2 /ɜː/ 3 /ɑː/ 4 /iː/ 5 /ɔː/

Listening (SB page 6)

1 1.05

- Ask the students whether or not they find it easy to remember people's names when they are first introduced. Then focus their attention on the photos and ask them to look at the people for a couple of minutes. Explain that they're going to hear the names of all these people on the recording and they must try to remember them, without writing anything down. Play the recording once.

- Ask the students to work individually to write down as many of the names as they can remember, either next to the photos in the book or with the numbers 1 to 9 in their notebooks. When they've finished, allow them to compare with a partner.

> 🌐 1.05
>
> *Study the faces of the people in the photographs. Listen and remember their names. Do not write anything.*
>
> *Number one is Charles.*   *Charles.*
> *Number two is Ann.*   *Ann.*
> *Number three is George.*   *George.*
> *Number four is Sophia.*   *Sophia.*
> *Number five is Pete.*   *Pete.*
> *Number six is Pearl.*   *Pearl.*
> *Number seven is Paul.*   *Paul.*
> *Number eight is Marge.*   *Marge.*
> *Number nine is Sue.*   *Sue.*

2

Play the recording for the students to check their answers. Find out who remembered the most names correctly. Ask this person if they have any special techniques for remembering names.

Reading (SB page 7)

1

- Tell the students they're going to read about some ways of improving their memory for names. Go through the headings with them first as this will give them a general idea of what the text is about. Then ask them to read the text and match the headings to the appropriate sections. Allow them to compare results in pairs or small groups before checking with the class. Give the students a chance to read the text

again, and answer any questions they may have about vocabulary.

- Ask them if they know of any other techniques for trying to remember other people's names. One method is to connect a person's name with a common word. For example, for the name Hannah, imagine her holding a handbag. For Robert, imagine him as a robber.

> 1 b) Pay attention
> 2 c) Use the name and repeat it
> 3 d) Visualise the name
> 4 a) Connect the name and the appearance

Cultural notes

Franklin D. Roosevelt /ˈfrænklɪn dɪ ˈruːsəvelt/ (1882–1945)
Franklin D. Roosevelt was an American politician and the 32nd President of the United States (1933–1945). His presidency oversaw the Great Depression of the 1930s and ended with the Second World War (1939–1945).

2

- Go through the questions with the whole class and make sure the students understand them before putting them into pairs to discuss them. Go round, monitoring and giving help.

- Ask the pairs to report back to the whole class on their discussions. Write any suggestions they make for remembering and learning new English words on the board. Encourage the students to make a note of these and try them out.

Grammar (SB page 7)

look(s) / look(s) like

1

- Focus the students' attention on the box of words. Point out the two examples: the adjective *friendly* and the noun phrase *a banker*. Ask the class for two or three more examples of adjectives and nouns or noun phrases. Then ask them to go through the box and write *N* or *A* for the remaining words and phrases. You may need to explain that a *noun phrase* or an *adjective phrase* is just a noun or adjective in combination with two or more words. As they do this go round, monitoring and giving help. Check answers with the class before moving on to the second part of the exercise.

- Ask the students to look at the information about the use of *look(s)* and *look(s) like* in the margin. Ask them what type of word you use after *look(s)* (adjective/ adjective phrase) and what type of word you use after *look(s) like* (noun/noun phrase). Ask the students to give some examples using both structures.

2

- Choose one of the photos on page 6 and ask the whole class to suggest sentences using *looks* and *looks like* to describe him or her.

- Then ask the students to work individually to write sentences about the other people on page 6. Go through the example with the class and point out that they should leave spaces for the people's names.

- Put the students in pairs and ask them to exchange their descriptions and try to complete their partner's sentences with the correct names.

Extra activity

If appropriate, repeat the activity using people in the class. Ask the students to choose three classmates and write sentences using *looks* and *looks like* to describe them. As they do this, go round, helping and making sure that no one writes anything hurtful or offensive. Put them in pairs to complete the sentences.

Reading (SB page 8)

1

- Tell the students they're going to complete a questionnaire about learning languages. Ask them first to read through the questionnaire and ask you if there's anything they don't understand.

- Ask them to work individually to decide their own answers to the questions. When they've finished, point out the *What your score means* section and ask them to work out their own score. Ask them to compare with a partner and discuss whether or not they think their scores are correct.

2

- Go through the tips with the whole class and make sure the students understand them. Give them a minute or two to match them to the questions in the questionnaire.

- Ask the students to suggest other tips for learning English. Write any suggestions on the board and encourage the class to try them out.

a) Question 3	e) Question 1
b) Question 6	f) Question 8
c) Question 2	g) Question 4
d) Question 7	h) Question 5

Speaking (SB page 8)

1

- Demonstrate the activity by using some of the alternatives to form new questions and ask various students around the class to answer them. If you don't want to pre-empt the questions the students will ask and answer in the exercise, put the following on the board and use it to demonstrate:

  How many **languages** can you **speak**?
  (musical instruments – play/people in the class – name/phone numbers – remember)

- Ask the students to work individually to make six new questions. As they do this, go round, monitoring and making sure they're forming the questions correctly. The alternatives are all correctly formed to slot into the questions, so the students shouldn't make any changes to the verb forms.

2

- Put the students into pairs and ask them to take turns asking and answering their questions. Tell them that they should try to remember any interesting answers which they can report back to the class.

- In a feedback session, ask the students to tell the class what they found out about their partners.

Grammar (SB page 9)

Question forms

1

- Focus the students' attention on the table. Read out each statement, followed by the corresponding question. Ask the students what they notice about statements and questions (the word order changes).

- Go through the questions one by one with the class, asking them to match them with the correct answers. Make sure they can identify the auxiliary verbs correctly and point out that auxiliary verbs are not used in questions with *be*. Explain also that you use *do/does/did* to form questions when there's no auxiliary verb in the corresponding statement.

- Put the students into pairs and tell them to take turns asking and answering the questions in the table.

a) 2	b) 3	c) 4	d) 1

Language notes

Grammar: word order

When making questions…

… the auxiliary comes before the subject, not after it (as in statements).

… if there is no other auxiliary verb, use *do*.

… if there is another auxiliary verb, don't use *do* (~~Do you can swim?~~).

… *What, Who, Where, How*, etc. (question words) come at the beginning.

2

- Ask the students to look carefully at the six questions and decide which ones are incorrect and need *do*, *does* or *did* to make them correct. Remind them that *do*, *does* and *did* are used when there's no auxiliary verb in the corresponding statement which can be used to form the question.
- Ask the students to work individually to write correct questions. Go round, monitoring and giving help.
- Put the students in pairs and ask them to take turns asking and answering their questions.

> a) *Do you* play the guitar?
> b) *Did you sleep* well last night?
> c) Can you drive?
> d) Where *does* your mother come from?
> e) Have you been to the Vatican?
> f) What's your favourite colour?

3

- Go through the example with the class and then ask the students to work individually to rewrite the questions in the correct order, but tell them not to ask their partners the questions. Allow them to compare their results in pairs before checking with the class.
- Ask the students to work in small groups and discuss in which situations is it OK to ask these questions. Ask them to make notes of their answers. In multinational groups, the answers may differ according to the nationalities of the students, so ask groups to note any differences and report these back to the class.
- Finally, find out what conclusions the groups came to. Ask if they think age, nationality or cultural background are factors in whether or not questions are acceptable.

> a) How old are you?
> b) Do you believe in life after death?
> c) How much do you earn?
> d) Have you ever broken the law?
> e) Which political party do you vote for?
> f) How many boyfriends or girlfriends have you had?

Cultural note

It's difficult to give hard and fast rules about which questions are or are not acceptable. Generally, in the UK, question a) would probably only be used with children. Adults might feel uncomfortable to be asked their age. Question b) might be acceptable amongst friends if the conversation had turned to such a topic. It would be unacceptable to ask this of a stranger. Questions c), d), e) and f) would make most people in the UK very embarrassed and wouldn't normally be asked, even by close friends.

4 Pairwork

- The pairwork exercise for this unit is on pages 116 and 121 of the Student's Book. Put the students in pairs and tell them who will be Student A, and who will be Student B.
- While they're doing the exercise, go round, monitoring and giving help. Take note of any errors which may need particular attention later, and also any examples of good language use which you can praise.

Student A	Student B
1 What – b	1 What – b
2 Where – c	2 Where – a
3 What – b	3 What – a
4 Who – a	4 Who – c
5 Which – c	5 Which – b
6 How – b	6 How – c

NB: Edinburgh /ˈedɪnbərə/; Buckingham Palace /ˈbʌkɪŋəm ˈpæləs/; The Tower of London /ðə ˈtaʊə əv ˈlʌndən/; The Houses of Parliament /ðə ˈhaʊzɪz əv ˈpɑːləmənt/; Queen Elizabeth /kwiːn ɪˈlɪzəbəθ/; The Sheriff of Nottingham /ðə ˈʃerɪf əv ˈnɒtɪŋəm/

5 Grammar *Extra* 1

Ask the students to turn to *Grammar Extra* 1 on page 126 of the Student's Book. Here they'll find an explanation of the grammar they've been studying and further exercises to practise it.

1
a) Do you like jazz?
b) Can you swim?
c) Did you go skiing last winter?
d) Are you wearing jeans today?
e) Have you been to Egypt?
f) Are you going to drive home after the lesson?

2
a) Yes, I do. / No, I don't.
b) Yes, I can. / No, I can't.
c) Yes, I did. / No, I didn't.
d) Yes, I am. / No, I'm not.
e) Yes, I have. / No, I haven't.
f) Yes, I am. / No, I'm not.

3
a) Does he like jazz? Yes, he does. / No, he doesn't.
b) Can he swim? Yes, he can. / No, he can't.
c) Did he go skiing last year?
   Yes, he did. / No, he didn't.
d) Is he wearing jeans today? Yes, he is. / No, he isn't.
e) Has he been to Egypt? Yes, he has. / No, he hasn't.
f) Is he going to drive home after the lesson?
   Yes, he is. / No, he isn't.

4
a) How far do you live from the school?
b) When did you last go to the theatre?
c) What are you going to do this evening?
d) How many cups of coffee have you had today?
e) What kind of pen are you using at the moment?
f) Where did you buy your shoes?

5
a) What do you do? – 3
b) Who do you work for? – 7
c) Which department do you work in? – 5
d) How do you get to work? – 2
e) When did you start working there? – 1
f) Why do you like working there? – 4
g) How much do you earn? – 6

6
a) Present continuous.   d) Future (be) going to
b) Past simple.   e) Present simple.
c) Present perfect.

a) We aren't studying Shakespeare in our English class.
b) My parents didn't name me after my uncle.
c) I haven't recently learnt to drive.
d) My friends aren't going to organise a party for me tomorrow.
e) I don't like getting up early in the morning.

Speaking: anecdote (SB page 9)

Anecdotes are features that occur regularly in this series. They're extended speaking tasks, where the students tackle a longer piece of discourse on a personal topic. There are questions to guide them and a model to listen to. For more information about how to set up, monitor and repeat Anecdotes, see page xx in the Introduction.

1 🌐 1.06

- Focus the students' attention on the photo of Dan. Explain that they're going to hear his friend Lee talking about somebody who is important to him.

- Go through the sentences and the choices with the class. Explain any unknown vocabulary. Then play the recording and ask the students to listen and decide which is the correct information. They should underline it in their books.

a) Dan Carter.
b) When we were five years old.
c) In Brussels.
d) a teacher
e) In the summer.
f) He knows me so well.
g) He's a really good listener.
h) late
i) On my birthday.

🌐 1.06

Dan Carter is my best friend. We met when we were five years old, because our parents were friends and we went to the same school. He lives in Brussels now – he's a teacher at the International School there. So I only see him in the summer when he comes home to visit his family. Of course, we stay in touch by email and phone. He's important to me because he knows me so well. When I'm feeling down or when I need to talk to somebody, I can always call him. Recently,

I had girlfriend problems and he was great. I'd say his best quality is that he's a really good listener. He just lets you talk and he listens. But he isn't perfect! He's always late for everything and he never says sorry. Never! One day last summer, we arranged to meet at seven o'clock to play football, and he arrived at half past nine! It was nearly dark! Oh well, nobody's perfect, are they? Last time I saw him was on my birthday, and we had a great time. We always have a great time.

2

- Give the students a minute or two to decide who they're going to talk about. Then ask them to look at the questions in Exercise 1 again. Allow them to make notes of what they're going to say about the person and how they're going to say it, but discourage them from writing a paragraph that they can simply read out. Go round, monitoring and giving help.

- Pairwork. Put the students in pairs and ask them to take turns to tell their partner about their important person. Encourage them to ask each other follow-up questions to get further information. Then ask some pairs to report back to the class about what they found out.

Useful phrases (SB page 10)

1 🌐 1.07

Focus the students' attention on the illustrations which show two friends discussing the weekend. Ask them what the difference is between the two pictures (in the first Beth looks bored; in the second she looks interested). Play the recording and ask the students to say which picture best illustrates the conversation.

The conversation matches picture 1.

🌐 1.07   (A = Adam; B = Beth)

A: *Did you have a good weekend?*
B: *Not bad. How about you?*
A: *I had a really good meal on Saturday night.*
B: *Oh.*
A: *Yes, we went to a new place in town – Edamame.*
B: *Ah.*
A: *They have a Japanese chef from Tokyo.*
B: *Uh huh.*
A: *And the menu is fantastic – they make their own sushi.*
B: *Oh.*
A: *Yes. It's the best sushi I've ever tasted.*
B: *Mm.*
A: *And it wasn't expensive. We had starters, main course, dessert and wine, and it only cost £25 each.*
B: *Ah.*
A: *I know. Unfortunately, when we got back to the car, we had a parking ticket.*
B: *Oh.*

2 ● 1.08

Tell the students they're going to listen to another version of the same conversation. Play the recording and ask them to say if Beth sounds more interested this time. Ask them to give reasons. (She doesn't just say *Oh, she uses other expressions to convey interest, she asks questions and reacts to what Adam says.*)

> Yes, she does.

3 ● 1.09

Play the recording. The students repeat the phrases after the speaker. Make sure that they match the speaker's intonation.

4

- Ask the students to complete the conversation with the phrases from Exercise 3. Allow them to work in pairs if they wish.
- After checking answers with the class, put the students into pairs and ask them to practise the conversation, taking turns to be Adam and Beth. Go round, monitoring and giving help. Tell the student playing Beth to use slightly exaggerated intonation in order to convey real interest. Ask any particularly good pairs to perform their conversations for the class.

> 1 Really?
> 2 I've never heard of it. (*also possible* That sounds interesting. That sounds great.)
> 3 That sounds interesting. (*also possible* Do they? That sounds great.)
> 4 Do they? (*also possible* That sounds interesting. That sounds great. Wow! That's brilliant.)
> 5 That sounds great. (*also possible* Wow! That's brilliant.)
> 6 Wow! That's brilliant. (*also possible* That sounds great.)
> 7 Oh no! That's terrible.

5

- Pairwork. Give the students a few minutes to write their conversations. Go round, monitoring and giving help. Encourage them to use as many of the useful phrases as possible. Then ask several pairs to perform their conversations for the class.

Vocabulary *Extra* (SB page 11)

Family and other relationships

1

Focus the students' attention on the table and point out that they're all family words. Then ask them to complete the table with the correct family words. Point out that the first one has been done for them. Check that the students can pronounce the words correctly.

> a) granddaughter   b) sister   c) grandfather
> d) parents   e) brother   f) cousin   g) sister
> h) father-in-law   i) stepmother   j) half-brother
> k) ex-husband   l) partner   m) twin

2

Pairwork. Demonstrate first with a confident student by getting them to ask you the first two questions. Then ask the students to work in pairs and take turns asking and answering the questions.

Focus on names

1

- Ask the students to work individually and underline the correct words. Then allow them to compare answers in pairs before checking with the class.
- Ask the students to tick the sentences that are true for them and compare with a partner.

> a) call   b) meaning   c) named   d) maiden
> e) initials   f) signature

2

Ask the students to complete the form for themselves. Go round, monitoring and giving help.

Further practice material

Need more writing practice?

→ Workbook page 9
- Filling in a form with personal information.

Need more classroom practice activities?

→ Photocopiable resource materials pages 151 to 153
  Grammar: *What's in a name?*
  Vocabulary: *Family puzzle*
  Communication: *Questions for me*
→ Top 10 activities pages xv to xx

Need DVD material?

→ DVD – Programme 1: *Names*

Need progress tests?

→ Test CD – *Test Unit 1*

Need more on important teaching concepts?

→ Key concepts in *New Inside Out* pages xxii to xxxv

Need student self-study practice?

→ CD-ROM – Unit 1: *Name*

Need student CEF self-evaluation?

→ CEF Checklists pages xxxvii to xliv

Need more information and more ideas?

→ www.insideout.net

2 Place Overview

Section & Aims	What the students are doing
⊕ Vocabulary **SB page 12** Places in a city	Finding features of a place in photos. Ordering the features near their school from nearest to furthest away.
⊕ Listening **SB page 13** Listening for gist	Listening to people talking about the places where they live and matching them to photos. Completing descriptions with adjectives.
Grammar & Vocabulary **SB page 13** *so/such, very/too*; adjectives to describe places	Identifying the uses of *so* and *such*. Completing an email. Then changing the email to sound negative. Identifying the uses of *very* and *too*. Then completing sentences.
Grammar **SB page 14** Countable and uncountable nouns	Matching questions and responses. Completing a table with nouns and discussing the plurals of nouns. Asking questions about cities and villages.
⊕ Vocabulary & Pronunciation **SB page 14** Country and nationality words; word stress	Completing a table with country and nationality words and marking the stress. Talking about countries they would like to visit.
Speaking **SB page 14** Fluency practice	Comparing things from different countries.
Reading **SB page 15** Reading for detail	Reading about holiday destinations and listing them in order. Answering questions in a competition. Writing a review of a holiday destination.
Reading **SB page 16** Reading for detail	Completing a description of a country. Identifying the country in the text.
Grammar **SB page 16** Quantity expressions	Matching quantity expressions with countable and uncountable nouns. Rewriting sentences to make them true for them. Asking and answering questions about daily habits.
Vocabulary **SB page 17** Location	Labelling the points of a compass. Matching location descriptions to cities.
⊕ Speaking: anecdote **SB page 17** Fluency practice	Talking about the best place they've ever visited.
⊕ Useful phrases **SB page 18** Useful conversational phrases for talking about where you are from	Reading and listening to a conversation to identify nationalities. Matching people with maps. Completing useful phrases, then listening and repeating them. Writing a conversation.
Vocabulary *Extra* **page 19** Revision of words from the unit: places; adjectives; like	Matching places in a picture with words. Categorising adjectives, then using them to describe their cities. Matching the uses of *like* with example sentences.
Writing **WB page 15**	Writing a web posting.

2 Place *Teacher's notes*

Warm-up

Think of a city that you and your students know well, or which is so famous that they're likely to know quite a lot about it. Tell them that you are thinking of a city and that they must ask you questions to find out where it is. Encourage them to ask about buildings and other features in the city as well as what country it's in. A student who identifies the city correctly can then think of a new city and answer questions from the class.

Vocabulary (SB page 12)

1

- Focus the students' attention on the photos. Ask them to look closely at the photos and to decide whether they would like to live in any of the places shown.

- Pairwork. Ask the students to discuss with a partner whether they would like to live in any of the places. Encourage them to give reasons why or why not.

- Go round, monitoring and giving help with vocabulary. Ask some students to report back on their discussion to the whole class.

Cultural notes

Venice /ˈvenɪs/
A city in the north east of Italy built on 118 small islands, separated by 150 canals. The main square is St. Mark's Square (Piazza San Marco), which features St. Mark's Basilica and The Doge's Palace (Palazzo Ducale). The city has a long association with the arts. The Venice Biennale has taken place there every other year since 1895, and the annual Venice Carnival is held in February, where people dress up in costumes and wear masks.

Rio de Janeiro /ˈriːəʊ də dʒəˈnɪərəʊ/
The second largest city in, and former capital of, Brazil. With a population of 5.6 million, Rio contains many of the sites famous to the rest of the world. These include Copacabana and Ipanema Beaches, Sugarloaf Mountain and the statue of Christ the Redeemer. Rio de Janeiro is also the venue of the famous carnival parade, which usually takes place every February.

La Bastide /læ bæˈstiːd/
This is a fictional city, created for the purposes of this exercise.

2 🌐 1.10

- Focus the students' attention on the words in the box. Point out that the underlining indicates the syllable of the word that has the strongest stress. Play the recording and ask the students to listen and repeat the words in the box. When they've done this chorally, ask several students to repeat the words individually. Check that the students can pronounce the words correctly.

- Give the students a few minutes to find as many of the items as they can in the photos. Check answers with the class and make sure that they can understand and pronounce all the items.

> a) Venice – a canal, a cathedral
> b) La Bastide – a church, a fountain, a square
> c) Rio de Janeiro – high-rise buildings, a hill, the sea, a statue

Language note

Vocabulary: places of worship

Traditionally a *church* or a *cathedral* is a place of worship associated with Christians, a *mosque* is a place of worship associated with Muslims and a *temple* is a place of worship associated with Hindus, Buddhists or Sikhs.

3

Ask the students first to tick the things that they can find near their school. They can then put them in order along the line. You may need to establish a distance for 'near', such as within two kilometres or within five kilometres. Point out the superlative form *nearest* from *near* and *furthest* from *far*.

Listening (SB page 13)

1 🌐 1.11

- Focus the students' attention on the photos in the margin. Tell them that they're going to listen to Paulo, Armelle and Luigi talking about the three places in the photos on page 12. Ask them to listen and match each person with one of the photos. Check answers before moving on to the next part of the exercise.

- See if the students can remember who does and who doesn't like living where they live without listening to the recording again. Encourage them to say what they can remember. Then play the recording again for them to check their answers.

> Paulo: c) Rio de Janeiro. He likes it apart from the summer.
> Armelle: b) La Bastide. She doesn't like it.
> Luigi: a) Venice. He hates living there.

🔊 **1.11**

Paulo
(I = Interviewer; P = Paulo)

I: *Do you like your city?*

P *Oh yes, I feel lucky to be living in a city that's so big and exciting.*

I: *What's the architecture like?*

P: *A mixture of old and new. There are too many high-rise buildings in some parts of the city. But there are plenty of cheap restaurants and interesting cafés and bars. And the nightlife is great. We also have the most famous beach in the world – Copacabana Beach.*

I: *Ah. What's the weather like?*

P: *It's great most of the time. The only time I don't like Rio much is in the summer: it's too hot and humid.*

Armelle
(I = Interviewer; A = Armelle)

I: *Where do you live?*

A: *Well, I live in a small village with my parents. My grandparents live here too, and my aunts and uncles. In fact, I think I'm related to about fifty per cent of the people in my village.*

I: *What's your village like?*

A: *It's very pretty. The countryside is beautiful, and the air is lovely and clean. But at night it's too quiet. I find it so dull and boring here – there aren't any discos or cinemas.*

I: *What are the people like?*

A: *Oh, they're kind and really friendly, but there aren't many young people. I want to go and live in the city. Soon.*

Luigi
(I = Interviewer; L = Luigi)

I: *What do you think of your city?*

L: *It is a very special place. It's such a romantic city.*

I: *What's the city centre like?*

L: *The buildings are beautiful, and we have San Marco, one of the most famous churches in the world. The Piazza San Marco is wonderful, and during carnival in February Venice is the best place in the world to be.*

I: *Do you like living here?*

L: *No, I really hate living here. It's horrible. There are too many tourists everywhere. It gets very noisy and crowded.*

I: *Oh dear. What are the shops like?*

> L: *Well, because of the tourists the shops are too expensive, and the canals are so dirty and polluted. My city is too small for all these people. Why don't they leave us in peace?*

2

- Go through the adjectives with the class and make sure that everyone understands them. Then ask them to work individually to complete the descriptions using the adjectives. Allow them to compare in pairs before checking with the class.

- Ask the students to say which of these adjectives they would use to describe the places where they live.

> a) exciting   b) humid   c) clean   d) boring
> e) romantic   f) crowded   g) polluted
> h) small

Language note

Vocabulary: *humid*

Humid describes a climate that is hot and wet in a way that makes you feel uncomfortable (i.e. Tokyo in summer). *Damp* describes a climate that is wet and slightly cold (i.e. London in winter).

Grammar & Vocabulary (SB page 13)

so/such and *very/too*

1

- Ask the students to find and underline the instances of *so* and *such a/an* in Exercise 2 of the Listening section. Ask several students to read out the sentences containing these words.

- Focus the students' attention on the rules and ask them to complete them using information from the sentences in Listening Exercise 2. Check answers with the class and go through the example sentences in the margin. Then ask the students to produce one or two more sentences using *so* or *such* to describe where they live.

> a) so   b) such

2

Ask the students to complete the email. Check answers with the class and then ask if they think the person is happy or unhappy.

1 such a		5 so
2 so		6 such an
3 so		7 so
4 such a		8 such a
They're happy.		

3

- Tell the students that they're going to rewrite the email in Exercise 2 to make it sound negative. Go through the example with the class and point out that *ugly* is the opposite of the adjective *beautiful*. Ask them what the adjective in the next sentence of the email is (*lucky*) and what its opposite is (*unlucky*). Then give them a few minutes to rewrite the rest of the email. Go round, monitoring and giving help.

- Allow them to compare their results in pairs before checking with the class. Accept any alternative versions that make sense. For example, the students may put *terrible* instead of *awful*, etc.

> *Model answer:*
> This is such an ugly place. We're so unlucky with our hotel. It's really far from the city centre and the staff are so unfriendly. Our room is horrible and dirty, and we have such a terrible view of the city. There aren't many good restaurants and bars, and they're so expensive. It's such a boring city. The museums and art galleries are awful, and we aren't going to visit the royal palace because it's closed. It's so boring. We're having such a bad time – we want to come home now.

4

- Ask the students to look back again at Exercise 2 in the Listening section. This time ask them to highlight the instances of *very* and *too*. Ask several students to read out the sentences containing these words.

- Focus attention on the rules and ask the students to complete them using information from the sentences in Listening Exercise 2. Then go through the information and example sentences in the margin. Ask the students to produce one or two more sentences using *very* or *too* to describe where they live.

> a) very   b) too

5

- Ask the students to work individually to complete the sentences.

- Ask the students to read their sentences again and tick any that are true for them. Then let them compare with a partner.

> a) very   b) too   c) very   d) very   e) too
> f) too

Grammar (SB page 14)

Nouns: countable/uncountable

1

- Focus the students' attention to the information in the margin. Point out that countable nouns have plural forms, but uncountable nouns don't.

- Ask the students to match the questions with the responses.

- Check answers with the class by getting one student to read out a question and another to read out the correct response. Then ask them to identify which of the nouns in the questions are countable (*shops, people*) and uncountable (*weather, architecture*).

> a) 4   b) 3   c) 2   d) 1

Language notes

Vocabulary: irregular plurals

There are a number of irregular plural forms in English. Here are some of the most common:

- Words ending in *-f* or *-fe* in the singular change to *-ves*. For example: *half – halves, loaf – loaves, wife – wives, life – lives*.

- Words ending in *-o* in the singular change to *-oes*. For example: *potato – potatoes, tomato – tomatoes*.

- Words ending in *-y* in the singular change to *-ies*. For example: *city – cities, activity – activities*.

- Irregular plural nouns: *woman – women, person – people, mouse – mice, child – children*.

Vocabulary: countable/uncountable

- Countable nouns are the names of individual objects, people or ideas which can be counted, e.g. *a man, two women, five chairs*. With countable nouns you can use numbers and the indefinite article *a/an* (*two cinemas and a church*). Countable nouns have plurals (*shop, shops*). You can use *some* with plural countable nouns: *some restaurants*.

- Uncountable or mass nouns are the names of materials, liquids, collections without clear boundaries, which aren't seen as separate objects, e.g. *water, weather, air*. Uncountable nouns don't have plurals (*weathers*). You can use *some* with uncountable nouns: *some water*.

- The distinction between countable and uncountable objects can seem a little difficult to determine in some cases. For example, you say *two chairs* and *three tables* (as both *chair* and *table* are countable), but you say *some furniture* (because *furniture* is uncountable in English). However, *furniture* is countable in some languages and this may confuse some students.

2

- Focus the students' attention on the table and point out that *cinema* is countable and has a plural form: *cinemas*, but *nightlife* is uncountable and doesn't have a plural form. Ask them to complete the table with the nouns in the box, in each case indicating what the plural form is, if it has one, and marking it countable or uncountable.

- Check answers with the class before asking the students to work in pairs and discuss the questions.

Singular form	Plural form	Countable or uncountable?
cinema	cinemas	countable
nightlife	–	uncountable
park	parks	countable
person	people	countable
public transport	–	uncountable
restaurant	restaurants	countable
traffic	–	uncountable

a) shops, buses, churches, cities, countries, leaves
b) person
c) men, women, children, feet, teeth

3

- Pairwork. Ask the students to choose two cities or villages they know well and to write down their names. Give them time to prepare the questions that they will ask each other.
- As they ask and answer their questions, go round, monitoring and giving help where necessary.

Vocabulary & Pronunciation
(SB page 14)

1 🌐 1.12

- Write *England* and *English* on the board. Explain or elicit that *England* is a noun and the name of a country, and *English* is an adjective which describes the nationality of someone from England.
- Focus attention on the table and point out that in each column, the country word is on the left and the corresponding nationality word on the right. Ask the students to complete the table. Check answers before moving on to the next part of the exercise.
- Point out that the underlining indicates the syllable of the word that has the strongest stress. Ask them to look at the words they've written in the table and to underline the stressed syllables in these words.
- Play the recording for the students to listen, check their answers and repeat the words. Ask them what they notice about the words stress in each set (A, B and C).

> **A**
> Cu<u>ba</u> – <u>Cu</u>ban
> <u>Tur</u>key – <u>Tur</u>kish
> Bra<u>zil</u> – Bra<u>zil</u>ian
> <u>Mo</u>rocco – Mo<u>roc</u>can
> Same stress.
>
> **B**
> <u>E</u>gypt – E<u>gyp</u>tian
> <u>I</u>taly – I<u>tal</u>ian
> <u>Hun</u>gary – Hun<u>gar</u>ian
> <u>Ca</u>nada – Ca<u>na</u>dian
> Stress different – moves to second syllable in nationality word

> **C**
> <u>Chi</u>na – Chi<u>nese</u>
> Viet<u>nam</u> – Vietna<u>mese</u>
> <u>Por</u>tugal – Portu<u>guese</u>
> <u>Ja</u>pan – Japa<u>nese</u>
> Stress different – moves to last syllable in nationality word

2

- Give the students a minute or two to write down six more countries and their nationalities. Go round, monitoring and giving help. Ask the students to mark the stress on their words. Check answers with the class, asking individual students to write their words and mark the stresses on the board.
- Ask the students to think about which countries they'd most like to visit. Put them in pairs to discuss with a partner.

Speaking (SB page 14)

1

Groupwork. Put the students into groups and ask them to discuss whether or not they agree with the two statements. If they disagree, ask them to substitute another nationality adjective for French or Japanese to make the statements into something they would agree with.

2

- Staying in their groups, the students discuss the nouns in the box and try to combine them with a nationality to produce statements with which they can all agree. As they do this, go round, monitoring and giving help.
- Ask a representative from each group to report back to the class on the statements they've agreed on and see if there is any consensus within the class as a whole.

Reading (SB page 15)

1

Focus the students' attention on the photos and ask them if any of these places represent their 'dream holiday' destinations. Ask them to read the short description of each place and then work individually to put them in order of which place they'd most like to go to and which they'd least like to go to. When they've finished, ask them to explain their choices to a partner.

2

- Explain that the descriptions they've read are part of a competition in a magazine. Point out that each is exactly 50 words long. Ask them to read the introduction and say what the prize for the competition is (a dream holiday for two in one of the places described).

- Ask the students to read the *How to enter* section and do Part A and Part B. Go round, monitoring and giving help with vocabulary where necessary. When they start Part B, remind them that their descriptions have to be exactly 50 words long. You may want to set this part of the exercise for homework.

3

The students can check their answers to Part A at the bottom of the page. Display the descriptions in the classroom and give the students time to read each other's work. Have a vote to determine the winner of the competition.

> 1 a Portuguese
> 2 b Turkey
> 3 a China
> 4 c Vietnam
> 5 b Spain
> 6 c Japan

Cultural notes

Shanghai /ʃæŋhaɪ/
Shanghai is situated on the east coast of the People's Republic of China. It has a population of nearly 19 million and is China's largest city. By the 20th century it had become the most important city in China and was the centre for popular culture. Since 1992, Shanghai has enjoyed renewed growth and modernisation.

Kenya
Bordered by five countries, Kenya is situated on the east coast of Africa. It has a population of 32 million and the two national languages are Swahili and English. The capital is Nairobi.

Dahab
Dahab is a town in Egypt, located around 85 km north of Sharm el-Sheikh on the Gulf of Aqaba, near the southern tip of Sinai. Until the 1960s, it was a sleepy Bedouin fishing village, but increased tourism has turned it into a busy resort and is popular with scuba divers.

Iceland
Iceland is a volcanic island in north-western Europe, situated in the north Atlantic. It has a population of 310,000. The capital is Reykjavik.

Ankara
Capital of Turkey since 1923, with a population of around 4.5 million. It's Turkey's second largest city after Istanbul and replaced it as the capital city of the newly founded Republic of Turkey under the leadership of its first president, Mustafa Kemal Atatürk.

The Alhambra Palace /ðiː əlˈæmbrə ˈpæləs/
Situated in Granada, in Andalusia, southern Spain, the Alhambra Palace is the fortress of the Moorish monarchs of Granada. It's a wonderful example of Islamic architecture and dates back to 900 A.D., although much of the present structure is probably from the 14th century.

Kyushu /kjuːʃuː/
Kyushu is the third largest island of the four main islands of Japan. It's the furthest west (and south) of the main four. The largest city on the island is Fukuoka, with a population of 1.4 million. The city of Nagasaki is notable for being one of two cities which were largely destroyed by atomic bombs in the Second World War.

Reading (SB page 16)

1

Ask the students to read the text and to complete it with the words in the box. Allow them to work in pairs if they wish. Go round, monitoring and giving help. Check answers with the class and answer any questions on vocabulary.

> 1 meat   2 cigarettes   3 coffee   4 wine
> 5 hours   6 sleep   7 people   8 cars   9 noise

2

Ask the students to discuss in pairs or groups which country they think the text describes. Ask them to give reasons why it could or couldn't be their own country. Ask one student from each group to report back to the class and see if they agree on where it might be.

Grammar (SB page 16)

Quantity expressions with countable and uncountable nouns

1

- Focus the students' attention to the information in the margin. Point out the two question forms *How many?* and *How much?* and ask the students to suggest nouns which could be used with each one. For example, *How many people? How much water?*

- Focus the students' attention on the categories in the table. Ask them to use the information in the margin to help them complete the headings.

A: countable
B: uncountable
C: countable, uncountable

2

- Ask the students to work individually to choose the correct alternatives. Then allow them to compare their results in pairs. When checking answers, ask the students to read out the complete sentences so that they get a feel for what sounds right.
- Ask the students to tick the sentences that are true for them and then to rewrite the others to make them true.
- When they've compared their sentences with a partner, ask them to report back to the class.

a) much	d) enough
b) lots of	e) a lot of
c) far too much	f) enough

Extra activity

Extend the activity by asking the students to create new sentences using other items of food and drink, e.g. *rice, pasta, wine, coffee, strawberry jam*, etc.

Language notes

Vocabulary: *little*

- Generally speaking, if a student makes a mistake with a quantity expression, they'll still be understood. If, for example, one of your students says *Bill Gates has many money*, although the sentence is grammatically incorrect, the meaning is clear. The word *little* presents a bigger problem: if used with a countable noun, *little* refers to the size of the noun; if used with an uncountable noun, it refers to the quantity. This can produce problems with meaning. It's therefore important that the teacher is aware that sentences like *There were little people at the party* are probably grammatically rather than politically incorrect, the desired sentence being *There were few people at the party*, or, more naturally *There weren't many people at the party*.

3

- Pairwork. Go through the example questions and answers with the class. Then elicit a few more questions using words from the box.
- Put the students in pairs and tell them to take turns asking and answering questions about their daily habits. Remind them that they can use their own verbs and nouns to make different questions if they wish. Go round, monitoring and giving help.

4 Grammar *Extra* 2

Ask the students to turn to *Grammar Extra* 2 on page 128 of the Student's Book. Here they'll find an explanation of the grammar they've been studying and further exercises to practise it.

1
a) names   b) places   c) menus   d) buses
e) families   f) wives   g) people   h) feet
i) days   j) mice   k) cameras   l) watches

2
Countable nouns: child, city, office, problem, tooth, woman
Uncountable nouns: advice, homework, information, money, news, weather

3
a) some   b) a   c) some   d) some   e) some
f) a   g) some   h) some

4
a) is   b) was   c) are   d) is   e) were
f) was

5
a) are a lot of   d) is a lot of
b) is a lot of   e) is a lot of
c) are a lot of   f) are a lot of
a) There aren't many parks.
b) There isn't much good nightlife.
c) There aren't many good restaurants.
d) There isn't much traffic.
e) There isn't much pollution.
f) There aren't many bookshops.

6
a) He drinks too much beer.
b) He eats too many pizzas.
c) He doesn't eat enough fruit and vegetables.
d) He smokes too many cigarettes.
e) He doesn't do enough exercise.
f) He watches too much television.
g) He doesn't get enough fresh air.

Vocabulary (SB page 17)

1

Focus the students' attention on the compass. Ask them to complete the labels.

a) North	b) East	c) South	d) South
e) West	f) North		

2

Focus the students' attention on the maps. Ask them to find each of the cities (Los Angeles, Ankara, London and Berlin) and match them with the descriptions. Remind them to refer to the compass they completed in Exercise 1 if they aren't sure of the direction words. Then check answers with the class.

a) 2	b) 4	c) 1	d) 3

3 Pairwork

- The pairwork exercise for this unit is on pages 116 and 121 of the Student's Book. Put the students in pairs and tell them who will be Student A, and who will be Student B.

- While they're doing the exercise, go round, monitoring and giving help. Take note of any errors which may need particular attention later, and also any examples of good language use which you can praise in a feedback session.

Speaking: anecdote (SB page 17)

For more information about how to set up, monitor and repeat Anecdotes, see page xx in the Introduction.

1 🔘 1.13

- Focus the students' attention on the photo of Emma. Explain that they're going to hear her talking about the best place she's ever visited. Go through the questions with the class. Explain any unknown vocabulary.

- Play the recording and ask the students to listen and tick the questions she gives information about.

> She talks about: a, b, c, d, e, f, g, h.

🔘 **1.13**

The best place I've ever visited is Buenos Aires, the capital of Argentina. It's a crazy city, but I really love it.

The first time I went there was on my summer holiday. It was the year before I went to university. So I was young and excited, and it was my first time in South America.

I flew there on my own, but I went to stay with friends. Of course I visited all the tourist places – the Colon Theatre, the Plaza de Mayo, La Boca, and my friends took me to watch a tango show. That was great. I even took some tango lessons, but I'm not very good.

I also went out dancing a lot – Buenos Aires nightlife is fantastic. The streets are crowded at three o'clock in the morning with people going to restaurants and discos. The discos are open until six or seven o'clock in the morning – in fact, Buenos Aires never sleeps!

Now I go back to Buenos Aires as often as possible. I've been there three times, and last year I went there for New Year.

What I particularly like about Buenos Aires is the people. Argentinian people are very special. They're loud and energetic and really good fun. I love them.

2

- Give the students a minute or two to decide on the place they're going to talk about. Then ask them to look at the questions in Exercise 1 again and decide how they'd answer them about their place. Allow them to make notes of what they're going to say and how they're going to say it, but discourage them from writing a paragraph that they can simply read out. Go round, monitoring and giving help.

- Pairwork. Put the students in pairs and ask them to take turns to tell their partner about the best place they've ever visited. Encourage them to ask each other follow-up questions to get further information.

- Ask some pairs to report back to the class about what they found out.

Useful phrases (SB page 18)

1 🔘 1.14

- Focus the students' attention on the illustration. Explain that the people in the picture are Josh, Matt and Erica. They're going to listen to them talking and they have to decide what nationality each of them is.

- Play the recording for them to listen and note down their answers. Encourage them to read the conversation as they listen.

> Josh is American.
> Matt is American.
> Erica is British.

Cultural notes

Manchester
A city in northwest England. Manchester is credited as the world's first industrialised city. It's the home to many modern bands, such as the Smiths, Stone Roses, Happy Mondays and Oasis and is also famous for its two football teams, Manchester City and Manchester United.

Los Angeles /lɒs ˈændʒəlɪs/
'The City of Angels' is on the west coast of the United States. Founded in 1781, Los Angeles was part of Spain. It became part of Mexico in 1821 and was then ceded to the United States in 1848. In the last 150 years, Los Angeles has become the film capital of the world.

2

Focus attention on the maps and ask the students to match each of the people with one of the maps. Tell them to put a cross to show exactly where each person comes from.

> Map 1: Erica   Map 2: Matt   Map 3: Josh

3 🔘 **1.15**

- Ask the students to complete the useful phrases. Remind them that they can look back at the conversation in Exercise 1 if they need help.
- Play the recording for the students to listen and check their answers. Then play it again for them to repeat the useful phrases.

---

a) Where are you from?
b) I'm originally from England.
c) Where exactly?
d) A small town just outside Manchester.
e) Manchester's in the north.
f) I live in New York but I'm actually from Los Angeles.
g) Which part of the city are you from?
h) Not far from the airport.
i) They live in the south.

4

Pairwork. Ask the students to write their conversations, using as many of the useful phrases as they can. Go round, monitoring and giving help where necessary. When they've finished, tell them to practise their conversations out loud. Ask a few confident pairs to perform their conversations for the class.

Vocabulary *Extra* (SB page 19)

Places

1

- Focus the students' attention on the list of words and point out that they're all to do with places. Check that the students can pronounce the words correctly.
- Ask the students to look at the places in the picture and match each one with one of the words. Point out that the first one has been done for them.

---

6 art gallery   10 car park   3 castle
7 church   5 library   1 mosque   2 museum
8 shopping centre   9 square   4 theatre

2

Pairwork. Go through the example question and answer with the class and then ask the students to take turns asking and answering similar questions using the places in Exercise 1.

Adjectives

1

Focus the students' attention on the adjectives in the box and tell them that all the adjectives describe cities. Ask the students to work individually and decide which words are positive and which are negative. Check answers with the class. Ask for choral and individual repetition to check that they're pronouncing the words correctly.

Possible answers
Positive: beautiful, (big), exciting, fabulous, interesting, (modern), romantic, spectacular
Negative: boring, crowded, dirty, dull, expensive, noisy, polluted
(Some people may regard *big* and *modern* as negative adjectives in this context.)

2

Pairwork. Ask the students to choose five adjectives to describe their own cities and to compare their choices with their partner.

Focus on *like*

1

Ask the students to look at the table. Go through the different uses of *like* with the class and then ask them to match them to the example sentences.

---

a) 4   b) 3   c) 6   d) 2   e) 1   f) 5

2

Ask the students to write a sentence of their own for each use of *like* in the table. Go round, monitoring and giving help. In a class feedback session, put some of their suggestions on the board.

Further practice material

Need more writing practice?
→ Workbook page 15
- Writing a web posting.

Need more classroom practice activities?
→ Photocopiable resource materials pages 154 to 156
   Grammar: *Categorise*
   Vocabulary: *Places in a city*
   Communication: *Worldsearch*
→ Top 10 activities pages xv to xx

Need progress tests?
→ Test CD – *Test Unit 2*

Need more on important teaching concepts?
→ Key concepts in *New Inside Out* pages xxii to xxxv

Need student self-study practice?
→ CD-ROM – Unit 2: *Place*

Need student CEF self-evaluation?
→ CEF Checklists pages xxxvii to xliv

Need more information and more ideas?
→ www.insideout.net

---

3 Love *Overview*

Section & Aims	What the students are doing
Listening SB page 20 Listening for specific information	Listening to two people talking about their relationship and answering questions. Matching sentences to people.
Vocabulary & Speaking SB page 20 Relationship expressions; fluency practice	Completing sentences with relationship expressions. Discussing statements about relationships.
Vocabulary SB page 21 Relationship expressions	Matching verb phrases with pictures. Putting the stages of a relationship in a logical order.
Grammar SB page 21 Past simple	Writing affirmative and negative past simple forms of verbs. Writing sentences with past simple verbs.
Pronunciation SB page 21 Irregular past simple forms	Categorising past simple forms according to their pronunciation.
Listening SB page 22 Listening for detail	Reading about a TV game show and answering questions. Listening to contestants and identifying the answers they give. Talking about the game show questions with a partner.
Grammar SB page 23 Past continuous	Identifying the uses of the past simple and past continuous. Writing sentences using past simple and past continuous to describe a picture.
Reading SB page 23 Reading for detail	Completing a story with past continuous or past simple verbs. Predicting the ending to the story.
Reading SB page 24 Reading for detail	Completing noun phrases. Reading stories and matching items to them. Then identifying the importance of the items to the stories.
Vocabulary & Speaking SB page 25 Time adverbials; telling a story	Finding time adverbials in stories and listing them in order. Retelling a story using time adverbials.
Grammar SB page 25 Adverbs of manner	Completing tables with adverbs and adjectives from stories. Rewriting sentences in the correct order.
Useful phrases SB page 26 Things in common	Listening to a conversation to determine whether the speakers know each other. Answering true/false questions. Completing useful phrases for talking about things in common. Writing and responding to comments with the useful phrases.
Vocabulary *Extra* SB page 27 Adjectives ending in *ed* or *ing*; *get*	Matching pictures with adjectives. Underlining the correct adjectives in sentences. Identifying the various uses of *get*. Writing example sentences using *get*.
Writing WB page 21	Writing a story.

3 Love *Teacher's notes*

Warm-up

- Prepare a number of labels, each with the name of one member of a famous couple that the students are likely to know, e.g. Romeo and Juliet, Bonnie and Clyde, Samson and Delilah, Minnie and Mickey Mouse. You can use ones from the students' own culture(s) to ensure that they are well-known. You can even get the students to prepare the labels themselves.

- Pin the labels to the backs of the students' clothing so they cannot see them. They then have to walk around the classroom asking questions to find out who they are – the only questions they can't ask are *Who am I?* or *What is my name?* They then have to find their other half. Pairs then report back to the class on what they know about their famous couple. You could ask them to do all the pairwork exercises in this unit as a couple.

Listening (SB page 20)

1 🌐 **1.16**

- Focus the students' attention on the photos. Ask the students what they notice about the photos (they show the same couple now and when they were younger). Ask them to say how old they think Fred and Edna are now and how old they were in the earlier photos.

- Go through the questions so that the students know what information to listen out for. Play the recording and ask them to answer the questions.

> a) Fifty years ago.   b) Last summer.

> 🌐 **1.16** (E = Edna; F = Fred)
>
> E: *We first met fifty years ago.*
>
> F: *I joined the army and I went to Blackpool in the north of England for my training. On the first day I went to the canteen, and this little lady was serving lunch.*
>
> E: *Yes, I was. I liked him so I gave him extra chips.*
>
> F: *Anyway we started talking. Then, one night, there was a party.*
>
> E: *I said to Fred, 'I'll be your girl tonight,' and that was it.*
>
> F: *Yes, we went out together for three wonderful months.*

> E: *We did.*
>
> F: *Then we both moved to different places. At first, we wrote to each other. We wrote twice a week.*
>
> E: *Yes, but then we stopped. I don't know why. But we lost touch with each other. Then we got married to other people. I had two children, and Fred had a daughter, didn't you?*
>
> F: *That's right. I was married for forty-eight years, and then my wife died.*
>
> E: *And I got divorced after thirty years of marriage.*
>
> F: *So, we were both single again.*
>
> E: *And one day, my grandson took me to Blackpool for the day. I visited all the old places and I thought about Fred. I wanted to find him.*
>
> F: *She didn't even know whether I was alive.*
>
> E: *No, I didn't. So I wrote a letter to the editor of the local newspaper.*
>
> F: *I have a cousin in Blackpool. She doesn't usually buy the newspaper. But on that day she did. She bought the paper and she saw the letter. And she realised that Edna was looking for me.*
>
> E: *He rang me up. I nearly had a heart attack. I said, 'Is that my Fred?' I was so happy.*
>
> F: *We met soon after that. We realised we were still in love and we moved in together a few months later.*
>
> E: *We got married last summer. I didn't want to lose him again!*

2

- Go through the example with the class, then ask the students to read the remaining sentences and complete them with *He, She* or *They*. Allow them to compare their answers in pairs before playing the recording again for them to check their answers.

- Ask the students for their reactions to this story. Can they imagine being in love and getting married in their seventies?

> a) They b) They c) He d) She e) She
> f) She g) She h) He i) They j) They

Vocabulary & Speaking (SB page 20)

1

Ask the students to read the sentences and complete them with the words in the box. Allow them to compare their sentences in pairs before checking answers with the class. Check answers by asking individual students to read their sentences aloud.

a) get   b) have   c) love   d) live   e) lose

2

Groupwork. Ask the students to discuss each of the statements in Exercise 1 and to decide whether they agree or disagree with them. Ask one member of each group to take notes on their discussion. The groups can then report back to the class on what they decided.

Vocabulary (SB page 21)

1

- Focus the students' attention on the pictures. Give them a minute or two to take in what they see. Then ask them to match the verb phrases to the pictures.

chat somebody up – b)   have a row – d)
fancy somebody – a)   move in together – c)

2

- This is an exercise about the different stages of a relationship. As such, you may need to adapt it to take into account the cultural sensitivities of your students. Point out that they have the option of adding or taking away any of the stages listed if they think it's necessary. You may find one of the alternative activities below more appropriate.

- Go through the stages of a relationship with the class and make sure everybody understands them. Ask them which of these stages comes first in a relationship. When they've identified that it's most likely d) *You fancy somebody*, ask them to work individually to work out the logical order of each of the other stages. There are no fixed answers to this and make it clear that they can add or take away any stages if they wish.

- Put the students in pairs and ask them to compare their ideas.

Grammar (SB page 21)

Past simple

1

- Go through the information in the margin on affirmative and negative past simple forms. Point out that *go* is an irregular verb and the past simple form is *went*. Ask several students to read out the sentences, questions and answers in the margin.

- Go through the list of verbs in the box. Ask the students to write the affirmative and negative past simple forms as in the example.

- Point out the double *t* in *chatted* and the change from *y* to *i* in *fancied* and *studied*.

be: was/were; wasn't/weren't
can: could; couldn't
chat: chatted; didn't chat
fancy: fancied; didn't fancy
get: got; didn't get
go: went; didn't go
have: had; didn't have
kiss: kissed; didn't kiss
meet: met; didn't meet
move: moved; didn't move
study: studied; didn't study
want: wanted; didn't want

2

- Do the first one with the class as an example and then ask the students to work individually to write the remaining sentences. Remind them that they should be true. Go round, monitoring and checking that the statements are being formed correctly.

- Go through the example question with the class. Then ask a student to form a question with the second statement. (With weaker classes, go through all the statements and get the students to change them into questions before moving into the pairwork stage.)
- Put the students in pairs and ask them to take turns asking and answering questions about the statements. Go round checking that all the questions are being formed correctly. Ask several pairs to report back to the class on what they learnt about their partners.

Statements
a) My mother and father met/didn't meet at university.
b) My grandparents got married/didn't get married in a church.
c) I had/didn't have a big breakfast this morning.
d) I went/didn't go skiing last winter.
e) I studied/didn't study German at school.
f) I was/wasn't very busy yesterday.

Questions
a) Did your mother and father meet at university?
b) Did your grandparents get married in a church?
c) Did you have a big breakfast this morning?
d) Did you go skiing last winter?
e) Did you study German at school?
f) Were you very busy yesterday?

Language notes

Grammar: *did* auxiliary

- In the past simple, the auxiliary *did/didn't* functions in exactly the same way as *do/does/doesn't* in the present simple. For example, *yes/no* questions and short answers: *Did you go to Liverpool yesterday? Yes, I did*. And in open questions and negative sentences: *Who did you meet? I didn't meet anyone.*

- Note that there's only one form *did* for first, second and third persons.

- Note also that you use the infinitive form of the verb after the auxiliary *did/didn't* rather than the past form. For example, *I didn't leave*, not *I didn't left.* and *Did he go?* not *Did he went?*

3 Grammar *Extra* 3 Part 1

Ask the students to turn to *Grammar Extra* 3 Part 1 on page 130 of the Student's Book. Here they'll find an explanation of the grammar they've been studying and further exercises to practise it.

1
a) worked, went, called, helped
b) took, made, woke, baked
c) tried, played, studied, copied
d) stopped, planned, chatted, walked

Odd ones out:
a) *go – went* because it's irregular.
b) *bake – baked* because it's regular.
c) *play – played* because the *y* doesn't change to an *i*.
d) *walk – walked* because it doesn't double the final consonant.

2
a) taught   b) sat   c) said   d) knew   e) spoke
f) made   g) began   h) rang   i) fell   j) learnt
k) caught   l) flew   m) sank   n) threw
o) swam   p) read   q) understood   r) brought
s) ran   t) slept   u) found   v) wore
w) bought   x) came   y) met   z) thought

3
a) My father didn't teach me how to drive.
b) I didn't go to a private school.
c) My parents didn't give me a present for my birthday.
d) I didn't have meat for dinner last night.
e) I didn't study English at school.
f) I didn't play basketball when I was young.

Pronunciation (SB page 21)

1 🌐 1.17

- Focus the students' attention on the table and explain that verbs which don't form their past simple by taking *-ed* are known as irregular. Point out that in each set, the infinitive is in the left-hand column and the past simple form in the right-hand column. Ask them to complete the table. Check answers with the class before moving on to the next part of the exercise.

- Point out that the irregular verbs have been grouped according to the pronunciation of their past simple forms. Read out the sounds in the instructions and make sure the students can identify them and say them correctly. You could write them on the board and ask the students to suggest words that contain each sound.

- Ask the students to label the past forms in each group with the sounds. Play the recording for them to check their answers, then play it again for them to listen and repeat all the words.

---

a) meant   b) meet   c) began   d) drank
e) buy   f) caught

Group 1 past forms: /e/
Group 2 past forms: /æ/
Group 3 past forms: /ɔː/

---

2 🌐 1.18

- Ask individual students to read out the verbs in the box. After each one, ask the other students to say what they think the past simple form is. When they produce the correct answer, ask them which group in the table they should add it to.

- Play the recording for them to check their answers. Then play it again for them to listen and repeat the words.

fight (fought): 3	sleep (slept): 1
read (read): 1	swim (swam): 2
sing (sang): 2	teach (taught): 3

Listening (SB page 22)

Warm-up

Ask the students to give you the names of some popular game shows that they watch on television. Ask them to explain what the contestants have to do and what they can win. Find out which game show they like best.

1

- Focus the students' attention on the photos and tell them that they show two people taking part in a TV game show called *Get Personal*.
- Go through the questions with the class so that they know what information they're looking for, then ask them to read the description of the show and answer the questions.
- Check answers with the class and answer any questions about vocabulary.

> a) Rosie and Dave
> b) £10,000
> c) They have to give the same answers to the same questions.

2 ⊚ 1.19

Go through the questions and answers with the class. Then ask the students to listen to the recording and choose the answers that Rosie gives. Play the recording twice if necessary.

> 1 a)   2 c)   3 b)   4 She b); He a)   5 b)

> ⊚ **1.19** (I = Introducer; BB = Bobby Brown; R = Rosie; D = Dave)
>
> I: *It's time for our popular competition, 'Get Personal', with your host, Bobby Brown.*
>
> BB: *Good evening and welcome to this week's 'Get Personal'. Let's meet our first couple, Rosie and Dave. As you know, Rosie and Dave are in separate studios – Rosie can't hear Dave, and Dave has no idea what Rosie is saying. But they can both hear me. OK, are you ready to play 'Get Personal'?*
>
> R&D: *Yes, Bobby.*

> BB: *Right, we'll start with you Rosie. We want you to remember exactly what was going on when you first met Dave. OK?*
>
> R: *OK, Bobby.*
>
> BB: *Now Rosie, how did you first meet Dave?*
>
> R: *Well, I was working as a nurse, and Dave was my patient. He came into the hospital for an operation.*
>
> BB: *OK, Rosie. I want you to think about the moment when you first met. What time of day was it?*
>
> R: *Um, I was working nights that week. So early evening.*
>
> BB: *Uh huh. And what was the weather like?*
>
> R: *Oh dear, I think it was raining. Yes, it was raining when I arrived at work.*
>
> BB: *What were you both wearing when you saw one another for the first time?*
>
> R: *Now, that's easy. I was wearing my nurse's uniform, and he was wearing pyjamas. Blue pyjamas. Or were they green? No, blue.*
>
> BB: *Finally, who spoke first and what did he or she say?*
>
> R: *Dave spoke first. In fact he shouted at me. He said, 'Nurse, I'm going to be sick.'*
>
> BB: *Oh well, that's very romantic! Thank you, Rosie.*

3 ⊚ 1.20

Go through the instructions with the class. Make sure they understand that they just have to circle the tick or the cross in the column for Dave's answers according to whether or not he gives the same answer as Rosie. Play the recording twice if necessary. Check answers with the class and ask how many points out of five Rosie and Dave scored.

> 1 ✓   2 ✓   3 ✗   4 ✓   5 ✗
> They scored three points out of five.

> ⊚ **1.20** (BB = Bobby Brown; D = Dave)
>
> BB: *Now, Dave, it's your turn. Where and how did you first meet?*
>
> D: *Well, I went into hospital for an operation, and Rosie was working there as a nurse.*
>
> BB: *What time of day was it?*
>
> D: *Oh, I don't know. Lunchtime? No, hang on, it was later than that. Early evening.*
>
> BB: *What was the weather like?*
>
> D: *Oh dear. It was summer, so I suppose the sun was shining.*
>
> BB: *What were you both wearing when you saw one another for the first time?*
>
> D: *Rosie was wearing her nurse's uniform and she was also wearing lovely perfume. I was wearing my favourite blue pyjamas.*
>
> BB: *Finally, Dave, who spoke first and what did he or she say?*
>
> D: *Rosie spoke first. She said, 'How are you feeling?' And I think I said, 'I feel terrible'.*

4

Pairwork. Ask the students to discuss the questions in pairs and then report back to the class.

Grammar (SB page 23)

Past continuous

1

- Go through the information in the margin, pointing out that the past continuous is formed with *was/were* plus the *-ing* form of the main verb. Ask several students to read out the full sentences in the margin (*I was working*, *You were working*, etc.).
- Read out the extracts from the interview with Rosie and ask the students to answer the questions about them. Go round, monitoring and giving help as they do this.

a) Past simple.	c) Past continuous.
b) Past continuous.	d) Past simple.

Extra activity

Ask the students to write the past simple forms of these verbs and answer the questions. For example: *be – was/were*.

be   can   get   go   have   kiss   want

1 Which verbs have irregular past forms?
2 How do you form the past simple of regular verbs?
3 How do you spell the past forms of these regular verbs: *move, fancy, chat*?
4 How do you make negatives for *be* and *can* in the past simple?
5 How do you make questions for *be* and *can* in the past simple?
6 How do you make negatives and questions for all other verbs?

Language note

Grammar: past continuous + *when* + past simple

The past continuous is used to talk about the circumstances surrounding an event in the past. It's often used with *when* in sentences where the event (in the past simple) interrupts the circumstances (in the past continuous): *It was raining when I arrived at work*. In these sentences, *when* is always followed by the event (in the past simple). It's possible to change the order of the clauses, putting *when* at the beginning of the sentence, without changing the meaning. Where this happens, the two clauses are separated by a comma: *When I arrived at work, it was raining*.

2 Pairwork

- The pairwork exercise for this unit is on pages 116 and 121 of the Student's Book. Put the students in pairs and tell them who will be Student A, and who will be Student B.

- While they're doing the exercise, go round, monitoring and giving help. Take note of any errors which may need particular attention later, and also any examples of good language use which you can praise.

3 🌐 **1.21**

- Focus the students' attention on the pictures. Explain to the class that they're going to listen to some sounds.
- Go through the example with the class. Point out the use of the past continuous for the action that was taking place when something else happened (past simple). Ask the students to work individually.
- Play the recording. Pause after each situation in the recording for the students to write sentences for them. When checking answers, make sure the students are using the past continuous and past simple correctly.

Possible answers
1 Jake was having a shower when his mobile phone rang.
2 Fiona and her friend were chatting at the disco when a man asked Fiona for a dance.
3 Jake and Fiona were having a meal when Jake asked Fiona to marry him.
4 Jake and Fiona were sleeping when the baby started to cry.
5 Jake and Fiona were having a row when somebody arrived.

4 Grammar *Extra* 3 Part 2

Ask the students to turn to *Grammar Extra* 3 Part 2 on page 130 of the Student's Book. Here they'll find an explanation of the grammar they've been studying and further exercises to practise it.

1
a) coming   b) eating   c) hitting   d) leaving
e) playing   f) putting   g) smoking   h) studying
i) swimming   j) waking   k) winning   l) working

2
a) 'Were you having breakfast?'
   'Yes, I was.' 'No, I wasn't.'
b) 'Were you driving to work?'
   'Yes, I was.' 'No, I wasn't.'
c) 'Was your mother working?'
   'Yes, she was.' 'No, she wasn't.'
d) 'Were you walking around town?'
   'Yes, I was.' 'No, I wasn't.'
e) 'Were your parents watching TV?'
   'Yes, they were.' 'No, they weren't.'

3

a) moved	d) was raining
b) were studying	e) switched on
c) started	f) was talking

Reading (SB page 23)

1

- Focus the students' attention on the picture and ask them what they think is happening in it.
- Ask the students to read the story and complete it with past continuous and past simple verbs. When they've finished, check their answers and then ask them to work in pairs to decide what the ending of the story is. Get various suggestions from around the class and write them on the board.

> 1 was filming
> 2 came
> 3 was talking
> 4 gave
> 5 continued
> 6 didn't come
> 7 was planning
> 8 went
> 9 found
> 10 shook

2 🌐 **1.22**

Play the recording for the students to listen and check their answers. Did any of them predict the original ending to the story?

> 🌐 **1.22**
>
> *A Hollywood director was filming an important film in the desert when an old Native American man came up to him and said, 'Tomorrow rain.'*
>
> *The next day it rained.*
>
> *A few days later, the director was talking to the cameraman about the next day's filming. The Native American went up to him and said, 'Tomorrow storm.'*
>
> *He was right again, and he saved the director thousands of dollars.*
>
> *The director was very impressed and gave the old man a job.*
>
> *The old man continued to predict the weather correctly, but then he didn't come for three weeks.*
>
> *The director was planning to film an important scene and he needed good weather. So he went to look for the Native American.*
>
> *When he found the old man, he said, 'Listen, I have to film an important scene tomorrow. What will the weather be like?'*
>
> *The old man shook his head and said, 'Don't know. Radio broken.'*

Reading (SB page 24)

1

- Focus the students' attention on the pictures. Ask them to read the words in the box and use them to complete the noun phrases.
- Check answers with the class and tell them that they're going to read two stories in which these things play an important part. Ask them to say what they think the stories might be about.

> a) paint   b) party   c) scissors   d) club
> e) bag   f) wine

2 🌐 **1.23**

- Give the students plenty of time to read the stories. Answer any questions they have about vocabulary.
- Tell the students to match the items in Exercise 1 with the correct stories and then decide why each thing is important to the story.

> Revenge is sweet: a), c), f)
> Dinner by post: b), d), e)

3

Pairwork. The students discuss which story they prefer. You could also ask them if they know any other stories about people who have taken revenge on their partners.

Vocabulary & Speaking (SB page 25)

1

- Focus the students' attention on the box and explain that these words are known as time adverbials; they tell us when or in what order things happened. Ask the students to look back through the stories on page 24 and underline the time adverbials.
- Draw the students' attention to the two lists and point out that the first time adverbial in each story has already been inserted in the lists. Ask them to write in the others in the order in which they appear in the stories.

> *Revenge is sweet*
> a) One day
> b) Then
> c) Next
> d) That night
> e) Finally
>
> *Dinner by post*
> 1 Last year
> 2 At first
> 3 At the end of August
> 4 That evening
> 5 The next morning
> 6 A week later

2

- Tell the students to choose one of the stories on page 24. Put them in pairs, preferably with students in each pair having chosen different stories.
- Ask the students to retell their story to their partner, using the list of time adverbials to prompt them and without looking back at page 24. Go round, monitoring and giving help. Take note of any students who do this particularly well and ask them to re-tell their stories to the class.

Grammar (SB page 25)
Adverbs of manner

1

- Go through the information in the margin, explaining that adverbs of manner tell us *how* something is or was done. Point out the spelling changes in *carefully* and *angrily*.
- Pairwork. Ask the students to work together to complete the tables with adverbs or adjectives from the stories on page 24. Check answers with the class. Then elicit answers from the class to the questions below the tables.

Revenge is sweet
a) unhappily   b) bad   c) angry
d) quickly   e) beautiful   f) carefully
g) quietly

Dinner by post
1 different   2 early   3 late   4 tidy
5 attractive   6 good   7 loudly

a) Add *ly*.
b) Delete *y* and add *ily*.
c) *well, early, late*

2

- Explain that it's important to put adverbs in the correct place in a sentence. Read out the example to the class and point out that the adverb is in the final position in the sentences. Explain that subject + verb + object + adverb is the usual order, though other positions are possible.
- Ask the students to work individually to rewrite the remaining sentences. As they do this, go round, monitoring and giving help where necessary. Check answers with the class before moving on to the next part of the exercise.
- Give the students a minute or two to decide which sentences are true for them and to change the ones that aren't to make them true. Then put them in pairs to compare their sentences.

---

a) I eat my lunch very quickly.
b) I drive my car very slowly.
c) I plan my days very carefully.
d) I spend my money very intelligently.
e) I play tennis very badly.

---

f) I clean my house very regularly.
g) I speak English very well.

Useful phrases (SB page 26)

1 🌐 **1.24**

- Focus the students' attention on the picture and ask them to describe the situation. Tell them that they're going to listen to a conversation between Tim and Anna, the people on the train, and all they have to do is decide whether they know each other or not.
- Play the recording. When you ask the students if they know each other, you could also ask what helped them decide (Tim's first words are *Excuse me*, which is a way of starting a conversation with a stranger).

They don't know each other.

🌐 1.24 (T = Tim; A = Anna)

T: *Excuse me. Do you know what time we arrive in London?*

A: *Yes, I think we get there at about 2.30.*

T: *Thanks. I see you're reading 'Pride and Prejudice'. Are you enjoying it?*

A: *Yes, I am.*

T: *I didn't like the film much.*

A: *Oh, I did. I thought it was great. I really like Keira Knightley.*

T: *Oh, so do I. I think she's really good in 'Pirates of the Caribbean'.*

A: *Me too. I love that film. Johnny Depp's brilliant.*

T: *I know. I'm going to see his new film tomorrow night.*

A: *Really? So am I. Where are you going to see it?*

T: *Piccadilly Circus.*

A: *Me too!*

T: *Oh, that's great. I don't know what time it starts.*

A: *No, neither do I. But my husband has the tickets, so he knows.*

T: *Oh. That's good.*

Cultural notes

Pride and Prejudice /praɪd ən ˈpredʒʊdɪs/
This novel by Jane Austen, published in 1813, tells the story of Mrs Bennett and her desperate attempts to get her five daughters to marry wealthy men, as there were no sons to inherit Mr Bennet's property and support the family should he die. Despite Mrs Bennet's interference in her daughters' love life, which leads to all sorts of misunderstandings, two of her daughters eventually get married to wealthy men.

Keira Knightley /ˈkɪərə ˈnaɪtlɪ/ (born 1985)
Keira Knightly was born in London. She plays the role of Elizabeth Swan in the *Pirates of the Caribbean* films. She also starred in the British films *Bend it Like Beckham* (2002), *Love Actually* (2003) and *Atonement* (2007).

Johnny Depp (born 1963)
Johnny Depp's film debut was in *Nightmare On Elm Street* (1984). He then acted in the popular TV series *21 Jump Street*, before starring in the film *Edward Scissorhands* (1990), directed by Tim Burton. His most popular films to date are probably acting as Jack Sparrow in the *Pirates of the Caribbean* trilogy.

2

- Read the sentences with the class. Tell them to decide whether they are true or false. You could do this by reading each one in turn and asking the students to stand up (and cheer) if they think it's true or remain seated (and boo) if they think it's false. Encourage them to try to persuade people who have made a different decision of their own point of view

- Play the recording for the students to check their answers.

a) True.   b) True.   c) True.   d) True.
e) False.

3 🌐 1.25

- Allow the students to work in pairs to complete the table.

- Play the recording for them to check their answers. Then play it again for them to listen and repeat the useful phrases.

1 Oh, I did.   4 So am I.
2 So do I.   5 Neither do I.
3 Me too.

4

Ask the students to work individually to write their comments. Explain that these can be on any subject they like. Elicit a few examples from the class before they begin to start them off, or put a few of your own on the board.

5

Pairwork. Demonstrate the activity first with comments of your own, encouraging the students around the class to respond by agreeing or disagreeing with your comments. Then put them into pairs to take turns reading out their sentences and agreeing or disagreeing with their partner's comments.

Vocabulary *Extra* (SB page 27)
Adjectives ending in *-ed* or *-ing*

1

Focus the students' attention on the list of words and point out that they are all adjectives to describe how people feel and adjectives to describe a situation (or people). Then focus the students' attention on the pictures and ask them to match them with the correct adjectives.

5   annoyed/annoying
1   bored/boring
10 confused/confusing
3   depressed/depressing
4   embarrassed/embarrassing
8   excited/exciting
6   frightened/frightening
2   interested/interesting
7   surprised/surprising
9   tired/tiring

2

- Go through the example with the class, explaining why the answer is *boring* not *bored* (you need an adjective that describes the situation rather than how the speaker feels). Then ask the students to choose the correct adjectives in the remaining sentences.

- Check answers with the class and then ask them to discuss in pairs whether any of the sentences are true for them.

1	bored	6	frightened
2	interesting	7	surprised
3	depressing	8	exciting
4	embarrassed	9	tired
5	annoying	10	confusing

Focus on *get*

1

- Ask the students to look at the table. Tell them that *get* is an extremely common word in English, but it can mean a variety of things, depending on the words that it's combined with.

- Focus the students' attention on the first use of *get* in the table and the examples for it. Then ask the students to read the other example sentences and match them with the correct uses of *get*. Go round, monitoring and giving help.

> a) 2   b) 5   c) 1   d) 3   e) 4

2

- Allow the students to work in pairs if they wish. Remind them that they can use a dictionary to help them. As they work, go round checking that their examples are accurate and are matched to the correct use of *get*. Check answers by taking a section at a time and asking several pairs to read out their own example sentences.

Further practice material

Need more writing practice?

→ Workbook page 21
- Writing a story.

Need more classroom practice activities?

→ Photocopiable resource materials pages 157 to 159
  Grammar: *A love story*
  Vocabulary: *Exciting or excited?*
  Communication: *A few quick questions*
→ Top 10 activities pages xv to xx

Need DVD material?

→ DVD – Programme 2: *Confessions*

Need progress tests?

→ Test CD – *Test Unit 3*

Need more on important teaching concepts?

→ Key concepts in *New Inside Out* pages xxii to xxxv

Need student self-study practice?

→ CD-ROM – Unit 3: *Love*

Need student CEF self-evaluation?

→ CEF Checklists pages xxxvii to xliv

Need more information and more ideas?

→ www.insideout.net

Review A *Teacher's notes*

These exercises act as a check of the grammar and vocabulary that the students have learnt in the first three units. Use them to find any problems that students are having, or anything that they haven't understood and which will need further work.

Grammar (SB page 28)

Remind the students of the grammar explanations they read and the exercises they did in the *Grammar Extra* on pages 126 to 131.

1

This exercise reviews language from Unit 1. Check answers before putting the students in pairs to ask and answer the questions.

> a) Have – Present perfect
> b) Do – Present simple
> c) did – Past simple
> d) are – Future (*be*) *going to*
> e) are – Present continuous
> f) Have – Present perfect
> g) do – Present simple

2

This exercise reviews *look(s)* and *look(s) like* from Unit 1. Check answers before the students work in pairs to compare and discuss their sentences.

> a) look like   d) look like
> b) looks   e) look like
> c) look   f) looks

3

This exercise reviews *such (a)*, *so*, *too* and *very* from Unit 2.

> 1 such a   2 too   3 very   4 so
> 5 such a   6 too   7 so   8 very

4

This exercise reviews *a lot*, *many* and *much* with countable and uncountable nouns from Unit 2.

> 1 many   2 many   3 much   4 much   5 lot
> 6 much   7 many   8 lot   9 many   10 lot

5

This exercise reviews the past simple and past continuous from Unit 3.

> a) was working, met   d) were chatting, came
> b) was raining, arrived e) was cooking, cut
> c) were having, rang   f) were watching, woke

6

This exercise reviews adjectives and adverbs. Check answers with the class before the students compare their sentences in pairs.

> a) regularly   b) well   c) quietly   d) early
> e) carefully

7

This exercise reviews structures used in Units 1, 2 and 3.

> 1 a) ~~What means your name?~~
> 2 a) ~~Did they been to Venice?~~
> 3 b) ~~How was the weather like in Greece?~~
> 4 b) ~~We eat far too many chocolate.~~
> 5 b) ~~You eat very slowly your food.~~
> 6 a) ~~They speak French very good.~~

Vocabulary (SB page 29)

1

This exercise reviews family words from Unit 1.

> 1 stepfather   6 brother-in-law
> 2 half-brother   7 niece
> 3 half-sister   8 nephew
> 4 daughter   9 uncle
> 5 stepmother

2

Check answers to the matching exercise with the class before the students answer the questions and discuss them in pairs.

> a) 2   b) 5   c) 4   d) 3   e) 1

3

This exercise review the names of places in a city.

> a) art gallery   f) fountain
> b) bridge   g) library
> c) canal   h) museum
> d) car park   i) park
> e) castle   j) shopping centre

4

This exercise reviews useful adjectives for describing places.

> a) crowded   e) expensive
> b) polluted   f) beautiful
> c) dull   g) spectacular
> d) romantic

5

This exercise reviews nationality words. Make sure students can pronounce them with correct intonation.

> -an: Brazilian, Canadian, Egyptian, Hungarian, Italian, Moroccan
>
> -ese: Chinese, Japanese, Portuguese, Vietnamese

6

This exercise reviews direction words. You might like to ask a student to draw a compass on the board and label it with the direction words before the students complete the exercise.

> Darwin is in the north.
> Cairns is in the north-east.
> Brisbane is in the east.
> Sydney is in the south-east.
> Melbourne is in the south.
> Perth is in the south-west.
> Alice Springs is in the centre.

Cultural notes

Alice Springs /ˈælɪs sprɪŋz/
A mining town in the Northern Territory of Australia, Alice Springs has a population of 27,000. It became important as the telegraph station on the overland route from Adelaide to Darwin.

Brisbane /ˈbrɪsbən/
Brisbane is the capital city of the Australian state of Queensland and has a population of 1.8 million.

Cairns /keənz/
A small city in northern Queensland with a population of 128,000, Cairns is a popular destination because it's close to many tourist attractions including The Great Barrier Reef, The Daintree National Park and Cape Tribulation.

Darwin /da:wɪn/
Darwin is the capital and most heavily populated city in the Northern Territory, with over 106,000 people. However, it's the least populated of Australia's capital cities. Its two main industries are mining and tourism.

Melbourne /melbən/
Melbourne has the second biggest population in Australia, with over 3.75 million people. It is the state capital of Victoria and is often referred to as Australia's sporting and cultural capital.

Perth /pɜ:θ/
The capital of the state of Western Australia, with 1.5 million residents, Perth is the fourth most populated city in Australia and is currently growing faster than any other Australian city.

Sydney /ˈsɪdni:/
With a population of 4.3 million, Sydney is the most heavily populated city in Australia. Sydney is the state capital of New South Wales and is the site of the first European colony, established in 1788. Famous landmarks in the city include Sydney Harbour Bridge and Sydney Opera House.

7

This exercise reviews words for stages of a relationship from Unit 3.

a) 2   b) 6   c) 1   d) 4   e) 7   f) 3   g) 5

Pronunciation (SB page 29)

1

Remind the students that the boxes show the syllables of a word and the large boxes indicate the stressed syllables. Here they are being asked to classify words according to how many syllables they have and where the main stress falls. Encourage them to say each word aloud to get a feeling for what sounds right.

2 🌐 **1.26**

Point out the main stresses in the example words which are underlined. Ask the students to do the same for the other words in the table. Then play the recording for them to check their answers. Play it a second time for them to listen and repeat.

1 and 2
A: an<u>noy</u>ed, Chi<u>nese</u>, <u>dess</u>ert, sur<u>prised</u>
B: <u>choc</u>olate, <u>cous</u>in, <u>per</u>fume, <u>Turk</u>ish
C: <u>beau</u>tiful, <u>grand</u>daughter, <u>uni</u>form, <u>veg</u>etables
D: ca<u>thed</u>ral, E<u>gyp</u>tian, ex<u>treme</u>ly, to<u>geth</u>er

Reading & Listening (SB page 30)

1 🌐 **1.27**

You could ask the students to read the questions first and point out that they need to answer each question for both pairs of friends.

a) Liz and Deb met on an internet chat site.
   Paul and Woody met at primary school.
b) Liz and Deb see each other once a week.
   Paul and Woody see each other every month.

2

Go through the sentences with the students before they read the texts again and see if they can identify the false statements. Then ask them to read the texts again, check their answers and correct the false statements.

a) True.
b) False. They liked each other immediately.
c) False. Liz is very similar to Deb.
d) True.
e) False. They were both very naughty and got into trouble a lot.
f) False. Woody was a punk. Paul liked rock music.
g) True.

3 🌐 **1.28**

Focus the students' attention on the photo. Play the recording and ask the students to identify Mark's nationality. Then focus attention on the information in the box. Play the recording again and ask the students to underline the correct information.

Mark is American.
1 At university.
2 Five years ago
3 She didn't like him.
4 Scuba diving.

🌐 1.28 (C = Carol; J = Jessica)

C: OK, so who's that in this photo, Jessica?

J: Oh, that's my friend, Mark.

C: Friend? Really?

J: OK, boyfriend!

C: Hmm. Where did you meet him?

J: At university in London – about five years ago.

C: Oh, right.

J: Yeah. I didn't actually like him at first. And I already had a boyfriend. But one day a group of us spent the day together at the beach. We went swimming and chatted and I discovered that Mark was a very interesting person and he really liked travelling.

C: You like travelling too, don't you?

J: Yes, I love it. Anyway, we talked all evening, and after that we became really good friends. But after university he went back to his home in the USA – he's American – and I stayed here.

C: Oh no!

J: Then Mark and I started emailing and phoning each other a lot because we wanted to go scuba diving in Egypt with friends.

C: Ah. In the Red Sea?

J: That's right. Anyway, I saw Mark in Egypt with all our friends. It was a lot of fun. Then, last summer I went to the USA to visit him. I asked him to come back to England with me, and he did.

C: Really? That's brilliant.

J: Yes, we're good together. In fact we're planning a trip to the Bahamas at the moment…

C: Hey, life is good!

4

Go through the questions with the students before playing the recording again. Elicit answers from the class.

a) They went swimming and chatted.
b) He went back to the USA.
c) They wanted to go scuba diving in the Red Sea.
d) Yes, she has.
e) Last summer.
f) The Bahamas.

Writing & Speaking (SB page 31)

1

Ask the students to work in pairs to match the questions and answers.

a) 3   b) 2   c) 5   d) 1   e) 4

2

Ask the students to read the text and match the different parts to the questions in Exercise 1.

a) My best friend …
b) We met on …
c) Adriana knew everybody …
d) We are very different …
e) We do everything together …

3

Give the students a minute or two to think of ideas, then ask them to make notes in answer to the questions in Exercise 1 about their own best friend. Discourage them from writing full sentences at this stage so that they don't simply read out their answers in Exercise 4.

4

Put the students in pairs to tell each other about their best friends. Go round, monitoring and giving help with vocabulary.

5

Remind the students that they can use the text in Exercise 2 as a model and that they should use long answers to the questions in Exercise 1 to structure their writing.

Further practice material

Need more classroom practice activities?

→ Photocopiable resource materials page 160, recording track 🌀 **1.29**
   Song: *Stand By Me*
→ Top 10 activities pages xv to xx

Need progress tests?

→ Test CD – *Test Review A*

Need more on important teaching concepts?

→ Key concepts in *New Inside Out* pages xxii to xxxv

Need student self-study practice?

→ CD-ROM – *Review A*

Need more information and more ideas?

→ www.insideout.net

4 Shopping *Overview*

Section & Aims	What the students are doing
Speaking SB page 32 Fluency practice	Discussing giving and receiving presents.
Reading SB page 32 Reading for specific information	Reading and answering questions on a text about presents. Rearranging words to make statements, then discussing them.
Vocabulary SB page 33 Collocations	Matching words to make common phrases. Talking about suitable items to give as presents.
Pronunciation SB page 33 Plural forms	Listening and repeating plural forms. Adding plural nouns to a table according to their pronunciation.
Grammar SB page 33 Adverbs of frequency	Studying the use and position of adverbs of frequency. Adding adverbs of frequency to sentences.
Speaking: anecdote SB page 34 Fluency practice	Talking about the last time they bought someone a present.
Grammar & Vocabulary SB page 34 Verb patterns (1)	Studying sentences with verbs with two objects. Completing a table. Completing questions with indirect objects.
Speaking SB page 35 Fluency practice	Completing statements and discussing them.
Grammar & Vocabulary SB page 35 Verb patterns (2)	Completing two interviews with *ing*-forms and the *to*-infinitive. Completing sentences and comparing with a partner.
Reading & Vocabulary SB page 36 Reading for detail Clothes and accessories	Completing texts describing designer clothes. Discussing designer clothes and their own shopping habits. Completing a table. Listening and repeating items of clothing. Completing sentences that are true for them.
Reading SB page 37 Reading for gist	Reading a text and deciding on the overall message. Completing a diagram. Discussing the cost of clothes and recycling.
Grammar SB page 37 Present simple and continuous	Matching present simple and continuous forms with uses. Writing present simple and continuous sentences in the negative.
Useful phrases SB page 38 Useful phrases in a clothes shop	Matching lines from a conversation with speakers. Completing a conversation with useful phrases. Writing and practising new conversations about shopping.
Vocabulary *Extra* SB page 39 Revision of words from the unit: clothes and accessories; verbs used with clothes	Matching pictures with descriptions. Matching verb phrases with meanings. Underlining appropriate verb phrases in sentences.
Writing WB page 27	Describing a shop.

4 Shopping *Teacher's notes*

Warm-up

- Bring to class several objects wrapped up in paper to make interesting-looking parcels. If possible, disguise the shapes a little. Ask the students to pass them around, feel them, shake them, smell them and talk about what they think is inside. Ask which one they would most like to receive as a present. Finally, allow them to open the parcels to reveal the contents.
- Focus the students' attention on the picture of a present on page 32. Ask them to say what they think might be inside.

Speaking (SB page 32)

1

- Groupwork. Go through the questions with the class, making sure that they understand them all. Then put the students in groups to discuss their answers. As they do this, go round, monitoring and giving help with vocabulary.
- Ask a representative from each group to report back to the class on their discussions.

Reading (SB page 32)

1

- Focus the students' attention on the title of the article and ask a number of students what they would like for their next birthday. Ask also if there is anything they definitely don't want.
- Go through the questions and then give the students time to read the article and discuss the answers in pairs or small groups. Check with the class and answer any questions they may have about the article.

> a) A woman.
> b) No.
> c) No.
> d) Women want jewellery and men want gadgets.

2

- Go through the example with the class and point out that all the jumbled sentences are from the article they've just read. Ask them to rearrange the words in the remaining statements.

- Check answers with the class before putting the students into pairs to discuss whether or not they agree with them.
- Go round, monitoring and giving help. If the discussion goes well, widen it to include the whole class.

> a) A real present is something you can keep.
> b) Cookery books are boring.
> c) Most women are not interested in gadgets.
> d) Women are sensitive and intuitive.
> e) Men don't usually want brightly coloured ties.
> f) Men like anything digital, electronic and fun.

Vocabulary (SB page 33)

1

Go through the example with the class and explain that all the words in column A can be matched with one of the items in each list in column B. Allow the students to work in pairs if they wish as they match the items. When checking answers, say the collocations aloud or get the students to say them so that they hear all the combinations of words.

> a) 4   b) 7   c) 1   d) 3   e) 2   f) 5   g) 8
> h) 6

Language notes

Pronunciation: sentence stress

- English is a stress-timed rather than a syllable-timed language. This means that the time it takes to say a sentence depends on the number of stressed syllables, not the number of syllables itself. This explains why students often think that native speakers of English speak very quickly, or swallow some of their words. The syllables that aren't stressed are shortened, and the schwa sound /ə/ is very common. For example, in the phrase *A bunch of flowers* the unstressed words *a* and *of* are pronounced /ə/ and /əv/.

2

- Pairwork. Go through the questions with the class and make sure they understand them all. Then put them in pairs to discuss their answers.
- If you have a multicultural class, make sure that you get feedback from a representative of each

nationality for the second and third questions. Be prepared to talk about your own country and your own experiences of present giving. You might like to mention that some people in the UK have stopped buying presents for their friends at Christmas and instead buy something from a charity catalogue, such as a goat, some farming tools or an emergency disaster kit to give to someone in a developing country. The friend then gets a card telling them that a gift has been bought in their name.

Pronunciation (SB page 33)

1 🌐 1.30

This exercise practises pronunciation of the endings of plural nouns. Focus the students' attention on the table which gives them three categories of plural nouns, those ending with the /s/ sound, those with /z/ and those with /ɪz/. Play the recording and ask them to listen and repeat the plural forms.

> ### Language notes
>
> **Pronunciation: *voiced* versus *unvoiced***
>
> - In this exercise, where possible, the plurals which end in an unvoiced sound are pronounced /s/; the plurals which end in a voiced sound are pronounced /z/, and where neither of these are possible the plural is pronounced /ɪz/.
>
> - One way to make your students more aware of the difference between voiced and unvoiced sounds is to get them to touch their throats as they are practicing. They should be able to feel the vibration as they make voiced sounds.
>
> - You can give extra practice by giving them the words that they've already met and asking them to classify them into voiced and unvoiced. For example:
>   Voiced: *the their them that there this these they*
>   Unvoiced: *thing third thirty think thank thirteen three Thursday*

2 🌐 1.31

- Focus the students' attention on the headings in the table and point out that there are rules which govern the pronunciation of plural endings. Explain that it's the sound that a word ends in that is important here, not the letter it ends with. So *cake* ends with the /k/ sound although the final letter is an *e*. Read out the sounds in each of the columns.

- Ask the students to say the words in the box aloud. Then allow them to work in pairs if they wish as they match them to the correct columns. Encourage them to say the words and their plural forms aloud as they work so they can match the final sounds to the columns more easily.

  Play the recording for the students to check their answers. Then play it a second time for them to listen and repeat all the words.

> A: /s/ grapes, pots, socks
> B: /z/ bars, keys, ties
> C: /ɪz/ bridges, bunches, pieces

Grammar (SB page 33)
Adverbs of frequency

1

- Focus the students' attention on the information in the margin. Read the adverbs of frequency aloud or ask a student to do it and point out the scale from 100% to 0%. Then go through the information about where the adverb goes in a sentence, pointing out the exception with the verb *be*.

- Ask the students to look back at the article on page 32. Point out that twelve adverbs of frequency are highlighted. Ask a number of students to read out the sentences that contain adverbs of frequency. Then ask the class to answer the true/false questions. If necessary, write some of the sentences on the board and label the adverbs, the main part of the verbs, the auxiliary verbs and instances of the verb *be*.

> a) True   b) True

> ### Language notes
>
> **Grammar: adverbs of frequency**
>
> - While the rule states that the adverb comes between the subject and the main verb (and after the verb *be*), it's possible to use some adverbs at the beginning of the sentence, to emphasise the frequency. From the selection in the Student's Book, adverbs which can start a sentence are: *usually, normally, sometimes* and *occasionally*.
>
>   ***Sometimes** I call her five times a day.* / *I **sometimes** call her five times a day.*
>
>   ***Normally** they cost £25.* / *They **normally** cost £25.*
>
>   It's probably as well not to mention this to your students at this stage, unless someone brings up the subject, as the rule in the Student's Book covers all adverbs of frequency.

2

- Go through the instructions with the class and make sure the students understand that they must not ask their partner for information. They should write their sentences based on what they think they know about the person next to them. Give them a few minutes to do this and discourage any talking or comparing of notes.

- Pairwork. The students work in pairs to check their sentences and see how many were true. Ask the pairs to report back to the class on how accurate their sentences were and how similar/different they are to each other.

Speaking: anecdote (SB page 34)

For more information about how to set up, monitor and repeat Anecdotes, see page xx in the Introduction.

1 🔊 1.32

- Ask the students to look at the photos. Ask the students if they know what the object is and what it's used for (a foot spa, used to massage and relax the feet). Then tell them that the man is called Eddie and they're going to hear him talking about the last time he bought someone a present.
- Go through the sentences and choices with the class. Explain any unknown vocabulary and ask the students to listen and underline the answers Eddie gives.
- Check answers with the class and ask them what they think about Eddie's story. Do they sympathise with him or with his sister?

a) sister	f) £50
b) birthday	g) Yes, I did.
c) On the internet.	h) No, she didn't.
d) No, I didn't.	i) Yes, it was.
e) A foot spa.	

🔊 1.32

The last present I bought was for my sister. It was her birthday. In fact, it was her thirtieth birthday. Thirty isn't very old, but she was quite upset. She liked being in her twenties and she thought thirty was really old. Anyway, I didn't know what to get her, so I went on the internet to find something. I didn't have any ideas, but I wanted something special. Eventually, I found a really good present. I thought it was unusual, and just perfect for her – it was a foot spa. My sister's a teacher and she stands up all day, so a foot spa is great for relaxing in the evening. It was expensive – about £50 – but she's my sister, and thirty is a special birthday. I bought a lovely card and wrote a funny message in it – I put, 'Now you're thirty you're too old to die young!' Ha ha. On her birthday, I gave her the present, but unfortunately she didn't like it – at all. She said that a foot spa is a good present for a grandmother, not for a young woman. I was really surprised – I'd love a foot spa. And then, when she read the card, she cried! What a disaster.

2

- Give the students a minute or two to decide what they're going to talk about. Then ask them to look at the questions in Exercise 1 again and decide how they would answer them. Allow them to make notes of what they're going to say and how they're going to say it, but discourage them from writing a paragraph that they can simply read out. Go round, monitoring and giving help.

- Pairwork. Put the students in pairs and ask them to take turns to tell their partner about the last time they bought someone a present. Encourage them to ask each other follow-up questions to get further information.
- Ask some pairs to report back to the class about what they found out.

Grammar & Vocabulary (SB page 34)
Verb patterns 1

1

- Remind the students they've just talked about when they last bought someone a present. Point out that *bought someone a present* is an example of a verb with two objects. Focus the students' attention on the information in the margin and point out that there are other verbs which can take two objects. Explain that in the sentence *I bought somebody something*, *somebody* is called the indirect object and *something* the direct object.
- Focus the students' attention on the two example sentences and either read them aloud or ask a student to read them. Elicit answers to the questions from the class.

a) Yes.	b) Blue.	c) Red.

Language notes
Grammar: Verbs with two objects

- The sentence *I bought a present* is an example of verb (*bought*) + object (*a present*). If you want to say who you bought it for, you need another object. *I bought my mother a present* is an example of verb (*bought*) + indirect object (*my mother*) + direct object (*a present*). The indirect object (usually the recipient) can be put after the direct object with *to* or *for* (*I bought a present for my mother*).
- Other verbs which can be followed by two objects include: *cost, give, leave, make, offer, play, promise, send, teach, tell, write*.

2

- Remind the students that the two sentences about Eddie in Exercise 1 were two ways of saying the same thing. Ask them to look at the table. Point out that *I never lend my car to anybody* and *I never lend anybody my car* also mean the same thing. The difference is in the position of the indirect object and the addition of *to* when the indirect object follows the direct object.
- Ask the students to complete the table and check answers with the class. Point out the use of *for* instead of *to* in the last sentence.

- Ask the students to tick the sentences that are true for them and to compare their results with a partner.

> a) I never lend anybody my car.
> b) My friends send me lots of texts.
> c) I sometimes buy my mum flowers.

3

Read the example to the class. Ask the students to complete the remaining questions and go round, monitoring and giving help as they do this. Check answers with the class before putting the students into pairs to take turns asking and answering the questions. As they do this, go round, making sure they are forming the questions correctly and that the indirect objects are in the right position.

> a) you bought your family presents?
> b) you made somebody a cup of coffee?
> c) your bank sent you a letter?
> d) you gave somebody a lift?
> e) you lent your best friend some money?
> f) a friend told you a joke?

4 Grammar *Extra* 4, Part 1

Ask the students to turn to *Grammar Extra* 4, Part 1 on page 132 of the Student's Book. Here they'll find an explanation of the grammar they've been studying and further exercises to practise it.

> **1**
> a) Anna gave Grandad some socks.
> b) John gave Tony an MP3 player.
> c) Dick gave Molly some chocolates.
> d) Sue gave Carla a cookery book.
> e) Becky gave Eric a CD.
> f) Jimmy gave Sally some earrings.
>
> **2**
> a) to   b) to   c) for   d) to   e) to   f) to
> g) for   h) to   i) for   j) to
>
> **3**
> a) Could you send me the money?
> b) (Not possible to change.)
> c) My dad bought me this for my birthday.
> d) I've told everybody that joke!
> e) (Not possible to change.)
> f) We showed him our holiday photos.
> g) Ian is getting us some ice creams.
> h) (Not possible to change.)
> i) I don't want to make him breakfast!
> j) Can you lend Sue your bike?

Speaking (SB page 35)

1

- Go throught the statements with the class and make sure they understand them all.
- Ask the students to work individually to decide whether each statement refers to men or women and to complete them accordingly.

2

- Pairwork. Ask the students to compare and discuss their answers to Exercise 1 with their partner. Do they agree on which ones describe men and which women?
- Ask the students to widen their discussion to include which of the statements are true for them and to report back to the class.

Grammar & Vocabulary (SB page 35)
Verb patterns 2

1 🔊 1.33

- Go through the information in the margin, pointing out that some verbs are followed by an *ing*-form and others by *to*-infinitive. Read out the example sentences or ask a student to do it. Then focus their attention on the statements they completed in Exercise 1 of the Speaking section on this page. Ask them to underline all instances of verb + *ing*-form and circle all those of verb + *to*-infinitive.

- Focus the students' attention on the photos of Conor and Jim. Tell them that these two men were interviewed about their attitudes to shopping. Ask the students to say, just by looking at the men, whether they think they would enjoy shopping or not.

- Tell the students that they have to complete the interviews with the *ing*-form or the *to*-infinitive of the verbs in brackets. Go through the example with the class, pointing out that it has to be *going* because *don't mind* is one of the verbs that takes an *ing*-form.

- Give them a few minutes to complete the rest of the text. Go round, monitoring and giving help. If students aren't sure which form they need, remind them that they can look back at lists of verbs in the margin.

- Play the recording for the students to check their answers. Then ask them to say whether they know of any men with similar attitudes.

- Pairwork. Ask the students to take turns asking and answering the questions from the interviews. Encourage them to report back to the class any interesting answers.

1 going	7 to buy	13 to go
2 to go	8 looking	14 to buy
3 going	9 to buy	15 buying
4 to go	10 going	16 to buy
5 going	11 to buy	17 having
6 reading	12 going	18 to find

I: *Right, OK. Question one. Do you mind going round the shops?*

C: *Not really. But after about an hour I want to go home.*

J: *Actually, I can't stand going round the shops. My girlfriend knows this, so she usually chooses to go without me.*

I: *Right, OK. Um let's see. Question two. What kind of shops do you enjoy going into?*

C: *Book shops. I spend a lot of time reading book reviews so I always have a list of books I'd like to buy.*

J: *I enjoy looking at electronic equipment but I can't afford to buy it. It's usually far too expensive.*

I: *Right. OK. Question three. Are there any kinds of shops you hate going into?*

C: *I hate supermarkets. I usually forget to buy the things I went there for, so I avoid going into them. Fortunately, I can do most of my food shopping online.*

J: *I refuse to go into shoe shops with my girlfriend. She tries on ten pairs and then decides to buy the first pair.*

I: *Right. OK. Last question. Question four. Do you enjoy buying clothes for yourself?*

C: *Not really. I only go into a clothes shop when I need to buy a new shirt or something. For me, shopping is a necessity, not a pleasure.*

J: *I love having new clothes, but I never manage to find time to go shopping.*

Language notes

Grammar: verbs + *ing*-form and *to*-infinitive

- Some verbs can be followed by an *ing*-form or by *to*-infinitive without changing the meaning. *He started running = He started to run.* Other verbs that follow this pattern include: *begin, continue, prefer.*

- Other verbs can be followed by an *ing*-form or by a *to*-infinitive, but the meaning changes in each case. Compare *He stopped smoking* (He stopped the action of smoking) with *He stopped to smoke* (He stopped what he was doing in order to smoke). Other verbs where there is a change of meaning include: *forget, remember, try.*

2

- Ask the students to work individually to complete the sentences. As they do this, go round offering help where needed.

- Put the students in pairs to compare their sentences.

Reading & Vocabulary (SB page 36)

1 1.34

- Focus the students' attention on the photos and ask them to cover the title and text accompanying each photo. Ask the students whether they find anything strange about the clothes the models are wearing.

- Ask the students to uncover the text and complete the descriptions, working in pairs if they wish.

- Play the recording for them to check their answers. Encourage them to keep a record of any new vocabulary in their notebooks. You could suggest that they have a special page for clothes words.

> 1 waistcoat   2 shirt   3 trousers   4 boots
> 5 top   6 skirt   7 scarf   8 earrings
> 9 necklace   10 sandals

> 1.34
> *Keiko is wearing a black silk waistcoat, a white cotton shirt, black woollen trousers and black leather boots.*
>
> *Robert is wearing a plain green linen top, a red cotton skirt, a light green silk scarf around his head, gold earrings, a gold necklace, and yellow leather sandals.*

2

Have a classroom discussion on what the students think about the clothes in the photos.

3

- Focus the students' attention on the table. Explain that they're going to complete it with words from the descriptions in Exercise 1. Explain *design, material* and *accessories* and elicit a few examples of words which can go in these columns before asking the students to complete the task.

Design/ Colour	Material	Clothes and accessories
black	silk	waistcoat
white	cotton	shirt
plain	woollen	trousers
(light) green	leather	boots
red	gold	top
		skirt
		scarf
		earrings
		necklace
		sandals

Language notes

Grammar: adjective word order

- When describing someone's clothes, it's often necessary to use two or more adjectives. When there are two or more adjectives, the order is:
  - size (*big, small*)
  - design (*plain, striped*)
  - colour (*black, red, cream*)
  - material (*cotton, leather, denim*)
- So, for example, you could say: *A small plain red cotton T-shirt.*

Vocabulary: *accessories*

- A small thing such as a piece of jewellery (*necklace, earrings, bracelet, brooch, a watch*, etc.) or an additional item of clothing (*a belt, a bag, a scarf*, etc.) that you wear with clothes to give them more style.

4 **1.35**

- Ask the students to look at the pictures. Then play the recording and ask them to listen and repeat the items of clothing.
- Tell the students to add the words to the table in Exercise 3.

Design: *striped, patterned, pinstriped, checked*
Material: *woollen, silk*
Clothes and accessories: *hat, tie, jacket, shirt*

1.35

a) *a striped, woollen hat*
b) *patterned silk ties*
c) *a pinstriped jacket*
d) *a checked shirt*

5

Go through the example with the class. Point out the position of *blue* in *I'm wearing a blue cotton top* and remind the students that you usually put colour words before material or design words. Ask the students to work individually to complete the sentences so that they are true for them. Go round, monitoring and giving help, then ask them to compare their sentences in pairs.

Extra activities

- Teach the word *bargain* and ask the students to describe the best bargain they ever bought.
- Ask the students to describe the oldest piece of clothing that they possess and which they still wear. Where did they get it? How much did it cost? What is so special about it that they've kept it for so long.

Reading (SB page 37)

1

- Tell the students that they're going to read an article about the real price of cheap clothes. Ask them to say what they think the 'real price' might refer to (environmental impact, sweatshop labour, etc.).
- Ask the students to read the article and say whether environmental groups think cheap clothes are good or bad.
- Check answers with the class. Encourage the students to explain why they are bad for the environment. Go through any difficult parts of the text with the class and answer any questions about vocabulary. Make sure the students understand the word *consumers*.

Cheap clothes are a bad thing.

Cultural notes

Primark /ˈpraɪmɑːk/
A chain of budget clothing department stores in the UK, Ireland and Spain. The first store opened in Dublin, Ireland in 1969 and was called Penneys. Stores opened in the UK in the 1970s and were rebranded as Primark. Their recent success is due to sourcing their clothes cheaply and having a very quick turnover.

Friends of the Earth
Founded in the United States in 1969, Friends of the Earth is an international network of autonomous environmental organisations. These organisations campaign for greater awareness of ecological concerns, including climate change, deforestation, etc.

2

- Focus the students' attention on the diagram and point out that it should be completed with *stores* or *consumers*, according to the information from the article the students have just read.

1 stores   2 consumers   3 consumers
4 stores   5 stores

3

- Pairwork. Answer the first question as a class, then go through the other questions with the students to make sure they understand them all. Then put them into pairs to discuss their answers.
- As they ask and answer the questions, go round, monitoring and giving help where necessary. Have a feedback session with the whole class.

Grammar (SB page 37)

Present tenses

1

- Focus the students' attention on the information in the margin and go through the form of the present simple and present continuous with the class. Read out the example sentences or ask students to read them out.
- Read the sentences in Exercise 1 to the class and ask them to match the underlined verb forms with their uses.

> 1 b   2 a   3 c

Language notes

Grammar: present simple versus present continuous

- The difference between the present simple and the present continuous can be confusing for students even at an advanced level. However, here the difference is clear. You use the present simple to talk about what you do regularly, and you use the present continuous to talk about what you are doing at, or around, the moment of speaking. Expressions like *at the moment* and *now* are commonly used in present continuous sentences. Adverbs of frequency (*sometimes*, *always*, *never*, etc.) are commonly used in present simple sentences.

- Further uses and differences will be met at higher levels. For the moment, pre-intermediate students need lots of practice to consolidate their understanding of this fundamental difference.

2

- Go through the example with the class and then ask them to write the remaining sentences in the negative. Check these answers with the class before asking the students to match them with the uses in Exercise 1.
- Ask the students to work individually to tick the sentences that are true for them. Point out that they can tick the affirmative sentences in the book or the negative ones that they've produced. They then compare with a partner.

> a) I'm not sitting near the door. = Use *b*
> b) My parents don't go to church. = Use *a*
> c) I'm not saving money for my next holiday.
>   = Use *c*
> d) My mother doesn't work in a shop. = Use *a*
> e) I'm not studying for an exam. = Use *c*
> f) It isn't raining. = Use *b*
> g) I'm not learning to play the piano. = Use *c*
> h) The cost of living isn't going up fast. = Use *c*

3 Pairwork

- The pairwork exercise for this unit is on pages 117 and 122 of the Student's Book. Put the students in pairs and tell them who will be Student A, and who will be Student B.
- While they're doing the exercise, go round, monitoring and giving help. Take note of any errors which may need particular attention later, and also any examples of good language use which you can praise.

> **Student A**
> a) He/She is trying to give up smoking.
> b) He/She is learning to type.
> c) He/She is writing a book.
> d) He/She is looking for a new place to live.
> e) He/She is applying for a job.
> f) He/She is lening to dance.
>
> **Student B**
> a) He/She is trying to do more excercise.
> b) He/She is learning to drive.
> c) He/She is planning a trip abroad.
> d) He/She is reading a good book.
> e) He/She is looking for a new job.
> f) He/She is learning to play the guitar.

4 Grammar *Extra* 4, Part 2

Ask the students to turn to *Grammar Extra* 4, Part 2 on page 132 of the Student's Book. Here they'll find an explanation of the grammar they've been studying and further exercises to practise it.

> **1**
> a) is   b) cries   c) does   d) goes   e) has
> f) hears   g) pays   h) pushes   i) says
> j) studies   k) takes   l) touches
>
> **2**
> a) becoming   b) choosing   c) cutting   d) flying
> e) living   f) meeting   g) shining   h) shutting
> i) sitting   j) starting   k) staying   l) wearing
>
> **3**
> a) Do you wear perfume? / Are you wearing perfume?
> b) Do you use an electronic dictionary? / Are you using an electronic dictionary?
> c) Do you plan your holidays? / Are you planning your holidays?
> d) Do your parents work? / Are your parents working?
> e) Does your teacher wear glasses? / Is your teacher wearing glasses?
> f) What do you do? / What are you doing?
>
> **4**
> a) Where do you come from?
> b) How many languages do you speak?
> c) What are you wearing today?
> d) Why are you learning English?
> e) What time do you usually go to bed?
> f) What colour pen are you using to do this exercise?

Useful phrases (SB page 38)

1 🌐 1.36

- Focus the students' attention on the picture and ask them what they can see. Explain that the young man is Russell and that he wants to buy a present for his girlfriend. The woman in the picture is a shop assistant. Go through the phrases and ask the students to decide who says them, Russell or the shop assistant.

- Before checking answers by playing the recording, you could read the phrases out one by one and ask the students to stand up if they think it's Russell and remain seated if they think it's the shop assistant. Tell the students to try to convince classmates who have made a different choice to change their minds.

- Play the recording for the students to check their answers. Then play it again for them to repeat the useful phrases.

> a) R   b) R   c) SA   d) R   e) SA   f) R
> g) SA   h) SA   i) SA   j) R

2 🌐 1.37

- Ask the students to read the conversation and decide where the useful phrases should go. Allow them to work in pairs if they wish.

- Play the recording for the students to check their answers.

- Put the students into pairs and ask them to practise the conversation, taking turns to be Russell and the shop assistant. Encourage them to exaggerate Russell's nervousness and desire to escape from the shop, and ask any particularly good pairs to perform their conversations for the class.

> 1   Can I help you?
> 2   I'm just looking, thanks.
> 3   What sort of thing are you looking for?
> 4   What colours do you have?
> 5   What size is she?
> 6   I'll take it
> 7   How would you like to pay?
> 8   By credit card
> 9   Here's your receipt
> 10 Can she exchange it if it doesn't fit?

> 🌐 1.37 (SA = Shop assistant; R = Russell)
>
> SA: *Can I help you?*
>
> R: *I'm just looking, thanks. Well, actually, I'm looking for something for my girlfriend.*
>
> SA: *What sort of thing are you looking for?*
>
> R: *I don't really know. A top?*
>
> SA: *OK, and what colour would you like?*
>
> R: *What colours do you have?*

> SA: *We have any colour you want, sir. Purple is very fashionable at the moment.*
>
> R: *Purple's fine.*
>
> SA: *Right. What size is she?*
>
> R: *Ah, well, she isn't very big, but she's not particularly small.*
>
> SA: *So, she's medium.*
>
> R: *Yes, medium.*
>
> SA: *Well, we have this rather nice purple top here …*
>
> R: *Good. I'll take it.*
>
> SA: *Are you sure you don't want to see any more …*
>
> R: *No, that's great. I'll take it. Thank you. How much is it?*
>
> SA: *That's £70, sir. How would you like to pay?*
>
> R: *Seventy?! By credit card, please.*
>
> SA: *Fine. If you could just sign …*
>
> R: *Here you are. Goodbye.*
>
> SA: *Just a minute, sir. Here's your receipt.*
>
> R: *Oh yes, er … Can she exchange it if it doesn't fit?*
>
> SA: *Yes, but she needs to keep the receipt.*

3

- Pairwork. Go through the instructions and explain anything that is unclear. Give the students a few minutes to write their conversations. Go round, monitoring and giving help. Encourage them to use as many of the useful phrases as possible and make sure they include at least six of the words in the box.

- Ask the pairs to practise their conversations and then perform them for the class.

Extra activity

Ask the students to discuss their shopping preferences. Do they like supermarkets where you can just take things off the shelves, put them in a basket or trolley and have no contact with the sales staff until you get to the checkout? Do they prefer shops with assistants who help you or do they prefer to be left alone to make their own choices? Have they ever felt uncomfortable in a shop where a shop assistant was too persistent, or showed too much interest in the items they were buying?

Vocabulary *Extra* (SB page 39)
Clothes and accessories

1

Focus the students' attention on the list of words and point out that they're all words used to describe clothes and accessories. Then focus the students' attention on the pictures and ask them to match them with the correct descriptions. When they've finished, ask them to complete the descriptions.

```
7   a checked scarf
9   brown leather gloves
11  a plain white cotton shirt
2   a blue denim jacket
8   a pinstriped suit
10  a silver necklace
12  a patterned woollen jumper
5   a floral top
6   gold earrings
1   striped tights
4   plastic sunglasses
3   a light blue silk dress
```

2

Pairwork. Demonstrate first with a confident student by getting them to ask and answer the example questions with you. Then ask the students to work in pairs and take turns asking and answering questions about the pictures.

Focus on verbs used with clothes

1

Ask the students to work individually to match the verb phrases with their meanings. Then allow them to compare answers in pairs before checking with the class.

```
a) 4   b) 1   c) 6   d) 3   e) 5   f) 2
```

2

Ask the students to underline the most appropriate verb phrases. Check answers with the class before asking the students to tick the sentences that are true for them and compare with a partner.

```
a) get dressed
b) wear
c) put on
d) trying on
e) suit
f) get changed
```

Further practice material

Need more writing practice?

→ Workbook page 27
• Describing a shop.

Need more classroom practice activities?

→ Photocopiable resource materials pages 161 to 163
  Grammar: *Let's talk!*
  Vocabulary: *What's the difference?*
  Communication: *Ten facts*
→ Top 10 activities pages xv to xx

Need progress tests?

→ Test CD – *Test Unit 4*

Need more on important teaching concepts?

→ Key concepts in *New Inside Out* pages xxii to xxxv

Need student self-study practice?

→ CD-ROM – Unit 4: *Shopping*

Need student CEF self-evaluation?

→ CEF Checklists pages xxxvii to xliv

Need more information and more ideas?

→ www.insideout.net

5 Fit *Overview*

Section & Aims	What the students are doing
🔘 Reading **SB page 40** Reading for detail	Reading and answering a questionnaire about fitness. Comparing scores with a partner.
Vocabulary **SB page 41** *how* + adjective/adverb	Completing a table about how long it takes them to do things. Completing questions with *How* + adjective/adverb.
🔘 Speaking: anecdote **SB page 41** Fluency practice	Talking about experiences of doing sport at school.
🔘 Listening **SB page 42** Listening for specific information	Matching famous sportspeople with their birthdates. Listening to a discussion and identifying which sportsman is chosen for an advertising campaign. Completing comparative sentences.
🔘 Grammar **SB page 42** Comparatives	Making comparisons in a general knowledge test. Making comparative statements with words in boxes.
🔘 Pronunciation **SB page 43** The schwa sound	Completing expressions with *as ... as*. Practising the schwa sound.
Grammar **SB page 43** Superlatives	Writing superlative forms for different groups of adjectives. Completing questions with superlative adjectives.
🔘 Vocabulary **SB page 43** Numbers	Listening and repeating fractions and decimals. Matching numbers to facts.
Reading **SB page 44** Reading for detail	Reading about ways to avoid stress and discussing the suggestions. Adding three more suggestions to the list.
Vocabulary **SB page 44** Phrasal verbs	Completing sentences with phrasal verbs from an article. Discussing the sentences with a partner.
Grammar **SB page 45** Phrasal verbs	Answering questions about the form and use of phrasal verbs. Putting words in the correct order to make answers to questions.
🔘 Listening & Speaking **SB page 45** Listening for gist; fluency practice	Listening to a radio programme about laughter clubs and marking statements true or false. Trying to make a partner laugh. Discussing questions about laughter.
🔘 Useful phrases **SB page 46** Useful conversational phrases for giving instructions	Listening to three conversations to identify sports. Matching people with sets of instructions. Completing a conversation with useful phrases, then listening and practising it with a partner.
Vocabulary *Extra* **SB page 47** Revision of words from the unit: sports; verbs with sports	Matching equipment with sports to complete a table. Adding more sports words to a table. Underlining the correct verbs in sentences. Completing verb phrases with *do, go* or *play* and adding more sports.
Writing **WB page 33**	Describing a sporting event.

Fit *Teacher's notes*

Warm-up

Write the word *sport* on the board and ask the students to suggest as many words and expressions as they can to do with sport. They should be able to name a number of sports, but try to widen the lexical field by prompting them to think of other aspects of sport such as health and fitness. Write all their suggestions in a spidergram, grouping them according to topic (all the sports together; words to do with health and fitness together; etc.).

Reading (SB page 40)

1

Focus the students' attention on the questionnaire. Look at the title and explain the expression *dangerously unfit*. Ask the students what the opposite of *unfit* is (*fit*). Tell them that they're going to answer a questionnaire to find out how fit they are. Ask them to work individually to do this. As they work, go round assisting with any vocabulary questions.

Language note

Vocabulary: *aerobic*

- *Aerobic* exercise is a very active type of exercise that makes your heart and lungs stronger.

2

When the students have answered all the questions, ask them to calculate their scores with the *How to score* section and then look at *What your score means*. In pairs, they should compare their answers and say if they agree with the results or not.

Vocabulary (SB page 41)

1

- Focus the students' attention on the photo in the margin. Ask them if this is a fair representation of their own morning routine or whether theirs is more leisurely.
- Ask the students to look at the table. Go through the activities listed and make sure everyone understands them. Put the students in pairs, but ask them to work individually to write down the time it takes them to do the activities. Ask them also to guess how long it takes their partner to do the activities. Ask them not to confer at this stage.

- When the students have finished completing the table, they can take turns asking each other about how long it takes them to do the activities to find out how accurately they guessed. You might like to complete the table for yourself and ask the students at the end to guess as a class how long it takes you to do these things.

Extra activity

Ask the students to brainstorm more questions with *How long …?* Then get the students to ask about other people in their family, e.g. *How long does it take your brother/sister to …?*

2

- Remind the students that the questions in Exercise 1 were all *How long does it take you to …*. Point out that this is a question about time using *How* plus the adjective *long*. Go through the words in the box and explain that these adjectives and adverbs can all be used with *How* to make questions.
- Ask the students to complete the questions. Check answers before the students take turns asking and answering the questions in pairs.

a) often	b) long	c) many	d) much
e) far	f) fast	g) old	h) well

Extra activity

- Extend the activity by getting the students to brainstorm another question for each *How +* adjective/adverb combination.

Speaking: anecdote (SB page 41)

For more information about how to set up, monitor and repeat Anecdotes, see page xx in the Introduction.

1 🔊 2.01

- Ask the students to look at the photos. Ask them if they think they both show the same woman and, if so, what they think she's going to talk about. Elicit or explain that she's going to talk about her experiences of sport at school.

- Go through the sentences and the answers with the class. Explain any unknown vocabulary and ask the students to listen and tick the answers Tina gives that are correct and put a cross against any that are wrong.
- Check answers with the class and ask them whether they had similar experiences to Tina of sport at school.

---

a) ✗ b) ✓ c) ✓ d) ✗ e) ✓ f) ✗ g) ✓

🌐 2.01

When I was at secondary school, we did sport every Wednesday afternoon. Two hours, from 1.30 to 3.30. Wednesdays were my worst day of the week. I hated doing sport at school. In summer we did swimming and tennis, and in winter we did hockey. I really, really hated hockey. It was always cold when we played hockey, but we wore shorts! Horrible, grey shorts. My legs were very thin and they were so cold that they turned blue. I was always happy when it was raining or snowing – then we stayed inside and did Scottish dancing. I loved that.

At my school we had a sports field and tennis courts and a swimming pool. I love swimming, but the swimming pool wasn't heated so it was freezing.

I didn't like my sports teacher, and she didn't like me. Her name was Miss Rockham. We called her Rocky. She looked like a boxer, and she had a very loud voice. She loved hockey. In fact, I think she played for the national hockey team.

Of course, I didn't play for the school hockey team, but I loved dancing so much that I joined a dance club after school. My best sporting moment was when my dance club won a competition for disco dancing. Rocky didn't think that dancing was a real sport, but I disagree. Dancing kept me fit, and I didn't have to wear grey shorts.

2

- Allow the students time to decide what experience they're going to talk about. Remind them that it could be a good or a bad experience. Then ask them to look at the questions in Exercise 1 again and decide how they would answer them about their experiences of sport at school. Allow them to make notes of what they're going to say and how they're going to say it, but discourage them from writing a paragraph that they can simply read out. Go round, monitoring and giving help.
- Pairwork. Put the students in pairs and ask them to take turns to tell their partner about their experiences. Encourage them to ask follow-up questions to get further information. Then ask some pairs to report back to the class about what they found out.

Listening (SB page 42)

1 2.02

- Draw the students' attention to the photos and ask them if they know anything about these sports stars. They may be able to say that Ronaldo, Beckham and Henry are footballers, Alonso is a racing driver and Nadal and Federer are tennis players. Then ask them to say who they think is the oldest and who the youngest. Don't confirm answers at this stage, but try to get the class to reach a consensus decision.
- Ask the students to try to match the sports stars with the list of birthdates. Allow them to discuss this in pairs or small groups and to try to come to a consensus.
- Play the recording for the students to check their answers. Ask them if they were surprised by any of the information.

02/05/75 – c)	08/08/81 – f)
17/08/77 – a)	05/02/85 – d)
29/07/81 – b)	03/06/86 – e)

🌐 2.02

David Beckham is the oldest. He was born in 1975. Thierry Henry's next. He was born in 1977. After that, it's Fernando Alonso, born in July 1981, then Roger Federer – a few days later in August 1981. Cristiano Ronaldo was born in 1985 and Rafael Nadal is the youngest. He was born in 1986.

Cultural notes

Thierry Henry /tiːˈjeriː ɒnˈriiː/ (born 1977)
French footballer. He played for Monaco and Juventus before moving to London to play for Arsenal in 1999. He was the club's top goalscorer almost every year since he joined the club, and has twice been nominated FIFA's World Player of the Year. He left Arsenal in 2007 to join Barcelona.

Fernando Alonso /fɜːˈnændəʊ əˈlɒnsəʊ/ (born 1981)
Spanish Formula One driver. In 2006, he won the world championship for the second time, making him the youngest double champion in the sport's history. He's driven for Minardi, Renault and McLaren.

David Beckham (born 1975)
(See notes about David Beckham in Unit 1, page 4.)

Cristiano Ronaldo /krɪstɪˈjɑːnəʊ rəˈnældəʊ/ (born 1985)
Portuguese footballer. He plays for Manchester United and Portugal. In 2007, he was awarded as Professional Footballers Association's Player of the Year.

Roger Federer /rɒdʒə ˈfedərə/ (born 1981)
Swiss tennis player. Possibly the greatest tennis player of all time. In 2006, he became the first and only man to have won three out of four Grand Slam singles titles three years running.

Rafael Nadal /ˈræfaɪjəl nəˈdæl/ (born 1986)
Spanish tennis player. Top ranked player Rafael
Nadal won the French Open in 2005, 2006 and 2007.
He was the first player to win three consecutive
French Open titles since Bjorn Borg. He's Federer's
main rival on the tennis circuit, although he's more
of a clay court player, whereas Federer excels on
grass.

2 🔘 2.03

- Explain the roles of a marketing director and an
  advertising executive. A marketing director is the
  person in a company who is responsible for making
  sure that its product sells well. Advertising is just
  one way of doing this and the marketing director
  will use an advertising executive from an advertising
  agency to help put together a campaign to get the
  product widely known. Ask the students how many
  advertising campaigns they can name which use
  famous sports stars to advertise a product.

- Tell the students that they're going to listen to a
  conversation between a marketing director and
  an advertising executive. They're discussing the
  marketing of a new energy drink called 'Iso-tonic'
  and they want to use a famous sportsman in the
  advertising campaign. Ask the students to listen and
  say who they choose.

- Check the answer and then go through the gapped
  sentences with the class. Play the recording again and
  ask the students to listen and complete the sentences
  with the names of the sportsmen in Exercise 1. Point
  out that they'll need to use some names more than
  once.

Cristiano Ronaldo

a) Beckham, Henry	d) Nadal, Federer
b) Beckham, Henry	e) Nadal, Federer
c) Beckham, Henry	f) Cristiano Ronaldo

🔘 2.03 (MD = marketing director;
AE = advertising executive)

MD: *OK, what are we looking for exactly?*

AE: *We're looking for the new face of 'Iso-tonic',
the new energy drink.*

MD: *Yes, I know ... but what kind of face are we
looking for?*

AE: *Ah, well, we need a sports celebrity. Probably a
man. Someone good-looking and healthy.*

MD: *Good. Do we have any ideas?*

AE: *Yes, we're thinking of David Beckham or
Thierry Henry.*

MD: *Hmm. Beckham is more famous than Henry ...*

AE: *Hmm. But he isn't as interesting.*

MD: *Are they the same age?*

AE: *Er, I think Beckham is a bit older than Henry.*

MD: *Hmm. I think we need a younger man.*

AE: *How about Fernando Alonso?*

MD: *Who's he?*

AE: *He's a Formula One champion – he's young,
successful ...*

MD: *But Formula One is too dangerous. We want
this man to be the face of 'Iso-tonic' for a few
years. How about tennis? Federer, Nadal ...?*

AE: *Hmm. Nadal isn't as successful as Federer.*

MD: *No, but Nadal's much younger than Federer, so
he could be more successful in future.*

AE: *Hmm.*

MD: *OK, who's your favourite sports star?*

AE: *Oh, Cristiano Ronaldo. I think he's the best-
looking, most interesting, most successful
sportsman in the world.*

MD: *Well, let's use him then. Perfect. I want you to
get in touch with him immediately.*

3

- Pairwork. Ask the students to list the most famous
  sportsmen and women in their country. If you have
  students from more than one country, make sure
  that the pairs are made up of students from the same
  country. If this isn't possible, allow them to make two
  lists.

- Ask the students to complete the exercise using the
  names they've listed and choosing one of them for
  a new sports car advertisement. As they do this, go
  round, monitoring and giving help. Make sure each
  pair has enough information to feed back to the rest
  of the class.

Extra activity

Ask the students to find a photograph of the
sportsperson they've chosen and to make their
advertisements. They'll need to think of slogans
and any other wording that will appear on them.
Display the finished adverts in the classroom for
everyone to see. Encourage discussion of them
using comparative adjectives.

Grammar (SB page 42)

Comparatives

1 🔘 2.04

- Remind the students that they used comparative
  structures to talk about the sportspeople in the last
  section. Go through the information in the margin to
  reinforce the structures.

- Focus the students' attention on the sentences and
  read out the example to the class. Ask the student
  to complete the remaining comparisons. Encourage
  them to work individually, but to compare their
  results with a partner when they've finished.

- Play the recording for the students to listen and check
  their answers.

a) is much higher than	d) is a bit busier than
b) isn't as wet as	e) isn't as big as
c) is much smaller than	f) a bit taller than

🌐 2.04

a) *At 5,894 metres, Mount Kilimanjaro is much higher than Mount Fuji, which is 3,776 metres.*

b) *Surprisingly, London isn't as wet as Rome. The annual average in London is 594 millimetres, whereas in Rome the annual average is 749 millimetres.*

c) *The US army is much smaller than the North Korean Army. There are 524,900 American soldiers compared to over one million North Koreans.*

d) *Heathrow Airport in London is a bit busier than Los Angeles International Airport. In one year, Heathrow serves 51,368,000 passengers and Los Angeles serves 51,030,000.*

e) *Ireland isn't as big as Cuba. Ireland is 83,030 square kilometres, but Cuba is 114,530.*

f) *Big Ben is a bit taller than the Statue of Liberty. Big Ben is 96 metres tall, and the Statue of Liberty is 93 metres tall.*

Language notes

Grammar: *a bit / much*

- Quantifiers *a bit* and *much* come between the verb *be* and the comparative adjective: *He's **much** older than his sister. It's **a bit** taller than Big Ben.* They help by giving more information about the differences between two things or people.

Grammar: comparative structures

- The comparative form can be divided into five categories:

  1) short adjectives (*old*) take -*r* / -*er* (*older*).

  2) adjectives that end in consonant-vowel-consonant (*th-i-n*) double the final consonant + -*er* (*thinner*).

  3) adjectives that end in -*y* (*happy*) drop the -*y* and take -*ier* (*happier*).

  4) longer adjectives (*interesting*) remain unchanged, but are preceded by *more* (*more interesting*).

  5) Some adjectives (*good* / *bad*) are irregular and don't follow any of the rules above (*better* / *worse*).

2

- Give the students time to choose the words they want to use and form their comparative statements. Remind them that they can use their own ideas if they wish and encourage them to work individually. Go round, monitoring and giving help where necessary.

- Ask the students to show their statements to a partner and discuss whether they agree or disagree with each other's comparisons. Ask a selection of pairs to report back on their statements to the class.

3 Grammar *Extra* 5, Part 1

Ask the students to turn to *Grammar Extra* 5, Part 1 on page 134 of the Student's Book. Here they'll find an explanation of the grammar they've been studying and further exercises to practise it.

1

a) kind – kinder than, nice – nicer than, strong – stronger than,

b) sad – sadder than, thin – thinner than, wet – wetter than

c) happy – happier than, lazy – lazier than, lucky – luckier than

d) bad – worse than, far – further than, good – better than

e) famous – more famous than, interesting – more interesting than, successful – more successful than

2

a) France is a bit bigger than Spain.

b) India is much hotter than the UK.

c) The River Nile is a bit longer than the Amazon.

d) Tokyo is much more expensive than Bangkok.

e) Rome is a bit further north than Barcelona.

f) Manila is much more crowded than Helsinki.

a) Spain isn't as big as France.

b) The UK isn't as hot as India.

c) The Amazon isn't as long as the River Nile.

d) Bangkok isn't as expensive as Tokyo.

e) Barcelona isn't as far north as Rome.

f) Helsinki isn't as crowded as Manila.

Pronunciation (SB page 43)

1

- Go through the example with the class and explain that there are several English expressions which use the structure *as … as*. Ask them to look at the expressions and try to decide on appropriate words to complete them. Emphasise that you don't expect them to know them all. Allow them to work in pairs if they wish and encourage them to be creative.

2 🌐 2.05

- Play the recording for the students to check their answers. Then play it again for them to listen to and ask them to notice how the schwa sounds are pronounced. Ask them to repeat after the speaker and try to copy these sounds exactly.

- Check that the students understand the meanings of these phrases, i.e.

  a) *It's as light as a feather.* = very light

  b) *He's as free as a bird.* = very free

  c) *They're as good as gold.* = very well-behaved (usually refers to children)

d) *She's as pretty as a picture.* = very pretty

e) *It's as solid as a rock.* = very strong, not likely to break (of a person = very reliable or calm)

f) *It's as old as the hills.* = very old

- Ask the students if they particularly like or dislike any of the expressions. Then find out if they can think of people or things they could use the expressions to describe. Write any good suggestions on the board. Ask if they have similar expressions in their own language(s).

---

a) feather   b) bird   c) gold   d) picture

e) rock f) hills

Extra activity

Point out that expressions with *as … as …* are known as similes and that the English language is full of them. Many are traditional, but new ones are being created all the time. One example that has become popular in recent years is *as sick as a parrot*, commonly used by football players to express how they feel after missing a penalty or losing a match. Although these similes are used more in daily conversation these days than proverbs are, students should be careful not to overuse them. However, they may be interested in knowing a few more. Here is a matching exercise to try; ask the students when they've matched them how appropriate they think the similes are.

1 as strong as	a) a pancake
2 as brave as	b) ice
3 as green as	c) two short planks
4 as cold as	d) a cucumber
5 as hot as	e) an ox
6 as flat as	f) a lion
7 as cool as	g) hell
8 as thick as	h) grass

---

1 e   2 f   3 h   4 b   5 g   6 a

7 d   8 c

Grammar (SB page 43)

Superlatives

1

- Remind the students that up till now they've compared two things. Tell them that now they're going to look at how to compare three or more things. Focus their attention on the information in the margin and go through the superlative forms with the class. If students ask how long an adjective has to be to be considered 'long', a good rule of thumb is three syllables or more, although there are exceptions and some adjectives which can be either 'long' or 'short' (e.g. *clever*). Focus their attention on the spelling change with *funny – funniest*.

- Go through the example in the exercise with the class. Elicit the superlative forms of *exciting* and *great* and then ask the students which superlative adjective in the group is formed in a different way from the other three (*the most exciting*). Ask them to complete the exercise, in each group underlining the one that is formed differently.

---

a) the oldest / the richest / <u>the most exciting</u> / the greatest

b) <u>the most valuable</u> / the biggest / the hottest / the thinnest

c) the funniest / <u>the most interesting</u> / the sexiest / the happiest

d) the worst / the furthest / the best / <u>the most talented</u>

Language notes

Grammar: superlatives

The superlative form can be divided into five categories:

1) short adjectives (*old*) take *-est* (*the oldest*).

2) adjectives that end in consonant-vowel-consonant (*th-i-n*) double the final consonant + *-est* (*the thinnest*).

3) adjectives that end in *-y* (*happy*) drop the *-y* and take *-iest* (*the happiest*).

4) longer adjectives (*interesting*) remain unchanged, but are preceded by *the most* (*the most interesting*).

5) Some adjectives (*good / bad*) are irregular and don't follow any of the rules above (*the best / the worst*).

2

- Tell the students that they can use the adjectives in Exercise 1 or their own ideas to complete the questions. However, the questions must make sense. As they complete them, go round, monitoring and giving help.

- Ask the students to work in pairs and ask their partner their questions.

Vocabulary (SB page 43)

1 🌐 2.06

- Ask the students what they notice about the numbers in the box. Teach the words *fraction* and *decimal*. In some countries, a comma is used instead of a decimal point, so draw their attention to the British usage.

- Play the recording and ask the students to listen and repeat the numbers. When they've done this chorally, ask for individual repetition of the numbers.

- Ask the students to find pairs of numbers with the same value. Read out the example to the class. When they've matched up the decimals and fractions, check answers by asking various students to read the pairs aloud. Then put them in pairs to practise saying the numbers.

> ¾ is the same as 0.75.   1½ is the same as 1.5.
> 0.25 is the same as ¼.   ⅛ is the same as 0.125.
> 0.33 is the same as ⅓.

2 🌐 2.07

- Play the recording and ask the students to listen and repeat the numbers in column A. When they've done this chorally, ask several students to repeat the numbers individually. Point out the way the first one can be written out in full. Ask the students to write out the others. Go round, monitoring and giving help.

- Focus the students' attention on column B and ask them to match these facts with the numbers. Allow them to discuss this in pairs or small groups.

> a) two hundred and forty-nine kilometres an hour
> b) forty-two point one nine five kilometres
> c) eight point two percent
> d) six million, one hundred and eighty-eight thousand
> e) thirty-two nil
> a) 4   b) 5   c) 2   d) 1   e) 3

Cultural notes

Cristiano Ronaldo
(See notes about Cristiano Ronaldo on page 46.)

Australia versus Samoa
The biggest football score ever was by Australia against Samoa. On April 11, 2001, in a FIFA World Cup qualifying round, Australia beat the American Samoa 32 goals to 0.

Andy Roddick (born 1982)
Andy Roddick is a professional tennis player. In 2007, he was the top-ranked player in the US. He recorded the fastest serve ever at 150 mph. He won the US Open in 2003. He reached three other Grand Slam finals, in 2004, 2005 and 2006, but lost to Roger Federer on each occasion.

3 Pairwork

- The pairwork exercise for this unit is on pages 117 and 122 of the Student's Book. Put the students in pairs and tell them who will be Student A, and who will be Student B.

- While they're doing the exercise, go round, monitoring and giving help. Take note of any errors which may need particular attention later, and also any examples of good language use which you can praise.

Student A	Student B
a) 30 km/h	a) 105 km/h
b) $80,137,000	b) $93,820,000
c) 7,120	c) 2,175
d) 20%	d) 2%
e) 40,075.16 km	e) 4,203 km
f) 194–0	f) 9–0

Reading (SB page 44)

1

- Teach the word *stress* and ask the students to suggest things in their lives that are stressful. They might come up with such things as exams, work, driving in heavy traffic, etc. Then ask them for ways in which they try to overcome stress, ways in which they relax. Write their suggestions on the board.

- Focus the students' attention on the photo and ask if they think the person in it is stressed or relaxed. Then ask them to read the list of ways to de-stress and think about their answers to the questions.

- Put the students in pairs to discuss their answers. Then ask several pairs to report back to the class.

2

Pairwork. Ask the students to work with the same partner and add three more suggestions to the list. Go round, monitoring and giving help. Then put some of the suggestions on the board.

Vocabulary (SB page 44)

1

- Remind the students that the phrasal verbs in the box were in the article in the previous section. Ask them to find and underline them.

- Allow them to work in pairs to complete the sentences. Go round, monitoring and giving help.

a) take off	e) switch on
b) switch off	f) throw away
c) put on	g) hang up
d) give up	

2

- Ask the students to discuss in pairs whether any of the sentences are true for them.

- Ask several pairs to report back to the class on their discussion.

Grammar (SB page 45)

Phrasal verbs

1

- Focus the students' attention on the information in the margin. Ask the students to identify the particles in the phrasal verbs in the margin (*down, off, after*).

Read the example sentences in the margin aloud or ask several students to read them. For more information on phrasal verbs, see the Language notes below.

- Put the students in pairs to look at the sentences and answer the questions. Go round, monitoring and giving help.

> a) sat down (sit down)
> b) took off (take off)
> c) ran after (run after)

2

Elicit the answer to the question from the class. Ask them to look at the example sentences in Exercise 1 and in the margin to help them decide.

> a) Between the verb and particle.
> b) After the verb and particle.

Language notes

Grammar: Phrasal verbs

- There are many phrasal verbs in English. When your students encounter a phrasal verb in a text, encourage them to try to guess the meaning from the context. This will help if they then look it up in a dictionary, as there can sometimes be several meanings of the same phrasal verb.
A good dictionary will tell you if the verb needs an object (transitive) or doesn't (intransitive). There are two types of transitive phrasal verbs, separable and non-separable.

- In separable phrasal verbs the object can separate the phrasal verb or come after it – **Throw** *the banana skin* **away**. / **Throw away** *the banana skin*.

  But if the object is a pronoun it must separate the phrasal verb – **Throw** *it* **away**.

- In non-separable phrasal verbs the object always comes after it – *Could you* **deal with** *the problem?* / *Could you* **deal with** *it?*

  If a phrasal verb has two particles (*get on with*), the object always comes after it – *My husband* **gets on with** *my parents.* / *He* **gets on with** *them.*

3

- Go through the example with the class, then ask the students to work individually to put the words in order in the answers for the questions. Allow them to compare answers in pairs before checking with the class. If the students don't have dictionaries to consult, answer any questions about vocabulary.

- Check answers by having one student read out a question and another give the appropriate answer.

> a) Throw it away.   d) Deal with it.
> b) Clear it up.   e) Fill it in.
> c) Hang them up.   f) Call it off.

4 Grammar *Extra* 5, Part 2

Ask the students to turn to *Grammar Extra* 5, Part 2 on page 134 of the Student's Book. Here they'll find an explanation of the grammar they've been studying and further exercises to practise it.

> **1**
> a) Can you turn the light off, please?
> b) She threw away my letter.
> c) I'd like to try this dress on, please.
> d Pick up all the papers before you leave!
> e) Write your name down, please.
> f) I gave his pen back.
>
> **2**
> a) take after her   e) put them away
> b) get on well with them f) make them up
> c) look after it   g) gave it up
> d) brought me up   h) look it up

Listening & Speaking (SB page 45)

1 🌐 2.08

- Focus the students' attention on the photo and ask them what the people are doing. Tell them that the people are at a laughter club and that they're going to listen to a radio programme about these clubs.

- Read the statements with the class and ask them if they can predict whether they are true or false. Encourage them to try to persuade other students to change their minds if they disagree with them.

- Play the recording for the students to listen and check their answers.

> a) True.   b) False.   c) True.   d) True.
> e) False.

> 🌐 2.08 (P = Presenter; A = Avril)
>
> P: *We all know the expression 'laughter is the best medicine'. But a recent study shows that adults don't laugh enough. The study shows that young children laugh up to four hundred times a day, while adults only laugh seventeen times a day. According to medical research, fifteen to twenty minutes of laughter a day really does keep the doctor away.*
>
> *Well now you can join one of the laughter clubs to get your regular twenty minutes of laughter.*
>
> *It sounds funny, and it even looks a little funny, but this is a laughter club. Avril is the teacher here. Avril, how did the laughter clubs start?*
>
> A: *They started in India eleven years ago. Dr Kataria started a club in Mumbai, and now there are hundreds of laughter clubs all over the world. In India, people are very serious about the benefits of laughter.*
>
> P: *And what are the benefits of laughter?* ➤

A: When you laugh, you release happy chemicals –
endorphins. This can reduce the effects of stress and
you feel more relaxed. Laughter boosts the immune
system and relaxes the mind. Also, laughing is good
for the heart and good for the lungs.

P: What happens in laughter club? What exactly
do you do?

A: We just laugh.

P: Do you listen to funny stories?

A: Oh no. We don't need anything to make us
laugh. We do exercises, and when you start
laughing, you can't stop.

P: What kind of exercises?

A: Well, we start the class with a laughing exercise
called ho ho ha ha ha.
After that, we do different kinds of laughing.
There's 'social laughter', silent laughter, and the
loud, explosive laugh which exercises the lungs.

2

- Tell the students they can use any reasonable means
to make their partner laugh, but not physical contact.
Elicit a few suggestions first for things they might try,
and put these on the board. You may have to start
them off with a few ideas of your own, e.g. tell a joke,
pull a funny face, make a funny noise, etc.

- Pairwork. In pairs, the students take turns to try to
make each other laugh. Give them a time limit. See
which methods are most successful and encourage
those students to try to make the whole class laugh.

3

Pairwork. Go through the questions with the class and
then ask them to discuss them in pairs. Encourage them
to report back to the class on anything interesting that
came out of their discussion.

Useful phrases (SB page 46)

1 🌐 2.09

- Focus the students' attention on the illustrations.
Explain that the people in the pictures are Sally,
Jimmy and Rebecca and they're each learning a sport.
They're going to listen to them talking and they have
to decide what sport each of them is learning.

- Play the recording for them to listen and note down
their answers.

a) windsurf   b) football   c) tennis

🌐 2.09

a)   (P = Paul; S = Sally)

P: OK, are you ready?

S: Yes.

P: Right. Stand up on the board.

S: OK. OOHHHHH!

P: Ha ha ha!

S: Don't be horrible.

P: Oh, sorry. OK, try again. Good! Great. Hold on.
Don't let go.

S: OHHHHH! It's too difficult. I can't do it.

P: Don't be silly. Of course you can do it. Be
patient. Come on, try again.

S: I look stupid.

P: Don't worry! Everyone looks stupid the first
time. Now, stand up on the board. That's it. Be
careful. Good. Well done. Now, don't go too fast,
Sally! Sally! Come back!

S: Wheeee!

b)   (F = Father; J = Jimmy)

F: OK, Jimmy, kick the ball to me.

J: Daddy, Daddy, look at me.

F: Oh, that's very good, Jimmy. Now, this time,
don't throw the ball – kick it.

J: Kick?

F: Yes, with your foot. Look, like this.

J: Like this?

F: No, no, don't pick it up – that's it. Now kick it.
No, don't touch the ball with your hand. Use
your foot. Yes, that's it. Ouch!

J: You OK, Daddy?

F: Aagh!

c)   (M = Mother; R = Rebecca)

M: Right, watch me. Throw the ball in the air.
Watch the ball, and hit it. OK? Now you try.
Throw the ball in the air and hit the – oh, OK,
try again. This time, don't look at me – look at
the ball. Throw the ball in the air. Watch the ball
and, … oh dear.

R: I hate this stupid game. I want to go horse-
riding. You're horrible.

M: Don't be rude, Rebecca. Pick up your racket and
try again.

2

Focus the students' attention on the instructions and ask
them to match each of the people with one of the sets
of instructions. Check answers with the class and point
out the use of the imperative in both the affirmative and
negative forms. If anyone asks about the use of do in
affirmative imperatives, tell them that this is only used
for very strong advice, as in Do be careful!

a) 2   b) 3   c) 1

Language notes

Vocabulary: sports equipment

- Tennis and squash players use a racket / racquet;
golfers use a club; table tennis and baseball
players use a bat and (wind)surfers use a board.

3

- Ask the students to complete the conversation by replacing the highlighted phrases with their equivalent from the box. Negative imperatives will be replaced with positive imperatives carrying the same meaning and vice versa. You may need to do the first one with the class as an example.

- Play the first conversation on the recording again for the students to listen and check their answers. Then ask them to practise the conversation with a partner.

1 Don't be horrible.	4 Don't worry.
2 Try again.	5 Be careful!
3 Be patient.	6 Come back!

Vocabulary *Extra* (SB page 47)

Sport

1

- Focus the students' attention on the table and look at all the items in the first row. Read them aloud and ask the students to repeat them. Make sure they get the stress right on *athletics* (/æθˈletɪks/) and *athlete* (/ˈæθliːt/). Point out that the final column (Equipment) is incomplete and there are illustrations of the missing equipment. Ask them to find the picture of the running shoes.

- Give the students a few minutes to identify the sports that the other pieces of equipment are associated with and to add them to the table.

- Check answers with the class, making sure they can pronounce all the items correctly.

1 running shoes	5 swimming trunks
2 a helmet	6 goggles
3 football boots	7 a tennis racket
4 golf clubs	8 a net

2

- Brainstorm another sport that could be added to the table and elicit the appropriate words to put in the person, place and equipment columns of the table. Then allow the students to work in pairs to add their own sports and words. Go round, monitoring and giving help.

- Ask several pairs to read out their answers to the class.

Focus on verbs used with sports

1

- Explain that you use different verbs to talk about doing different sports. There are no hard and fast rules, but *play* tends to be used with ball games and games played in teams, such as ice-hockey, or between two opponents, such as chess; *go* is used with sports that end in *-ing*, such as swimming, and *do* with other sports, such as athletics. Explain that

practise refers to spending time working on a sport in order to improve one's performance.

- Ask the students to underline the appropriate verbs in the sentences. Check answers with the class before putting them into pairs to discuss how many are true for them.

a) do   b) been   c) go   d) did   e) played   f) practise

2

Ask the students to complete the table. Check answers with the class before asking them to add more sports to each list. Go round, monitoring and checking that they put the new sports in the correct columns.

a) go   b) do   c) play

Extra activities

- Write the following stems on the board and ask the students to complete them to make true statements about their participation in sports and then compare with a partner.
  a) *I often …*   b) *I sometimes …*   c) *I don't …*
  d) *I've never …*   e) *I'd like to …*

- Discuss the various things you can do with a ball: *throw, catch, pass, kick, head, hit, smash*, etc.

Further practice material

Need more writing practice?

→ Workbook page 33
- Describing a sporting event.

Need more classroom practice activities?

→ Photocopiable resource materials pages 164 to 166
  Grammar: *As fit as a fiddle*
  Vocabulary: *Sports crossword*
  Communication: *Numbers, numbers, numbers*
→ Top 10 activities pages xv to xx

Need progress tests?

→ Test CD – *Test Unit 5*

Need more on important teaching concepts?

→ Key concepts in *New Inside Out* pages xxii to xxxv

Need student self-study practice?

→ CD-ROM – Unit 5: *Fit*

Need student CEF self-evaluation?

→ CEF Checklists pages xxxvii to xliv

Need more information and more ideas?

→ www.insideout.net

6 Job *Overview*

Section & Aims	What the students are doing
Listening SB page 48 Listening for specific information	Listening to people and identifying the question they're asked. Ticking the jobs each person mentions.
Speaking SB page 48 Fluency practice	Listing all the jobs they, their parents and their grandparents have done. Discussing questions about jobs.
Reading SB page 49 Reading for detail	Matching words with either modelling or snowboarding and reading a text about a woman with two jobs to check answers. Talking about having two jobs.
Grammar SB page 49 *can / can't, have to / don't have to*	Matching the beginnings and endings of sentences. Matching verbs and meanings.
Reading SB page 50 Reading for specific information	Reading about bad experiences in the workplace. Answering questions on the text.
Vocabulary SB page 50 Collocations (work)	Adding further words and phrases to sets of collocations about jobs. Writing sentences about themselves.
Grammar SB page 51 Present perfect	Identifying the uses of the present perfect. Completing a table and completing sentences with time expressions.
Pronunciation SB page 51 Past participles of irregular verbs	Completing a table with past participles and categorising them according to vowel sound. Then practising saying them.
Speaking SB page 51 Fluency work	Forming questions using the present perfect. Asking and answering questions about past experience.
Listening SB page 52 Listening for specific information	Listening to an interview with a businessman and answering questions. Deciding if statements are true or false.
Vocabulary SB page 52 Job-related words	Using job-related words from a text to complete sentences. Identifying the meaning and use of *should*. Discussing statements about working practices.
Writing SB page 53 A letter of application	Improving a job application letter. Writing their own letter of application for a dream job.
Speaking: anecdote SB page 53 Fluency practice	Talking about someone who has a good job.
Useful phrases SB page 54 Presenting yourself	Listening and underlining the correct information. Completing presentations for three other people. Writing a short presentation.
Vocabulary *Extra* SB page 55 Office equipment; uses of *work* and *job*	Matching pictures with words. Completing sentences with *work* or *job*. Writing questions using *work* and *job*.
Writing WB page 39	Writing a letter of enquiry.

6 Job *Teacher's notes*

Warm-up

- Ask the students how easy they think it is to decide what someone's job is just by looking at them. Ask what things can give them a clue, e.g. someone's clothes, perhaps a uniform they wear, their voice, whether or not they have a suntan, the condition of their hands, etc.
- Encourage them to tell the class of any times when they've correctly or incorrectly guessed someone's job and what the consequences were, if any.

Listening (SB page 48)

1 🌐 **2.10**

- Focus the students' attention on the photos. Ask the students if they think that the people in the photos look as if they do these jobs and to give reasons why.
- Tell the students they're going to hear the four people each answering the same question. Ask them to listen and identify the question.

> *Possible answers:*
> What did you want to be when you were a child?
> What job did you want to do when you were a child?
> When you were a child, what did you want to be when you grew up?
> When you were a child, what job did you want to do when you grew up?

> 🌐 **2.10**
>
> a) Mark, a company director
> *I think I wanted to be a solider – I liked the uniform, and lots of boys want to be soldiers when they're young, don't they? Later on I thought of being an engineer, but I didn't do any work at school so I couldn't go to university. In the end I started working with my father and now I'm the director of my own company, so I'm quite pleased with the way things turned out.*
>
> b) Lucy, a surgeon
> *I've always wanted to be a surgeon, right from when I was a small child. It's my vocation. When I was at school, my best friend wanted to be a ballet dancer, but even then I knew what I wanted to do. There's never been a doctor in our family but my father's a butcher, so I suppose it's similar!*

> c) Frank, a teacher
> *When I was five, I wanted to be a farmer or a vet because I loved animals. Later, I wanted to be a pilot, but my eyes weren't good enough. When I was at university I wanted to be a snowboarder, but I wasn't good enough to be a professional. After university I had no idea what I wanted to do so I became a teacher, and I love it.*
>
> d) Mia, a model
> *My dream was to be an archaeologist. My family went on holiday to Egypt and I loved the Pyramids so much that I became really interested in ancient history. But when I was sixteen I had the chance to earn a lot of money as a model, so I stopped studying, and I've been working as a model for five years now. I want to start studying again when I'm thirty.*

2

- Go through the job choices in each line and make sure the students understand and can pronounce them all.
- Play the recording again and ask the students to tick the ones that each person mentions.
- Have a class discussion about what the students wanted to be when they were children. Depending on the age of the students, find out if they did, in fact, become what they wanted to be, or whether they now have different ambitions.

> a) Mark: a soldier, an engineer, a company director
> b) Lucy: a surgeon, a ballet dancer, a doctor, a butcher
> c) Frank: a farmer, a vet, a pilot, a snowboarder, a teacher
> d) Mia: an archaeologist, a model

Speaking (SB page 48)

1

Ask the students to call out the jobs and write them on the board. Give help with any vocabulary they need. (Depending on the age of the students, you could widen this to include siblings and friends.)

2

Groupwork. Go through the questions with the class and make sure everyone understands them. Then put the students into small groups and ask them to discuss the questions with reference to the jobs listed on the board. Ask one member of each group to act as a secretary and take notes on their discussion. The groups can then report back to the class on what they decided.

Reading (SB page 49)

1

- Focus the students' attention on the photos. Explain that they show a woman called Charlotte Dutton who has two jobs. She's both a model and a snowboarder.

- Read out the words in the box and explain any the students don't understand. Ask them to say if they associate each one with modelling or snowboarding, then ask them to read the article to check their ideas.

- Ask the students for their reaction to the text. Do they think Charlotte has a good life? Would they like to do what she does?

> modelling: designer clothes, Paris, slim
> snowboarding: crash helmet, freezing, muscles,
> strong, warm, baggy clothes

2

- Give the students a few minutes to decide on two jobs that they'd like to do. Ask them to think about how easy it would be to combine them.

- Pairwork. Put the students in pairs and ask them to compare their ideas.

Grammar (SB page 49)

1

- This exercise focuses on *can* and *can't* for permission and *have to* and *don't have to* for necessity. Go through the information in the margin. Point out the difference between *can* and *can't* and read out the example sentences. If students ask, tell them that the form of *can* and *can't* is the same for talking about ability, but here the focus is permission.

- Go through the information in the margin about *have to* and *don't have to*. Emphasise that *you don't have to do something* isn't the same *as you mustn't do it*. Read out the example sentences.

- Ask the students to match the beginnings and endings of the sentences in the exercise.

> a) A snowboarder has to wear a crash helmet.
> b) A club DJ can get up late.
> c) A flight attendant doesn't have to pay for flights.
> d) A tour guide has to know a lot of history.
> e) A model can't eat fattening food.
> f) A cook has to have very clean hands.

2

- Go through the example with the class and then ask the students to work individually to match the remaining sentences with their meanings. Go round, monitoring and giving help where necessary.

- Check answers with the class before asking them to say which sentences are true for them.

> a) 4   b) 2   c) 1   d) 3

3 Grammar *Extra* 6, Part 1

Ask the students to turn to *Grammar Extra* 6, Part 1 on page 136 of the Student's Book. Here they'll find an explanation of the grammar they've been studying and further exercises to practise it.

> **1**
> a) can   e) can
> b) don't have to   f) have to
> c) can   g) can
> d) can't   h) don't have to

Reading (SB page 50)

1 🌐 6.02

- Pairwork. Make sure the students understand all the jobs, then ask them to list all the bad experiences they think you could have in these jobs. You may need to start them off with a few ideas. For example, an au pair could have a job with a family where the house is very dirty; a vet could be kicked by a horse. Get the pairs to report back on their ideas to the class.

- Play the recording and ask the students to read the article as they listen. Ask them if any of their ideas were similar to the experiences Polly and Leo describe.

Language note

Vocabulary: *nightmare*

- *Nightmare* has two meanings: 1) a frightening and unpleasant dream; 2) an extremely difficult situation. The meaning in the title of this text is 2).

2

- Ask the students to cover the text and try to answer the questions from memory. Allow them to work in pairs if they wish.
- When they've finished, ask them to uncover the text, read it and check their answers.

> a) Leo   b) Polly   c) Polly   d) Leo
> e) Leo   f) Polly

3

- Elicit the sort of questions the students could ask to find somebody who has had the same experiences as Leo and Polly. For example: *Have you worked as a vet? Have you been bitten by a dog? Have you worked in a factory?* Write these on the board.
- Ask the student to mingle and try to find someone who has had the same experiences.

Vocabulary (SB page 50)

1

- Tell the students that collocations are pairs or groups of words that commonly occur together. Read the first set of collocations aloud, substituting the middle part, i.e. *some time, two weeks, a day,* so that the students hear the complete collocation each time. Point out that *to have a day off* is a collocation from Polly's story in the article. She says *I never had a day off.*
- Ask the students to find collocations in the article to complete the other sets. Go round, monitoring and giving help as they do this. It may be helpful if they underline the collocations in the article as they find them.
- Check answers with the class and answers any questions about vocabulary.

> a) a day   d) part-time
> b) get   e) break
> c) living   f) permission

2

Demonstrate the activity and get the students started by writing some sentences about yourself on the board using the collocations from Exercise 1. Then give the students time to write some sentences of their own. Encourage them to work individually and allow them to compare with a partner when they've finished. Ask several students to read out their sentences to the class.

Grammar (SB page 51)

Present perfect

1

- Read the two sentences in the exercise to the class and ask them to answer the questions underneath.
- Ask the students to look at the information in the margin about the form of the present perfect. Focus their attention on the meaning and use of *ever* which is commonly used in present perfect questions, but point out that it isn't used in the answers to them. Also point out that the main verb (*worked*) isn't repeated in short answers to present perfect questions. Ask the students to look back at the questions in the article on page 50, all of which use *ever* and the present perfect.

> a) Sentence 1. Past simple.
> b) Sentence 2. Present perfect.

Language note

Grammar: present perfect

- Many students have difficulty with the present perfect tense. To some students (e.g. French, Spanish, Italian, German) the tense may look similar to a composite tense (auxiliary *have/ be* + past participle) they use in their own language. However, these students will find that the present perfect in English is used rather differently from the tense they know.
- The present perfect has many different usages. In the Speaking exercise the focus is on questions about past experience (completed events in the past) using the adverb *ever* (*What's the best party you've ever been to?*). In this context, *ever* means *at any time* (*in your life up to now*). The present perfect is never used with precise past time references, and so any answer requiring precise time references must revert to the past simple.
- In contrast with the present perfect, the past simple is used to describe completed events in the past where a precise time (e.g. *at 10.00 a.m., yesterday, two days ago*) is specified.
- *been* is the past participle of *be*, but it's often used as a past participle of *go* (or *come*). Note that this use of *been* is only for completed visits, i.e. gone and returned (*She's been to New York many times … but now she's in London.*) If the visit does not involve a return trip, then *gone* should be used (*She's gone to New York … and she's still there.*)

2

- Focus the students' attention on the headings in the table. Explain that you can categorise time expressions according to whether they refer to time which has already finished or to time 'up to now'. They've already seen that *ever* is used to refer to time 'up to now'.

- Read out each time expression in turn and ask the students to decide which column of the table it should go in.
- Explain that you use the past simple to talk about finished time and the present perfect to talk about time 'up to now'.

> Finished time: a few moments ago, in 2005, last week, recently, when I was a student, years ago
>
> Time 'up to now': in the last two weeks, never, over the years, recently, today, this week

Language note

Grammar: *recently* and *today*

- *Recently* is in both columns because although it's very often used with the present perfect, it can also be used with past simple, e.g. *I saw a great film recently* (describing a past event).

- Although *today* belongs in the time 'up to now' column, it can be sometimes be used with the past simple if we're talking at the end of the day, or distancing ourselves from the earlier part of the day. This will depend on whether what happened is still affecting us now. Compare *I've had a bad day today* with *I bought a new dress today*.

- Note that it's often possible to use the 'time up to now' adverbials with both tenses in the affirmative: i.e. *I've been to the cinema recently – I went to the cinema recently*. It's much more unusual to use the past simple with these adverbials in the negative or question forms: *I didn't go to the cinema recently – Did you go to the cinema recently.*

3

- Remind the students that you use the past simple for finished time and the present perfect for time 'up to now'. Do the first sentence with the class as an example, then ask them to complete the remaining sentences.
- Go round, monitoring and giving help as they work. Make sure they are using appropriate tenses and time expressions. Take note of any particularly good sentences and ask the students to write them on the board.

> a) bought/'ve bought
> b) didn't go/haven't been
> c) met/'ve met
> d) spent/'ve spent
> e) didn't see/haven't seen
> f) did/done
> g) read/'ve read
> h) lost/'ve lost

4 Pairwork

- The pairwork exercise for this unit is on pages 117 and 122 of the Student's Book. Put the students in pairs and tell them who will be Student A, and who will be Student B.
- While they're doing the exercise, go round, monitoring and giving help. Take note of any errors which may need particular attention later, and also any examples of good language use which you can praise.

> *Questions:*
> **Student A**
> a) Have you ever broken your leg?
> b) Have you ever sung karaoke?
> c) Have you ever ridden a horse?
> d) Have you ever been fishing?
> e) Have you ever drunk whisky?
> f) Have you ever bought a painting?
>
> **Student B**
> a) Have you ever been to the USA?
> b) Have you ever given a speech?
> c) Have you ever broken the speed limit?
> d) Have you ever cut somebody's hair?
> e) Have you ever cried at the cinema?
> f) Have you ever forgotten your mother's birthday?

5 Grammar *Extra* 6, Part 2

Ask the students to turn to *Grammar Extra* 6, Part 2 on page 136 of the Student's Book. Here they'll find an explanation of the grammar they've been studying and further exercises to practise it.

> **1**
> 1 been   2 done   3 taken   4 drunk
> 5 broken   6 seen   7 eaten   8 written
> 9 forgotten   10 ridden   11 become
> 12 stood   13 given   14 gone   15 been
> **2**
> a) I haven't been on television.
> b) I haven't sung karaoke.
> c) I haven't driven a sports car.
> d) I haven't met a famous person.
> e) I haven't climbed a mountain.
> f) I haven't phoned a TV programme.
> **3**
> a) Have you been on television?
> b) Have you sung karaoke?
> c) Have you driven a sports car?
> d) Have you met a famous person?
> e) Have you climbed a mountain?
> f) Have you phoned a TV programme?
> **4**
> a) 've never been
> b) didn't do
> c) haven't phoned
> d) 've never eaten
> e) went
> f) had

Pronunciation (SB page 51)

1

- Explain that the present perfect tense is formed with the auxiliary verb *have* and the past participle of the main verb. With regular verbs, this is formed by adding *-ed* to the infinitive. Tell the students to look back at the example sentences in Exercise 1 of the previous section and point out the past simple form of the irregular verb *do*: *did* and the past participle: *done*.

- Ask the students to look at the table. Read the first four infinitive forms aloud, following each one with its past participle so that the students hear them together. Then read the past participle forms only and ask the students to identify the one with the different vowel sound (*been*).

- Tell the students to write the past participle forms of the remaining verbs in the right-hand column. Suggest that they say them aloud as they do this. Then ask them to underline the one in each line that has a different vowel sound.

2 🔘 **2.12**

Play the recording for the students to check their answers. Then play it again for them to listen and repeat. When they've done this chorally, ask for individual repetition of the past participle forms.

---

a) said, read, fed, <u>been</u>
b) known, <u>bought</u>, flown, grown
c) rung, sung, <u>brought</u>, hung
d) <u>drunk</u>, taught, thought, fought

Speaking (SB page 51)

1

- Read the example aloud and remind students of the use of *ever* in present perfect questions about people's experiences up till now.

- Pairwork. Put the students in pairs to make the remaining questions from the prompts. Go round, monitoring and giving help as they do this.

---

a) What's the best/worst party you've ever been to?
b) What's the best/worst holiday you've ever been on?
c) What's the best/worst meal you've ever eaten?
d) What's the best/worst joke you've ever heard?
e) What's the best/worst car you've ever been in?
f) What's the best/worst T-shirt you've ever worn?
g) What's the best/worst bed you've ever slept in?

2

- Give the students a moment or two to choose their questions. Emphasise that they should choose either the best or the worst in each case. Demonstrate the example dialogue with a confident student. Point out the switch to the past simple in the answer (to talk about a specific finished event in the past) and in the follow-up question.

- Put the students in pairs and ask them to take turns asking and answering their questions. As they work, go round making sure they are using the tenses correctly. Encourage them to use follow-up questions to elicit more information, and to report back to the class on what they found out about each other.

Listening (SB page 52)

1 🔘 **2.13**

- Pairwork. Focus the students' attention on the photo of Mr Reynold and ask the students to discuss the questions in pairs.

- Play the recording for them to check their answers. Then ask them if they were surprised by anything they heard.

---

a) A department store.
b) In 1948.
c) He's 85 (nearly 86).

🔘 **2.13** (P = Radio presenter; I = Interviewer; Mr R = Mr Reynold)

P: *... And this week, in our regular report from England, we visited a department store with a difference ...*

I: *Mr Reynold, can you tell us what is so special about your department store?*

Mr R: *Well, Reynold's is a large department store and you can find everything you want for the home here. Oh, and it stays open late on Thursdays and Saturdays.*

I: *Yes, that's right, but isn't there something special about the staff – you know – has anybody retired recently?*

Mr R: *Ah, oh, I see. No. Nobody has retired recently, and we never force anybody to retire here.*

I: *How old is your oldest employee?*

Mr R: *Well, that's Arthur. Arthur is our cleaner, and he's 87.*

I: *87! And he cleans the store every day?*

Mr R: *Well, not alone, no. He works with two other cleaners. They're not so old – Mabel's 70 and Ivy's 75 – no 76. That's right, she's just had her birthday.*

I: *And they don't want to retire?* ➤

> Mr R: No, I think they enjoy the work, and it keeps
> them young. Also, we pay a decent salary,
> and they get four weeks' paid holiday a year.
>
> I: So how many workers do you have who are
> over retirement age?
>
> Mr R: Well, we employ a staff of 105 and half of
> those are over 65. The young ones work in the
> office – we've got computers now you know.
>
> I: Really? Has the store changed much over
> the years?
>
> Mr R: No, not really. I started working here in 1948
> and I've only had two secretaries in all that
> time. Edith, my first secretary, resigned when
> she was 72.
>
> I: Oh, why did she leave Reynold's so young?
>
> Mr R: Well, she was getting married to someone
> who lived in another town.
>
> I: Jeez! That's amazing … Do you think you
> will ever retire, Mr Reynold?
>
> Mr R: Oh yes. I'm nearly 86! My son's going to take
> over the business next year. He's only 64.

2

- Go through the statements with the class so the students know what information they are listening out for.
- Play the recording again and ask the students to mark the statements true or false. Tell them to correct the false statements to make them true.

> a) True.
> b) False. The oldest employee at Reynold's is 87.
> c) True.
> d) False. Employees get four weeks' paid holiday.
> e) False. About half the staff are over the retirement age.
> f) True.
> g) False. Mr Reynold's son is going to run the business from next year.

Vocabulary (SB page 52)

1

- Tell the students to look back at the statements in Exercise 2 in the previous section. Ask them to use the underlined words to complete the sentences. Allow them to compare their answers in pairs before checking answers with the class.

> a) weeks' paid holiday   d) to retire
> b) a decent salary   e) run
> c) retirement age   f) resign

2

- Point out the use of should in each of the sentences in Exercise 1. Ask several students to read the sentences containing should aloud.

- Ask them to decide which adjectives best describe the meaning of should in these statements.

> a good idea

3

Groupwork. Put the students in small groups to discuss whether or not they agree with the statements in Exercise 1. Ask a representative from each group to report back to the class on their group's decisions.

Writing (SB page 53)

1

- Focus the students' attention on the letter and explain that the highlighted parts are those where Enid has used either the wrong word or expression, or one that isn't suitable for a formal letter. Explain the concept of formal and informal language and establish that a letter of application for a job requires formal language. Point out the example: formal letters to someone you don't know should begin *Dear Sir or Madam. Dear Mr Reynold* would be acceptable in a less formal letter, but *Dear Reynold* is wrong.

- Read out the expressions in the box and ask the students to use them to improve the letter by replacing the highlighted parts. Go round, monitoring and giving help.

> 1 Sir or Madam
> 2 would like to apply for
> 3 enclosed
> 4 reached retirement age
> 5 a new challenge
> 6 look forward to hearing

2

- This exercise could be set for homework. Explain the concept of a dream job – the one that you would most like to have. Give the students a minute or two to decide what their dream job would be. You could start by telling them about your own dream job.

- Point out the different sections of Enid's letter in Exercise 1. She begins by saying that she saw the advertisement and makes it clear which job she's applying for. In the second paragraph, she talks about her experience – why she would be a suitable candidate for the job – and refers to her CV. In the third paragraph, she explains why she wants the job. In the fourth paragraph, she says when she's available for a job interview.

- Ask the students to write their own letter of application for their dream job. Tell them that they can use Enid's letter as a model, but remind them to keep the language formal and appropriate and to change the details to match the job they have in mind.

Speaking: anecdote (SB page 53)

For more information about how to set up, monitor and repeat Anecdotes, see page xx in the Introduction.

1 🌐 2.14

- Ask the students to look at the photo. Explain that Kim, a friend of the woman in the photo, is going to talk about her friend's job. Go through the questions and the answer choices with the class. Explain any unknown vocabulary and ask the students to listen and underline the answers Kim gives.

- Check answers with the class and ask them whether they would like a job like Hannah's.

---

a) Hannah
b) personal trainer
c) She's self-employed.
d) 7.00
e) £35
f) She helps people to get fit.
g) Yes, because she doesn't have to work in an office.

🌐 2.14

My friend Hannah has the best job in the world – she's a personal trainer. She has about ten clients, and she writes an exercise programme for each person. She doesn't work for anybody – she's self-employed.

She starts work very early every day because some of her clients like to do exercise before they go to work. I think she starts her first client at seven o'clock in the morning.

I think it's a great job, because Hannah loves sport and so she gets money for doing what she loves. She earns a reasonably good salary. I think she charges £35 an hour, so her salary depends on the number of hours she works. She loves her job because she helps people to get fit and healthy.

I'd love to do her job, because she doesn't have to work in an office all day and she doesn't have to go to the gym in her free time either. She's her own boss so she can go on holiday when she wants, and she always looks fantastic in a swimming costume.

2

- Give the students a minute or two to decide who they're going to talk about. Then ask them to look at the questions in Exercise 1 again and decide how they'd answer them about the person and the job they're going to talk about. Allow them to make notes on what they're going to say and how they're going to say it, but discourage them from writing a paragraph that they can simply read out. Go round, monitoring and giving help.

- Pairwork. Put the students in pairs and ask them to take turns to tell their partner about the person they know who has a good job. Encourage them to ask each other follow-up questions.

- Ask some pairs to report back to the class about what they found out.

Useful phrases (SB page 54)

1 🌐 2.15 & 2.16

- Focus the students' attention on the picture and ask them to describe the situation. Tell them that all these people are in a group that is trying to give up smoking. This is their first meeting and they're going to introduce themselves. Give them a minute or two to read through the information.

- Play the first recording and ask the students to underline the correct information for each person. Then check answers with the class.

- Play the second recording for the students to check again and to listen and repeat the useful phrases.

Layla: audio equipment; sales and promotion
Mike: unemployed; publishing
Jack: London; a lot of foreign travel
Elsie: the photography department; taking photographs

🌐 2.15 (C = Chair; L = Layla; J = Jack; E = Elsie; M = Mike)

C: *Good afternoon everybody. Welcome to 'Quit Smoking'. I'm John and I'm an ex-smoker. Can you tell the group who you are, and what you do.*

L: *Hello. My name's Layla. I work for a big company and we produce high quality audio equipment. I'm responsible for sales and promotion.*

M: *Good morning. My name's Mike. I've just left university and at present I'm unemployed. I'm looking for a job in publishing.*

J: *Hi. I'm Jack and I work as a bodyguard. I'm self-employed and I'm based in London, but my job involves a lot of foreign travel. I have to take important clients safely from one place to another.*

E: *My name's Elsie. I'm a photographer and I work for a music magazine. We're based in Brighton. I run the photography department and I'm in charge of taking photographs of rock stars and bands, so I travel a lot, especially to the United States.*

C: *Thank you. Right, let's get this meeting started. Coffee is at …*

🌐 2.16

Layla
I work for a big company and we produce audio equipment.
I'm responsible for sales and promotion.

Mike
At present I'm unemployed.
I'm looking for a job in publishing.

Jack
I work as a bodyguard and I'm based in London.
My job involves a lot of foreign travel. ➤

---

2 🌐 2.17

- Focus the students' attention on the next set of pictures. Tell the students that these people are also joining the Quit Smoking group, but they're late. Ask the students to look through the notes and complete their presentations with words from Exercise 1.

- Allow them to compare their answers in pairs before you play the recording for them to check.

> 1 as   2 for   3 charge   4 for   5 involves
> 6 looking   7 in   8 run   9 produce
> 10 based

3

- Ask the students to work individually to write their presentations. Remind them that they can use the ones in Exercises 1 and 2 as a model and that they can invent information if they wish, based on their ideal job.

- As they work, go round, monitoring and giving help. Make sure they use at least three of the useful phrases from Exercise 1.

- Ask the students to make their presentations to the class.

Vocabulary *Extra* (SB page 55)

Office equipment

1

- Focus the students' attention on the list of words and point out that they're all words to do with office equipment. Check that the students can pronounce the words correctly.

- Ask the students to match the pictures with the words. Let them use dictionaries if they wish.

16	a bin	8	a mouse
15	a briefcase	6	a note pad
5	a calculator	2	paper clips
11	a desk lamp	12	a photocopier
13	a filing cabinet	3	Post-its®
14	a folder	1	a printer
9	a hole punch	7	a screen
10	a keyboard	4	a stapler

2

Pairwork. Demonstrate the example dialogue to the class with a confident student. Then put them in pairs to continue asking and answering questions about office equipment.

Focus on *work* and *job*

1

- Tell the students that *work* and *job* are used slightly differently in English. *Work* is usually used as a verb and *job* is a noun.

- Ask them to complete the sentences in pairs.

> a) job   b) work   c) job

2

- Elicit a few example questions around the class. Then ask the students to write at least six more questions using the words in the box. Go round checking that they are using *work* and *job* correctly.

- Put them in pairs to take turns asking and answering six questions each.

> *had* can be replaced with: *applied for, looked for, lost, resigned from*
>
> *abroad* can be replaced with: *from home, in marketing, outdoors*
>
> *dangerous* can be replaced with: *badly-paid, boring, stressful, well-paid*

Further practice material

Need more writing practice?

→ Workbook page 39
- Writing a letter of enquiry.

Need more classroom practice activities?

→ Photocopiable resource materials pages 167 to 169
  Grammar: *Have you ever done it?*
  Vocabulary: *In an ideal world*
  Communication: *What's my job?*
→ Top 10 activities pages xv to xx

Need DVD material?

→ DVD – Programme 3: *A bad day*

Need progress tests?

→ Test CD – *Test Unit 6*

Need more on important teaching concepts?

→ Key concepts in *New Inside Out* pages xxii to xxxv

Need student self-study practice?

→ CD-ROM – Unit 6: *Job*

Need student CEF self-evaluation?

→ CEF Checklists pages xxxvii to xliv

Need more information and more ideas?

→ www.insideout.net

Review B *Teacher's notes*

These exercises act as a check of the grammar and vocabulary that the students have learnt in Units 4–6. Use them to find any problems that students are having, or anything that they haven't understood and which will need further work.

Grammar (SB page 56)

Remind the students of the grammar explanations they read and the exercises they did in the *Grammar Extra* on pages 132 to 137.

1

This exercise reviews adverbs of frequency from Unit 4. Check answers with the class before the students rewrite the sentences to make them true for them.

a) We always get up at 7.00 a.m.
b) You never get to class on time!
c) We occasionally eat meat.
d) They are often at home on Sunday evenings.
e) Yuko hardly ever goes out in the evening.

2

This exercise reviews sentences with two objects from Unit 4.

a) My son bought me this pen.
b) Could you lend me your mobile?
c) They gave their money to their children.
d) I'm making a cake for my dad.
e) Did you send them an email?

3

This exercise reviews verbs which take *ing*-form and those which take a *to*-infinitive from Unit 4.

Verbs + *ing*-form: avoid, can't stand, don't mind, enjoy, like, love, spend time

Verbs + *to*-infinitive: agree, choose, decide, forget, need, want, would like

4

This exercise reviews comparative and superlative forms from Unit 5.

a) fittest
b) sensitive
c) expensive
d) best-looking
e) cheapest
f) noisier

5

This exercise reviews the present simple and present continuous from Unit 4.

1 love
2 like
3 have
4 doesn't understand
5 has
6 wear
7 'm trying
8 'm not buying
9 'm saving
10 look

6

This exercise reviews *can, can't, have to* and *don't have to* from Unit 6.

1 have to
2 have to
3 can
4 can't
5 have to

7

This exercise reviews past simple and present perfect verb forms from Unit 6.

1 Have you worked
2 've done
3 Have you had
4 've been
5 worked
6 went
7 left

8

This exercise reviews structures used in Units 4, 5 and 6.

1 a) I like always to read on trains.
2 b) He bought for me a very nice book.
3 b) Do you want go out tonight?
4 a) Athens is more older than Paris.
5 b) It's too late for TV now. Please turn off it.
6 a) I've seen that new show on TV last week.

Vocabulary (SB page 57)

1

This exercise reviews collocations in Unit 4.

a) chocolates, tissues   d) biscuits, crisps
b) flowers, keys   e) perfume, wine
c) beans, petrol

2

Go through the example first and explain that *necklace* is the odd one out because it's the only one that is jewellery; the others are all materials. Ask the students to give explanations of their choices for the other items in the exercise.

a) necklace   c) boots   d) woollen   b) checked

3

This exercise reviews questions with *How ...?* from Unit 5. Check answers with the class before the students work in pairs to ask and answer the questions.

a) 6   b) 5   c) 4   d) 1   e) 3   f) 2

4

This exercise reviews percentages, fractions, decimals and large numbers.

a) a half
b) nought point four five
c) three quarters
d) fifty-eight percent
e) twenty-three million dollars

5

This exercise reviews questions with phrasal verbs from Unit 5.

a) 2   b) 4   c) 1   d) 3

6

This exercise reviews job-related collocations.

a) part-time   b) a pay-rise   c) decision
d) time   e) lost

Pronunciation (SB page 57)

1

Remind the students that the boxes show the syllables of a word and the large boxes indicate the stressed syllables. Here the students are being asked to classify words according to how many syllables they have and where the main stress falls.

2 🌐 2.18

Point out the main stresses in the example words which are underlined. Ask the students to do the same for the other words in the table. Then play the recording for them to check their answers. Play it a second time for them to listen and repeat.

1 and 2
A: <u>a</u>dult, <u>flow</u>ers, <u>mo</u>bile, <u>pack</u>et, <u>pre</u>sent
B: ad<u>vice</u>, <u>a</u>fford, au <u>pair</u>, a<u>void</u>, re<u>ceive</u>
C: <u>horr</u>ible, <u>in</u>terested, <u>qual</u>ity, <u>tal</u>ented, <u>val</u>uable

Reading & Listening (SB page 58)

1

Ask the students to read the statements first so that they know what information they're looking for when they read the text. When you've checked their answers, ask them to correct the false information.

a) False. (Helena is older than Kate.)
b) True.
c) False. (Kate hates going to the gym.)
d) False. (Kate is a researcher for a TV company. Helena is a company director.)
e) False. (Helena wears sophisticated designer clothes; Kate wears jeans and a T-shirt.)

2

Go through the questions first to see if the students can answer any of them. Then ask them to read the text again and find the answers to any remaining questions.

a) Helena
b) She walks to work and climbs the stairs.
c) Four times a week.
d) No. (Helena does. Kate doesn't.)
e) Yes.
f) Now, it is good, but not when they were younger.
g) Kate.

3 🌐 2.19

Tell the students they're going to hear Tom and Patsy (shown in the photos) talking about their relationship. Go through the questions so that they know what information they're listening for. Play the recording again and ask the students to answer the questions.

a) They're husband and wife.
b) She loves him.

2.19 (T = Tom; P = Patsy)

T: *Patsy and I are very different …*

P: *Yes, very different. In fact we're complete opposites. Tom's water and I'm air. He's a Scorpio and I'm an Aquarius.*

T: *Mm, I don't really believe in all that …*

P: *And Tom's much older than me. I think that also makes a difference.*

T: *I don't see what difference …*

P: *The clothes he wears make him look older, too.*

T: *That's true. On the other hand, Patsy dresses like a teenager.*

P: *No, I don't. But I do enjoy finding fashionable clothes at good prices. I always buy him really good clothes but, he never wears them.*

T: *We've been married for twenty-two years …*

P: *Is it that long?*

T: *… and sometimes we can't understand why we've stayed together …*

P: *Yes. He likes watching sport on TV, whereas I like getting out there and playing it. I can't stand watching it on TV.*

T: *She loves shopping, but I prefer sitting in my garden with a newspaper.*

P: *So, why are we together? Simple – I love him. He's a good husband and a good father to our children. And he's one of the funniest people I've ever met.*

T: *I think I'm the luckiest person I know.*

4

Go through the choices with the students before playing the recording again. Ask them to underline the correct information.

> a) younger   d) never
> b) Tom   e) likes
> c) always   f) very funny

Writing & Speaking (SB page 59)

1

Go through the questions with the class, then ask the students to read the text and tick the ones that are answered.

> Questions *a*, *b*, *c*, *d*, *e*, *g* and *h* are answered.

2

Ask the students to read the text and underline the words from the box as they find them. When they've finished, ask them to complete the rules with these words and phrases.

> a) both
> b) whereas, but
> c) However, On the other hand

3

Encourage the students to read the sentences aloud to get a feel for what sounds right.

> a) However,   c) On the other hand,
> b) whereas   d) but

4

Check answers with the class before putting the students into pairs to discuss whether or not the sentences are true for them.

> a) We both love dancing. (*both* comes before the main verb)
> b) We have both been to America (*both* comes after the auxiliary)

5

Give the students a minute or two to decide who they're going to talk about. Remind them that they can choose questions from Exercise 1 to answer. Give them time to prepare what they're going to say and allow them to make notes if they wish, but discourage them from writing a script.

6

Remind the students that they can use the text in Exercise 1 as a model. Go round, monitoring and giving help, and encourage them to use expressions to describe contrast and similarity.

Further practice material

Need more classroom practice activities?
→ Photocopiable resource materials page 170, recording track ● 2.20
  Song: *Suspicious Minds*
→ Top 10 activities pages xv to xx

Need progress tests?
→ Test CD – *Test Review B*

Need more on important teaching concepts?
→ Key concepts in *New Inside Out* pages xxii to xxxv

Need student self-study practice?
→ CD-ROM – *Review B*

Need more information and more ideas?
→ www.insideout.net

Section & Aims	What the students are doing
Reading & Vocabulary SB page 60 Reading for detail Climate change	Reading about a protest march and identifying true and false statements. Matching phrases with similar meaning. Talking about climate change.
Listening & Vocabulary SB page 61 Listening for gist Opinions	Matching four protesters with their opinions. Completing sentences which state opinions and discussing them.
Grammar SB page 61 Subject questions	Studying the structure and use of subject questions. Writing subject and object questions.
Pronunciation SB page 62 Words ending in *tion*	Completing a table with words ending in *tion*. Listening and repeating the words.
Grammar SB page 62 Dynamic and stative meanings	Studying verbs with dynamic and stative meanings. Writing sentences using the present continuous. Completing sentences describing actions and states.
Speaking SB page 63 Fluency practice	Discussing what's good or bad for the environment. Conducting a survey on environmental issues.
Writing SB page 63 Writing a report	Completing a survey report on green issues. Writing a survey report.
Reading & Listening SB page 64 Reading for detail Listening for specific information	Discussing voluntary work. Matching projects from a volunteer website with duties. Listening and identifying which project a volunteer is going to join.
Grammar SB page 64 Future: *be going to*	Correcting mistakes in sentences. Studying the future *be going to*. Writing and asking questions about the future.
Listening SB page 65 Listening for detail	Listening and identifying the speakers' feelings. Listening and underlining the correct information.
Grammar SB page 65 Future: present continuous	Studying the present continuous to talk about the future. Deciding when you can use *be going to* or the present continuous.
Useful phrases SB page 66 Useful phrases on the telephone	Underlining appropriate expressions in a phone conversation. Listening and repeating useful phrases. Practising a phone conversation.
Vocabulary *Extra* SB page 67 Revision of words from the unit: environmental problems and solutions; *have / have got*	Matching pictures with phrases. Categorising expressions and adding their own ideas. Completing sentences with *do, don't, have* and *haven't*. Writing questions with *have / has got*. Comparing the use of *have / has* and *have / has got*.
Writing WB page 45	Making written suggestions.

Reading & Vocabulary (SB page 60)

1

Focus the students' attention on the photos, which show people demonstrating about climate change. Then ask the questions in the exercise.

2

- Ask the students to read the article. Give them plenty of time to do this.
- Go through the statements one by one and ask the students to say whether they're true or false and to correct the false statements.

a) False. (The world leaders were taking part in talks about climate change; the protesters were ordinary people.)
b) True.
c) True.
d) False. (They delivered a letter to the British Prime Minister asking him to do something about climate change.)
e) True.
f) False. (They didn't go shopping; they smashed shop windows and tried to set fire to a supermarket.)

3

- Focus attention on the highlighted phrases. Ask the students to work in pairs to match them to similar phrases in the statements in Exercise 2.

took part in = participated in
slogans = political messages
made their way = went
demanding urgent action on = asking world leaders to do something immediately about
swarming with people = extremely crowded
buzzing with activity = very busy
broke away from = separated from

4

Pairwork. Ask for some suggestions from the class and put them on the board before putting the students in pairs to discuss the questions. Go round, monitoring and helping with vocabulary. Note any interesting vocabulary and expressions on the board. Encourage the pairs to report back to the class on their discussions

Listening & Vocabulary (SB page 61)

1 🔊 2.21

- Tell the students that they're going to listen to four protesters at the climate change march described in the article on page 60. Ask them to look at the photos and encourage them to speculate on what kind of people they are and what their interests might be.
- Before you play the recording, go through the opinions with the class and make sure everyone understands them.
- Play the recording and ask the students to match the people with their opinions.

1 Jake   2 Debbie   3 Ronny   4 Jo

2.21

Jo, 26
I work for an organisation called Eco Holidays, and we're demonstrating against mass tourism. I'm not against tourism but I believe in responsible tourism. We're against big hotels and package holidays. With Eco Holidays you can really experience the local culture. We organise accommodation with local families. Would you like some information about our holidays?

Jake, 14
I'm having fun with my friends. It's my first demonstration. I don't feel strongly about politics, but I'm worried about global warming. I don't really care about people – they can look after themselves. I'm in favour of protecting wild animals – I want to help polar bears and penguins. If the ice caps melt, where will they live?

Debbie, 37
I'm here because we're destroying the planet. I'm protesting against multinational companies. They're polluting our rivers and oceans and they're causing global warming. I'm in favour of small family-run companies. I'm against food imports. I support local farmers and I buy food from farmers' markets, not supermarkets.

Ronny, 27
I'm riding my bicycle today because I'm against big cars in the city. I'm not anti-cars – in fact, I have a car – but I just think more people should use public transport. Leave your car at home – ride a bicycle!

2

- Give the students a minute or two to complete the sentences.
- When checking answers, make sure that the students understand all the sentences. Then put them into pairs to discuss whether or not they agree with them. Go round, monitoring and giving help. See if there's any consensus regarding the sentences.

a) anti	e) against
b) really care	f) support
c) in favour	g) don't feel
d) believe	

Grammar (SB page 61)

Subject questions

1

- Focus the students' attention on the information in the margin. Point out that the statement *John hates cars* can generate two different questions, one focusing on the subject of the sentence and the other on the object.
- Go through the information and questions with the class.

a) Who	b) Jo	c) No.

Language note
Grammar: subject questions

If a question word (i.e. *who*) is the subject of the question, you don't use *do*, *does* or *did*. Compare:
Who went to the party? (*Who* is the subject)
Who did you go with? (*Who* is the object – *you* is the subject)
Who saw him? (*Who* is the subject)
Who did he see? (*Who* is the object – *he* is the subject)

2

- Look at the two example questions with the class and make sure that the students understand the principles. Then ask them to work individually to complete the exercise.
- Check answers with the class before putting the students into pairs to take turns asking and answering the questions.

a) What did Mahatma Gandhi believe in?
b) Who said, 'I have a dream' in a famous speech?
c) What does 'slogan' mean?
d) Which organisation has a boat called 'Rainbow Warrior'?
e) What did thirty-six million people protest against in 2003?
f) Who fought against apartheid for over fifty years?
a) Non-violent protest.
b) Martin Luther King.
c) Political message.
d) Greenpeace
e) The Iraq war.
f) Nelson Mandela.

Cultural notes

Mahatma Gandhi /məˈhætmə ˈɡændiː/ (1869–1948) Political and spiritual leader in India who helped his country, through peaceful resistance, to achieve independence in 1947 from the British Empire. Gandhi was committed to non-violence, and so his assassination at the hands of an extremist Hindu (Gandhi's own faith) gunman was all the more ironic.

Martin Luther King, Jr /ˈmɑːtɪn ˈluːðə kɪŋ/ (1929–1968) One of the leaders of the American civil rights movement, Luther King was a Baptist minister who, inspired by Gandhi's success in India, advocated civil disobedience to gain rights for the black citizens of the United States. Luther King was also assassinated by a gunman's bullet in 1968.

Greenpeace /ˈɡriːn piːs/
An international environmental organisation founded in Canada in 1971. It's well known for its campaigns against whaling. Its boat, *Rainbow Warrior*, often makes the news around the world for its efforts on behalf of marine ecology.

Nelson Mandela /'nelsən mæn'delə/ (born 1918) Nelson Mandela was President of South Africa from 1994 to 1999. Before that he was in prison for 27 years (from 1962 to 1989) for his involvement with the armed wing of the African National Congress. In earlier life, Mandela had been inspired by Gandhi's non-violent protest, but was eventually brutalized by the apartheid system in South Africa and took up arms against it.

Pronunciation (SB page 62)

1

- Ask the students to look at the table. Remind them that the boxes show the syllables of a word and the large boxes indicate the stressed syllables. Read the word *demonstration* aloud and ask the students to repeat it. Make sure that they're pronouncing it correctly.
- Ask the students to put the words in the box in the correct columns of the table according to how they are pronounced. Encourage them to say the words aloud so they get a feeling for what sounds right.

> A: destruction, pollution, solution
> B: demonstration, education, explanation, revolution
> C: globalisation, modernisation, organisation

2 🌐 2.22

Play the recording for the students to check their answers to Exercise 1. Then play it a second time for them to listen and repeat the words. When they've done this chorally, ask individual students to repeat the words after you, and check that they're putting the stress on the correct syllables.

Grammar (SB page 62)

Dynamic and stative meanings

1

- If necessary, explain the difference between a verb with dynamic meaning (one describing an action when something happens) and one with stative meaning (one describing a state, not something that happens).
- Focus attention on the information in the margin and go through the example sentences. Point out that there are some verbs which can have both meanings.
- Focus attention on the two example sentences in the exercise and ask the students to answer the questions in pairs.

> a) Actions.
> b) The present continuous.

Language notes

Grammar: dynamic and stative verbs

- Stative verbs describe states or conditions which continue over a period of time. *Like, love, hate, want, need, hear* and *see* are examples of stative verbs. These verbs aren't normally used in the continuous form.
  I want to be an engineer one day, not *I'm wanting to be an engineer one day*.
- Dynamic verbs describe things which happen within a limited time. *Come, bring, buy, get* and *learn* are examples of dynamic verbs.
  I'm learning English at the moment, not *I learn English at the moment*.
- Some verbs, like *have, look* and *think* can have both stative and dynamic meanings.

Compare:
1 *I have an old car* (state) with *I'm having a great time!* (something happening within a limited time).
2 *He looks tired* (condition) with *That woman is looking at me in a strange way*. (something happening within a limited time).
3 *Do you think Brazil will win the World Cup?* (state) with *I'm thinking of going into the city centre today*. (something happening within a limited time).
* Recently there's been a fashion to make the verbs *like* and *love* take a dynamic form but retain a stative meaning. Thus *I'm really liking that song!* is a modern colloquial way of saying *I really like that song!* Burger chain McDonald's have introduced the slogan '*I'm lovin' it!*' with the intention of appealing to the 15–24 age group market.

2

- Ask the students to work individually to complete the sentences. When checking answers, make sure that the students have spelt *making* and *chatting* correctly. Then ask whether the sentences describe actions or states or both.

> a) A phone is ringing.
> b) A teacher in another class is talking.
> c) The traffic is making a lot of noise.
> d) A clock is ticking.
> e) Birds are singing.
> f) Rain is falling.
> g) A student is laughing.
> h) People are chatting.

- Tell the class that they must stay absolutely silent for the next 15 seconds and to tick any of the things that they hear during that time, and to write sentences using the present continuous to describe anything else that they notice is happening. Agree a signal for the beginning and end of the 15 seconds. Make sure the students are completely silent before you begin.

- See if everyone agrees on which things were happening and ask several students to read out their additional sentences.

3

- Read the example sentences to the class. Ask the students to look at the verbs in these sentences and answer the questions.

> a) States.
> b) The present simple.
> c) No.

4

- Remind the students that some verbs can have both dynamic and stative meanings. Go through the two examples with the class and get the students to identify that sentences a) describes an action and sentence b) a state. Point out the use of the present continuous in a) and the present simple in b).
- Ask the students to work individually to complete the remaining sentences. Go round, monitoring and helping anyone who's having difficulty.
- Check answers with the class before asking the students to replace the names in the sentences with those of members of the class. Emphasise that they should try to make true sentences and encourage them to ask each other questions as in the examples.
- Get several students to read their sentences aloud and ask the subjects of those sentences to confirm whether or not they're true.

> a) is thinking   e) looks
> b) thinks   f) is looking
> c) has   g) likes
> d) is having   h) knows

5 Grammar *Extra* 7, Part 1

Ask the students to turn to *Grammar Extra* 7, Part 1 on page 138 of the Student's Book. Here they'll find an explanation of the grammar they've been studying and further exercises to practise it.

> **1**
> a) is having   f) thinks
> b) 's thinking   g) looks
> c) 's listening   h) knows
> d) has   i) 's planning
> e) loves   j) seems

Speaking (SB page 63)

1

- Groupwork. Put the students in groups and ask them to look at the list of activities and decide which ones are good for the environment and which are bad. Go round, monitoring and giving help with any difficult vocabulary.
- When the students have finished, ask them to make a list of any other activities they can think of which are good or bad for the environment.
- In a feedback session, find out if there is consensus of opinion and encourage the groups to share their other suggestions with the class.

> Good for the environment: a, c, g, i, k
> Bad for the environment: b, d, e, f, h, j, l

2

- Go through the instructions with the class and then ask them to work in the same groups. Tell them to follow the instructions to prepare their surveys. Go round, monitoring and giving help.
- When the students are ready, tell them to go round the class asking their questions and noting down the answers. When they write down the results of their survey in their groups, make sure each member takes a copy as they'll need this in the next section.

Writing (SB page 63)

You might like to discuss the various meanings of the word *green* as an introduction to this section. It can mean new and naïve, as in *He's only recently joined the company and he's still very green*, as well as concerned with protecting the environment, the meaning used in this section.

1

- Go through the information in the margin, pointing out the different expressions for referring to larger or smaller numbers of people.
- Focus attention on the Greenville survey and the title *How green are you?* If you haven't already done so, explain the meaning of *green* to the class. Ask the students to read the report and complete it with either *very green* or not *very green*.

> not very green

2

- Remind the students of the survey that they did in the previous section. Ask them to take the results of that survey and use it to rewrite the Greenville survey, making any changes that are necessary. Encourage them to use the expressions in the margin.
- Go round, monitoring and giving help. Ask several students (from different groups) to read out their reports and find out how green the class is.

Reading & Listening (SB page 64)

1

- Introduce the idea of projects involving volunteers that try to help people in developing countries. Ask the students if it's common for people in their countries to do unpaid voluntary work either at home or overseas.

- Ask the students to read the list of duties that people volunteer to do. Explain any that they don't understand.

- Put the students into pairs to discuss which of the duties they feel they could and couldn't do and have a class feedback session on the most popular and least popular duties.

- Then ask the students to read the information from the website and match the duties to the projects. Point out that some of the duties aren't mentioned.

> Project 1: g, h
> Project 2: a, b
> Not mentioned: c, d, e, f

Language note

Orphanage – an institution where children with no parents live.

Cultural note

Organic farming describes a method of farming that doesn't use artificial chemicals. It claims to be better for the environment as it doesn't use fossil fuels, and it's kinder to animals. Organic produce is growing in popularity in Britain. Many people believe organic food is healthier for you and it tastes much better.

2 🔘 2.23

Tell the students that they're going to listen to Helen, a young woman who's going to volunteer to join one of the projects in Exercise 1, talking to a friend. Ask them to listen and decide which project Helen is going to join.

> Project 2.

> 🔘 2.23 (H = Helen; C = Carole)
>
> H: *I've decided I'm going to change my life.*
>
> C: *Yeah, me too. I want a bigger house, a bigger salary and a better boyfriend.*
>
> H: *No, I'm serious. I'm going to do something important.*
>
> C: *What do you mean?*
>
> H: *I want to help people less fortunate than me – I'm going to go abroad and work with children.*
>
> C: *Oh. Well, that's um … Where are you going?*
>
> H: *Ghana.*

> C: *Ghana? What about the animals?*
>
> H: *No, I'm not going to work with animals – I want to help people.*
>
> C: *No, I mean the dangerous animals – crocodiles, lions, snakes, …*
>
> H: *Oh, I see. I'm not just going there alone. I've joined an organisation, and they're going to arrange everything for me. I'm going to work in an orphanage.*
>
> C: *Good for you. How much are they going to pay you?*
>
> H: *Nothing. I'm a volunteer. In fact, I'm going to pay them £25 a week.*
>
> C: *You're going to pay them. I see. When are you going?*
>
> H: *Soon – next month.*
>
> C: *Wow. How exciting. I'd love to visit South America.*
>
> H: *Africa. Ghana's in Africa.*
>
> C: *Oh, is it? There are a lot of dangerous animals in Africa.*
>
> H: *I told you I'm not …*

3

Ask the students to listen to Helen again and to tick the things she says she's going to do. After checking answers with the class put the students into pairs to talk about which projects they'd like to be involved with.

> ✓: a, c, e

Cultural note

Ghana /ɡɑːnə/
West African country with a population of 24 million. It gained independence from the UK in 1957. The country is rich in natural resources including oil, gold, timber, cocoa and diamond. The official language is English.

Grammar (SB page 64)

Future: be going to

1

Focus the students' attention on the information in the margin. Explain that *be going to* is one of the ways you can use to talk about the future, and that it's usually used to talk about decisions people have made about the future. Go through the examples and then ask the students to look at the incorrect sentences in the exercise and tell them to correct them.

> a) 'I<u>'m</u> going to change my life.'
> b) 'I'm not <u>going</u> to work with animals.'
> c) 'How much are they going <u>to</u> pay you?'

2

Do this exercise with the class, but give all the students a chance to decide how the sentence should be completed before you ask for the answers.

> 1 past   2 future

3

- Ask the students to work individually to write their questions. Go round, monitoring and giving help as they do this.

- Check answers with the class before putting the students into pairs to take turns asking and answering the questions.

> a) Are you going to drive home after the lesson?
> b) Are you going to watch TV this evening?
> c) Are you going to learn another foreign language one day?
> d) Are you going to buy any new clothes this weekend?
> e) Are you going to do anything interesting next week?
> f) Are you going to travel abroad next year?

Listening (SB page 65)

1 🌐 2.24

- Remind the students that in the last section they heard Helen talking to a friend about her plans to join a volunteer project. Elicit that she's going to Ghana to work in an orphanage. Ask the students what Helen's friend's reaction to the news was (surprised, uncomprehending, concerned). Ask them to predict what Helen's mother's reaction will be when she hears Helen's news.

- Check that the students understand all the options in the sentences. Then play the recording and ask them to underline the ones that they think are correct.

> a) confident   b) worried

> 🌐 2.24 (M = Mum; H = Helen)
>
> M: *Who's picking you up at the airport?*
>
> H: *I've told you, Mum.*
>
> M: *I know, but I'm worried. Ghana's a long way from here.*
>
> H: *OK. Let's go through it again. I'm arriving in Accra at ten o'clock in the morning, and the volunteers' coordinator is meeting me. That's Bob White. He's taking me to my accommodation.*
>
> M: *And you're staying with a family.*
>
> H: *Yes, I'm staying with a Ghanaian family.*
>
> M: *Don't you want to stay in a hotel?*
>
> H: *No, I want to have an authentic experience, so I'm staying with the Odoi family.*
>
> M: *You must write down their name and address for me.*
>
> H: *Yes, don't worry. Then, I'm starting work on Monday.*
>
> M: *And where exactly are you working?*
>
> H: *In a small town near Accra.*
>
> M: *How are you getting there?*
>
> H: *By bus. Mrs Odoi's going to make sure I get the right bus.*
>
> M: *When are you coming back?*
>
> H: *On 15th September. Just in time for your birthday.*

2

- Go through the options with the class, then play the recording again and ask them to choose and underline the correct information.

- Check answers with the class. Then ask the students to give examples of situations in which their parents worry about them.

> | | |
> |---|---|
> | a) a.m. | d) Monday |
> | b) accommodation | e) small |
> | c) Ghanaian | f) mum's |

Grammar (SB page 65)

Future: present continuous

1

- Remind the students about the use of *be going to* to talk about future decisions. Explain that the present continuous can also be used to talk about the future. It's generally used to talk about future arrangements. Focus attention on the information in the margin and read the example sentences aloud to the class or ask students to read them out.

- Focus attention on the sentences in Listening Exercise 2 and ask them if the explanation is true or false.

> True.

Language notes
Grammar: present continuous

- Using the present continuous is the most common way to talk about future arrangements. It's usually used when you've already made plans (with someone else) to do something in the future.
  Compare:
  I'm going to learn Chinese one day. (intention/decision)
  I'm seeing an old friend on Friday. (arrangement)
- The present continuous is often used with a time expression to make the future meaning clearer.
  I'm having dinner with a friend this evening.

2

- Remind the class that *be going to* is used to talk about decisions made about the future and the present continuous is used for future arrangements. Explain that sometimes the two overlap and both forms are possible. Focus attention on the two examples. Explain that in the first sentence both options are possible because the sentence describes both a decision that has been made about the future and an arrangement that has been made. However, in the second sentence, a decision to start guitar lessons has been made but no actual arrangement has been made, so the present continuous isn't possible. Point out that time expressions like *one day* and *one of these days* aren't sufficiently concrete to establish an arrangement.
- Ask the students to work in pairs and look at the remaining sentences. They should decide whether both options are possible or not. Check answers with the class. You may need to explain in sentence f) that the present continuous isn't possible because it's impossible to predict precisely the outcome of a tennis match, so even though the time expression suggests an arrangement, no arrangement is possible.
- Students tell their partner if any of the sentences are true for them.

> a) ✓   b) ✗   c) ✓   d) ✓   e) ✗   f) ✗
> g) ✓   h) ✗

3 Pairwork

- The pairwork exercise for this unit is on pages 118 and 123 of the Student's Book. Put the students in pairs and tell them who will be Student A, and who will be Student B.
- While they're doing the exercise, go round monitoring and giving help. Take note of any errors which may need particular attention later, and also any examples of good language use which you can praise.

4 Grammar *Extra* 7, Part 2

Ask the students to turn to *Grammar Extra* 7, Part 2 on page 138 of the Student's Book. Here they'll find an explanation of the grammar they've been studying and further exercises to practise it.

> **1**
> a) I'm going to join the Green Party.
> b) I'm going to start yoga classes.
> c) I'm going to get a better job.
> d) I'm not going to eat so much fast food.
> e) I'm going to change my hairstyle.
> f) I'm not going to watch so much TV.
> g) I'm going to give up smoking.
> h) I'm going to spend less time on the computer.
>
> **2**
> 1 I'm going to the dentist
> 2 I'm meeting Mum in town
> 3 I'm having lunch with Vicky
> 4 I'm playing tennis
> 5 I'm collecting the children from school
> 6 I'm having a drink with Tim

Useful phrases (SB page 66)

1 🌐 2.25

- Focus the students' attention on the picture and ask the students what they can see. Explain that the young man is Matt Walker and that he's speaking on the phone to the receptionist at a big chemical company. Ask them to read the conversation and underline the most appropriate expressions to complete it.
- Play the recording for the students to check their answers. Explain that these choices are correct because they're more polite and more formal than the other options. On the phone, particularly when you're talking to strangers, more formal polite language is usually used.

> 1 Could I speak to the Managing Director, please?
> 2 Who's speaking?
> 3 I'll try to put you through.
> 4 I'm afraid Mr Carr is out at the moment.
> 5 Would you like to leave a message?
> 6 Hold on a moment, please.

2 🌐 2.26

Ask the students to listen and repeat the useful phrases. When they've done this chorally, ask several students to repeat the words individually and make sure that they're using the correct pronunciation and intonation.

3

- Pairwork. Ask the students to practise the conversation, taking turns to be Matt and the receptionist. They may find it helpful to sit back to back so that they cannot see each other as they do this.

Students write another phone conversation using the useful phrases given in Exercise 2.

Go through the example with the class and then ask the students' write the remaining questions. Check answers before putting them into pairs to take turns asking and answering the questions.

> a) Have you got any brothers and sisters?
> b) Have you got more than one credit card?
> c) Have you got a pet?
> d) Have you got a headache?
> e) Has your mother got the same eyes as you?
> f) Has your father got any hobbies?

Vocabulary *Extra* (SB page 67)
Environmental problems and solutions

1

Focus the students' attention on the pictures and ask them to match the pictures with the phrases.

> 3 a bottle bank
> 8 a carbon footprint
> 1 environmentally-friendly products
> 7 global warming
> 6 mass-produced clothes
> 2 organic vegetables
> 5 a plastic container
> 4 public transport
> 9 renewable energy

3

Look at the example with the class and elicit how sentence a) would be formed using *have got* instead of *have* (*Have you got a laptop?*). Ask the students to look at the remaining sentences and decide whether *have/has got* could be used in them. When checking answers, if students say that *have/has got* can be used, ask them to produce the sentence. When you've finished, get the students to write down the sentences with *have got*.

> ✓: a, c, d, e
>
> a) Have you got a laptop?
> c) My mother has got short, grey hair.
> d) I haven't got an MP3 player.
> e) Have you got any children?

2

Focus attention on the table and point out that global warming is a problem for the world, and organic vegetables represent a solution to the problem of introducing too many chemicals into the environment. Ask the students to categorise the other expressions from Exercise 1 as either problems or solutions. Encourage them to say what problems the various solutions apply to and to add their own ideas to each list.

> Problems: global warming , a carbon footprint, mass-produced clothes, a plastic container
>
> Solutions: a bottle bank, environmentally-friendly products, organic vegetables, public transport, renewable energy

Focus on *have / have got*

The use of *have* or *have got* for talking about possession is largely a matter of personal taste, but the forms are manipulated in slightly different ways and *have got* can only be used when talking about possession.

1

* Go through this exercise with the class, eliciting the correct words to fill the gaps. Explain that when *have/has* means to own or possess, you can also use *have/has* got.

> a) 'Do you have a car?'
>   Yes, I *do*. No, I *don't*.
> b) 'Have you *got* a car?'
>   Yes, I *have*. No, I *haven't*.

Further practice material

Need more writing practice?
→ Workbook page 45
• Making written suggestions.

Need more classroom practice activities?
→ Photocopiable resource materials pages 171 to 173
    Grammar: *Thirty-second futures*
    Vocabulary: *How green are you?*
    Communication: *Manifesto*
→ Top 10 activities pages xv to xx

Need DVD material?
→ DVD – Programme 4: *The audition*

Need progress tests?
→ Test CD – *Test Unit 7*

Need more on important teaching concepts?
→ Key concepts in *New Inside Out* pages xxii to xxxv

Need student self-study practice?
→ CD-ROM – Unit 7: *Eco*

Need student CEF self-evaluation?
→ CEF Checklists pages xxxvii to xliv

Need more information and more ideas?
→ www.insideout.net

8 Education *Overview*

Section & Aims	What the students are doing
Reading SB page 68 Reading for detail	Reading about a trainee geisha and identifying true and false statements. Talking about their families' hopes for their future.
Vocabulary SB page 69 Education and training	Completing sentences with words from the Reading section. Discussing whether statements are true for their country.
Pronunciation SB page 69 Stress in school subjects	Saying names of school subjects with correct stress. Discussing their attitudes to school subjects.
Speaking: anecdote SB page 69 Fluency practice	Talking about favourite school subjects.
Reading SB page 70 Reading for gist and for detail	Matching quotes with the person who said them. Answering questions about the text. Talking about how life has changed over the generations.
Grammar SB page 71 *could* for permission and *had to* for obligation	Completing a table with *can* and *have to*. Completing questions and answers. Discussing permission and obligation in their own families.
Listening SB page 71 Listening for gist	Identifying topics discussed in a conversation. Writing sentences about then and now. Talking about permission and obligation in their own countries.
Reading & Listening SB page 72 Reading for detail Listening for main ideas	Deciding on important advice for a friend. Labelling the paragraphs with advice. Listening and identifying the advice the person follows.
Vocabulary SB page 72 Words from a text	Completing sentences with words from a text. Discussing sentences with a partner.
Grammar SB page 73 *should* and *must* for advice	Matching phrases with meanings. Completing sentences with *must* and *should*.
Reading & Speaking SB page 73 Reading for detail Fluency practice	Completing advice on being the perfect girlfriend or boyfriend. Discussing the advice with a partner.
Useful phrases SB page 74 Useful conversational phrases for giving opinions	Identify topics from a conversation. Completing sentences from the conversation. Listening to and practising useful phrases. Putting phrases for agreeing and disagreeing in order. Rewriting statements to show their own opinions.
Vocabulary *Extra* SB page 75 Revision of words from the unit: education stages; words used with education	Matching photos with stages of education. Comparing the stages with those in their countries. Describing their own education. Completing questions about education and discussing them.
Writing WB page 51	Writing a personal letter.

8 Education *Teacher's notes*

Warm-up

Write the word *school* on the board and ask the students to think back to their first day at school. What can they remember about it? Start them off by telling them about your first day at school (or a memorable incident in your early school years).

Reading (SB page 68)

1

Focus the students' attention on the photo. Look at the title of the article and explain that the photo shows a geisha (a professional Japanese entertainer). Read the sentences aloud to the class and, as you read each one, ask the students to discuss in pairs whether they think it's true or false.

2

Ask the students to read the article and see whether they were right about the statements in Exercise 1. Explain any difficult vocabulary and ask the students to say if they were surprised by any of the information in the text.

a) False	b) True	c) True	d) True
e) False	f) False	g) True	

3

Ask the students whether Makiko's parents were happy about her becoming a geisha. (Not really – they would have preferred her to go to university and become a doctor.) Then ask them to think about what their parents and/or grandparents wanted them to study at school. Go through the example with the class and then ask the students to work in pairs to discuss their answer to the question. (If your students are still at school, they can discuss what their parents' hopes for their future are and whether they'll follow their advice or not.)

Cultural note

Geisha /ˈɡeɪʃə/

Geishas are female Japanese entertainers. They're skilled in all traditional Japanese arts. They wear expensive, silk kimonos and paint their faces a vivid white. Eighty years ago there were more than 80,000 geishas in Japan. Now there are fewer than a thousand. Geishas these days are likely to be hired for special events.

Vocabulary (SB page 69)

1

• Tell the students that the words they need to complete the sentences are all in the article on page 68. They should use the line references to locate them

a) training	b) become	c) study	d) cost
e) move	f) take	g) pass	h) role

2

Groupwork. If you have a multinational class, put students from the same country in the same group. Ask the students to discuss whether the statement in Exercise 1 are true for their country or not, and then report back to the class on their decisions.

Pronunciation (SB page 69)

1 🔊 2.27

• Focus the students' attention on the table and remind the students that the large boxes show stressed syllables and the small boxes unstressed syllables.

• Play the recording and ask the students to listen and repeat the school subjects.

• When they've done this chorally, ask individual students to repeat the subjects. Check that everyone understands them. Find out which subjects the students study or studied at school.

Language note

Vocabulary: *Maths*

Maths is British English and is short for *Mathematics*. In American English the school subject *Mathematics* is shortened to *Math*.

2

• Pairwork. Go through the categories with the class and then put the students into pairs to discuss and categorise the school subjects in Exercise 1.

• Ask some pairs to report back to the class about what they decided.

Speaking: anecdote (SB page 69)

For more information about how to set up, monitor and repeat anecdotes, see Practical methodology, page xx in the Introduction.

1 **2.28**

- Ask the students to look at the photo. Explain that Andy, the man in the photo, is going to talk about his favourite school subject.

- Go through the questions and the answer choices with the class. Explain any unknown vocabulary and ask the students to listen and underline the answers Andy gives.

- Check answers with the class and ask them whether their art classes are/were as enjoyable as Andy's.

---

a) Art
b) I was good at it
c) Miss Lewis
d) had long black hair and wore bright colours
e) interesting and varied
f) three
g) still love taking photos

2.28

I wasn't very academic at school, but I loved art. Yes, art was my favourite subject because I was good at it. We had a wonderful teacher – she was called Miss Lewis, and I remember the first day she arrived at school. She didn't look like a teacher. She had long black hair, and she wore bright colours. She was quite young – thirty, thirty-one, something like that, and we all fell in love with her – boys and girls! She wasn't just beautiful – she was a really good teacher, too. Her lessons were interesting and varied. We only had three hours of art each week on Wednesday afternoons. Miss Lewis loved photography and she taught us how to develop our own photographs. I really enjoyed that, and for a while I wanted to be a professional photographer. In the end, I realised that it was difficult to make a living as a photographer so I went to university and studied engineering. But I still love taking photos and recently I won a competition – Miss Lewis would be proud of me!

2

- Give the students a minute or two to decide what they're going to talk about. Then ask them to look at the questions in Exercise 1 again and decide how they'd answer them about the school subject they're going to talk about. Allow them to make notes on what they're going to say and how they're going to say it, but discourage them from writing a paragraph that they can simply read out. Go round, monitoring and giving help.

- Pairwork. Put the students in pairs and ask them to take turns to tell their partner about their favourite school subject. Encourage them to ask each other follow-up questions to get further information.

- Ask some pairs to report back to the class about what they found out.

Reading (SB page 70)

1 **2.29**

- Focus the students' attention on the three men in the photos and explain that they show three generations of the same family: grandfather, son and grandson.

- Read out the three quotes about fathers and ask the students to decide which person said each one. Allow them to discuss this in pairs or small groups if they wish.

- Play the recording and ask the students to read the text as they listen.

---

a) 3   b) 2   c) 1

2

- Give the students time to read the article in more detail. Then ask them to answer the questions.

- Check answers with the class and explain any difficult vocabulary.

---

a) Because there was no other way of getting there.
b) Because he had to go to church.
c) Because he had to do his homework every night.
d) Because the government gave him a grant to study.
e) Because Louise found out she was pregnant.
f) To pay for the luxuries he wants.

3

Look at the example with the class, then put the students into pairs to discuss how life has changed in their families over the generations. Encourage them to report back to the class on their discussions.

Grammar (SB page 71)

could and *had to*

1

- Go through the information in the margin with the class and explain the difference between permission (you're allowed to do something) and obligation (you're required to do something). Point out that the negative forms of *have to* mean lack of obligation rather than prohibition. Ask several students to read out the example sentences.

- Focus attention on the table and ask the students to complete it with the correct forms of *can* and *have to*.

> 1 can
> 2 could
> 3 can't
> 4 couldn't
> 5 have to
> 6 had to
> 7 don't have to
> 8 didn't have to

Language notes

Grammar: *could*

- *Could* is a modal verb. In this unit, *could* is used to talk generally about permission in the past (i.e. that you were allowed to do something over a period of time in the past).

- As with all other modal verbs, *could* is followed by the infinitive (without *to*), and doesn't use *do/did* to form questions and negative statements.

  ***Could you** smoke at school?* (i.e. were you allowed to smoke?)

  *No, **we couldn't**. It was against the rules.* (i.e. we weren't allowed to smoke).

Grammar: *have to*

- *Have to* is used to talk about obligation/necessity (i.e. that you're required to do something).

- *Have/had to* is followed by the infinitive. You use *do/did* to form questions and negative statements.

  ***Did you have to** do homework every day?* (i.e. was is necessary to do homework every day?)

  *No, we **didn't have to** do it every day. Three times a week, usually.* (i.e. it wasn't necessary to do it every day).

2 🌐 2.30

- Go through the example with the class and then ask the students to work individually to complete the other sentences. Go round, monitoring and giving help.

- Play the recording for students to check their answers and repeat the sentences, before asking them to check with the article on page 70 and choose the correct answers to the questions.

> a) 'Did Gordon have to obey his dad without question?'
>   'Yes, he did.' 'No, he didn't.'
> b) 'Did Gordon have to go to church on Sundays?'
>   'Yes, he did.' 'No, he didn't.'
> c) 'Could Gordon bring his girlfriends home?'
>   'Yes, he could.' 'No, he couldn't.'
> d) 'Did Tony have to do his homework every night?'
>   'Yes, he did.' 'No, he didn't,'
> e) 'Could Scott come home at any time?'
>   'Yes, he could' 'No, he couldn't.'
> f) 'Does Scott have to hide things from his dad?'
>   'Yes, he does.' 'No, he doesn't.'
>
> a) Yes, he did.
> b) Yes, he did.
> c) No, he couldn't.
> d) Yes, he did.
> e) Yes, he could.
> f) No, he doesn't.

3

- Go through the example with the class and demonstrate how the questions need to be altered to make them suitable for asking other members of the class.

- Put the students in pairs to take turns asking and answering the questions.

4 Pairwork

- The pairwork exercise for this unit is on pages 118 and 123 of the Student's Book. Put the students in pairs and tell them who will be Student A, and who will be Student B.

- While they're doing the exercise, go round monitoring and giving help. Take note of any errors which may need particular attention later, and also any examples of good language use which you can praise.

5 Grammar *Extra*, Part 1

Ask the students to turn to *Grammar Extra* 8, Part 1 on page 140 of the Student's Book. Here they'll find an explanation of the grammar they've been studying and further exercises to practise it.

1
a) I didn't have to make my bed every morning.
b) I couldn't wear whatever I wanted.
c) I didn't have to keep my bedroom clean and tidy.
d) I didn't have to help my parents in the house.
e) I didn't have to travel everywhere by bicycle.
f) I couldn't invite friends home at the weekend.
g) I couldn't stay out after 10.00 p.m.
h) I couldn't play music as loud as I wanted.

2
a) Did you have to make your bed every morning?
b) Could you wear whatever you wanted?
c) Did you have to keep your bedroom clean and tidy?
d) Did you have to help your parents in the house?
e) Did you have to travel everywhere by bicycle?
f) Could you invite friends home at the weekend?
g) Could you stay out after 10.00 p.m?
h) Could you play your music as loud as you wanted?

Listening (SB page 71)

1 🌐 **2.31**

- Focus the students' attention on the photos. Play the recording and ask the students to note which of the topics Gordon and Scott talk about.

> They talk about: road travel, money, military service, appearance, air travel.

> 🌐 **2.31** (S = Scott; G = Gordon)
>
> S: Fasten your seatbelt, Grandad.
>
> G: But I'm sitting in the back.
>
> S: Yes, and you have to fasten your seatbelt in the back now.
>
> G: Oh dear. All these rules and regulations. In my day, we didn't have to wear seatbelts at all.
>
> S: And it was much more dangerous.
>
> G: But we didn't drive so fast. And there weren't so many cars on the road. In my day, we couldn't drive fast because there weren't any motorways.
>
> S: I thought you drove a horse and cart in your day.
>
> G: Hmm, very funny. Actually, I had a beautiful motorbike – a Triumph – and I didn't have to wear a helmet. Not like nowadays.
>
> S: Do you really think life was better in your day, Grandad?
>
> G: Well, life was less complicated. For example, we didn't have all these credit cards in my day. We had to use cash to buy things
>
> S: But not everything was better, Grandad. You had to do military service – I wouldn't like that.

> G: I was proud to do military service. In my day, a man had to be a man. Not like these days – men and women look exactly the same to me. In my day, you couldn't have long hair, or wear earrings or carry a handbag like some men do nowadays.
>
> S: Ha ha. But some things were more difficult in your day, Grandad – like travelling.
>
> G: That's right, we couldn't travel by air like you do today – it was too expensive. But we travelled by train and bus. I remember the first time I went to France …

2

- Go through the example with the class and emphasise the different forms of the verbs for 'then' and 'now'.
- Ask the students to work individually to write sentences for the other prompts. Go round, monitoring and giving help.
- Play the recording again for the students to check and amend their answers if necessary. Then check answers with the class.

> a) Now: You have to wear a seatbelt.
>   Then: You didn't have to wear a seatbelt.
> b) Now: You have to wear a helmet.
>   Then: You didn't have to wear a helmet.
> c) Now: You don't have to use cash.
>   Then: You had to use cash.
> d) Now: You don't have to do military service.
>   Then: You had to do military service.
> e) Now: You can have long hair.
>   Then: You couldn't have long hair.
> f) Now: You can wear earrings.
>   Then: You couldn't wear earrings.

3

- Elicit a few changes from the class and put them up on the board before you put the students into pairs to discuss the differences. In multinational classes it may be helpful to have pairs of students from the same country. Encourage them to think of any other differences between then and now and to report back to the class.

Reading & Listening (SB page 72)

1

- Ask the students if they would like to tell the class about a situation in which they met a girlfriend's/boyfriend's parents for the first time.
- Explain the situation and tell them that they have to decide which of the pieces of advice is most important. Ask them to discuss this in pairs and report back to the class.

2

- Explain that the pieces of advice in Exercise 1 have been removed from the reading text. Ask the students to read the text and paragraphs with the pieces of advice from Exercise 1.
- Check answers with the class and ask them for ideas about any other advice to give.

> 1 e – Do some research
> 2 c – Wear the right clothes
> 3 a – Make a good first impression
> 4 b – Tell the truth
> 5 d – Avoid controversial topics of conversation
> 6 f – Be prepared to answer questions

3 🌐 2.32

- Tell the students that they're going to hear the young man in the photo meeting his girlfriend's parents for the first time. Ask them to tick the advice he follows and put a cross next to the advice he doesn't follow.
- Allow the students to compare notes in pairs before checking answers. You may need to play the recording more than once. Then ask them as a class to suggest ideas about how the evening continued.

> 1 e) ✗   2 c) ✗   3 a) ✓   4 b) ✗   5 d) ✓
> 6 f) ✓

🌐 2.32 (L = Liz; M = Martin; A = Anne; J = John)

L: This is my mum, and this is my dad.

M: Hello, Mrs Farley … Mr Farley.

J: Nice to meet you, Martin. Please call us John and Anne.

A: Come in. Take a seat.

J: That's a very smart suit. Have you come straight from work?

M: Oh, no, I usually wear jeans at work!

J: Oh … what do you do?

M: Ah, er, I'm a um sort of, interior design consultant.

L: He works in a furniture shop.

A: Oh, that's nice. Um, Liz tells us you were in France recently.

M: Yes, that's right, I went to Paris last month.

A: Lovely. Did you like it?

M: Well, it's a beautiful city, but the people were very rude.

A: Oh. Did you know John's mother's from Paris?

M: Oh dear, no, I didn't. I'm sorry. I didn't mean … um …

J: Don't worry, my mother's very rude too. Now Martin, would you like a beer?

M: Oh, yes, please. Um, is that a photo of Liz when she was younger? What was she like when she was a child?

J: Oh, she was a lovely little girl. Would you like to see some more photos?

L: Oh, Dad!

M: Oh, yes please, er … John.

A: OK, John, you get the photo albums out, and I'll chat to Martin. So Martin, what are you going to do in the future?

M: Well, in my free time I'm studying at the college. I'm hoping to do a diploma in interior design and after that …

Vocabulary (SB page 72)

1

- Remind the students that the words and phrases in the box come from the article on this page.
- Ask the students to work individually to complete the sentences with the items in the box. Then allow them to compare with a partner.

> a) common   d) career
> b) effort   e) share
> c) tidy

2

Pairwork. Ask the students to discuss whether the sentences are true for them. Invite them to report back to the class.

Grammar (SB page 73)

should and *must*

1

- Read out the sentences in the margin with *should* and *must*. Then focus the students' attention on the matching exercise.
- Allow the students to work in pairs to match the sentences and their meanings. Go round, monitoring and giving help. Then check answers with the class and ask them to choose the correct alternative in the sentence.

> a) 4   b) 1   c) 2   d) 3
> When you're giving advice, *must* is stronger than *should*.

2

- Go through the sentences with the class. Point out that the choice of *should* or *must* depends largely on the importance of the situation in which the advice is given or the status of the person giving it. Ask them to decide which situations require *must* and which *should*.

- Ask the students to complete the sentences. Check answers with the class, then put the students into pairs to discuss situations where they've heard similar sentences.

  a) should do
  b) must do
  c) must hold
  d) mustn't forget
  e) must speak (*or* should speak)
  f) shouldn't watch (*or* mustn't watch)

3 Grammar *Extra* 8, Part 2

Ask the students to turn to *Grammar Extra* 8, Part 2 on page 140 of the Student's Book. Here they'll find an explanation of the grammar they've been studying and further exercises to practise it.

  1
  a) mustn't   b) should   c) shouldn't
  d) must   e) should   f) shouldn't   g) must

  2
  a) a parent   e) an old man
  b) a doctor   f) a best friend
  c) a teenage boy   g) an airport announcer
  d) a parent

Reading & Speaking (SB page 73)

1

Ask the students for a couple of ideas about what they think the perfect girlfriend or boyfriend would be like. Ask them to read the two texts. Then ask the students to work in pairs and complete the text with the words in the box. Go round, monitoring and giving help.

2 🔊 2.33

Play the recording for the students to check their answers to Exercise 1. Then have a class discussion about whether or not they agree with the advice. Elicit ideas about what makes a successful date and put them on the board. (If the subject of dating is too sensitive an issue in your class, choose one of the subjects from the extra activity below instead.)

  The perfect girlfriend
  a) clothes   b) stomach   c) work   d) shoes
  e) directions

  The perfect boyfriend
  a) time   b) pay   c) funny   d) silent
  e) women

Useful phrases (SB page 74)

1 🌐 2.34

- Focus the students' attention on the illustration. Explain that the students are going to hear a conversation between the women in the picture. Go through the list of topics and ask the students to try to predict which ones they'll talk about.

- Play the recording for them to listen and tick the topics mentioned.

> a) Looking after children ✓
> c) Marriage ✓
> d) Leaving home ✓

> 🌐 2.34 (J = Jean; E = Elaine)
>
> J: How are your children?
>
> E: Oh, Jenny's very well. She's a dentist now.
>
> J: Oh, very good.
>
> E: Yes, it's a good job, but I don't think she should work.
>
> J: Oh, why?
>
> E: Well, her son's only three. I think mothers should stay at home and look after the children.
>
> J: Oh yes, I agree. I think children need their mothers at home.
>
> E: Absolutely. My daughter thinks fathers should stay at home and look after the children.
>
> J: Oh no, I don't agree with that. It's a woman's job.
>
> E: Exactly. Now, what about your son? Is he married yet?
>
> J: No, but he's living with his girlfriend.
>
> E: Oh, dear. I don't think couples should live together before they get married.
>
> J: Oh, I'm not so sure. I don't think my son's ready to get married.
>
> E: No, he's like my Simon. He's thirty-six and he's still living at home.
>
> J: Really? I think young people should leave home when they're eighteen.
>
> E: Well, it depends. Simon can't afford to leave home.
>
> J: Well, when we were young, …

2

- Ask the students to work in pairs and discuss how they think each of the sentences should be completed.

- Play the recording again for them to listen and check their answers. Focus the students' attention on the language for expressing opinions and for agreeing and disagreeing with someone else's opinion.

> a) I think   d) I don't think
> b) I think   e) I think
> c) My daughter thinks

3 🌐 2.35

Ask the students to listen and repeat the useful phrases.

4

Put the diagram on the board and ask the students to call out their answers or come to the board and put the phrases in the correct place.

> Agree – *Absolutely. – Oh yes, I agree. – Well, it depends. – Oh, I'm not sure. – Oh no, I don't agree with that. – Disagree*

5

Ask the students to work individually to rewrite the statements according to their own opinions. Then put them in pairs to compare notes and discuss the statements.

Vocabulary *Extra* (SB page 75)

Stages of education

1

- Focus the students' attention on the photos and look at the list of stages. Read these aloud and ask the students to match them to the photos.

- Check answers with the class, and explain any new vocabulary.

> 7 Age 3–5. …
> 6 Age 5. …
> 1 Age 11. …
> 4 Age 16. …
> 5 Age 16–18. …
> 2 Age 18. …
> 8 Age 18+. …
> 3 Age 21+. …

2

In single-nationality classes, put the students into pairs and ask them to discuss the question and report back to the class. In multinational classrooms, have a class discussion with people from different countries volunteering information.

3

Give the students a few minutes to think about their own education and to decide how they would describe it. Allow them to make notes but discourage them from writing a script. Then ask several students to describe their education to the class.

UK education system and exams

In the UK, it's currently compulsory for students to attend school between the ages five and sixteen, although in 2007 the government made plans to change this to five to eighteen.

School exams

At sixteen years old students take GCSE (General Certificate of Secondary Education) exams in a range of subjects (including Maths, English and Science) which they've been studying for two years. At eighteen years old students take A-level (Advanced level) exams, usually in three or four specialised subjects).

University exams

Degree courses in England usually take three years, while in Scotland they take four years. There are two types of university: the traditional ones, which are long-established and offer traditional subjects in the Arts and Sciences; and the modern universities, which offer a range of vocational subjects like Business studies, Engineering and Tourism.

At the end of their university studies, students are awarded a degree. A standard degree is called a Bachelor's degree (BA), a Master's degree (MA), involves between one and two years of further study, and a Doctoral degree (Ph.D), involves research and usually takes between two and three years.

Focus on words used with education

1

- Allow the students to work in pairs to complete the sentences.
- Check answers and explain any difficult vocabulary.

a) go	e) gap
b) primary	f) study
c) leave	g) taken
d) apply	h) fail

2

Ask the students to answer the questions individually and then compare their answers with a partner. Encourage them to report back to the class any particularly interesting information.

Further practice material

Need more writing practice?

→ Workbook page 51
- Writing a personal letter.

Need more classroom practice activities?

→ Photocopiable resource materials pages 174 to 176
  Grammar: *Schooldays*
  Vocabulary: *Education wordsearch*
  Communication: *What's your advice?*
→ Top 10 activities pages xv to xx

Need DVD material?

→ DVD – Programme 5: *Schooldays*

Need progress tests?

→ Test CD – *Test Unit 8*

Need more on important teaching concepts?

→ Key concepts in *New Inside Out* pages xxii to xxxv

Need student self-study practice?

→ CD-ROM – Unit 8: *Education*

Need student CEF self-evaluation?

→ CEF Checklists pages xxxvii to xliv

Need more information and more ideas?

→ www.insideout.net

9 Smile *Overview*

Section & Aims	What the students are doing
Reading SB page 76 Reading detail	Discussing smiling for photographs. Reading and completing an article about smiling.
Vocabulary SB page 76 The face	Matching adjectives with parts of the face. Discussing facial features that they like.
Reading SB page 77 Reading for gist	Matching headings to paragraphs. Matching descriptions to people they know.
Vocabulary SB page 77 Character adjectives	Repeating adjectives and matching them with their meanings. Listening and choosing adjectives to describe six people. Doing a personality test.
Reading SB page 78 Reading for detail	Reading and answering a questionnaire. Talking about the results of the questionnaire.
Grammar & Vocabulary SB page 78 Verb patterns	Underlining the correct structures in sentences. Writing more true sentences about themselves.
Reading & Speaking SB page 79 Fluency practice	Describing their country. Completing a text about Thailand and discussing holiday destinations.
Listening SB page 79 Listening for specific information	Completing statements about holidays with the correct names. Writing more true sentences.
Listening SB page 80 Listening for specific information	Identifying people's jobs from a radio programme. Identifying true and false statements. Talking about countries they'd like to live in.
Grammar SB page 80 *for, since* and *been*	Completing sentences with *for* or *since* and completing a table. Studying the use of *been*. Writing true sentences about their own experiences.
Grammar SB page 81 Present perfect simple & continuous	Studying the form and use of the present perfect simple and continuous. Completing sentences with the present perfect simple and continuous. Asking questions with *How long ...?*
Pronunciation SB page 81 Sentence stress	Underlining stressed words in sentences. Listening to and repeating a chant.
Speaking SB page 81 Fluency practice	Talking about how long they've known people, been going to places, etc.
Useful phrases SB page 82 Useful body idioms	Reading conversations and underlining the correct alternatives. Matching phrases with their meanings and writing a conversation.
Vocabulary *Extra* SB page 83 Parts of the body, verbs + *ing*-form or *to*-infinitive	Matching pictures with words. Choosing the correct alternatives and completing a table.
Writing WB page 57	Writing a travel blog.

9 Smile *Teacher's notes*

Reading (SB page 76)

1

- Focus the students' attention on the speech bubble. Ask the students to discuss the questions in groups. You'll need to check that they know the answer to the first one (they say it when they want people to smile for a photograph) before they go on to answer the others.

- In a multinational class, you may get several answers to the second question. Ask the students to write the words used in their language up on the board. Then let them all have a go at saying them. Find out which one produces the best smile.

2

- Give the students time to look at the photo and the facial features that are labelled.

- Ask the students to read the title of the text and say what they think it means (people prefer the company of those who are happy to the company of those who are sad).

- Ask the students to read the article and complete it with words for facial features from the photo. Allow them to compare their answers in pairs or small groups before checking with the class.

> 1 tooth   2 cheeks   3 mouth   4 eyes
> 5 dimples

3

Ask the class how many smiles are mentioned and the names of them. Then put the students in pairs to practise doing all the smiles. Choose any particularly talented students to demonstrate their smiles to the class.

> Four different smiles are mentioned (listener/response, polite, miserable, genuine smile of enjoyment).

Vocabulary (SB page 76)

1

Ask the students to work individually to match the adjectives to the features. Then let them compare their results in pairs before checking with the class.

> a) 2   b) 6   c) 5   d) 3   e) 1   f) 4

2

Groupwork. Ask the students to discuss the question in groups and then report back to the class. Find out how much agreement there is within the class about features liked on a man and on a woman.

3 Pairwork

- The pairwork exercise for this unit is on pages 119 and 124 of the Student's Book. Put the students in pairs and tell them who will be Student A, and who will be Student B.

- While they're doing the exercise, go round monitoring and giving help. Take note of any errors which may need particular attention later, and also any examples of good language use which you can praise.

> **Picture 1**
> Student A: the man has straight hair and thin eyebrows.
> Student B: the man has curly hair and thick eyebrows.
>
> **Picture 2**
> Student A: the woman has long blond hair and dimples.
> Student B: the woman has short blond hair and no dimples.
>
> **Picture 3**
> Student A: the woman has big brown eyes and full lips.
> Student B: the woman has big blue eyes and thin lips.
>
> **Picture 4**
> Student A: the man has slightly crooked teeth and wrinkles on his forehead and cheeks.
> Student B: the man has straight teeth and no wrinkles.

Reading (SB page 77)

1

- Focus the students' attention on the photos. Explain that they show four different types of smile. Ask the students to say which one they like best.
- Give the students time to read the article and then ask them to match the headings to the paragraphs and read it again to check their answers.
- Check answers with the class and answer any questions about difficult vocabulary.

> a) 3   b) 1   c) 4   d) 2

2

- Give the students a few minutes to think about and visualise their family, friends and colleagues. Ask them to imagine them smiling and try to match them with one of the descriptions.
- Pairwork. Put the students in pairs and ask them to tell each other about the people they've matched with the descriptions. Encourage them to ask each other follow-up questions to find out more about these people.

Vocabulary (SB page 77)

1 ⊙ 3.01

- This exercise focuses on adjectives describing character which were used in the reading text in the previous section.
- Play the recording and ask the students to listen to the adjectives and repeat them.
- Encourage the students to find the adjectives in the reading text and use the context to work out what they mean.

> a) 3   b) 6   c) 1   d) 7   e) 2   f) 4
> g) 8   h) 5

2 ⊙ 3.02

- Tell the students that they'll hear six people talking. They should listen and choose the most appropriate adjective to describe each one. You may need to play the recording more than once and pause it between speakers to allow the students time to decide which adjective they'll use.
- Allow the students to compare their results in pairs before checking answers with the class.

> a) sociable
> b) bossy
> c) confident
> d) ambitious
> e) easygoing
> f) sensitive

> ⊙ 3.02
>
> 1   *I'd love to meet your friends – let's make a date now. We could try that new restaurant in town.*
>
> 2   *No, no, don't do it like that. Do it like this. Go on, do it again, and, oh, then get me a cup of tea.*
>
> 3   *No problem – I'm sure I can win. I know I'm faster than the others.*
>
> 4   *I'm working here to get some experience, but I'm going to start up my own company soon.*
>
> 5   *Yeah, whatever – I really don't mind. I'll be happy if we go out. I'll be happy if we stay in. Let's do whatever you want to do.*
>
> 6   *Look, are you sure you're OK, because I can stay longer if you want. Anyway, you know where I am if you need me. Take care.*

3 ⊙ 3.03

- Ask the students to work individually to choose and write down the adjectives they'd use to describe each thing. Remind them that they can use their own ideas if none of the adjectives in the box is right for them.
- Play the recording so the students can find out the meaning of their choices. Put them in pairs to discuss whether or not they agree with the analysis.

> ⊙ 3.03
>
> *Your description of a dog is your own personality.*
> *Your description of a cat is your partner's personality.*
> *Your description of a rat is your enemy's personality.*
> *Your description of coffee is how you see love.*
> *Your description of an ocean is your own life.*

Reading (SB page 78)

1

- Explain optimist and pessimist and then ask the students to work individually to answer the questionnaire. Discourage them from reading the analysis section until they've answered all the questions. Go round, monitoring and answering any questions the students may have.

- When the students have answered the questions, ask them to calculate their scores and read what they mean. Allow them to compare with a partner and discuss whether they agree with the analysis.

2

- You could ask the students to stand in line according to the score they got on the questionnaire. Insist that they ask and answer questions in English to ascertain their place in the line.

- When they've finished, ask them if they agree that the person at the head of the line is more optimistic than the person at the end.

Grammar & Vocabulary (SB page 78)

Verb patterns 3

1

- Focus attention on the information in the margin. Read out the example sentence for the verbs which take verb + *ing*-form or ask a student to read it aloud. See if the students can come up with example sentences for one or two of the other verbs in the list.

- Do the same for the verbs which take *to*-infinitive.

- Ask the students to look at the sentences in the exercise and underline the correct structures. Remind them that they can look at the examples in the questionnaire in the previous section to help them.

a) to get	d) to spend
b) to travel	e) worrying
c) speaking	f) going out

Language notes

Grammar: verbs with *ing*-form and *to*-infinitive

- Although the Grammar section on page 78 doesn't deal with those verbs which can take either the *ing*-form or the *to*-infinitive, there's work in the *Focus on …* section of the *Vocabulary Extra* on page 83 which does.

- Verbs like *begin*, *hate*, *like*, *love*, *prefer* and *start* can take both the *ing*-form and the *to*-infinitive with virtually no change in meaning:
  It started to rain at lunchtime.
  It started raining at lunchtime.

- With *stop*, *try* and *remember/forget* there's a marked difference in meaning depending on whether you use the *ing*-form or the *to*-infinitive:
  *He **stopped** smoking.* (= He gave it up.) Refers to the action someone has stopped.
  *He **stopped** to smoke.* (= He stopped what he was doing in order to have a cigarette.) Refers to the reason why someone has stopped an action.
  *Sue **remembered** feeding the cat.* (= Sue fed the cat and, at a later date, she recalled doing it.)
  *Sue **remembered** to feed the cat.* (= Sue had to feed the cat and she did.)

2

Read the example sentence with the class and give the students examples of sentences that are true for you. Then ask them to write their sentences. Allow them to compare them in pairs or small groups and ask some students to read their sentences out to the class.

Reading & Speaking (SB page 79)

1

- Pairwork. If you have a multinational class, try to form pairs with students from the same country.

- Ask the students to take each topic in turn and note down some of the adjectives they'd use to describe them to people from another country. Then ask the students to form sentences using those adjectives.

- Get several pairs to read their sentences to the class.

2

- Focus the students' attention on the photo and the title of the article. Find out if anyone has been to Thailand. If so, ask them if they agree that it's 'the land of smiles'.

- Give the students time to read the article and complete it with the words in the box in Exercise 1.

- Check answers with the class and answer any questions the students may have.

1 The people
2 The food
3 The mountains
4 the beaches
5 The capital city
6 the historical sites

3

- Pairwork. Give the students a few minutes to decide which places they're going to talk about and the language they'll need to do this. Go round, giving help with vocabulary where necessary.

- Put the students in pairs and ask them to take turns describing the various places they've chosen. Go round, monitoring and giving help. Take note of any particularly good descriptions and ask the students to repeat them to the class.

Listening (SB page 79)

1 🌐 **3.04**

- Focus the students' attention on the photos and explain that all the people shown are on holiday in Thailand. Ask the students to think about what kind of people they are and what their interests might be. Go through the statements and ask the students to guess which people match each statement.

- Play the recording and ask the students to complete the statements with the names. You may need to play the recording more than once or pause it after each speaker to give the students time to make their choices.

a) Cindy	d) Kath
b) Hans	e) Kath and Roy
c) Cindy	f) Hans

🌐 3.04 (P = Presenter; K = Kath; R = Roy; C = Cindy; H = Hans)

P: *Welcome to 'The Holiday Programme'. We start off with a report from Thailand. In this report, we spoke to tourists on the beach in Ao Nang in the south of Thailand. We asked them what they were doing in Thailand.*

First, we spoke to Kath and Roy.

K: *We're on our honeymoon and we're staying in the Rayavadee hotel. It's wonderful. They put rose petals in our bath.*

R: *Next week we want to go to the north. I want to go trekking in the jungle, and Kath wants to do a cookery course. We both love Thai food, so I think it's a great idea.*

P: *Then we spoke to Cindy.*

C: *I'm on holiday and I'm doing a scuba diving course. I like swimming in the sea so I spend most of my day on the beach, and then in the evening I go shopping. I have a shop back home in Sydney so I'm always looking for things to take back there.*

P: *Finally, we spoke to Hans.*

H: *I'm living here at the moment. I come from Germany but I've rented a house here for six months because I'm writing a novel. I think Thailand is a perfect place to live – it's cheap, hot and inspiring. My girlfriend isn't very happy about it though – I have a dog in Germany, and she had to stay at home and look after it!*

2

- Elicit the kinds of questions the students will need to find out the necessary information from their classmates. With weaker classes, put these on the board. Then let the students mingle to ask questions and note down names.

- When they've got all the information they need, ask them to rewrite the sentences in Exercise 1, using the names of students in the class. Find out who has the most sentences and ask this student to read them aloud and get the students named to confirm that the information is correct.

Listening (SB page 80)

1 🌐 **3.05**

- Focus the students' attention on the photos of Becky and Jeff. Explain that Becky and Jeff went to Thailand on holiday and liked it so much that they decided to stay.

- Tell the students that they're going to hear a radio programme about tourists who have stayed in Thailand and that they should listen and note down what jobs Becky and Jeff now do in Thailand.

Becky runs a bar.
Jeff works in a dive centre.

🌐 3.05 (P = Presenter; B = Becky; J = Jeff)

P: *In our second report from Thailand, we met two people who came here on holiday and never went home. Becky, how long have you been here in Thailand?*

B: *I arrived here in 2004. I only came here for a holiday, but I liked it so much I stayed.*

P: *What have you been doing here since 2004?*

B: *I've been running a bar on the beach. It was difficult at first, because I opened my bar two months before the tsunami in December 2004. Our bar was OK, but tourists stayed away for a long time after that, and I almost had to close the bar. But I've had a lot of support from my husband, and now the bar is going very well.*

P: Did you get married here?

B: Yes, my husband's Thai, and we've been married for two years now.

P: Do you go back to the UK often?

B: I haven't been to the UK for a few years.

P: What do you miss about home?

B: Certainly not the weather, or the food. I guess I miss my family and friends, but they love coming here.

P: Jeff, how long have you been here?

J: For about six months.

P: What have you been doing here since you arrived?

J: I've been working in a dive centre.

P: Have you learnt the language?

J: Thai? Ha ha. No, it's really difficult. I've been having lessons for a few months, but I'm not a very good student.

P: What do you like most about living in Thailand?

J: Apart from the obvious things like the weather, the food and the laid-back lifestyle, I like the fact that it's close to other interesting places. I've been to Laos, Cambodia, Bali and Malaysia. But I always like coming back to Thailand. I'm not going home for a long time.

Cultural notes

- There are more than 10,000 British people living as permanent residents in Thailand.
- In 2004, the Indian Ocean tsunami devastated the west coast of Thailand and claimed the lives of 230,000 people in Thailand, India, Sri Lanka, Myanmar and Indonesia.

2

- Go through the statements with the class. As you read each one aloud, ask the students to raise their hands if they think it's true and to do nothing if they think it's false. Encourage students who disagree to try to convince the others of their point of view. Note the majority decision on the board.

- Play the recording again for the students to check their answers. Encourage individual students to correct the false statements.

---
a) False. (She came for a holiday.)
b) True.
c) False. (She says her bar was OK.)
d) True.
e) True.
f) False. (He says he's not going home for a long time.)

3

- Give the students a minute or two to think of their answer. Remind them that they'll need to give reasons as well as simply naming the country.

- Put the students into pairs and ask them to take turns talking about which country they'd like to live in and why. Go round, monitoring and encouraging students to answer the question as fully as they can.

Grammar (SB page 80)

for, since and *been*

1

- Focus attention on the information about *for* and *since* in the margin. Explain the difference between a period of time (*24 hours, three days, ten minutes, six years*, etc.) and a point in time (*yesterday, this morning, last week, Saturday, last year*, etc.)

- Ask the students to complete the two sentences in the exercises and check their answers.

---
a) since   b) for

2

- Look at the diagram with the class and ask the students to work individually to complete the table.

- Go round, monitoring and checking that everyone has understood the difference between *for* and *since*.

- Ask the students to add more examples of expressions used with *for* and *since* to the table. Get several students to read theirs aloud to the class.

3

- Focus attention on the information about *been* in the margin and read out the two example sentences.

- Pairwork. Put the students in pairs to discuss the questions.

---
a) Present perfect simple.
b) Sentence *b*.
c) Sentence *a*.

Language notes

Grammar: *been* and *gone*

- You may need to explain that *gone* is also a past participle of *go*.
  Write on the board:
  John has gone to London.
  John has been to London.

- The first sentence means that John went to London and he's still there. The second means that at some time in his life, John went to London, but he isn't necessarily there at the moment.

4

- Go through the examples with the class, then ask them to work individually to write three true sentences for each item. Go round, monitoring and giving help. Make sure that everyone is using *for* and *since* and the present perfect simple correctly.
- Put the students in pairs to compare their sentences. Ask some students to read theirs aloud to the class.

Student A	Student B
Have you ever been to Zara?	*No, never. What/Where is it?*
Have you been to Zara recently?	*Yes, I went there last Saturday.*

Grammar (SB page 81)

Present perfect simple & continuous

1

- Go through the information in the margin with the class. Remind the students that they studied verbs with dynamic and stative meanings on page 62.
- Ask them to look at the table in the exercise and decide which facts describe how long each activity has continued. Allow them to compare their answers in pairs before checking with the class.

> 3 Present perfect facts

Language notes

Grammar: present perfect simple and continuous

- The present perfect can be used to talk about past experience (completed actions in the past). *I've been to France, but I haven't been to Paris.* Note that no precise time is given for the action in the past and only the present perfect simple form is used when speaking about past experience.
- The present perfect can also be used to speak about actions which started in the past and are still happening now. In these cases it's possible to mention time, using *for* and *since*. Use *for* when you give the length of time – duration – (*for a few days, for years*). Use *since* when you give the beginning of the time – starting point – (*since Tuesday, since 1967*). You usually use the continuous form for verbs with dynamic meanings (*I've been going to the same dentist for years.*). However, you can't use the continuous form for verbs with stative meanings (*I've*

known him since he was born, not ~~I've been knowing him since he was born.~~). See page 138 in the Student's Book for a list of verbs with stative meanings.

- Occasionally you can use the simple form with verbs with dynamic meanings to indicate unchanging, 'permanent' situations. Compare: *I've been working here since the beginning of summer* with *I've worked here all my life.*

2

Pairwork. Ask the students to discuss the questions in pairs.

> a) be
> b) present perfect simple
> c) work
> d) present perfect continuous

3

- Ask the students to work individually to complete the sentences. Go round, checking that everyone is using the correct verb forms.
- Allow the students to compare their answers in pairs before checking with the class. Then ask them to make changes to the sentences to make them true. Ask several students to read out their new sentences to the class.

> | a) 've been studying | d) 've had |
> |---|---|
> | b) 've been | e) 've been using |
> | c) 've known | f) 've wanted |

4

Pairwork. Put the students in pairs to discuss how long they've been doing the things in Exercise 3. Go through the example question with the class first, and with weaker classes, elicit more of the questions they'll need. If necessary, write the questions up on the board.

5 Grammar *Extra* 9

Ask the students to turn to *Grammar Extra* 9 on page 142 of the Student's Book. Here they'll find an explanation of the grammar they've been studying and further exercises to practise it.

> 1
> a) for b) for c) since d) for e) since
> f) since g) since h) for
>
> 2
> | a) stealing, stolen | h) getting, got |
> |---|---|
> | b) growing, grown | i) telling, told |
> | c) selling, sold | j) costing, cost |
> | d) driving, driven | k) hearing, heard |
> | e) sending, sent | l) losing, lost |
> | f) paying, paid | m) building, built |
> | g) feeling, felt | n) lending, lent |

3
a) We've been married since 2007.
b) I've been reading the newspaper for half an hour.
c) He's liked jazz since he was at university.
d) She's been learning to swim since September.
e) She's worked/been working in a shop since last May.
f) They've lived/been living together since last summer.
g) I've been playing the guitar since I was eight.
h) We've had a motorbike for three years.

4
a) How long have you known your best friend?
b) How long have you been wearing the same sunglasses?
c) How long have you been going to the same dentist?
d) How long have you been listening to the same kind of music?
e) How long have you been in the same job?
f) How long have you been driving the same car?
g) How long have you been living in the same house?
h) How long have you been doing your shopping in the same supermarket?

Pronunciation (SB page 81)

1

- Explain that two words in each line of the chants should be stressed. Ask the students to decide which two words these are and to underline them.

- Allow the students to compare their answers in pairs but don't check them with the class at this stage.

2 ⊕ 3.06

Play the recording for the students to check their answers to Exercise 1. Then play it again for them to repeat the chants.

A
How <u>long</u> has she been <u>cooking</u>?
How <u>long</u> has she been <u>cleaning</u>?
How <u>long</u> has she been <u>shopping</u>?
How <u>long</u> have you been <u>sleeping</u>?

B
How <u>long</u> has he been <u>reading</u>?
How <u>long</u> has he been <u>playing</u>?
How <u>long</u> has he been <u>eating</u>?
How <u>long</u> have you been <u>waiting</u>?

Speaking (SB page 81)

1

Ask the students to work individually to write the names of all the places, people and things. If the students ask about the underlining, tell them not to worry about it at this stage.

2

- Focus the students' attention on the underlined words in Exercise 1 and go through the example, showing them how these words can be used to write sentences describing how long each activity has gone on.

- Ask the students to work individually to write sentences for each of the places, people and things they chose in Exercise 1. Go round, monitoring and giving help. Remind them to use the underlined words to help them.

- Put the students into pairs and ask them to take turns telling their partner about what they've written.

Extra activity

- Set up a class survey to find out who in the class has done each activity in Exercise 1 the longest.

- Ask each student to choose one 'fact' from Exercise 2 and practise the questions they'll ask. For example, *What is your neighbour's name? How long have you known him/her?*

- Tell the students to ask everybody in the class their questions and make a note of the answers. They should then report the results back to the class.

Useful phrases (SB page 82)

1

- Focus the students' attention on the pictures and ask them to speculate about the situation. Then tell them to read the conversations in pairs and decide who is getting married.

Adam and Dawn

---

2 ⊕ 3.07

- Focus the students' attention on alternatives given in the conversations. Ask them what all these have in common (they're all body parts). Explain that there are several expressions (called *idioms*) in English which use parts of the body. An idiom is a fixed expression whose meaning cannot always be guessed from an understanding of the meaning of its constituent parts.

- Ask the students to underline the correct alternative to complete each phrase.

- Play the recording for the students to check and ask if anyone was surprised by the answers. Find out if they have any similar expressions in their own language(s).

---

a) fingers   d) a hand
b) an arm and a leg e) eye to eye
c) leg

---

3 🌐 3.08

- Ask the students to work individually to match the phrases and their meanings.
- Check answers with the class and then play the recording for the students to listen and repeat.
- When they've done this chorally, ask for individual repetition of the useful phrases.

a) 3   b) 1   c) 4   d) 5   e) 2

4

- Pairwork. Ask the students to work in pairs to write their conversations. Go round, monitoring and giving help with vocabulary. Make sure the useful phrases are being used correctly.
- Ask the pairs to perform their conversations for the class.

Vocabulary *Extra* (SB page 83)

Parts of the body

1

Ask the students to match the pictures with the words. Let them use dictionaries if they wish. Check answers with the class. Then check that the students can pronounce the words correctly.

14 ankle	12 knee
11 bottom	3 lip
2 cheek	18 nail
7 chest	5 neck
4 chin	6 shoulder
20 elbow	8 stomach
16 finger	17 thumb
1 forehead	14 toe
15 heel	9 waist
10 hip	19 wrist

2

Ask the students to discuss the questions in pairs and then present their lists to the class.

bottom
chest
chin (unless someone has a 'double chin', a fold of
    skin which give the appearance of two chins!)
forehead
neck
stomach
waist

Extra activity

In classes where it's culturally acceptable to do so, ask the students to test each other on the parts of the body by asking a partner to touch parts of his or her body.

Focus on verbs + *ing*-form or *to*-infinitive (with a change in meaning)

1

- Remind the students that they studied verbs which take *ing*-form or the *to*-infinitive on page 78. Explain that so far they've practised using verbs with either *ing*-form or the *to*-infinitive. However, there are some verbs which can use either structure, depending on the context, though the meaning changes.
- Ask the students to choose and underline the correct alternatives.

a) to post   b) getting   c) kissing
d) raining   e) to lock   f) to buy

2

- Go through the table with the class. Ask them to complete it with the sentences from Exercise 1.
- Check answers with the class, then ask the students to write their own sentences using the same verbs. Go round, monitoring and giving help. Write some of their sentences on the board.

1: Sentences b and c
2: Sentences a and e
3: Sentence d
4: Sentence f

Further practice material

Need more writing practice?

→ Workbook page 57
- Writing a travel blog.

Need more classroom practice activities?

→ Photocopiable resource materials pages 177 to 179
    Grammar: *For and since*
    Vocabulary: *Character crossword*
    Communication: *Smile!*
→ Top 10 activities pages xv to xx

Need progress tests?

→ Test CD – *Test Unit 9*

Need more on important teaching concepts?

→ Key concepts in *New Inside Out* pages xxii to xxxv

Need student self-study practice?

→ CD-ROM – Unit 9: *Smile*

Need student CEF self-evaluation?

→ CEF Checklists pages xxxvii to xliv

Need more information and more ideas?

→ www.insideout.net

Review C *Teacher's notes*

These exercises act as a check of the grammar and vocabulary that the students have learnt in Units 7–9. Use them to find any problems that students are having, or anything that they haven't understood and which will need further work.

Grammar (SB page 84)

Remind the students of the grammar explanations they read and the exercises they did in the *Grammar Extra* on pages 138 to 143.

1

This exercise reviews subject and object questions from Unit 7.

> a) What did Al Gore make a film about?
> b) Which country is the world's biggest polluter?
> c) How much litter does the UK produce every year?
> d) Who wants Virgin Airlines to go green?
> e) How many people travel on passenger jets every year?
> f) Which organisation protests against global warming?

Cultural notes

Al Gore /æl gɔː/ (born 1948)
An American businessman, politician and environmentalist, Al Gore was the 45th Vice President of the United States from 1993 to 2001, under Bill Clinton. In 2000, he ran for President against George W. Bush in the US Presidential elections but just lost. Since then he's emerged as champion of environmental causes and won the Nobel Peace Prize and an Oscar for his film about climate change, *An Inconvenient Truth*, in 2007.

Richard Branson /ˈrɪtʃəd ˈbrænsən/ (born 1950)
A British businessman, who started up Virgin Records when he was 20 years old. In 1984, the Virgin brand grew when he formed Virgin Atlantic Airways. His worth is estimated today at around £4 billion.

Alliance for Climate Protection
An American organisation which aims to persuade people that it's important to make changes to the way we live in order to reduce the negative effect we're having on the world's climate. The founder of the alliance is former US Vice President Al Gore.

2

This exercise reviews verbs with dynamic and stative meanings from Unit 7.

> a) 's having   d) look like
> b) have   e) 're thinking
> c) believe   f) thinks

Cultural note

Beyoncé Knowles (born 1981)
(See notes about Beyoncé Knowles in Unit 1, page 4.)

3

This exercise reviews future forms for arrangements and intentions from Unit 7. Check answers with the class before asking the students to tick the sentences that are true for them and to compare with a partner.

> a) 'm seeing   d) are coming
> b) 'm going to visit   e) 'm going to buy
> c) 'm going   f) 'm having

4

This exercise reviews verbs which take *ing*-form or the *to*-infinitive from Unit 9. Check answers with the class before asking the students to tick the sentences that are true for them and to compare with a partner.

> a) walking   d) to go
> b) to take   e) watching
> c) doing   f) to spend

5

This exercise reviews *could* for permission and *had to*, *should* and *must* for obligation from Unit 8. Check answers with the class. Then ask the students for their views on the clothes they have to or had to wear at school.

> 1 Did you have to   4 didn't have to
> 2 couldn't   5 should
> 3 had to   6 mustn't

6

This exercise reviews the present perfect simple or continuous with *for* and *since* from Unit 9.

> a) They've been living in France since 2005.
> b) We've been learning the violin for two months.
> c) She's wanted to be a vet since she was six.
> d) He's been studying Chinese for a year.
> e) I've known him since we were at school.
> f) She's had a motorbike for three weeks.

7

This exercise reviews structures used in Units 7, 8 and 9.

> 1 b) ~~Who does like George Clooney?~~
> 2 b) ~~Don't worry — I'm believing you.~~
> 3 a) ~~We're visiting the USA one day.~~
> 4 a) ~~Did you had to clean your room?~~
> 5 b) ~~I'm looking forward to meet you.~~
> 6 a) ~~She's been here since four years.~~

Cultural note

George Clooney (born 1961)
An American actor, director, producer and screenwriter. He also has a keen interest in politics and environmental issues. Clooney uses the money he earns in blockbuster films like *Ocean's Eleven* (2001), *Ocean's Twelve* (2004) and *Ocean's Thirteen* (2007) to fund smaller budget, political films like *Good Night, and Good Luck* (2005), which he directed, produced and starred in. He was voted 'Sexiest Man Alive' by People Magazine in 1997 and again in 2006.

Vocabulary (SB page 85)

1

This exercise reviews words connected to protesting and demonstrations from Unit 7.

> 1 buzzing   2 part   3 way   4 away
> 5 swarming   6 slogans   7 action

Cultural notes

Trafalgar Square /trəˈfælgə skweə/
Trafalgar Square, in the centre of London, commemorates the Battle of Trafalgar (1805). During the most significant battle of the Napoleonic Wars, a Royal Navy fleet of 27 ships, led by Admiral Lord Nelson, defeated a combined French and Spanish fleet of 33 ships. Nelson died late in the battle, after victory had been won.

Trafalgar Square is now a popular site for tourists and for political demonstrations.

Nelson's Column /ˈnelsənz ˈkɒləm/
Nelson's 5.5 m statue stands on a 46 m column in the centre of Trafalgar Square. The statue was sculpted in 1838. Four large bronze lions were added at the foot of the column in 1867.

Jubilee Gardens /ˈdʒuːbɪliː ˈgɑːdənz/
From Trafalgar Square, Whitehall (a road) leads down to the Houses of Parliament. Next to the Houses of Parliament, Westminster Bridge crosses the River Thames to London's South Bank, on which stands the London Eye (a large ferris wheel). Behind the London Eye are the Jubilee Gardens, a grassed park created in 1977 to mark Queen Elizabeth II's Silver Jubilee.

2

Go through the example with the class first and then ask them to complete the exercise by putting the other sentences in order. Check answers with the class before asking the students to tick the statements which they agree with and then compare with a partner.

> a) I'm anti-nuclear power.
> b) I'm against using big cars in the city.
> c) I don't feel strongly about global warming.
> d) I'm in favour of more money for farmers.
> e) I don't really care about politics.
> f) I support the protection of wild animals.

3

This exercise reviews vocabulary to do with education and training from Unit 8. Check answers with the class before asking the students to think about their own country and tick the statements which are true. They should then compare with a partner.

> a) 3   b) 1   c) 4   d) 2   e) 6   f) 5

4

This exercise reviews collocations in an educational context.

> 1 effort   2 career   3 common   4 opinions
> 5 avoid   6 tidy

5

This exercise reviews adjectives for describing facial features from Unit 9.

> 1 curly   2 thick   3 full   4 rosy
> 5 square   6 white

6

This exercise reviews character adjectives from Unit 9.

a) ambitious   b) bossy   c) confident
d) easygoing   e) independent   f) loyal
g) mysterious   h) selfish

Pronunciation (SB page 85)

1

Remind the students that the boxes show the syllables in a word and the large boxes indicate the stressed syllables. Here the students are being asked to classify words from Units 7–9 according to how many syllables they have and where the main stress falls. Encourage them to say each word aloud to get a feeling for what sounds right. Don't confirm answers at this stage.

2 🌐 3.09

Point out the main stresses in the example words which are underlined. Ask the students to do the same for the other words in the table. Play the recording for the students to check their answers. Then play it a second time for them to listen and repeat the words.

1 and 2
A: <u>cur</u>ly, <u>eye</u>brows, <u>fore</u>head, <u>poin</u>ted
B: a<u>gainst</u>, be<u>lieve</u>, de<u>gree</u>, su<u>pport</u>
C: <u>con</u>fident, <u>ear</u>lier, <u>so</u>ciable, <u>tour</u>ism
D: a<u>ffec</u>tionate, bi<u>ol</u>ogy, de<u>moc</u>racy, res<u>pon</u>sible

Reading & Listening (SB page 86)

1 🌐 3.10

Give the students plenty of time to read the article about Phil and Hazel Green. Then go through the statements with the class and ask the students to say who they think made them, Phil or Hazel.

a) Hazel.   b) Phil.   c) Hazel.

2

Go through the questions with the students before they read the texts again and see if they can answer any of them. Then ask them to read the text again and find the answers to any remaining questions.

a) Last summer.
b) Phil.
c) From local farmers, and from their garden.
d) Because they don't buy things they don't need.
e) Holidays in warm places.
f) Hazel.
g) The south coast of Wales.

3

Pairwork. Ask the students to discuss what they've read in pairs and talk about whether they could make similar changes in their lives.

4 🌐 3.11

Go through the choices with the students before playing the recording. Ask them to underline the correct information.

a) is   b) is

🌐 3.11 (I = Interviewer; K = Kyle; N = Naomi)

I: *Tell me, Kyle, how did your family decide to go green?*

K: *It was Dad's idea, really. When we were young, Dad had an important job with an oil company. He was very ambitious, and we didn't see him a lot, because he was always flying around the world. But when he was forty-three, he lost his job. After he lost his job, he changed completely. His hair got long ... he grew a beard. He started working as a gardener, met new friends and that's how he became interested in green issues.*

I: *Very different from his old life?*

K: *Yeah. He actually became a bit of a rebel. So when he asked us about going green, I wasn't surprised.*

I: *How did you feel about the changes you had to make, Naomi?*

N: *I was very happy. Last year Dad and I took part in a demonstration about climate change in London. It was fun, and I had a great day, but when I went back home I felt I needed to do more. These are serious problems. We all have to make changes to our lives now!*

I: *What about you, Kyle?*

K: *Mostly it's OK. I don't mind walking and cycling. I agree with recycling bottles and paper and all that, but I get tired of eating potatoes, salad and apples. Sometimes I just want to eat a hamburger, turn all the lights on in every room in the house, and have a big bath. And I'd really like to get a motorbike when I'm older.*

I: *What about your friends, what do they think?*

N: *They're all very worried about climate change. At my school I've started an environmental group. We're trying to persuade people to change their lives. My friends think I'm very bossy, but all this is too important! We must do something before it's too late. We mustn't close our eyes to this problem.*

K: *My friends think my dad is crazy – I think he's crazy too sometimes – but all my friends agree that climate change is a real problem and we should do everything we can to stop it. I hope the changes my family is making can help, but I'm not sure.*

5

Go through the statements before you play the recording again and ask the students to think about whether they are true or false. Then play the recording for them to check. Encourage them to correct the false statements.

> a) False. (He worked for an oil company.)
> b) True.
> c) False. (She was very happy about the changes.)
> d) False. (He says he would like to get a motorbike.)
> e) True.
> f) False. (He says his friends agree that climate change is a real problem.)

Writing & Speaking (SB page 87)

1

Ask the students to read the email and complete it with the words in the box.

> 1 ... I bought a lottery ticket **last** week, ... I**'m** so excited.
> 2 ... starting with **my** job. ... I've always wanted to be a doctor, **but** my parents ... Now I **can** finally do it!
> 3 ... We **have** nothing in common, ... I'm going to **be** too busy with my studies!
> 4 ... I'm looking **forward** to that. ... Do you think I **should** give some money to my sister?
> 5 ... I'm **going** to give some money to Greenpeace. But first I'm planning a **holiday** in a warm place. ... I'll pay **for** your ticket!
> You mustn't **tell** Kenny I won this money.

2

Ask the students to read the text again and match the headings to the paragraphs.

> a) Paragraph 4   d) Paragraph 1
> b) Paragraph 5   e) Paragraph 3
> c) Paragraph 2

3

Explain the situation and ask the students to work individually to decide on the changes they're going to make to their lives. Go round, offering help with vocabulary and encouraging them to put something for each of the items in Exercise 2.

4

Pairwork. Go through the example sentence with the class and then ask the students to work in pairs and take turns to tell each other about the changes they plan for their lives following their big win.

5

Remind the students that they can use the text in Exercise 1 as a model. Go round, monitoring and giving help. Encourage the use of the headings in Exercise 2 for structuring the email.

Further practice material

Need more classroom practice activities?

→ Photocopiable resource materials page 180, recording track 🌐 3.12
   Song: *Money*
→ Top 10 activities pages xv to xx

Need progress tests?

→ Test CD – *Test Review C*

Need more on important teaching concepts?

→ Key concepts in *New Inside Out* pages xxii to xxxv

Need student self-study practice?

→ CD-ROM – *Review C*

Need more information and more ideas?

→ www.insideout.net

10 Lifestyle *Overview*

Section & Aims	What the students are doing
Reading & Vocabulary SB page 88 Reading for detail Collocations	Predicting a text by guessing answers to questions. Completing collocations. Discussing lifestyles.
Listening & Grammar SB page 89 Listening for gist *will*	Answering questions about a telephone enquiry. Completing questions and answers. Talking about health spas.
Grammar SB page 89 Future time clauses	Studying future time clauses. Underlining the correct structures and rewriting the sentences so they are true for them.
Vocabulary SB page 90 Food and cooking	Checking items bought in a shopping list. Giving opinions about food.
Pronunciation SB page 90 Vowel sounds in food words	Listening and repeating food words. Matching words according to pronunciation of vowel sounds.
Reading & Vocabulary SB page 91 Reading for detailed information	Reading a text and categorising vocabulary. Talking about their favourite dish.
Speaking: anecdote SB page 91 Fluency work	Underlining the correct information from a description. Talking about the fittest/healthiest person they know.
Reading SB page 92 Reading for detail	Matching descriptions with photos. Answering questions about the text from memory. Talking about first experiences with cars.
Vocabulary SB page 93 Cars and driving	Finding names of car parts in a reading text. Putting features of cars in order of importance.
Grammar SB page 93 *used to* + infinitive	Identifying the meaning and usage of *used to* + infinitive. Replacing the past simple with *used to* + infinitive and changing the sentences so they are true for them.
Speaking: anecdote SB page 93 Fluency practice	Underlining the correct information about a woman's dream car. Talking about their own dream car.
Useful phrases SB page 94 Idioms with food	Matching conversations with pictures. Underlining the correct alternatives. Replacing phrases in sentences with food idioms. Listening to and repeating sentences. Talking about which sentences are true for them.
Vocabulary *Extra* SB page 95 Revision of words from the unit: cars; words used with driving	Matching pictures with words. Asking and answering questions. Matching sentence halves to complete definitions. Completing questions, then discussing them with a partner.
Writing WB page 63	Writing a narrative.

Lifestyle *Teacher's notes*

Reading & Vocabulary (SB page 88)

1

- Ask the students to cover the text and look at the photo. Go through the questions with the class and ask them to guess the answers. Allow them to discuss in pairs or small groups if they wish. Find out how much consensus there is in the class, particularly with regard to the woman's age. Note the highest and lowest estimates of her age on the board.
- Give the students time to read the text and find out if their guesses were correct. Ask them if they're surprised by how old Chiako is. Answer any questions they may have about vocabulary.

a) 7.00 a.m.	d) A low-calorie diet.
b) 102 years old.	e) No.
c) Okinawa.	

2

- Ask the students if they can complete any of the collocations without looking back at the article. For number 2 they may suggest *live a healthy life*; point out that this is possible, but the word used in the article is more common. When they've done all they can, allow them to look through the article and complete the remainder.
- Check answers with the class before putting the students into pairs to discuss their answers to the questions and the similarities and differences between their lives and those of the people of Okinawa. Get several pairs to report back to the class on their discussions.

a) brisk	b) lead	c) arts	d) hurry
e) sunset	f) family	g) network	h) keep

Listening & Grammar (SB page 89)

1 🔊 3.13

- Ask the students to look at the picture and describe what they see. Prompt them to say which of the people shown they think is the healthiest. What might the man do to get fit?
- Tell the students that they're going to hear the woman's phone conversation with the receptionist at the New Life Centre, a health spa. Explain the word *health spa* and ask the students to suggest a few of the things that you might find in a health spa (a gym, a pool, therapy rooms, etc.). Before you play the recording, go through the questions with the class so they know what they are listening for.
- Play the recording and ask the students to answer the questions.

a) She wants to give her husband a surprise for his birthday.
b) No, he won't, because he isn't very fit.

3.13 (R = Receptionist; W = Woman)

R: *New Life Centre. Can I help you?*

W: *Yes. Could you give me some information about your centre?*

R: *Certainly. When would you like to come?*

W: *Actually it's not for me. It's for my husband. It's a surprise for his birthday.*

R: *Ah, lucky man!*

W: *Yes. Could you tell me something about the programme?*

R: *Sure. As soon as he arrives here he'll take a fitness test.*

W: *Right. Um, he isn't very fit.*

R: *Well, we start every day at 7.30 a.m. He'll do a yoga class before breakfast.*

W: *Ha ha. He usually has a cigarette before breakfast!*

R: *Oh dear. If he has a cigarette here, he'll be in big trouble. It's a strictly no smoking area.*

W: *Well, it's a good idea for him to give up smoking. He says he'll give up as soon as he feels more relaxed.*

R: *Oh well, this is the ideal place to relax. After the morning walk, he'll have a sauna and jacuzzi.*

W: *Oh, he'll enjoy that. But what's this walk?*

R: *They go for a brisk walk in the morning from 8.30 to 12.30. That's four hours.*

W: *Four hours! He hates walking. He only walks from the front door to his car.*

R: *Oh, don't worry. When they get to the top of the mountain, they have a twenty-minute break before they come down again.*

W: *And what about the afternoon? Will he relax?*

R: *No, not really. He'll go to the gym in the afternoon. But he'll have time to relax in the evening.*

W: *Oh my goodness. I don't think he'll thank me for this.*

R: *Believe me, when he finishes the week, he'll feel like a new man.*

W: *If he finishes the week!*

2 3.14

- Go through the information about *will* in the margin and explain that it's used to talk and ask questions about the future. So far the students have used *going to* to talk about decisions that have been made for the future and the present continuous for future arrangements. Here, the future isn't definitely decided or arranged yet – *will* is a more general way of referring to the future. Spend some time making sure the students can pronounce *won't* /wəʊnt/ correctly and make sure that they can distinguish it from *want* /wɒnt/.

- Ask the students to complete the questions and answers and then play the recording for them to check.

a) 'Will he take a fitness test?'
   'Yes, he will.' 'No, he won't.'
b) 'Will he do yoga?'
   'Yes, he will.' 'No, he won't.'
c) 'Will he have a cigarette?'
   'Yes, he will.' 'No, he won't.'
d) 'Will he have a sauna and a jacuzzi?'
   'Yes, he will.' 'No, he won't.'
e) 'Will he go for a four-hour walk?'
   'Yes, he will.' 'No, he won't.'
f) 'Will he have time to relax in the afternoon?'
   'Yes, he will.' 'No, he won't.'

Language notes

Grammar: *will*

- *Will* is a modal verb and is used to express a number of functions such as offers (*I'll help her*), promises (*She'll be there at 10 a.m.*), requests (*Will you get me a newspaper?*), orders (*I'll have the steak*) and predictions (*It'll rain tomorrow – it always rains at the weekend*). *Will* is also used to make general statements (of fact) about the future (*The stadium will be used for all national events*). In this unit *will* is used to express predictions and to make statements of fact about the future.

- The negative of *will* is *will not*. The contraction of *will* is *'ll* and the contraction of *will not* is *won't*. The contractions *'ll* and *won't* are more commonly used than the full form in statements, while in questions and short answers the full form is always used.

  Statement: He'll do a yoga class.
  Question: Will he relax?
  Short answer: Yes, he will. (not ~~Yes, he'll.~~)

- *Will* is always followed by the infinitive without *to*.

3

- Pairwork. Ask the students to take turns to ask and answer the questions in Exercise 2 according to what they heard on the recording.

- Still in the pairs, students discuss health spas or the equivalent in their country and whether or not they would like to go to one. Go round, monitoring and giving help with vocabulary.

a) Yes, he will.
b) Yes, he will.
c) No, he won't.
d) Yes, he will.
e) Yes, he will.
f) No, he won't.

Grammar (SB page 89)

Future time clauses

1

- Focus the students' attention on the information in the margin. Read out the first two example sentences and make sure everyone notices the present form verb in the subordinate clause and the future form in the main clause. Point out that the order of the clauses can be reversed.

- Go through the examples in the table with the class and ask them to discuss the questions in pairs.

a) Future time.	d) if
b) will	e) when
c) Present simple.	f) as soon as

Language notes

Grammar: Future time clauses with *if, as soon as, when*

- It is important to establish that in future time clauses, after the conjunctions *if, as soon as* and *when*, you use a present simple form. (*If it rains, we'll play indoors* not ~~If it will rain, we'll play indoors~~).

- It is the main clause that takes the future form and can be placed at the beginning or at the end of a sentence. For example:
  He'll take a fitness test as soon as he arrives.
  As soon as he arrives, he'll take a fitness test.

  Note the difference in punctuation in the two sentences.

2

- Ask the students to work individually to underline the correct verb forms.

- Go round as they do this and help anyone who's having difficulty. Check answers with the class before asking them to rewrite the sentences so that they are true for them. Ask several students to read out their new sentences.

a) 'll go	d) 'm
b) finishes	e) have
c) go	f) 'll go

3 Grammar *Extra* 10, Part 1

Ask the students to turn to *Grammar Extra* 10, Part 1 on page 144 of the Student's Book. Here they'll find an explanation of the grammar they've been studying and further exercises to practise it.

1	2
a) I'll lend	a) finishes
b) you won't be	b) meets
c) Dom will love	c) gets home
d) Anna will get	d) rains
e) We won't arrive	e) goes
f) They won't play	f) leaves

Vocabulary (SB page 90)

1

- Ask the students to look at shopping list and the photos. Tell them to tick the items on the shopping list which are shown in the photos (the items that Nick bought). They should then have five items unticked (the ones he forgot). If you wish, you could have the students work in pairs and make this a race, with the first pair to identify the five forgotten items as the winners.

- Check answers with the class and help them with any items that presented difficulties.

> Forgotten: oranges, tomatoes, carrots, sardines and tea

2

Ask the students to work individually to look at the list again and follow the instructions in the task. When they've finished, allow them to compare their results in pairs. Then have a class feedback session. Find out which are the most popular and the least popular food items on the shopping list.

Pronunciation (SB page 90)

1 🌐 3.15

- Point out that the vowels sounds which are featured here are printed in red. Focus attention on the example. Students may be surprised that *lettuce* and *spinach* both contain the same vowel sound /ɪ/.

- Play the recording and ask the students to listen and repeat, paying particular attention to the vowel sounds in red.

- When they've done this chorally, ask for individual repetition. Make sure everyone can pronounce the more difficult items, such as *lettuce* /ˈletɪs/, *aubergine* /ˈəʊbəʒiːn/, *spinach* /ˈspɪnɪdʒ/ and *cauliflower* /ˈkɒliːflaʊə/ correctly.

2 🌐 3.16

- Ask the students to work individually to match the words in the two columns. Encourage them to say the words aloud as they do this in order to get a feel for what sounds right.

- Play the recording for them to check their own answers and then check with the class.

- See if everyone agrees on which word is the most difficult to say. Give extra practice in saying this word.

> a) 3   b) 1   c) 5   d) 4   e) 6   f) 2

Reading & Vocabulary (SB page 91)

1

- Find out by a show of hands who in the class likes or doesn't like bananas. Ask them to give details about how they eat them. For example, do they peel the skin down in strips (if so, how many), hold it by the end and bite bits off, or do they take the whole skin off and slice it with a knife? If students show interest in this, extend the questions to how they prepare and eat other fruit, such as apples (e.g. Do they eat the peel? Can they get the peel off in one long strip? Do they slice the apple before eating it? Do they eat the core?). Ask similar questions about oranges and grapes.
- Ask the students to read the text about bananas and mark the dishes they would and wouldn't like to try.
- In a feedback session, find out if there is consensus on which dishes are preferred and if the students know of any other dishes that are made with bananas.

2

- Ask the students to work individually to find the words in the text.
- Allow them to compare their results in pairs before checking with the class.

> a) peel, cut, mix, slice, chop
> b) boil, fry, grill, bake
> c) raw

Extra activity

- Ask the students to think about food items from the previous page which they can boil, peel, fry, etc. For example, you can peel an orange, an apple, a potato, a carrot, etc.
- Select one item of food and ask the students to decide how many things you can do with it, e.g. *an onion – peel it, slice it, chop it, fry it,* etc.

3

- Give the students a minute or two to think about their favourite dish. Emphasise that it doesn't have to contain bananas. Ask them to think about the questions and make brief notes (but not write down whole sentences). Go round, monitoring and giving help with vocabulary.
- Put the students into pairs and ask them to use their notes as prompts to help them talk about their favourite dishes.

Speaking: anecdote (SB page 91)

For more information about how to set up, monitor and repeat Anecdotes, see page xx in the Introduction.

1 3.17

- Ask the students to look at the photo of Darren. Explain that someone called Josh is going to talk about Darren, who's the fittest/healthiest person he knows.
- Go through the questions and the answer choices with the class. Explain any unknown vocabulary and then ask the students to listen and underline the answers Josh gives.
- Check answers with the class and ask them whether they know anyone like Darren.

> a) cousin   e) runs up mountains
> b) 26   f) high-calorie
> c) an army officer   g) really lazy
> d) tall and well-built

> 🌐 3.17
>
> *The fittest person I know is my cousin, Darren. He's twenty-six and he's training to be an army officer. Darren's tall and well-built and he looks fantastic in his uniform. He's also very strong, and he has amazing stamina. For his training, he has to do really difficult exercises. For example, he has to run up mountains carrying about forty kilos of equipment on his back. That's almost like carrying a person! He has to eat a really high-calorie diet, but he's always loved his food so that's not too difficult for him. He says he's enjoying the training, but it's hard to believe because he used to be so lazy. When he was a student, he never got up before midday, and he never did any housework. Now, he gets up at 5.30 in the morning, and he has to iron his uniform every day!*

2

- Give the students a minute or two to decide who they're going to talk about. Then ask them to look at the questions in Exercise 1 again and decide how they'd answer them about the person they're going to talk about. Allow them to make notes of what they're going to say and how they're going to say it, but discourage them from writing a paragraph that they can simply read out. Go round, monitoring and giving help.
- Pairwork. Put the students in pairs and ask them to take turns to tell their partner about the fittest/healthiest person they know. Encourage them to ask each other follow-up questions to get further information.
- Ask some pairs to report back to the class about what they found out.

Reading (SB page 92)

Warm-up

Introduce the idea of cars by finding out the students' attitudes to them. Ask them to arrange themselves in a line with people who positively dislike cars at one end, those who are fairly indifferent to them and just regard them as a convenience, somewhere towards the middle, and those who love them and see them as objects of beauty at the other end. Go along the line and ask for a few individual opinions.

1 ● 3.18

- Go through the instructions with the class and then ask them to read the descriptions as they listen to the recording and match them to the photos.
- Check answers with the class and answer any questions about vocabulary.

> a) 2   b) 3   c) 1

2

Ask the students to cover the descriptions and see if they can answer the questions from memory. Read each question aloud in turn and ask the students to say which car they think it is. Allow people with different opinions to try to persuade each other to change their minds. At the end, ask them to uncover the descriptions and check their answers.

> a) Citroen 2CV
> b) Porsche
> c) Citroen 2CV
> d) VW Beetle
> e) Porsche
> f) VW Beetle

3

Pairwork. Put the students into pairs to talk about their first car or their first experience of travelling in a car. Encourage them to report any interesting experiences to the class.

Vocabulary (SB page 93)

1

- You could set this up as a race with the first student or pair of students to find all six car parts as the winners.

> windscreen wiper, sunroof, engine, boot, steering wheel, seats

Extra activity

Draw the outline of a car on the board and ask the students to label it with the words from Exercise 1. Then invite them to add any other car parts they know.

2

Go through the features in the box with the class and make sure that they understand all of them. Then ask the students to work individually to categorise the features according to how important they think they are. Put them in pairs to compare answers and find out how much consensus there is around the class.

Grammar (SB page 93)

used to + infinitive

1

- Go through the information in the margin with the students and explain that you use *used to* to talk about repeated actions that happened (or states that were true) in the past, but which no longer happen (or are true) now. Draw their attention to the fact that the question form is *Did he use to ...?* and not *Did he used to ...?*
- Ask the students to look at the extracts from the texts on page 92 in pairs and to match the underlined verbs with the descriptions.
- Check answers with the class and then ask them if it's possible to use *used to* + infinitive to talk about a single action in the past.

> a) 2   b) 1   c) 3
>
> No, it isn't possible to use the structure to talk about a single action in the past.

2

- Pairwork. Go through the example with the class. You may like to point out that the past simple has been underlined in each sentence. Ask the students to work in pairs to replace it with *used to* or *didn't used to* + infinitive where this is possible.

- Check answers with the class and then ask the students to work individually to change the sentences so that they are true for them. They can then compare with a partner before you ask several students to read out their altered sentences.

> a) my parents used to have …
> b) my mother used to drive …
> c) I didn't use to like; I used to get …
> d) –
> e) my father never used to wash; It always used to look …
> f) – ; –

3 Pairwork

- The pairwork exercise for this unit is on pages 119 and 124 of the Student's Book. Put the students in pairs and tell them who will be Student A, and who will be Student B.

- While they're doing the exercise, go round monitoring and giving help. Take note of any errors which may need particular attention later, and also any examples of good language use which you can praise in a feedback session.

4 Grammar *Extra* 10, Part 2

Ask students to turn to *Grammar Extra* 10, Part 2 on page 144 of the Student's Book. Here they'll find an explanation of the grammar they've been studying and further exercises to practise it.

1	2
1 did your dad use to do	a) –
2 used to be	b) used to live
3 Did he use to enjoy	c) used to share
4 used to say	d) used to have
5 didn't use to like	e) used to watch
6 used to leave	f) used to give
7 didn't use to arrive	g) –
8 used to get	h) didn't use to
9 Did your dad use to earn	enjoy
10 used to have	
11 used to eat out	
12 used to tell	

Speaking: anecdote (SB page 93)

For more information about how to set up, monitor and repeat Anecdotes, see page xx in the Introduction.

1 🔘 3.19

- Ask the students to look at the photo. Tell them that a woman called Patti is going to talk about her dream car. Explain that the expression *a dream car* is used to refer to the car that you'd most like to own, not to a car you've seen in a dream. Similar common expressions include *dream kitchen*, *dream holiday*, *dream job*, etc.

- Go through the questions and the answer choices with the class. Explain any unknown vocabulary and ask the students to listen and underline the answers Patti gives.

- Check answers with the class and ask them whether their dream car would be like Patti's.

> a) Chevrolet
> b) old
> c) black
> d) spacious
> e) Brown leather
> f) Elvis
> g) My friends
> h) Down 5th Avenue in New York

> 🔘 **3.19**
>
> *My dream car is an old car. I love cars from the fifties or sixties, and my favourite is a Chevrolet. A really big, old Chevrolet. It has to be black – definitely black – with a silver bumper and big flashy headlights. Inside, it's really spacious with plenty of room to stretch your legs. The seats are soft and made of leather. Red leather. No, brown leather. Brown is more sophisticated. Oh, and there's a beautiful old radio with Elvis playing really loud. I love Elvis. I'd like to take all my friends out in my car. I can imagine wearing glamorous evening clothes and going to a fancy restaurant in New York. As we drive down Fifth Avenue, everybody turns to look at our fabulous car …*

Cultural notes

Elvis Presley /elvɪs ˈprezli/ (1935–1977)
An American singer, musician and actor, Elvis Presley is known as 'The King' (of Rock and Roll). The teenage Presley got his break in 1953. Over the next two decades Presley became an international star with recordings like *Jailhouse Rock* (1957), *It's Now or Never* (1960) and *Suspicious Minds* (1969). From 1973, Presley's health declined. He put on weight and became increasingly dependent on prescription drugs. In 1977 he died of a heart attack at the age of forty-two.

George Clooney (born 1961)
(See notes about George Clooney in Review C, page 94.)

2

- Give the students a minute or two to decide what their dream car would be like. Then ask them to look at the questions in Exercise 1 again and decide how they'd answer them about their dream car. Allow them to make notes of what they're going to say and how they're going to say it, but discourage them from writing a paragraph that they can simply read out. Go round, monitoring and giving help.

- Pairwork. Put the students in pairs and ask them to take turns to tell their partner about their dream car. Encourage them to ask each other follow-up questions to get further information.

- Ask some pairs to report back to the class about what they found out.

Useful phrases (SB page 94)

1

- Focus the students' attention on the pictures and ask the students what they can see.

- Ask the students to read the conversations and match them to the pictures. Tell them not to worry about the alternatives at this point.

a) 2	b) 4	c) 5	d) 1	e) 3

2 🌐 3.20

- Focus the students' attention on the choices in the conversations. Point out that these are parts of idioms involving food. Ask them what they think the first one means: they should be able to guess from the context that it means the opposite of *tired* – something like *lively* or *energetic*. Then ask them to say which of the choices they think might convey this idea (*beans*).

- Ask the students to work in pairs or small groups and to use the same technique (deciding on meaning from context and then choosing the most likely-sounding option) to complete the remaining expressions.

- Play the recording for the students to check their answers. You may need to point out that *packed in like sardines* comes from the way sardines are traditionally sold in the UK, lying in tight rows in a tin. Ask them if they think any of the idioms are particularly appropriate, and whether they have any idioms like these in their own language(s).

a) beans	b) cheese	c) tea	d) cake
e) sardines			

3 🌐 3.21

- Ask the students to work individually to replace the underlined phrases with the food idioms from the conversations in Exercise 1.

- Play the recording for them to check their answers and then play it a second time for them to listen and repeat the sentences.

- Ask the students to discuss in pairs whether the sentences are true for them or not.

a) a piece of cake	d) full of beans
b) packed in like sardines	e) not my cup of tea
c) like chalk and cheese	

Extra activity

Ask the students to write another conversation using at least two of the useful phrases.

Vocabulary *Extra* (SB page 95)

Cars

1

- Focus the students' attention on the list of words and point out that they're all to do with parts of a car. Remind students that the underlining indicates the syllable of the word that has the strongest stress. Check that the students can pronounce the words correctly.

- Ask students to look at the pictures and ask them to match the numbers in the pictures with the car parts.

4 bonnet	12 seat belt
3 boot	10 steering wheel
5 bumper	1 sunroof
11 gear stick	7 tyre
13 handbrake	8 wheel
6 number plate	2 windscreen
14 seat	9 windscreen wipers

2

Pairwork. Ask the students to cover the words and take turns to test each other by pointing at parts of the pictures and asking what the things are. Go through the example questions with the class first.

Focus on words used with driving

1

Go through this exercise with the class, reading out each sentence half in turn and asking the students to match it with the correct ending.

a) 2	b) 5	c) 1	d) 6	e) 3	f) 4

2

Ask the students to work individually to complete the questions. Check answers before putting them into pairs to take turns asking and answering the questions.

a) overtaking b) down c) petrol
d) hour e) jams f) lift

Further practice material

Need more writing practice?

→ Workbook page 63
• Writing a narrative.

Need more classroom practice activities?

→ Photocopiable resource materials pages
  181 to 183
  Grammar: *Then or now?*
  Vocabulary: *Features of a car*
  Communication: *Food*
→ Top 10 activities pages xv to xx

Need progress tests?

→ Test CD – *Test Unit 10*

Need more on important teaching concepts?

→ Key concepts in *New Inside Out* pages
  xxii to xxxv

Need student self-study practice?

→ CD-ROM – Unit 10: *Lifestyle*

Need student CEF self-evaluation?

→ CEF Checklists pages xxxvii to xliv

Need more information and more ideas?

→ www.insideout.net

11 Animals *Overview*

Section & Aims	What the students are doing
Reading & Speaking SB page 96 Reading for detail	Reading and answering a questionnaire about animals. Discussing their opinions about animals. Commenting on their discussions.
Listening SB page 97 Listening for specific information	Talking about animals they like and dislike. Listening and ticking the animals the people mention. Underlining correct information and rewriting the sentences so they are true for people in the class.
Vocabulary SB page 97 Adjective + preposition	Adding prepositions to sentences and completing them to make some true and some false. Guessing which of a partner's statements are true.
Vocabulary SB page 98 Animals	Matching animals with their defining characteristics. Listing animals or insects for every letter of the alphabet.
Reading & Vocabulary SB page 98 Reading for gist and detail	Matching animals to descriptions and checking answers in a text. Identifying true and false sentences. Replacing words in sentences with expressions from stories.
Grammar SB page 99 Defining relative clauses	Studying the structure and use of defining relative clauses. Using *that* to combine sentences and replacing *that* with *which* or *who*. Correcting sentences. Matching sentences to words.
Pronunciation SB page 100 Words with the same sound but different meaning	Listening to and repeating pairs of words. Matching words with the correct meanings.
Listening SB page 100 Listening for detail	Identifying the questions which an interviewer asks about pets. Ticking the characteristics of pets mentioned. Talking about characteristics they look for in pets and people.
Grammar SB page 101 Unreal conditionals	Studying the structure and meaning of unreal conditional sentences. Completing a table with conditional sentences. Completing moral dilemmas and discussing their answers.
Speaking: anecdote SB page 101 Fluency practice	Talking about pets.
Useful phrases SB page 102 Useful conversational phrases for making polite requests	Finding out who's going to look after someone's pet snake. Completing a table with useful phrases. Listening to and repeating useful phrases. Writing and practising conversations.
Vocabulary *Extra* SB page 103 Revision of words from the unit: animals; insects; *that*	Matching pictures with words. Completing a table with examples using *that* and writing their own examples.
Writing WB page 67	Giving opinions.

11 Animals *Teacher's notes*

Reading & Speaking (SB page 96)

1

- Focus the students' attention on the photos and ask what's different about the circumstances of the three animals shown (one is domesticated, one in a zoo and the other in the wild).
- Tell the students to read the questionnaire and tick the options that best describe their own attitudes to animals. Ask them to work individually.

2

Groupwork. Ask the students to work in small groups and discuss their opinions. Go round, monitoring and giving help with vocabulary. Ask one student in each group to make notes of their discussion as these will be needed for the next exercise.

3

Ask a representative from each group to present the results of their discussion to the class.

Listening (SB page 97)

1

- Ask the students to look at the animals and insects in the photos. Ask them which ones are pets, which ones you can find in a zoo and which in the wild.
- Pairwork. Ask the students to discuss which animals they like or dislike.

2 🔘 **3.22**

- Ask the students to listen to three people talking about animals and to tick the animals in Exercise 1 that they mention. You may need to play the recording more than once.

> bull, lion, crocodile, mouse, frog, eagle, cat, horse, dog

🔘 **3.22** (I = Interviewer; R = Richard; A = Alicia; H = Harry)

Richard

I: So, Richard, which animals do you like or dislike?

R: I like dogs and I hate cats.

I: Oh, why?

R: Because I'm allergic to cats.

I: Oh I see.

R: But I'm interested in wild birds. In fact I'm writing a book on South American eagles. I find the Black-chested Buzzard Eagle particularly fascinating.

I: Gosh. Um, are there any animals you're afraid of?

R: Yes, bulls. I once went camping in southern Spain. When I put the tent up, there weren't any animals in the field, but when I woke up, I could see this shadow outside the tent – a big shadow. And I could hear heavy breathing.

I: Oh my goodness. A bull?

R: No, actually it was a cow. A very big cow. But I thought it was a bull.

Alicia

I: Which animals do you like or dislike, Alicia?

A: Well, I like most animals but I'm particularly keen on horses. I think they're wonderful, beautiful animals. I don't like mice, obviously. And I really can't stand frogs. Urggh, they're horrible.

I: Are you afraid of frogs?

A: Afraid? I'm terrified of them.

I: Are there any other animals you're afraid of?

A: Well, most wild animals. I don't think I'd like to meet a lion or a crocodile in the street. I enjoy watching documentaries about them, but I wouldn't have one as a pet. ➤

Harry

I: *And Harry, which animals do you like or dislike?*

H: *I'm fond of all animals.*

I: *Have you ever had any experience of wild animals?*

H: *Yes. I used to work in a zoo.*

I: *Oh, lovely.*

H: *You wouldn't think it was lovely if you were an animal. How would you like to live in a cage?*

I: *Oh no, that would be, um … Are there any animals you're afraid of?*

H: *No, I'm afraid of humans.*

I: *Well, thank you for your help. Bye.*

3

• Go through the sentences with the class and make sure everyone understands them. You may need to explain *allergic* (a condition in which certain things, such as cats, pollen, certain foods, etc. make the sufferer come out in a rash, start sneezing or make their eyes water, etc.).

• Play the recording again and ask the students to underline the correct alternatives. Check answers with the class before asking the students to rewrite the sentences using the names of people in the class. Then go through the example question and answer with the class, and with weaker classes elicit the questions they'll need to find out the other information. Allow the students to mingle and check how many they got correct.

a) cats	d) frogs
b) wild birds	e) all animals
c) horses	f) humans

Vocabulary (SB page 97)

1

• Focus the students' attention on the example and point out that the sentence has been completed with the preposition *on* and a noun *football*. Ask various students around the class if they're keen on football, keen on animals, etc.

• Ask the students to work individually to complete the remaining sentences. Remind them that they need a preposition and a noun each time and that some of their sentences should be true and some false. Go round, monitoring and giving help.

2

• Pairwork. Ask the students to work in pairs and to exchange the statements they wrote in Exercise 1.

• Ask them to read their partner's statements and to decide which ones they think are true and which false. They can then check with their partner.

Vocabulary (SB page 98)

1

• Look at the example with the class and then give the students time to read the defining characteristics and match them to the animal they refer to.

• Allow the students to compare results in pairs before checking answers with the class. Answer any questions about vocabulary and ask if the students know any more surprising facts about animals. If they know a lot, perhaps they could prepare a matching activity like the one in this exercise to test other students.

| a) 4 b) 6 c) 2 d) 1 e) 3 f) 5 |

2

• Groupwork. Look at the example with the class and then give the groups three minutes to prepare their lists.

• When the three minutes is up, stop the class and find out which group has the longest list. Ask them to read out their list to the class. Invite other teams to call out alternative animals that they put on their lists.

• If you want to make this more of a competition, award one point for every correct animal or insect that each team has listed, and an extra point if it's an animal or insect that no other team got. Explain the points system in advance so that the teams can choose whether to spend time thinking of unusual animals for each letter, or to simply list as many as they can in the time limit.

Extra activity

As an alternative to Exercise 2, students could be encouraged to brainstorm as many animals as they know in the following categories:

• in houses (domestic)
• in the countryside
• on a farm
• in the sea/rivers
• in the wild/a zoo

Reading & Vocabulary (SB page 98)

1 🌐 3.23

• Focus the students' attention on the three photos. Read out the three descriptions, or get individual students to read them out, and ask the students to decide which animal goes best with each description.

• Play the recording and ask the students to read the stories as they listen.

a) mynah bird (story 1)
b) cow (story 3)
c) cat (story 2)

Cultural note

Mozart /ˈməʊtsaːt/ (1756–1791)
An Austrian composer with precocious talent,
by the age of six Wolfgang Amadeus Mozart was
writing his own compositions. By the time he
died, in 1791, at the age of thirty-five, he'd already
written over 600 compositions. People have long
believed Mozart's music to have a relaxing effect
and an aid to concentration. But recently a Spanish
farmer has found that playing Mozart to his cows
has significantly improved how much milk his
cows produce. His yield has increased between one
and six litres a day in a phenomenon now known
as the 'Mozart Effect'.

2

- Give the students time to read the stories again.
Then ask them to decide if the statements are true
or false. (Tell them to ignore the underlined words
at this stage.) You might like to read each one aloud
in turn and get the students to vote on whether it's
true or false.

- Check answers with the class and explain any
difficult vocabulary.

a) True.   b) False.   c) False.   d) True.
e) False.   f) False.   g) True.

3

Ask the students to look at the underlined words in
each statement in Exercise 2. Ask them to look back at
the stories and find words and expressions which they
can use instead of the underlined parts. Check answers
before asking the students to comment on the stories
and tell a partner any other animal stories they know.

a) travels away from home – goes away
b) contacts – gets in touch with
c) arrive – turn up
d) look after – keep an eye on
e) typed – keyed in
f) stop the car – pull up
g) left – walked off

Grammar (SB page 99)
Defining relative clauses

1

- Go through the information in the margin with the
class and read out the example sentences. Point
out that the relative clauses are used to combine
ideas to make one sentence. Do the first part of the
exercise with the class, reminding them to refer to the
information in margin to see which relative pronouns
can and can't be used.

- Then ask the students to work individually to
complete the rules.

a) that / ~~which~~ / who
b) that / which / ~~who~~
1 who   2 which   3 that

Language notes

Grammar: Defining relative clauses

- A defining relative clause gives essential
information about the noun or noun phrase it
describes. The defining relative clause joins two
ideas together with a relative pronoun (*who*,
which, *that*).

  For example these two sentences: *I've got a friend.
  He lives in the United States,* become one sentence
  when the relative pronoun *who* replaces the
  pronoun *he*: *I've got a friend **who** lives in the
  Unites States*.

  The relative pronoun *who* is used when talking
  about people (and replaces the pronoun *he* or
  she); *which* is used when talking about things (and
  replaces the pronoun *it*). The relative pronoun
  that can be used to talk about people or things in
  a defining relative clause, although it's mainly
  used in spoken English rather than written.

2

- Go through the example with the class and then ask
the students to work individually to combine the
other sentences. Go round, monitoring and giving
help.

- Check answers with the class before asking the
students to do the second part of the exercise. When
checking answers, find out which sentences are true
for the students.

a) I've got a dog that likes going for long walks.
b) I've got a car that isn't very easy to park.
c) I've got a sister that works in a shop.
d) I've got an espresso machine that makes great coffee.
e) I've got a friend that lives in the USA.
f) I've got some shoes that are too small for me.

a) which   b) which   c) who   d) which
e) who   f) which

3

• Look at the example with the class and explain that each sentence has one word that isn't needed.

• Check answers to the first part of the exercise before asking the students to match the words to the definitions.

a) A person who she treats sick animals.
b) The only animal – apart from humans – which it gets sunburn.
c) A name for people who they are afraid of spiders.
d) A person who he studies birds.
e) The scientist who he developed the theory of evolution.
f) The largest animal that it has ever lived.

1 c)   2 d)   3 a)   4 e)   5 b)   6 f)

Cultural note

Charles Darwin /tʃɑːlz ˈdɑːwɪn/ (1809–1882)
A British naturalist whose travels by sea around the world resulted in his theory of evolution as set out in the book *On the Origin of Species* (1859). Darwin's work had a tremendous impact on religious thought. Many people strongly opposed the idea of evolution because it conflicted with their religious convictions.

4 Pairwork

• The pairwork exercise for this unit is on pages 120 and 125 of the Student's Book. Put the students in pairs and tell them who will be Student A, and who will be Student B.

• While they're doing the exercise, go round monitoring and giving help.

5 Grammar *Extra* 11, Part 1

Ask students to turn to Grammar Extra 11, Part 1 on page 146 of the Student's Book. Here they'll find an explanation of the grammar they've been studying and further exercises to practise it.

1
a) 'A camel is a horse *that* has been designed by a committee.'
b) 'Everybody knows how to raise children – except the people *who* have them.'
c) 'How can you govern a country *that* has 246 varieties of cheese?'
d) 'Go on, get out! Last words are for fools *who* haven't said enough.'
e) 'Life is something *that* happens when you can't get to sleep.'
f) 'A bank is a place *that* will lend you money if you can prove you don't need it.'
g) 'Women *who* want to be equal with men don't have ambition.'
h) 'People *who* get nostalgic about childhood were obviously never children.'

2
a) Most of the people who work with me speak perfect English.
b) People who complain all the time make me angry.
c) I've met lots of people who have the same name as me.
d) We should ban cars that use too much petrol.
e) I think dictionaries that don't give good examples are useless.
f) The family who live next door have a dog and a cat.

Pronunciation (SB page 100)

1 🌐 **3.24**

• Focus the students' attention on the pairs of words in the left-hand column. Play the recording once and ask the students to say what they notice about the pairs of words.

• Play the recording again and ask the students to listen and repeat the pairs of words. When they've done this chorally, ask for individual repetition of the words.

The two words are pronounced the same but are spelt differently.

Language note

Pronunciation: homophones

Words which are pronounced the same but have different spellings are called *homophones*. This activity focuses on some common homophones. For more, see Activity 11 *Communication: Homophones* in the Resource Materials section at the back of this Teacher's Book.

2

- Ask the students to match the words in Exercise 1 with their meanings.
- Check answers with the class and then ask about words in their own language(s) which sound the same but have different spellings and meanings.

> a) 3   b) 1   c) 2   d) 5   e) 4

Listening (SB page 100)

1 🌐 3.25

- Ask the students to look at the photos and explain that they show three people and their pets. Ask them whether they think these are unusual pets or not. You might like to ask if they'd like any of these animals as a pet.
- Explain that they're going to listen to the three people being interviewed about their pets. Ask them to read the questions and then listen and decide which questions the interviewer asked.
- Check answers with the class and see what the students can remember about what each person said about their pet.

> a, c, e, and f

> 🌐 3.25
>
> Tim
> (I = Interviewer; T = Tim)
> I: Can you describe your pet?
> T: She's very fat and not very pretty. But she's got a lovely curly tail.
> I: Is she a good companion?
> T: Yes, absolutely. I always tell her my problems, and she listens.
> I: Do you and your pet look alike?
> T: I hope not.
> I: If you were an animal, what would you like to be?
> T: A dolphin. I love the sea, and dolphins are intelligent and funny – like me!
>
> Gus
> (I = Interviewer; G = Gus)
> I: Can you describe your pet?
> G: He's black and has eight hairy legs.
> I: Is he a good companion?
> G: Yeah. He's like a friend. But other people are afraid of him. He frightens people away.
> I: Do you and your pet look alike?
> G: I'm not that hairy – but I think he looks cool, like me.
> I: If you were an animal, what would you like to be?
> G: A lion, because they're big and tough and they rule.

> Maxine
> (I = Interviewer; M = Maxine)
> I: Can you describe your pet?
> M: She's very fluffy and very loveable. My boyfriend doesn't like her because she bit him – she doesn't like men.
> I: Is she a good companion?
> M: Yes, she's good company for me when my boyfriend goes away on business. And she enjoys doing the same things as me – she loves to sleep all day and party all night long.
> I: Do you and your pet look alike?
> M: I think that she's better looking than me – who could resist those brown eyes?
> I: If you were an animal, what would you like to be?
> M: I am an animal. Miaow.

Extra activity

In pairs, students interview each other about their pets using the questions in Exercise 1.

2

- Go through the characteristics with the class and ask them to tick the things that they think Tim, Gus and Maxine mentioned in their interviews. Allow them to work in pairs if they wish.
- Play the interviews again for the students to check their answers.

> ✓: a), b), d), f), g)

3

- Pairwork. Ask the students to discuss the questions in pairs. Go round, monitoring and giving help. Ask several pairs to report back to the class.
- In a follow-up feedback session, allow students to share information about their own pets if they wish.

Grammar (SB page 101)
Unreal conditionals

1

- Remind the students that one of the questions in the interviews in the previous section was *If you were an animal, what would you like to be?* Ask the students if it's possible to be an animal. Point out that it's possible to talk about imaginary situations: it's true that no one can actually be an animal, but they can talk about what kind of animal they'd like to be if they could be one.
- Go through the example sentences in the margin and ask the students what they'd like to be if they were animals.

- Focus the students' attention on the table and go through the structure of unreal conditional sentences with the class. Elicit answers to the questions under the table.

- Check answers and then ask the students to make further questions using the words in the box or their own ideas. Put them in pairs to take turns asking and answering their questions.

> a) Imaginary situation.
> b) Now.
> c) Past simple.

Language notes

Grammar: unreal conditionals

- The type of conditional in this unit is also known as the 'second conditional'. There are two clauses in this type of sentence: the *if* clause (*if* followed by the verb in the past simple form), and the main clause (*would* followed by the infinitive without *to*). For example:
  If I *was* an animal, (*if* + past simple form) **I'*d be* a cat.** (*would* + infinitive).

- The clauses can be reversed without changing the meaning, but the punctuation changes:
  When the *if* clause comes after the main clause they aren't separated by a comma.
  When the *if* clause comes before the main clause they are separated by a comma.

- The examples in this unit relate to a hypothetical or imaginary present, and not the past. *If* is followed by the past simple form to 'remove it one step from reality', not because the situation relates to the past.

2

- Ask the students to work individually to complete the right-hand column with conditional sentences. As they work, go round offering extra help to anyone who's having difficulties with the concept or structure of unreal conditionals.

- When they've finished, ask them to compare their sentences with a partner. Put any particularly good or imaginative sentences on the board.

3

- Introduce the idea of a 'moral dilemma': a situation in which several courses of action are possible and a person is required to choose what to do. That choice may be 'moral', in that it's the right thing to do (by society's standards of right and wrong), or the thing that will cause the least harm to anyone. Alternatively, some people may choose the course of action that will benefit themselves the most.

- Go through the situations with the class and make sure that everyone understands them. Ask the students to complete them with the correct verb forms. Check answers with the class before moving on to the next stage of the exercise.

- Put the students into small groups to discuss what they'd do in these situations. When they've finished, ask them to think of some more moral dilemmas. Get them to write these out properly and check that they've formed their questions correctly. You can then ask them to exchange them with other groups and discuss each other's new moral dilemmas. Have a feedback session in which groups report back to the class on what they decided.

> a) found   c) gave
> b) would you tell   d) would you look

4 Grammar *Extra* 11, Part 2

Ask students to turn to *Grammar Extra* 11, Part 2 on page 146 of the Student's Book. Here they'll find an explanation of the grammar they've been studying and further exercises to practise it.

> a) could sing; 'd join
> b) won; 'd give
> c) was/were; wouldn't be
> d) had; 'd read
> e) didn't work; wouldn't be
> f) lost; 'd have to

Speaking: anecdote (SB page 101)

For more information about how to set up, monitor and repeat Anecdotes, see page xx in the Introduction.

1 🌐 3.26

- Ask the students to look at the photo. Explain that someone called Mandy is going to talk about her friend in the photo and his pet.

- Go through the questions and the answer choices with the class. Explain any unknown vocabulary and then ask the students to listen and underline the answers Mandy gives.

- Check answers with the class and ask them whether they know anyone like Angus who has an unusual pet.

> a) iguana
> b) Angus
> c) Iggy
> d) five
> e) green and almost a metre long
> f) the curtains
> g) Vegetables
> h) goes for walks in the park

3.26

I know somebody who's got an iguana as a pet. It's a man I work with called Angus. The iguana is called Iggy and it's probably about five years old – that's how long I've known Angus and he got it soon after we met. It was a birthday present from his wife. It's almost a metre long from the tip of its nose to the end of its tail and it's a lovely green colour. Like all reptiles, iguanas never stop growing, so Iggy will get bigger and bigger. It's quite shy and nervous, which is exactly the opposite of Angus, who's very outgoing and confident. It's definitely better looking than Angus though. Iggy doesn't sleep in a cage. At the moment, it lives at the top of the curtains in Angus' living room. When it was young, it ate crickets, but now it's adult it doesn't need so much protein – in fact it's completely vegetarian. Angus takes it for walks in the park on a lead. It's funny – when it's frightened, it runs up Angus's body and sits on his head.

2

- Give the students a minute or two to decide what they're going to talk about. Then ask them to look at the questions in Exercise 1 again and decide how they'd answer them about the pet they're going to talk about. Allow them to make notes of what they're going to say and how they're going to say it, but discourage them from writing a paragraph that they can simply read out. Go round, monitoring and giving help.

- Pairwork. Put the students in pairs and ask them to take turns to tell their partner about their pet or a pet they know. Encourage them to ask each other follow-up questions to get further information.

- Ask some pairs to report back to the class about what they found out.

Useful phrases (SB page 102)

1 3.27

- Focus the students' attention on the illustration. Explain that the students are going to hear telephone conversations between Sarah, the women in the picture, and four people she's going to ask to take care of her pet this weekend.

- Play the recording for them to listen, read and decide who will look after Molly. Check answers with the class and ask if any of the students would be willing to look after a friend's pet snake.

Mrs Harvey is going to look after Molly.

2 3.28

- Ask the students to work in pairs to complete the table.

- Check answers with the class, then play the recording for them to listen and repeat the useful phrases.

1 Could you look after Molly?
2 Oh, I'm afraid I can't.
3 Do you think you could look after Molly?
4 I'd really like to help, but I'm afraid I can't.
5 Oh yes, that's no problem at all.
6 That's wonderful.

3

Ask the students to look closely at the phrases in the completed table in Exercise 2 and to choose the correct alternative to complete the sentence.

more

4

- Pairwork. Go through the situations with the class. Then ask them to work in pairs and to choose one of the situations to write a conversation about.

- As they write their conversations, go round, giving help with vocabulary and making sure that they incorporate some of the useful phrases.

- When they've finished, ask them to practise their conversations. It may help to have them sitting back-to-back to simulate a real phone conversation. Choose some pairs to perform their conversations to the class.

Vocabulary *Extra* (SB page 103)

Animals

1

- Focus the students' attention on the pictures and the names of the baby animals. Read these aloud and ask the students to match them to the names of the adult animals.

5 a kitten: a cat	6 a chick: a hen
2 a calf: a cow	4 a foal: a horse
1 a puppy: a dog	3 a lamb: a sheep

2

Pairwork. Put the students in pairs. Go through the example question and answer with the class and then ask them to cover the words and pictures and take turns to test each other with similar questions.

Insects

1

- Focus the students' attention on the pictures and the insect names. Remind students that the underlining indicates the syllable of the word that has the strongest stress. Read the insect names aloud and ask the students to match the pictures to them.

- Check answers with the class and check that everyone can pronounce the names correctly.

4	an ant	8	a fly
5	a bee	7	a mosquito
1	a butterfly	3	a spider
6	a cockroach	2	a wasp

2

Pairwork. Put the students in pairs. Go through the example question and answer with the class and then ask them to cover the words and take turns to test each other with similar questions.

Focus on *that*

1

- Allow the students to work in pairs to complete the table.

- Check answers and explain any difficult vocabulary.

1	What's that strange noise?
2	Look at that car. It's going too fast.
3	The woman that phoned me spoke French.
4	Where are the photos that were on my desk?
5	Yes, that's right.
6	That's all right.

2

Ask the students to write their own example sentences. Go round, monitoring and giving extra help to anyone that needs it.

Further practice material

Need more writing practice?

→ Workbook page 67
- Giving opinions.

Need more classroom practice activities?

→ Photocopiable resource materials pages 184 to 186
   Grammar: *Find the mistake*
   Vocabulary: *Find someone*
   Communication: *Homophones*
→ Top 10 activities pages xv to xx

Need DVD material?

→ DVD – Programme 6: *My humans*

Need progress tests?

→ Test CD – *Test Unit 11*

Need more on important teaching concepts?

→ Key concepts in *New Inside Out* pages xxii to xxxv

Need student self-study practice?

→ CD-ROM – Unit 11: *Animals*

Need student CEF self-evaluation?

→ CEF Checklists pages xxxvii to xliv

Need more information and more ideas?

→ www.insideout.net

Before the next lesson ...

You'll need dice for each pair of students for the activity for the Reading & Speaking activity on page 109 of the Student's Book. Depending on the size of your class, you may need to ask the students to bring their own to the next lesson.

12 Incredible *Overview*

Section & Aims	What the students are doing
Reading SB page 104 Reading for detail	Reading two stories and inserting missing sentences. Identifying true and false statements. Discussing incredible but true stories.
Grammar **SB page 105** Past perfect	Studying the form and use of the past perfect. Underlining actions that happened first in sentences. Talking about emotions and what had happened previously to cause them.
Vocabulary **SB page 105** Collocations with *have, make* and *take*	Finding collocations in stories and completing statements with them. Discussing the statements.
Reading **SB page 106** Reading for specific information	Matching figures with meanings from a text. Answering questions on the text.
Grammar SB page 107 Passives	Studying the form and use of the passive. Completing questions and answers. Asking and answering questions.
Speaking: anecdote SB page 107 Fluency practice	Talking about the most incredible building they've ever seen.
Vocabulary & Listening **SB page 108** The weather	Completing a table with weather words. Underlining the correct information in a weather forecast. Inventing a weather forecast for their own country.
Grammar **SB page 108** *will* and *might* for future possibility	Completing predictions about the weather with *will* and *might*. Making predictions about people in the class and discussing them.
Reading & Speaking **SB page 109** Reading for detail	Playing a fortune-telling game, then discussing predictions for the future. Writing sentences about their future.
Useful phrases SB page 110 Useful conversational phrases for making exclamations	Ticking the topics mentioned in a conversation. Completing a conversation with *very* and *absolutely*. Listening to and repeating useful phrases. Completing a table with adjectives that take *very* and *absolutely*. Continuing and practising a conversation with adjectives and their own ideas.
Vocabulary *Extra* **SB page 111** Revision of words from the unit: *weather; do, get, go, have, make* and *take*	Matching pictures with words. Completing a list of nouns and adjectives to do with the weather. Studying expressions for talking about temperature. Completing collocation tables with *do, get, go, have, make* and *take*.
Writing **WB page 71**	Describing a building.

Warm-up

Explain that the title of this unit is *Incredible* and this word can be used to refer to anything that is so amazing that it's difficult to believe. Elicit from the students any amazing stories from their own country or culture. If they don't have any specific examples, they may be able to talk about TV programmes that they've watched which tell incredible stories.

Reading (SB page 104)

1 🔊 3.29

• Focus the students' attention on the photos, tell them that they're going the read two incredible stories and ask them to predict what might be in these stories.

• Give the students plenty of time to read the stories and then ask them to decide where the missing sentences might go. Allow them to discuss this in pairs before playing the recording for them to check their answers.

• Teach the word *coincidence* (when two things unexpectedly happen at the same time) and ask what the coincidences were in Story B (Amy and Ian both decided to cross the world to see each other at the same time; they were both sitting in the airport in Singapore at the same time).

> a) – Story B. Position 1
> b) – Story A. Position 2

Cultural notes

Sydney
(See notes on Sydney in Review A, page 31.)

Singapore /sɪŋgəpɔː/
An island at the southern tip of the Malay Peninsula, Singapore is the smallest country in southeast Asia and has a population of 4.5 million. The official languages of the country are: Malay, English, Mandarin and Tamil. It's a transit stop for travellers flying between the UK and Australia for several airlines including Singapore Airlines and Qantas.

2

Ask the students to work individually to mark the statements true or false. Allow them to compare in pairs before checking with the class. Encourage them to correct the false statements.

> a) True.
> b) True.
> c) False. (They had the same name; they were the same age; they both had the same pets.)
> d) False. (They had been together for five years.)
> e) False. (They didn't meet in Singapore, even though they were sitting a few metres away from each other.)
> f) True.

3 Pairwork

• The pairwork exercise for this unit is on pages 120 and 125 of the Student's Book. Put the students in pairs and tell them who will be Student A, and who will be Student B.

• While they're doing the exercise, go round monitoring and giving help. Take note of any errors which may need particular attention later, and also any examples of good language use which you can praise in a feedback session.

> **Text before marriage**
> A clairvoyant had once told Emily Brown that she would meet her husband when she was 21. She was now nearly 22 and hadn't met the love of her life yet.
>
> One day, she tapped the text message, 'Do you want to talk?' into her mobile. She then invented a number and sent the message.
>
> She didn't know that the number belonged to her future husband. Peter Baldwin was at work 140 miles away when he got the message.
>
> He phoned Emily, and they chatted for about an hour. They found that they had lots in common and made arrangements to meet.
>
> They got married six months later.

4

Groupwork. Put the students into groups to discuss the questions. Go round, monitoring and giving help with vocabulary. Ask a representative from each group to present any interesting stories to the class.

Grammar (SB page 105)

Past perfect

1

- Go through the form of the past perfect in the margin with the class. Then put the students into pairs to look at the sentences and answer the questions. As they do this, go round giving extra help to students who need it.

- Check answers with the class and make sure that everyone understands that the past perfect is used to help express the order in which actions happened in the past.

  a) arrived = past simple; had been = past perfect
  b) the past perfect
  c) 1 He didn't arrive
     2 Did he arrive?
     3 She hadn't been
     4 Had she been?

Language note

Grammar: Past perfect

You use the past perfect when you're talking about the past and want to talk about something that happened before the time you're speaking about. It's an 'earlier' past. It's formed with *had* + past participle.

2

- Go through the example with the class. Explain that in the first sentence, the person had breakfast in the office after they arrived at work. In the second, they had breakfast, probably at home, before they arrived at work. Ask the students to read the other pairs of sentences and decide which actions happened first. As they do this, go round, offering extra help to students who are having difficulty.

- Check answers with the class and then read out the example sentence using *already* with the class. Ask the student to rewrite the other sentences using already. Go round, monitoring and giving help. Check answers with the class and ask the students which sentences are true for them.

a) 1 I had breakfast when I got to work this morning.
   2 I'd had breakfast when I got to work this morning.
b) 1 When I got home yesterday, my mum made dinner.
   2 When I got home yesterday, my mum had made dinner.
c) 1 When I started learning English, I'd been to England several times.
   2 When I started learning English, I went to England several times.
d) 1 This lesson started when I arrived.
   2 This lesson had started when I arrived.

a) 2 I'd already had breakfast when I got to work this morning.
b) 2 When I got home yesterday, my mother had already made dinner.
c) 1 When I started learning English, I'd already been to England several times.
d) 2 This lesson had already started when I arrived.

3

- Go through the emotions with the class and make sure everyone understands them. As you read each one aloud, you could ask the students to mime the feeling or show by their facial expression that they understand it.

- Give the students a few minutes to think about times when they've felt these emotions and what had happened to make them feel that way. Allow them to make brief notes if they wish.

- Put the students into pairs. Read the example aloud and point out the use of the past perfect to say what the person had done to make them feel tired. Then ask the students to take turns to tell each other about the emotions and what had caused them. Go round, monitoring and taking note of any particularly good sentences which can be put on the board or reported to the class.

4 Grammar *Extra* 12, Part 1

Ask students to turn to *Grammar Extra* 12, Part 1 on page 148 of the Student's Book. Here they'll find an explanation of the grammar they've been studying and a further exercise to practise it.

1
1 had lived   7 had died
2 had died   8 had seen
3 were   9 met
4 had been   10 hadn't seen
5 had lived   11 reminded
6 realised   12 had been

Vocabulary (SB page 105)

1

- Remind the students that collocations are words that frequently occur together. Point out that *have*, *make* and *take* are very common verbs in English and that they occur in several fixed expressions.

- Ask the students to work individually to find the collocations in the stories on page 104 and to complete the sentences. Go round, monitoring and giving help. Check answers with the class and then ask the students if they know of any other collocations with these verbs. They may know *take a taxi*, *have dinner*, *make plans*, etc.

> had an idea, have lots in common, made arrangements, took her seat
>
> a) have a go　　　d) take photos
> b) take risks　　　e) make money
> c) have a laugh　　f) make a promise

Language note

Vocabulary: Collocations

Many words in English exist as part of a group of words which commonly occur together in a certain order. Verbs like *have*, *make*, *take* and *do* are all commonly used in collocations. *Have breakfast* is much more natural than *eat breakfast*; you *make a mistake*, you don't ~~do a mistake~~; you *take a photograph*, you don't ~~make a photograph~~ and you *do your homework*, you don't ~~make your homework~~.

2

- Pairwork. Ask the students to work in pairs and to decide which of the statements in Exercise 1 they agree or disagree with.

- Ask the students to report back to the class on their decisions.

Reading (SB page 106)

1

- Focus the students' attention on the photos and tell them that these are pictures of an unusual hotel in Sweden. Give them a minute or two to look at the photos and then ask them what they think is unusual about this hotel (it's made of ice).

- Ask the students to look at the figures in column A and the explanations in column B and to try to match them up. Explain that they should do this by guessing, not looking at the text, and that they aren't expected to get everything correct.

- Have a class feedback session before asking the students to read the text and check their guesses. Allow them time to comment on what they've read and to say what they found the most surprising. Would they like to stay in this hotel?

> 40,000 = The number of tons of ice and snow used to build the hotel.
> 1990 = The year the first hotel was built.
> 64 = The number of rooms in the hotel.
> 14,000 = The number of hotel guests last year.
> $^-$30 = The temperature outside the hotel.
> $^-$5 = The temperature inside the hotel.

Cultural notes

Torne River /tɔːn ˈrɪvə/, **Sweden**
A river in northern Sweden, the Torne is around 520 km long. Half the length of the river forms half of the border between Sweden and Finland. The river flows into the Gulf of Bothnia, which separates Sweden and Finland.

Jukkasjärvi, Sweden
A small town in northern Sweden with a population of around 600. The village is a popular tourist destination and is famous for its ice hotel, which is open from December to April every year. A room in the hotel costs around US $200 per night.

2

- Pairwork. Put the students into pairs and ask them to take turns asking and answering the questions about the Ice Hotel. You could give them a few minutes beforehand to look through the text and decide on their answers to the questions. All these questions are in the passive which the students will study in the next grammar section.

- Check answers with the class before asking them to talk about the best or worst hotel they've ever stayed in. Go round, monitoring and taking note of any interesting information which can be shared with the class.

> a) On the shores of the Torne River (in the old village of Jukkasjärvi, Sweden).
> b) Ice and snow.
> c) Ice.
> d) Reindeer skins.
> e) Different artists from around the world.
> f) Stunning, beautiful, unique.

Grammar (SB page 107)

Passives

1

- Focus the students' attention on the information in the margin and explain that the sentences are all examples of the passive. You may like to point out that all the sentences they've studied in earlier units have been in the active, but that the questions in Exercise 2 of the previous section were in the passive. The text on page 106 has many examples of the passive in use. You could ask the students to look through this text and underline the passive sentences.

- Go through the sentences in the table with the class and point out the differences between the active sentences and the passive ones.
- Ask the students to decide if statements a–c are true or false.

a) True.   b) True.   c) True.

2 🌐 3.30

- Go through the first example with the class and ask several students this question about their own houses. Then ask them to complete the remaining questions and answers.
- Play the recording for the students to check their answers. Then play it again for them to listen and repeat the questions and answers. When they've done this chorally, ask individual students to repeat the questions and answers.

a) 'Was your house built before 1980?'
   'Yes, it was.' 'No, it wasn't.'
b) 'Were your shoes designed in Italy?'
   'Yes, they were.' 'No, they weren't.'
c) 'Is your salary paid by cheque?'
   'Yes, it is.' 'No, it isn't.'
d) 'Were you invited to any parties last week?'
   'Yes, I was.' 'No, I wasn't.'
e) 'Is your name spelt the same in English?'
   'Yes, it is.' 'No, it isn't.'
f) 'Was your mobile phone made in Japan?'
   'Yes, it was.' 'No, it wasn't.'

3

Pairwork. Put the students into pairs and ask them to take turns asking and answering the questions in Exercise 2.

4 Grammar Extra 12, Part2

Ask students to turn to *Grammar Extra* 12, Part 2 on page 148 of the Student's Book. Here they'll find an explanation of the grammar they've been studying and further exercises to practise it.

1
a) was opened   d) was painted
b) is parked   e) is pronounced
c) is cleaned   f) was made

2
a) Was this school opened in the 1990s?
b) Is your car parked outside your house every day?
c) Is your house cleaned once a week?
d) Was our classroom painted recently?
e) Is your name pronounced differently in English?
f) Was your watch made in Switzerland?

3
1 is called   5 was completed
2 was built   6 was designed
3 is connected   7 is considered
4 was started

Speaking: anecdote (SB page 107)

For more information about how to set up, monitor and repeat Anecdotes, see page xx in the Introduction.

1 🌐 3.31

- Ask the students to look at the photo. Explain that this is Curro and he's going to talk about the most incredible building he's ever seen.
- Go through the questions and the answer choices with the class. Explain any unknown vocabulary and then ask the students to listen and underline the answers Curro gives.
- Check answers with the class and ask them whether they've ever been to the Alhambra and if so, what they thought of it.

a) Alhambra
b) the South of Spain
c) When I was eighteen
d) In the 13th or 14th century
e) The style is Moorish
f) location
g) Four times

🌐 3.31

The most incredible building I've ever seen is the Alhambra. It's a beautiful palace in Granada in the south of Spain. The first time I saw the Alhambra Palace was when I was eighteen – I went to visit my brother who was studying at university in Granada. I think it was built in the thirteenth or fourteenth century for the Moorish kings. Alhambra is an Arabic name – it means 'red', probably because of the colour of the walls. It's an enormous building, I don't know who the architect was, but the style is Moorish, or Islamic. I love the gardens – water is very important. You can hear water running wherever you go. But it isn't only the building that's so great. I think the location is the most incredible thing about it. It's built on a hill overlooking Granada with the Sierra Nevada mountains in the background. I've been there four times, and each time I think it is more beautiful. In my opinion, it is definitely one of the seven wonders of the modern world.

Cultural notes

Colosseum /kɒləˈsiːjəm/, Rome
A Roman amphitheatre built between 70 AD and 80 AD, the Colosseum could seat 50,000 spectators and was used for public spectacles such as dramas and gladiator fights. Although the last known entertainment took place in 465 AD, it remained in use, even inhabited, until the early 19th century. In 2000, a new floor was installed in part of the arena for smaller events. Larger events are played outside, using the Colosseum as a backdrop.

The Alhambra Palace
(See notes on the Alhambra Palace on page 16.)

2

- Give the students a minute or two to decide which building they're going to talk about. Then ask them to look at the questions in Exercise 1 again and decide how they'd answer them about the building they're going to talk about. Allow them to make notes of what they're going to say and how they're going to say it, but discourage them from writing a paragraph that they can simply read out. Go round, monitoring and giving help with vocabulary.

- Pairwork. Put the students in pairs and ask them to take turns to tell their partner about the most incredible building they've ever seen. Encourage them to ask each other follow-up questions to get further information.

- Ask some pairs to report back to the class about what they found out.

Vocabulary & Listening (SB page 108)

1

- Ask the students how they'd describe the weather today. Elicit words for temperature as well as weather conditions. Then focus their attention on the table. Ask them to work individually to try to complete it with suitable words to describe the weather.

- Ask the students to compare notes with a partner before checking answers with the class.

> 1 sun   2 cloudy   3 rain   4 foggy
> 5 wind   6 storm

2 🌐 3.32

- Ask the students to look at the photo of the North Pole in winter. Tell them to read the text and decide which of the alternatives is most likely.

- Allow them to compare their answers in pairs before playing the recording for them to listen and check. Ask the students whether they would prefer to live in a very hot climate or a very cold climate.

> 1 cold   2 minus 30   3 windy   4 snow
> 5 dark   6 warmer

Cultural note

North Pole
The North Pole is the most northerly point on Earth and is in the middle of the Arctic Ocean in waters that are usually covered with ice. As the ice is constantly moving, it isn't possible to build any permanent structure on it (unlike the South Pole, which is located on the continent of Antarctica, and on which there's a permanent structure, the Amundsen-Scott South Pole Station).

3

- Remind the students that they can use the text in Exercise 2 as a model and just change the highlighted words to match a particular season in their own country. Encourage them to work individually to do this.

- Put the students into pairs to read the weather forecasts and guess the season. Alternatively, collect in the forecasts and read them aloud to the class, asking the students to guess collectively which season is being described.

Grammar (SB page 108)

will and *might* for future possibility

1

- Go through the sentences in the margin and explain that *will* and *might* are both used to talk about future possibility. (See Language notes below.) Ask the students to look at the weather forecast in Exercise 2 of the previous section and underline *will* and *might*.

- Go through the example with the class, then ask the students to complete the remaining predictions. As they do this, go round checking that everyone has understood. Point out that *probably* (in sentences b and f) expresses less certainty than *definitely*, but still gives an idea of what the speaker is pretty sure will happen.

- Check answers with the class before asking the students to rewrite the sentences so they are true for them and to compare them in pairs.

---

a) The south will definitely have better weather than the north.
b) Tomorrow will probably be warmer than today.
c) I think we'll have a lot of snow next winter.
d) It might rain later today.
e) I don't think there will be any storms tomorrow.
f) It probably won't be so sunny tomorrow.
g) It definitely won't freeze tomorrow.

Language notes

Grammar: *will* and *might*

- *Will* and *might* are both modal verbs and so they follow the same grammatical rules as other modal verbs. They're followed by the infinitive without *to* and they don't take the third person *s*. For example:

  It might rain tomorrow. Not: ~~It might to rain tomorrow. It mights rain tomorrow. It might rains tomorrow.~~

- The meaning of *will* and *might* can differ depending on the context in which they're used. In this unit, *will* and *might* are used to make predictions about the future. *Might* is used to express a 50% possibility, whereas the meaning of *will* is broader and depends on other words (*definitely*, *probably*, *think*, *don't think*) that are used with it and which modify it:

  – *It will **definitely** happen* is a strong prediction and indicates a degree of certainty from the speaker.
  – *It will **probably** happen* indicates confidence, but isn't as strong.
  – *I **think** it will happen* is less confident than the previous two examples but still more confident than *It might happen*.

- The modifying words *definitely* and *probably* come after *will* but before *won't*:

  *It **will definitely** happen.*
  *It **definitely won't** happen.*

2

- Pairwork. Go through the prompts with the class and then ask the students to discuss which people in the class they can make these predictions about.

- Go round, monitoring and giving help. Encourage them to use all the expressions in the box at least once.

- Check answers by having pairs read their sentences aloud and ask the people named whether or not they agree with the prediction.

Reading & Speaking (SB page 109)

1

- The Oracle is a lighthearted way of looking at predictions for the future

- Go through the instructions with the class, making sure they understand all the questions. Then put the students in pairs, each with a dice.

- Allow the students time to play the game and react to the results they get. In a class feedback session, find out how likely or unlikely they think the predictions they got are. Encourage them to use expressions like *I think*, *will definitely*, *might*, *probably*, etc.

2

- Ask the students to work individually to write their sentences. As they work, go round offering extra help to anyone who is having difficulties with the concept or structure of making predictions.

- When they've finished, ask them to compare their sentences with a partner and discuss their predictions. Put any particularly good sentences on the board.

Useful phrases (SB page 110)

1 🌐 3.33

- Focus the students' attention on the illustration and ask the students where Agnes and Betty, the two women, are (at the hairdresser's). Ask the students if women at the hairdresser's in their country talk to each other. Teach the word *gossip* and ask for other situations in which people gossip and the sorts of things they gossip about.

- Go through the list of topics, then play the recording and ask the students to tick the topics that the two women talk about.

They talk about: celebrities, clothes and houses.

2

- Explain that *very* and *absolutely* are both used to make adjectives stronger. Ask the students to read the conversation and try to complete it with *very* and *absolutely*.

- Play the recording again for the students to check their answers. Ask them if they notice anything about when you use *very* and when you use *absolutely*. They may notice that you use *absolutely* with adjectives which are already strong.

1 very	2 absolutely	3 very	4 absolutely
5 very	6 absolutely	7 very	8 absolutely
9 very	10 absolutely	11 very	
12 absolutely	13 very	14 absolutely	

3 🌐 3.34

- Ask the students to look closely at the useful phrases. Point out that some adjectives are stronger than others. For example, *pretty* and *gorgeous* have similar meaning, but *gorgeous* is much stronger than *pretty*. Here the adjectives are paired by meaning. In each pair, *very* is used with the weaker adjective and *absolutely* with the stronger one.

- Play the recording and ask the students to repeat the phrases, trying to imitate the intonation of the speakers. When they've done this chorally, ask individual students to repeat the words and encourage them to exaggerate their intonation to match the speakers.

4

- Focus the students' attention on the adjectives in the box. Ask the students to decide which have strong meanings and which weaker meanings.

- As the students put the adjectives into the table, go round, monitoring and giving help.

- Check answers with the class, asking students to read their answers aloud using appropriate intonation.

1 impossible	2 funny	3 good
4 delicious		

5

- Remind the students that Agnes and Betty were looking at a magazine at the hairdresser's. Ask them to imagine that they're now looking at a different page of the magazine and to continue their conversation. Practising their new conversations will be easier if you allow them to work in pairs to do this. Go round, offering help with ideas and vocabulary. Encourage them to use the adjectives in Exercises 3 and 4 and their own ideas.

- Ask the students to practise their conversation aloud and then perform them for the class. Allow them to sit side by side at the front of the class with magazines open as if in a hairdresser's as they do this.

Vocabulary *Extra* (SB page 111)

Weather

1

- Focus the students' attention on the list of words and point out that they're all to do with the weather. Check that the students can pronounce all the words correctly.

- Ask the students to look at the pictures and match each one to the weather words. Point out that the first one has been done for them.

1 and 2	
9 breeze – breezy	5 mist – misty
11 cloud – cloudy	2 rain – rainy
6 fog – foggy	1 shower – showery
7 heat – hot	3 storm – stormy
8 humidity – humid	12 sun – sunny
4 ice – icy	10 wind – windy

2

Go through the example with the class and explain that you can say such things as *There is a breeze today* or *It is breezy today*. Ask them to complete the table with the other corresponding nouns and adjectives.

3

- Read the words in the box aloud to the class or get one or two of the students to read them out. Ask them to work individually to decide what temperature is, for them, the equivalent of each of these terms.

- You might like to point out that the terms are in order in the box, with *freezing* referring to extreme cold and *boiling* to extreme heat, and that when you say *It's freezing* or *It's boiling*, this isn't a literal statement of fact.

- Allow the students to compare results with a partner and see if they agree on the temperatures.

- You could revise *very* and *absolutely* with the class. Ask the students which adjectives they can use with *very* (*cold/chilly, warm* and *hot*) and which with *absolutely* (*freezing* and *boiling*).

Focus on *do, get, go, have, make, take*

Note: there's some overlap in the use of these verbs. For example, you could also say *get lunch* or *get a bus* or *get the shopping* or *get home*. However, the collocations given here are the most frequent ones.

1

- Allow the students to work in pairs to complete the tables, if they wish. Encourage them to say each of the collocations aloud to see what sounds right.

- Check answers and answer any questions the students may have.

a) get b) have c) take d) make
e) do f) go

2

Ask the students to use their dictionaries to find other collocations for these verbs.

Extra activity

Ask the students to produce sentences using some of the collocations.

Further practice material

Need more writing practice?

→ Workbook page 71

- Describing a building.

Need more classroom practice activities?

→ Photocopiable resource materials pages 187 to 189

Grammar: *What happened?*
Vocabulary: *Shout it out!*
Communication: *Let's talk about …*

→ Top 10 activities pages xv to xx

Need progress tests?

→ Test CD – *Test Unit 12*

Need more on important teaching concepts?

→ Key concepts in *New Inside Out* pages xxii to xxxv

Need student self-study practice?

→ CD-ROM – Unit 12: *Incredible*

Need student CEF self-evaluation?

→ CEF Checklists pages xxxvii to xliv

Need more information and more ideas?

→ www.insideout.net

Review D *Teacher's notes*

These exercises act as a check of the grammar and vocabulary that the students have learnt in Units 10–12. Use them to find any problems that students are having, or anything that they haven't understood and which will need further work.

Grammar (SB page 112)

Remind the students of the grammar explanations they read and the exercises they did in the *Grammar Extra* on pages 144 to 149.

1

This exercise reviews the *will* future from Unit 10.

a) will help	d) Will Sarah be
b) won't have	e) won't eat
c) 'll send	f) Will you see

2

This exercise reviews future time clauses from Unit 10.

a) If	d) When
b) When	e) If
c) as soon as	f) as soon as

3

This exercise reviews *used to* and *didn't use to* from Unit 10. Check answers with the class before asking the students to write new sentences, including one false one. They then see if they can identify their partner's false sentence.

a) I used to live in a flat.
b) –
c) I didn't use to have a bicycle.
d) –
e) my family didn't use to watch TV.
f) I didn't use to like classical music.

4

This exercise reviews defining relative clauses from Unit 11.

a) She has a cat which never stops eating.
b) I have a friend who lives in Australia.
c) I have a phone which takes good photos.
d) Where are the eggs which were in the fridge?
e) Those are the people who bought my old house.
f) She has a boyfriend who is a doctor.

5

This exercise reviews unreal conditionals from Unit 11. When you've checked the answers, ask the students to practise the conversation in pairs.

1 would you do	6 wouldn't buy
2 won	7 Would you give
3 'd buy	8 had
4 won	9 'd give
5 'd get	

6

This exercise reviews the past perfect from Unit 12.

a) 4   b) 1   c) 5   d) 3   e) 2   f) 6

7

This exercise reviews the past passive from Unit 12. Check answers with the class before asking the students to answer the questions. Then put them into pairs to compare their results.

a) Was your car made in Spain?
b) Was your house built in the 20th century?
c) Were your shoes made in Brazil?
d) Was your jacket designed by Armani?
e) Was your watch made in Japan?
f) Was your computer manufactured in China?

8

This exercise reviews structures used in Units 10, 11 and 12.

1 b) ~~Did you used to visit the zoo?~~
2 b) ~~A teacher is a person which works in a school.~~
3 a) ~~If you would have a pet, what would it be?~~
4 a) ~~When I got home I had made lunch.~~
5 a) ~~This watch is make of gold.~~
6 b) ~~It might to rain tomorrow.~~

Vocabulary (SB page 113)

1

This exercise reviews words connected to lifestyles from Unit 10. Check answers with the class before asking the students to tick the statements that are true for them and then compare with a partner.

a) a healthy life
b) extended family
c) a brisk walk
d) in a hurry
e) a good network
f) fit

2

This exercise revises food vocabulary from Unit 10.

Fruit and vegetables: garlic, lettuce, onion, orange, peach, tomato
Meat and fish: chicken, prawns, sausage, trout
Other: beans, nuts, soup, tea

3

This exercise reviews vocabulary to do with food preparation from Unit 10.

1 Peel, Boil
2 Chop
3 Put
4 Slice
5 Bake

4

This exercise reviews prepositions. Check answers with the class before asking the students to tick the statements that are true for them and then compare with a partner.

a) of   b) of   c) on   d) of   e) to   f) in

5

This exercise reviews animal vocabulary from Unit 11. Ask the students which ones people keep as pets.

E	R	A	V	C	A	T	I	P	D
A	S	H	A	R	K	H	N	E	O
G	W	L	I	O	N	F	R	O	G
L	E	B	M	C	I	A	T	W	Z
E	X	R	D	O	L	P	H	I	N
H	W	A	Q	D	X	B	A	T	M
O	A	T	L	I	F	U	I	Y	O
R	S	J	F	L	P	L	D	E	U
S	P	I	D	E	R	L	U	N	S
E	O	G	Y	V	S	N	A	K	E

6

This exercise reviews collocations with *take*, *have* and *make* from Unit 12. Check answers with the class before asking the students to answer the questions and then compare with a partner.

a) make   b) have   c) take   d) make
e) have   f) take

7

This exercise reviews weather words from Unit 12. Start by asking the students what the weather is like today.

a) rainy, snowing, sunny, wet, windy
b) clouds, snow, storms, the sun

Pronunciation (SB page 113)

1

Remind the students that the boxes show the syllables of a word and the large boxes indicate the stressed syllables. Here the students are being asked to classify words from Units 10–12 according to how many syllables they have and where the main stress falls. Encourage them to say each word aloud to get a feeling for what sounds right.

2 🌐 3.35

Point out the main stresses in the example words which are underlined. Ask the students to do the same for the other words in the table. Then play the recording for them to check their answers. Play it a second time for them to listen and repeat.

---

1 and 2
A: fitness, healthy, lettuce, promise, rainy
B: afraid, arrive, enjoy, relax, sardine
C: animal, dangerous, gardening, holiday, terrified

Reading & Listening (SB page 114)

1 🌐 3.36

Give the students plenty of time to read and listen to the article. Then ask them to match the animals to the distances. Make sure the students can pronounce the names of the animals and the numbers correctly. Ask them which journey they find most surprising.

---

a) 40,000 kilometres   d) 2,000 kilometres
b) 8,000 kilometres   e) 3,000 kilometres
c) 3,500 kilometres

Cultural note

Serengeti /serən'geti:/
The Serengeti is a savanna which covers 60,000 square kilometers in Tanzania and Kenya, in east Africa. The Serengeti region contains several national parks and is home to over two million grass-eating animals including; wildebeest, gazelles, zebras and buffalo. There are also thousands of meat-eating animals including: lions, cheetahs and hyenas.

2

Go through the items with the students before they read the texts again and see if they can identify which animals they refer to. Then ask them to read the text again and find any remaining answers.

---

a) Albatross   d) Humpback whale
b) Wildebeest   e) Green turtle
c) Monarch butterfly

---

3 🌐 3.37

Go through the statements with the students before playing the recording. Then ask them to listen and say which statements are true and which false. Encourage them to correct the false statements.

---

a) False. (Emma went on holiday with Dom.)
b) True.
c) True.
d) False. (They didn't sleep well as they were woken at 3 a.m. and had to get off the train and wait for a bus.)
e) False. (The coffee was terrible.)
f) True.
g) False. (It rained when they were setting off on the boat, but it stopped quickly and the sun came out.)

🌐 3.37 (D = Dom; L = Lou)

D: *That's incredible! I'm just reading about albatrosses, Lou. Did you know that they fly around the world at least once a year? That's 40,000 kilometres!*

L: *Wow! That's a long way. What's the longest journey you've been on, Dom?*

D: *Not as far as an albatross. I think it was in Thailand.*

L: *Oh, yeah?*

D: *Emma and I were living in Bangkok and we decided to go to Koh Tao for our holidays.*

L: *Koh Tao?*

D: *Yeah. It means 'Turtle Island' in Thai. It's near Koh Samui.*

L: *Ah, I see.*

D: *Anyway, we had to take a night train from Bangkok to Chumphorn in the south of Thailand and then a boat from there to Koh Tao.*

L: *How exciting!*

D: *So, we were taken to the train station in Bangkok and then we waited there for two hours. We left the station at around 7.30 p.m.*

L: *Oh right.*

D: *Yeah. At first we felt really excited, but after about an hour we started feeling quite tired. It was noisy and hot. I think I got to sleep at around 11.30 p.m.*

L: *Oh, that's not so bad.*

D: *Mm. The next morning, at three o'clock, the train stopped, and we were told to get off. It was the middle of the night, so it was still dark. We had to wait in a small station for a bus to take us to the boat.*

L: *How did you feel?*

D: *Really tired! And hungry and thirsty, but the only place we could get a drink was from an old lady who served terrible coffee.*

L: *Oh, poor you.*

D: Then the mosquitoes started biting us – and they were hungry, too! Well, they bit me but they didn't really bite, Emma.

L: Oh, dear!

D: Four hours later the bus arrived, and we were taken to the boat. Then it started raining as the boat moved out into the open sea.

L: Oh, how annoying!

D: Suddenly, as quickly as it had started, the rain stopped, and the sun came out.

L: Aha! A happy ending!

D: Yes, it was. Eventually we arrived at Koh Tao, seventeen hours after our journey had begun.

L: Ahh. Were you tired?

D: Absolutely exhausted, but really happy.

4

Go through the choices with the students before playing the recording again. Ask them to match the linkers to the correct events.

a) 2   b) 6   c) 5   d) 4   e) 3   f) 1

Writing & Speaking (SB page 115)

1

Ask the students to read the story and complete it with the words in the box.

1	Two years ago	5	Then
2	At first	6	suddenly
3	The next day	7	Eventually
4	four days		

2

Ask the students to put the words in order to make questions. Check answers with the class before asking them to look back through the text and see which of these questions it answers.

a) Where did you start your journey?
b) Where did you go?
c) How did you get there?
d) Where did you stay at night?
e) Did you have any problems?
f) Did you enjoy your journey?
g) How long did the journey take?
h) Would you do it again?

Questions a)–e) were answered in the text.

3

Go through the instructions with the class and make sure everyone understands what they have to do. Ask them to work individually at first to think of ideas. Allow them to make brief notes if they wish, but discourage them from writing out a script. Remind them to look at the expressions in Exercise 1. Go round, offering help with vocabulary. Then ask the students to get into pairs and take turns to describe their journeys.

4

Remind the students that they can use the text in Exercise 1 as a model and should incorporate some of the organising expressions in the box. Go round, monitoring and giving help and encourage them to use the questions in Exercise 2 to help them structure their work. You could then display the finished accounts around the classroom.

Further practice material

Need more classroom practice activities?
→ Photocopiable resource materials page 190, recording track 🔘 3.38
   Song: *I Have a Dream*
→ Top 10 activities pages xv to xx

Need progress tests?
→ Test CD – *Test Review D*

Need more on important teaching concepts?
→ Key concepts in *New Inside Out* pages xxii to xxxv

Need student self-study practice?
→ CD-ROM – *Review D*

Need more information and more ideas?
→ www.insideout.net

Resource materials

Worksheet	Activity and focus	What the students are doing
Unit 1		
1 Grammar *What's in a name?*	Pairwork: personal information Present simple and word order in questions	Asking questions. Describing people.
1 Vocabulary *Family puzzle*	Pairwork: word puzzle Family relationships	Completing a word puzzle using picture clues.
1 Communication *Questions for me*	Individual and groupwork: mixed tense questions	Finding out and sharing personal information.
Unit 2		
2 Grammar *Categorise*	Groupwork: categorising words countable/uncountable nouns	Putting words from a list into correct categories.
2 Vocabulary *Places in a city*	Groupwork: *Pelmanism* game Places, buildings and monuments in a city	Matching words and picture clues.
2 Communication *Worldsearch*	Pairwork and groupwork: crossword Country names and stress patterns	Writing clues with information about a country and completing a crossword.
Unit 3		
3 Grammar *A love story*	Pairwork: information gap Past simple and continuous	Writing and asking questions to complete a story with missing information.
3 Vocabulary *Exciting or excited?*	Whole class: mingle activity *-ed* and *-ing* adjective endings	Forming adjectives correctly to ask questions about feelings.
3 Communication *A few quick questions*	Whole class: mingle activity Question forms and revision	Asking about lifestyles and feelings of other students.
Review A *Stand By Me*	Pairwork: song Revision of grammar and vocabulary from Units 1–3	Listening to and reading a song and discussing interpretation.
Unit 4		
4 Grammar *Let's talk!*	Groupwork: board game Gerunds and infinitives	Playing a board game asking questions correctly.
4 Vocabulary *What's the difference?*	Pairwork: picture description Clothes, accessories, patterns *is/isn't wearing*	Finding twelve differences in a pair of pictures.
4 Communication *Ten facts*	Pairwork: guessing game Adverbs of frequency	Guessing a partner's habits correctly.

Unit 5

5 Grammar *As fit as a fiddle*	Group or pairwork: dominoes game Comparative and superlative forms Health and fitness	Playing a dominoes game to match sentence halves correctly.
5 Vocabulary *Sports crossword*	Group or pairwork: crossword Sports, locations, equipment Present simple	Writing clues about a sport so that other students can complete their half of a crossword correctly.
5 Communication *Numbers, numbers, numbers*	Groupwork: quiz Superlatives Numbers	Matching correct answers with questions about unusual facts.

Unit 6

6 Grammar *Have you ever done it?*	Whole class: mingle activity Present perfect and past simple Experiences	Asking and talking about personal experiences.
6 Vocabulary *In an ideal world*	Individual or pairwork: opinions *Should*	Discussing feelings and opinions about friends, jobs and partners.
6 Communication *What's my job?*	Whole class: mingle activity Adverbs of frequency *Have to* Jobs	Asking about job details in order to guess the job.
Review B *Suspicious minds*	Pairwork: song Revision of grammar and vocabulary from Units 4–6	Listening to and reading a song and vocabulary work.

Unit 7

7 Grammar *Thirty-second futures*	Groupwork: board game Present continuous and *going to* for future	Playing a board game talking about future events in their lives.
7 Vocabulary *How green are you?*	Individual and group or pairwork: questionnaire Green issues	Answering a questionnaire to find out how good they and their classmates are at being 'green'.
7 Communication *Manifesto*	Groupwork: preparing a manifesto Topical issues Expressing opinions	Working in groups to think of and write statements for a presentation to the class.

Unit 8

8 Grammar *Schooldays*	Individual and groupwork: questioning and reporting *Could/couldn't/had to/didn't have to* Permission and obligation	Making questions to ask each other about schooldays.
8 Vocabulary *Education wordsearch*	Groupwork: word puzzle Education	Completing a wordsearch puzzle.
8 Communication *What's your advice?*	Groupwork: writing problems and advice *Should*	Completing a problem creatively and writing advice for other groups.

Worksheet	Activity and focus	What the students are doing
Unit 9		
9 Grammar For *and* since	Whole class: mingle activity *How long…?*+ present perfect simple/continuous *For/since*	Asking and answering about the length of time they have been doing certain things.
9 Vocabulary *Character crossword*	Groupwork: completing a crossword Character adjectives	Helping each other complete a crossword and talking about people.
9 Communication *Smile!*	Groupwork: board game Vocabulary and verb patterns from Unit 9	Playing a board game and choosing the correct alternatives.
Review C *Money*	Pairwork: song Revision of grammar and vocabulary from Units 7–9	Listening to and reading a song and discussing money expressions.
Unit 10		
10 Grammar *Then or now?*	Pair or groupwork: discussion *Used to* + infinitive Opinions and agreement	Talking about differences in life 100 years ago and discussing opinions.
10 Vocabulary *Features of a car*	Group or pairwork: dominoes game Car parts and accessories	Playing dominoes by combining car part expressions.
10 Communication *Food*	Groupwork: board game Food and drink	Playing a board game and talking about food-related topics.
Unit 11		
11 Grammar *Find the mistake*	Pairwork: error correction Grammar revision	Correcting grammar mistakes and checking with a partner.
11 Vocabulary *Find someone*	Whole class: mingle activity Adjectives and dependent prepositions	Completing statements with the correct preposition and finding someone who fits the statement.
11 Communication *Homophones*	Pair or groupwork: *Pelmanism* game Homophones	Playing a game to match different picture cards which have the same sound.
Unit 12		
12 Grammar *What happened?*	Pairwork: completing and ordering a story Narrative tenses	Working together to complete an unusual experience story and ordering events.
12 Vocabulary *Shout it out!*	Groupwork: team game Vocabulary revision	Playing a team game to guess vocabulary in different categories.
12 Communication *Let's talk about …*	Groupwork: board game Language revision	Playing a board game and talking about different subjects for thirty or sixty seconds.
Review D *I Have a Dream*	Pairwork: song Revision of grammar and vocabulary from Units 10–12	Listening to and reading a song and talking about dreams.

Teacher's notes

1 Grammar What's in a name?

Page 151

Activity

Pairwork: asking questions.

Focus

Present simple question forms and word order in questions.

Preparation

Make one copy of the worksheet for each pair of students and cut into two as indicated.

Procedure

• Demonstrate the activity by writing the first name of a member of your family on the board. Invite questions from the students about this person, helping them if necessary with words like *who?* or *how old?* or *job?*

• Tell the students they are going to do the same, in pairs, with the worksheets. Divide the class into equal numbers of Student As and Student Bs. Give a copy of the A worksheet to Student A and the B worksheet to Student B. Ask them not to show their worksheets to their partner.

• Ask the students to complete the 'Names' section of the worksheet. They then tear off this section and exchange it with their partner's.

• Ask the students to ask their partner three or more questions about each of the names their partner wrote down. They can use the example prompts on the worksheets to help them. Go round the class and make sure students form the questions correctly.

• When most students have finished, ask two or three students to describe one person from their partner's list.

Note: If some pairs finish early, ask them to swap partners and start again.

1 Vocabulary Family puzzle

Page 152

Activity

Pairwork: word puzzle.

Focus

Family and relationship vocabulary.

Preparation

Make one copy of the worksheet for each pair of students in the class.

Procedure

• Divide the class into pairs and give each pair a copy of the worksheet.

• Explain to the students that they should look at the pictures and discuss what relationship each one shows. When they have agreed, they should write in the word on the puzzle. You could make it into a race with the first pair to finish as the winner.

• When the first pair has finished, check the answers with the class to find out the two hidden family-related words.

The hidden family-related words are *nephew* and *cousin*.

1 Communication Questions for me

Page 153

Activity

Individual and groupwork: sharing personal information.

Focus

Mixed tense question forms.

Preparation

Make one copy of the worksheet for each student in the class.

Procedure

- Tell the students they are going to write some questions for each other. Explain that each question has been started, so they will need to think how to finish it.

- Give one copy to each student in the class and ask them to write their names at the bottom where it says *These questions are for me. My name is _____ .* Then tell them to pass their worksheet to the student on their left. Explain that the questions they write will be for the student whose name is at the bottom of the worksheet.

- Ask the students to complete the first question and write their name on the right. This is very important. Then ask them to fold the worksheet back, along the dotted line, so that their question is hidden, and then pass the worksheet to the student on their left who repeats the same procedure. (If the class is small and a student sees his/her name at the bottom of the worksheet, he/she should pass it to the left without writing a question.)

- When all the questions have been written, ask the students to return the worksheet to the student whose name is at the bottom of the worksheet.

- Ask the students to unfold their worksheets and read the questions. Ask them to find the person who asked each question and answer it giving more information if they want to.

  For example:

  Student A to B: *You asked 'Have you been to Paris?' My answer is 'Yes, I've been to Paris three times. The last time was a year ago…'*

Alternative

For a more controlled activity, ask students to work in pairs. Each student writes questions to ask his/her partner.

2 Grammar Categorise

Page 154

Activity

Group or pairwork: categorising words.

Focus

Revision of countable and uncountable nouns from Unit 2 *New Inside Out* Pre-intermediate Student's Book.

Preparation

Make one copy of the worksheet for each student in the class.

Procedure

- Divide the students into pairs or small groups. Give each group a worksheet.

- Ask students to put all the words on their worksheet under the seven headings. The winner is the first group to categorise the words successfully. Go round the class helping with any vocabulary problems.

- Write the seven headings on the board and ask one student from each group to come up to the board and write the words under the headings. Or, for a more competitive alternative, see *Variation* below.

- Tell students to read the categorised words and mark each word with a U for uncountable and C for countable. The winning pair or group is the first to finish.

Variation

Play *Back to the board*.

1 Divide the class into two teams, A and B. Ask one student from each group to come to the front and sit, facing their own teams, with their backs to the board.

2 The teacher writes a word from the worksheet on the board. The teams then call out descriptions of the word until one of the two students guesses the word on the board.

3 The team that guessed the word score one point and both students go back to their teams and are replaced by two more.

4 The game continues for as long as the students want. The team with the most points at the end of the game are the winners.

Follow-up

This will be suitable for practising words describing quantity from this unit.

1 Ask students to get into pairs (this will work best if the students are from different countries or different regions of a country).

2 Ask them to talk about the first six categories: *Transport, buildings, geography, going out, food and drink.* Write examples on the board:

People don't drink much tea, but they drink a lot of coffee.
Not many people live in houses.
There are lots of mountains.

Transport: bus (C), car (C), taxi (C), traffic (U)
Buildings: castle (C), church (C), house (C),
    office block (C)
Geography: canal (C), coast (C), mountain (C),
    sea (C/U)
Going out: cinema (C), disco (C) , nightlife (U),
    theatre (C),
Food: bread (U), cake (C/U), fruit (U), meat (U),
    rice (U), vegetables (C)
Drink: beer (C/U), coffee (C/U), juice (U),
    tea (C/U), water (U), wine (U)
Countries: Brazil (C), Egypt (C), Greece (C),
    Ireland (C), Malta (C), Turkey (C)

2 Vocabulary Places in a city

Page 155

Activity

Group or pairwork: *Pelmanism* game.

Focus

Vocabulary of buildings, monuments or places in a city.

Preparation

Make one copy of the worksheet for each group of four students in the class and cut up as indicated.

Procedure

- Tell your students they are going to play a game matching a word to a picture.

- Divide the class into pairs and ask one pair to play against another pair. Give each group of four a copy of the worksheet, cut into cards as indicated. Ask them to put all the cards face down on the table.

- Each team takes it in turns to turn two cards over. The object of the game is to turn over two matching cards (i.e. a card with a picture of a bridge together with a card that has 'bridge' written on it.) If a player does this, he or she keeps the pair of cards. As the player turns over each card, he or she must say what they see (i.e. *bridge* and *bridge*), otherwise they cannot claim the pair.

- If the cards are not a matching pair, they are turned over and left for the next pair to try. The team with the most pairs of cards at the end of the game are the winners.

2 Communication Worldsearch

Page 156

Activity

Group and pairwork: crossword.

Focus

Country names and their stress patterns.

Preparation

Make one copy of the worksheet for each pair of students in the class and cut in half as indicated. It would be useful to have a map of the world/atlas/encyclopedia as a reference.

Procedure

- Write on the board: *It is famous for wine, food and romance. There is a famous tower in the capital city.* Ask students to guess the country (*France*). Tell the students they are going to write some similar sentences as clues for a crossword.

- Divide the class into Team A and Team B. Explain that you are going to give each group the same crossword but that Team A will have the 'down' words already written in and Team B will have the 'across' words already written in. They have to write the clues for the words written on their crosswords.

- Give a copy of crossword A to each student in Team A and a copy of crossword B to each student in Team B. Ask the students to work together with people in their group to write a clue for each country.

- To help your students prepare the clues, encourage them to think particularly about: a) geographical location, b) what the country produces, c) what it's famous for and d) what its capital city is called.

- When they have finished writing their clues, students should work with a partner from the other group. They must not show each other their crossword.

- Ask them to sit facing each other and take it in turns to ask their partner for clues to the missing countries on their crossword. At the end they can look to check their answers.

Follow up

Give one copy of this to each student in the class:

Put each country from your crossword in the right column for its stress pattern.

◻◼   ◻◼   ◻◻◼
_____   _____ Japan   _____

◼◻◻   ◻◼◻◻   ◻◻◼◻
_____   _____   _____ Venezuela

Ask students, with their partner, to work out which country name goes into which column, depending on word stress. Explain there is room for only two countries in each column. Go round the class, helping students if necessary. Check answers with the class.

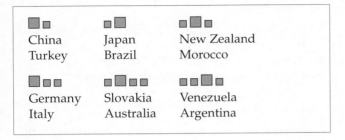

China	Japan	New Zealand
Turkey	Brazil	Morocco
Germany	Slovakia	Venezuela
Italy	Australia	Argentina

3 Grammar A love story

Page 157
Activity
Pairwork: Completing a story using questions and answers.

Focus
Making questions and statements using the past simple and past continuous.

Preparation
Make one copy of the worksheet for each pair of students in the class and cut in half as indicated.

Procedure
• Divide the class into two groups, Group A and Group B. Give one copy of worksheet A to each student in Group A and one copy of worksheet B to each student in Group B.

• Tell your students they have the same story (the story is actually about Marie and Pierre Curie) but there is some information missing from each worksheet. Explain that they are going to ask a member of the other group some questions to help them complete the text, but first they need to prepare the questions.

• Ask the students to work together to prepare and write down the questions they need to ask to complete the text.

• When all the students have prepared their questions, ask each student from Group A to work with a student from Group B. They should take it in turns to ask and answer the questions they have prepared and write the answer in the space in their text.

• When both students have finished asking and answering, allow them to compare worksheets. Find out if your students recognised the characters as being Marie and Pierre Curie, famous for their work in the field of radioactivity.

> *Suggested questions:*
> 1 Where was Maria born?
> 2 When was Maria born?
> 3 When did she (Maria) go to Paris?
> 4 What did she (Maria) go to Paris to study?
> 5 Where was she (Maria) studying when she met Pierre?
> 6 When did they (Maria and Pierre) get married?
> 7 What did the French call her (Maria)?
> 8 When did Pierre die?
> 9 What was Pierre doing when the cart hit him?
> 10 What did Maria win?
> 11 When did Maria die?
> 12 Where was she (Maria) resting when she died?

3 Vocabulary Exciting or excited?

Page 158
Activity
Class mingle: finding out about feelings.

Focus
Using -ed and -ing adjective endings.

Preparation
Make one copy of the worksheet for each group of twelve students in the class and cut up as indicated.

Procedure
• If there are more than twelve students in the class, divide them into groups. Give one card to each student in the class and ask them to complete the adjective with an appropriate ending, either -ed or -ing.

• Tell the students to find the answer to the questions on their card by speaking to everybody in their group. Make sure the students know which form the adjective on their card should take, -ed or -ing.

• Ask the students to go round the class (or their group) asking and answering questions. Tell them that they may need to make notes on a separate piece of paper.

• When they have spoken to everyone in the class (or their group), they should take it in turns to report back to the class (or group) on the information they have found out.

3 Communication A few quick questions

Page 159
Activity

Class mingle: sentence completion.

Focus

Consolidation of questions and the topics and language from Units 1–3 of *New Inside Out* Pre-intermediate Student's Book.

Preparation

Make one copy of the worksheet for each student in the class.

Procedure

- Fold the worksheet so only the left column is visible. Give one worksheet to each student in the class.

- Ask the students to write a different classmate's name on each line of the left column. If there are fewer than ten students in the class, ask them to repeat some names. However, they must not write their own name in this list.

- Students then unfold the worksheet to show incomplete statements about their classmates. For example:

  Thierry feels _____ today.
  Emily is named after _____ .

- Give students time to prepare and write a question for each statement. If necessary, demonstrate an example with one of the students to encourage them to ask the first question.

  Suggested questions:
  How do you feel today? Who are you named after?
  Who / Which famous person do you look like?
  What do your friends sometimes call you?
  What's your favourite country?
  Which country / place would you really like to visit?
  Who would you love to go on a date with?
  Who's your favourite celebrity?
  What is your dream holiday?
  How would you describe your life?

- The students then mingle around the classroom, asking and answering the questions they have written and completing the statements. For example:

  Thierry feels *worried about his exam* today.
  Emily is named after *her grandmother*.

- Encourage students to ask further questions to find out more information.

- When all the sentences have been completed, the students, in pairs or small groups, tell each other what they've learnt. Ask the students to report anything interesting to the class.

Review A Stand By Me

Page 160
Activity

Pairwork: song.

Focus

Revision of grammar and vocabulary from *New Inside Out* Pre-intermediate Student's Book, Units 1–3.

Preparation

Make one copy of the worksheet for each student in the class. Get the recording ready.

Procedure

- Explain that you're going to listen to a song called *Stand By Me* by Ben E. King. Students may be familiar with this song. Although it is quite old (it has been recorded many times), it was used in the film of the same name, which students may have seen.

- Encourage students to read the lines aloud to see which words don't sound right and disrupt the rhythm. Do not check answers at this stage, but allow students to compare notes in pairs or groups. Play the recording for students to check their answers. If they would like, play it again for them just to listen and enjoy.

- Allow students time to discuss the best interpretation of the song in 2 and report their views back to the class.

- Ask students to work in pairs. Give students time to consider the question in 3 before they start speaking.

> **1** 1 good   2 Disney   3 flashing
>   4 probably   5 ever   6 up   7 blue
>   8 over   9 Rocky   10 out   11 big
>   12 up
>
> **2** The best interpretation of the song is c)

4 Grammar Let's talk!

Page 161
Activity

Groupwork: board game.

Focus

Gerunds and infinitives after particular verbs.

Preparation

Make one copy of the worksheet for each group of three to five students in the class. Each group will need dice and counters.

Procedure

- Write two examples on the board – one which requires the gerund and one the infinitive:

  Do you like _____ (go) to the theatre? (going)
  Have you decided _____ (go) out tonight? (to go)

  Ask the students to complete the gaps correctly.

- Divide the class into groups of three to five and explain the rules of the game:

  1 Students throw the dice and move around the board.

  2 If they land on a question, the student must form the question correctly using the gerund or infinitive form. They then ask this question to another member of the group who must give a suitable answer.

  3 If the student lands on a one-word prompt, for example, DECIDE, then any other member of the group must form a question for them to answer. The question must use the key word in a suitable tense and with the correct verb pattern e.g.

  When did you decide to come to England?

  4 The game ends when someone has finished. If there is time, they can start again in new groups.

---

2 Do you enjoy <u>speaking</u> English?
3 Do you spend a lot of time <u>reading</u> in English?
4 What kinds of music do you hate <u>listening</u> to?
6 What kind of house would you choose <u>to live</u> in when you're 60?
7 Are there any household jobs you can't stand <u>doing</u>?
8 Do you need <u>to go</u> anywhere special this evening?
10 Are there any sports you hate <u>playing</u>?
11 What kind of job do you want <u>to have</u> in five years' time?
13 Do you mind other people <u>smoking</u> next to you in public places?
14 What countries do you want <u>to visit</u> next year?
16 Do you like <u>going</u> to the same place on holiday every year?
17 When did you start <u>learning</u> English?
19 What do you love <u>doing</u> on Friday evenings?
20 What sports do you enjoy <u>watching</u> but not <u>doing</u>?
21 Do you mind <u>going</u> to the dentist?
22 Do you like <u>going</u> out on a rainy day?
23 When was the last time you agreed <u>to help</u> someone?
25 What do men waste time <u>doing</u> in your country?
27 Which shops do you avoid <u>going</u> into?

---

4 Vocabulary What's the difference?

Page 162

Activity

Pairwork: finding and describing differences.

Focus

Vocabulary of clothes, accessories and patterns from Unit 4 *New Inside Out* Pre-intermediate Student's Book.

Preparation

Make one copy of the worksheet for each pair of students in the class and cut in half as indicated.

Procedure

- Divide the class into pairs. Tell your students they are going to look at a picture which is almost the same as their partner's, but there are some differences (you can either tell them there are twelve, or let them find as many as they can).

- Give a copy of Worksheet A to each Student A and a copy of Worksheet B to each Student B. Tell them they must not look at each other's worksheet. Ask them to take it in turns to describe what they see on their worksheet, paying special attention to clothes, accessories and patterns.

- Each time they find a difference, they should mark it on their worksheet and be prepared to explain it later.

- When students have finished describing their pictures to each other, ask them how many mistakes they found (if you didn't tell them at the start) and check answers with the class. Only at this stage can students compare their pictures.

(from left to right)
1) In A the girl is wearing floral pyjamas; in B she's wearing plain pyjamas.
2) In A the girl is wearing checked slippers (shoes); in B she's wearing floral slippers.
3) In A the girl is wearing a bracelet; in B she isn't wearing a bracelet.
4) In A the boy is wearing a plain cap; in B he's wearing a floral cap.
5) In A the boy is wearing a striped vest; in B he's wearing a striped T-shirt.
6) In A the boy is wearing striped socks; in B he's wearing plain socks.
7) In A the man isn't wearing a scarf; in B he's wearing a checked scarf.
8) In A the man isn't wearing a raincoat; in B he's wearing a plain raincoat.
9) In A the man is wearing a floral waistcoat; in B he's wearing a plain waistcoat.
10) In A the woman is wearing a floral scarf; in B she's wearing a checked scarf.
11) In A the woman isn't wearing (any) earrings; in B she's wearing earrings.
12) In A the woman is wearing a checked skirt; in B she's wearing a striped skirt.

---

4 **Communication** Ten facts

Page 163

Activity

Pairwork: guessing a partner's habits.

Focus

Adverbs of frequency.

Preparation

Make one copy of the worksheet for each student in the class.

Procedure

- Divide the class into pairs. Tell your students they are going to read ten statements and they have to think about the statements from their own point of view and from the point of view of their partner.
- On the right of the page there are some adverbs of frequency. Ask your students to think about the first statement (*I go to bed early*) and tick (✓) an adverb of frequency which makes the statement true for themselves. For example a student who always goes to bed around midnight would tick the adverb 'never'.
- Once they have done this, ask them to guess which adverb their partner would choose, by ticking one of them. However, they must not ask their partner yet.
- When all students have ticked the statements for themselves and their partner, ask them to take it in turns to read each statement about themselves, including the adverb of frequency (in the correct position!) so that the other student can check their guess. For example: *I **never** go to bed early*. A correct guess scores one point.
- Students continue until they have read out all ten statements to each other and checked their guesses. The student who guessed most statements correctly is the winner.

5 **Grammar** As fit as a fiddle

Page 164

Activity

Group or pairwork: dominoes game.

Focus

Comparative and superlative forms from Unit 5 of *New Inside Out* Pre-intermediate Student's Book.

Preparation

Make one copy of the worksheet for each group of three students in the class and cut up as indicated.

Procedure

- Explain to the students that they are going to play a game of dominoes by matching two halves of a sentence about fitness, and that the object of the game is to get rid of all their dominoes.
- Ask the students to work in groups of three and give each group a set of dominoes. Ask them to deal out three dominoes each and to leave the rest in a pile, face down.
- Before they start, explain the instructions:
  1 Player A puts down any one of their dominoes face up.
  2 The player on their left must put down one of their dominoes, making sure that one of their sentence halves matches one on either side of Player A's domino.

ng fatter.	More people join a gym in January …	… than at any other time of year.	It's impor thirty min exercise ..

  3 If a player can't put down one of their dominoes, they take a domino from the top of the pile and put it down if they can.
  4 The winner is the first player to get rid of all their dominoes. When they have finished the game, students can shuffle the dominoes and play again if they like.

5 **Vocabulary** Sports crossword

Page 165

Activity

Group or pairwork: completing a crossword.

Focus

Sports, where you do sports, and what equipment you need.

Preparation

Make one copy of the worksheet for each pair of students in the class and cut in half as indicated.

Procedure

- Write: *You play it with a bat and a ball. The pitch is a diamond shape.* Ask students to guess the sport (*baseball*). Tell the students they are going to write some similar sentences as clues for a crossword.
- Divide the class into two groups, Group A and Group B. Explain that you are going to give each group the same crossword but that Group A will have the 'down' words in pictures and Group B will have the 'across' words in pictures. Their task is to write the names of the sports on their crosswords and then write clues for the words written on their crosswords.
- Give a copy of crossword A to each student in

Group A and a copy of crossword B to each student in Group B. Ask the students to work together with people in their group to write the names of the sports pictured on their worksheet on their crosswords.

- Then ask them to work together to write clues for each of the sports. Encourage them to think about where it's played (*pitch, court, track, pool,* etc.) and what equipment you need to play it (*ball, racket, stick, club, goggles, special shoes/boots, trunks, net,* etc.). If they need to, they can refer to the Student's Book page 47. Go round the class and help them if needed.

- When they have finished writing their clues, students should work with a partner from the other group. They must not show each other their crossword.

- Ask them to sit facing each other and take it in turns to ask their partner for clues to the missing words on their crossword.

- When they have asked and answered all the questions and completed their crosswords, they can look at each other's worksheet to check their spellings.

5 **Communication** Numbers, numbers, numbers

Page 166

Activity

Groupwork: number quiz.

Focus

Consolidation and practice of numbers and superlatives.

Preparation

Make one copy of the worksheet for each group of three students in the class and cut up as indicated.

Procedure

- Put the students into groups of three and give a different set of questions and answers to each student. The students must not show each other their worksheets.

- Student A reads out the first question on his or her list. Students B and C look at their list of answers and try to agree which is the correct one. The clues (e.g. *kph, litres, centimetres* etc.) should help them. Student A writes the answer in the answers column.

- Then Student B reads out the first question on his or her list and Students A and C try to find the correct answer.

- They continue taking turns to ask their questions until all the questions have been asked.

- Check the answers with the class. The group with the most correct answers is the winner.

Student A: 1 206   2 200,000   3 in the 1850s
4 272 centimetres

Student B: 1 250   2 38 litres   3 1948   4 58°C

Student C: 1 100,000 times a day   2 12,756 km
3 900 years ago   4 1,670 kph

- You may like to copy the additional information below and give it to each group with the answers.

Additional information

Student A

1 The adult body has 206 bones, but we are born with 300.

2 This was at the World Cup final in Brazil in 1950.

4 The world's tallest person was Robert Wadlow, an American, who died in 1940.

Student B

1 This is the same as 4.2 babies per second, 360,500 per day or 131,500,000 per year. The population was 6,000,000,000 in the year 2000 and will reach 10,000,000,000 by the year 2050. In contrast, there are only 105 deaths per minute.

3 The shop was opened in California.

4 The hottest temperature ever was recorded at Al'Azizyah in Libya in 1922.

Student C

1 That's the same as 3 billion times in an average lifetime.

3 Sunglasses were first worn by Chinese judges to hide their eyes so that people couldn't tell what they were thinking.

6 **Grammar** Have you ever done it?

Page 167

Activity

Class mingle: asking and talking about experiences.

Focus

Present perfect for experience and past simple to give more details.

Preparation

Make one copy of the worksheet for each student in the class.

Procedure

- Give one copy of the worksheet to each student. Explain that they are going to ask questions about experiences and then find out more details.

- Direct your students' attention to the first question, 'Have you ever won a prize?' and then to the two questions on the right which have been completed as examples. Point out that the verb changes from the present perfect form in the first question to the past simple form when asking for more specific details.

- Divide the class into pairs and ask students to work together to complete the questions in the 'Details' column. Be ready to offer help at this stage.

- Once the students have completed the questions, ask them to stand up and mingle, asking as many different people their questions as they can. Tell them to write down only the name of the person whose answer to the first question is 'Yes'. If the person answers 'No', there is no need to continue with the other questions.

- When the first student has completed their questionnaire, stop the activity and talk about any interesting experiences with the class.

Extension

Ask students to write a short sentence about an experience they've had on a piece of paper, fold it up and put it in a hat. For example: *'I've held a baby lion'*.

They can repeat this between three and five times, writing a different experience on each piece of paper.

When all students have put their experiences into a hat, each one in turn takes a piece of paper out, unfolds it, and reads it. Then they go around the class asking each person the question until they find the owner of the piece of paper. For example: *'Have you ever held a baby lion?'*

When they have found the owner, they ask more questions to find out the details. For example: *'When did you hold it? Where were you? What was it like? Did it bite you?'* You can end by talking with the class about the biggest surprises.

6 Vocabulary In an ideal world

Page 168

Activity

Individual and pair or groupwork: giving opinions.

Focus

Using the modal verb *should* for talking about what you think is right.

Preparation

Make one copy of the worksheet for each student in the class.

Procedure

- Tell your students they are going to read some statements about what they think makes a good friend, an ideal job and a life partner (husband/wife/girlfriend/boyfriend).

- Give each student a copy of the worksheet and ask them to read each statement and tick (✓) a box (ranging from *very important* to *not at all important*) depending on how strongly they feel about the statement.

- Once students have finished reading all the statements and have a ticked a box for each, divide the class into pairs or small groups and ask students to compare and discuss their answers.

- Talk about the answers with the class. Did anyone find out anything interesting?

6 Communication What's my job?

Page 169

Activity

Class mingle: finding out job details to guess jobs.

Focus

Job-related questions, adverbs of frequency, *have to*.

Preparation

Make one copy of the worksheet for each student in the class. Write names of 'jobs' on separate post-it™ notes. You will need one job and post-it note per student.

Possible examples of jobs:
accountant, butcher, clown, dentist, farmer, fashion designer, fire fighter, gardener, hairdresser, mechanic, musician, nurse, photographer, pilot, plumber, pop star, postman, priest, scientist, soldier, taxi driver, translator, waiter, window cleaner, writer

Procedure

- Explain to the students that they will be given a job but they won't know what it is. They have to find out.

- Give each student a copy of the worksheet. Ask the students to read the instructions and questions.

- Tell the students that if they want to they can add three extra questions of their own at the bottom. Help with vocabulary problems, for example: *admire, tips, laboratory*.

- Ask the students to come to your desk to get a job stuck on their back.

- Tell students to walk around the class asking each person a couple of questions and noting down the answers. Go round and help when necessary.

- After ten minutes of questioning (or when the first student has correctly guessed their job), stop the activity and ask students to write down what they think their job is.

- Check what they think and see if they were right.

Follow up

The students can write about 'their job' for homework: e.g. *Positive and negative aspects of being a (taxi driver), My working day as a (taxi driver)*, etc.

Note: To help students feel more comfortable with the activity, you can ask one student to write a job and stick it on your back, and you can go round the class asking questions too.

Review B Suspicious minds

Page 170

Activity

Pairwork: song.

Focus

Revision of grammar and vocabulary from *New Inside Out* Pre-intermediate Student's Book, Units 4–6.

Preparation

Make one copy of the worksheet for each student in the class. Get the recording ready.

Procedure

- Find out how much students know about Elvis Presley. Perhaps divide the class into teams and award points for every fact they can produce and two points for titles of his songs. If your students have no interest at all in Elvis Presley, find out who they think the most romantic singer at the moment is. Ask them to tell you everything they know about this singer.

- Ask students to decide which choice describes someone with a suspicious mind.

- Ask students to look at the two pictures on the page. Tell them they are going to listen to the song and decide which picture, A or B, goes with the song. Play the recording.

- Allow students to discuss their answers in pairs/ groups. Check answers with the class.

- Give your students plenty of time to think about what they are going to say in 5. You might like to set the preparation for homework.

---

1 A person with a suspicious mind **doesn't believe** what you tell them.

2 Picture B goes with the song.

3 a) doesn't want   b) unhappy   c) thinks
   d) never lies

4 a) walk out   b) a word   c) go on
   d) drops by   e) dry the tears from your eyes

   The singer said *a, c* and *e*.
   The suspicious lover said *b* and *d*.

---

7 Grammar Thirty-second futures

Page 171

Activity

Groupwork: talking about your future.

Focus

Present continuous and *going to* for future arrangements and plans.

Preparation

Make one copy of the worksheet for each group of three or four students in the class. Each group will need one coin. Each student will need one counter.

Procedure

- Show students the board game. Demonstrate how to play: toss a coin and explain that one side of the coin (heads) means move two spaces; the other (tails) means move one space. Move your counter onto a square and speak for 30 seconds about what is written on the square.

- You may like to write a couple of examples on the board of different future forms that students can use, for example, your next holiday:

  I'm staying with friends.
  I'm going to sunbathe.

- Divide the students into groups of three or four. Give one board and one coin to each group, and one counter to each student.

- Go round the class while the students play the game, noting down any mistakes that you can talk about and correct later.

- Continue the game until all or nearly all of the groups have got to the finish.

Note: Encourage students to ask further questions to the speaker each time.

7 Vocabulary How green are you?

Page 172

Activity

Individual and pair or groupwork: questionnaire.

Focus

Vocabulary related to green issues in Unit 7 *New Inside Out* Pre-intermediate Student's Book.

Preparation

Make one copy of the worksheet for each student in the class and one copy of the *Scores* (page 142) for each pair or group.

Procedure

- Check or remind your students of the following items: *household waste, recycling, on standby, environmentally-friendly, low energy lightbulbs, carbon emissions, electrical appliance, switch/turn on/off.*

- Give each student a copy of the worksheet and ask them to read each question and circle the answer which best describes them.

Scores

1 More than 80% of our waste could be recycled but only a small amount is. The top five countries in the world for recycling are: Sweden, Austria, Switzerland, Germany and the Netherlands.
   a) 4   b) 2   c) 0

2 Always switch electrical appliances off. Many use as much electricity on standby as they do when they're switched on.
   a) 0   b) 2   c) 4

3 We usually end up drinking the water that goes down our drains. Non environmentally-friendly cleaning products can be poisonous and almost impossible to remove completely from our drinking water.
   a) 4   b) 2   c) 0

4 Always turn your lights off, even if it's just for ten minutes.
   a) 0   b) 2   c) 4

5 Food usually comes to you from other countries by plane. Planes produce more carbon than any other form of transport, so it's much better for the planet if you buy locally.
   a) 4   b) 2   c) 0

6 Your car produces carbon emissions. If you can walk or cycle, it's better for your health and the health of the planet.
   a) 4   b) 2   c) 0

7 Low-energy lightbulbs last 8-10 times longer than standard lightbulbs and can save you 50% on your lighting bills.
   a) 4   b) 2   c) 0

8 See 5
   a) 4   b) 2   c) 0

9 See 6
   a) 4   b) 2   c) 0

10 A five-minute shower uses 35 litres of water compared to a bath that uses 80 litres. The less water you use to wash yourself the more environmentally-friendly you are, but you may not be very popular in a small room with no windows.
   a) 1   b) 3   c) 4

- Once students have finished reading all the questions and have a circled an answer for each, divide the class into pairs or small groups and ask students to compare and discuss their answers. Give each pair or group a copy of the Scores (below) so that they can work out how green they are.

- Ask the whole class if anyone found out anything interesting from their partner/group.

7 Communication Manifesto

Page 173

Activity

Groupwork: preparing statements about a cause.

Focus

Vocabulary connected with topical issues and pressure groups; language of expressing opinions.

Preparation

Make one copy of the worksheet for each group of three to five students in the class.

Procedure

- Explain that the students are going to form their own pressure groups connected with a cause of their choice. These could include: *against globalisation, against cruelty to animals, against nuclear weapons, against school fees, against destruction of the environment, against unequal pay for women,* etc.

- Divide the class into groups of three to five students.

- Ask the students to decide which cause they represent. Tell them to think of a suitable name for their group and to choose a leader. Explain that the leader will present the group's ideas to the class at the end and that a vote will be taken on the best manifesto.

- Either draw a framework of the manifesto leaflet on the board or photocopy it onto an OHT. Do an example with the class and ask them for possibilities to fill the gaps.

- Give out one worksheet per group and choose a secretary who will write down the group's ideas.

- Go round and listen, helping with ideas where necessary.

- Ask each party leader to present their manifesto to the class.

- Take a class vote on the best manifesto.

Follow up

The manifestos could form the basis of a poster/leaflet competition. Students could use the basic ideas from the manifestos to produce a more detailed and colourful poster/leaflet for their party. Encourage the use of computer graphics, cut-up magazines, etc.

8 Grammar Schooldays

Page 174

Activity

Individual and groupwork: asking about schooldays.

Focus

Could/couldn't for permission and *had to/didn't have to* for obligation.

Preparation

Make one copy of the worksheet for each student in the class.

Procedure

- Tell your students they are going to write and ask each other some questions about when they were at school. (If your students are still at school, ask them to think about the last school they were at.)

- Draw their attention to the first question, which has been given as an example. Ask students the questions for 2 and 3 (*Did you have to go to school on Saturdays?* and *Could you run in the school buildings?*) and then ask students to write the questions for the rest.

- When they have finished writing the questions, ask students to write *Yes* or *No* in the first of the right-hand columns, as a true response for themselves to each question.

- After they have answered each question, divide the class into groups of three. Ask students to write the name of the other two people in the group at the top of the remaining two right-hand columns. Then they take it in turns to ask and answer the questions.

- When the first group have finished, ask students to report back their findings to the class. For example:
  All of us had to do homework every day.
  Two of us had to go to school on Saturdays, but one didn't have to.
  None of us could smoke at school.

---

2   Did you have to go to school on Saturdays?
3   Could you run in the school buildings?
4   Did you have to switch off your mobiles before class?
5   Did you have to start classes at 8.30 a.m.?
6   Did you have to do homework every day?
7   Could you eat in the classrooms?
8   As a punishment, did you have to stay an extra hour?
9   Could you bring radios to school?
10 Did you have to give your homework in on time?
11 Could you smoke?
12 Did you have to call your teachers 'Sir' and 'Miss'?

---

8 Vocabulary Education wordsearch

Page 175

Activity

Groupwork: word puzzle.

Focus

Vocabulary related to education from Unit 8 *New Inside Out* Pre-intermediate Student's Book.

Preparation

Make one copy of the worksheet for each student in the class.

Procedure

- Give each student in the class a copy of the worksheet and then divide the class into groups of three.

- Ask your students to work together to find as many of the sixteen words as they can and then write them in the correct column in the table.

- Check the answers with the class.

I	X	Y	N	T	D	M	E	K	A	P	A	S	O	F	L	M
O	S	–	G	B	G	E	N	P	D	T	R	Y	R	O	G	Z
A	B	J	R	U	G	D	G	M	Z	–	X	I	X	N	–	P
E	L	U	Z	S	H	I	I	R	D	Q	U	V	M	A	G	I
B	A	A	Y	I	M	C	N	H	E	U	P	A	Y	A	R	J
A	N	I	W	N	G	I	E	S	A	E	X	V	O	T	R	C
P	G	X	M	E	T	N	E	E	D	H	I	S	T	O	R	Y
S	U	I	X	S	L	E	R	C	S	I	F	G	S	U	G	J
Z	A	X	T	S	D	S	I	R	E	B	P	G	K	R	O	U
V	G	W	–	E	R	N	N	E	C	V	S	L	E	I	R	N
X	E	C	U	U	A	O	G	T	O	W	–	T	O	S	A	I
G	S	H	Z	O	G	I	V	A	N	W	M	M	Y	M	D	O
B	X	H	Z	E	N	A	L	R	D	R	O	J	U	B	A	R
A	–	L	E	V	E	L	S	I	A	L	B	H	K	N	R	H
W	K	I	N	D	E	R	G	A	R	T	E	N	O	Q	Y	I
Q	M	G	M	B	D	S	N	L	Y	G	K	J	L	A	X	G
C	E	R	T	I	F	I	C	A	T	E	B	E	V	O	L	H

Types of school: Primary, Secondary, Junior High, Kindergarten. Note: High schools are found in North America and Asia. Secondary is the British equivalent. Kindergartens are for children of pre-primary age.

Vocational subjects: Secretarial, Tourism, Business, Engineering.

Qualifications: Certificate, A-levels, Degree, Diploma. Note: High school diplomas are qualifications in the USA and Canada, High school certificates (HSC) in Australia, and 'A' levels in the UK.

Classic subjects: Law, Medicine, Languages, History.

8 **Communication** What's your advice?

Page 176
Activity

Groupwork: writing problems and advice.

Focus

Should for advice.

Preparation

Make one copy of the worksheet for every three groups of three, then cut into three as indicated and give each group one third.

Procedure

- Introduce the topic and briefly discuss the purpose of problem pages. Then divide the class into groups of three (or pairs or groups of four if you have fewer or more students in your class).
- Give each group one section of the worksheet and ask them to complete the problem. Encourage them to be as imaginative and/or amusing as they can.
- When each group has finished their problem, ask them to pass it to the group on their left. This group should then write some advice for the problem, on a separate piece of paper. At this stage, encourage them to use *should*.
- When each group has finished writing their advice, they pass the problem to the group their left, who writes some advice for the problem. This continues until all groups have written advice for the other problems.
- When the groups have finished writing, they should hand the problem back to the original group, as well as their advice. Each group can then choose the best piece of advice for their problem.

9 **Grammar** *For* and *since*

Page 177
Activity

Class mingle: finding out personal information.

Focus

Questions with *How long ...?* + present perfect simple/continuous, and answers with *for/since*.

Preparation

Make one copy of the worksheet for each student in the class.

Procedure

- Give one copy of the worksheet to each student in the class. Explain that they are going to ask a question and then write down two versions of the answer.
- Choose a student to help demonstrate the first question. See if they can ask the question *Do you live in a flat?* If the answer is *Yes*, write the name of the student in the middle column. Ask the students what the next question is: *How long have you been living there?* to which the answer could be *Two years*.
- In the third column write a period of time after the word *for* (two years) and the point in time when the action started after *since* (2006, for example).
- Ask the students to tell you the '*Do you...?*' questions, to establish that your students are all asking similar questions, and then ask the students to stand up and mingle around the class, asking and answering the questions.
- When the first student has completed their questionnaire, stop the activity and ask the class to make sentences about another student, e.g. *Monica has been living in her flat for two years.*

9 **Vocabulary** Character crossword

Page 178
Activity

Groupwork: completing a crossword.

Focus

Character adjectives, their synonyms and antonyms, from Unit 9 *New Inside Out* Pre-intermediate Student's Book.

Preparation

Make one copy of the worksheet for each student in the class.

Procedure

- Give one copy of the worksheet to each student.
- Divide the class into pairs or small groups and ask them to work together to complete the crossword with character adjectives from Unit 9 of the Student's Book. Allow the students to check in the Student's Book if necessary.
- Stop when the first pair or group have finished and check answers with the class.

Follow up

Ask students to stay in their pairs or groups and talk about someone they know using the adjectives in the puzzle.

Across		Down	
1	loyal	2	annoying
3	selfish	3	shy
6	easygoing	4	sociable
7	calm	5	confident
8	faithful	9	pessimistic
10	bossy		
11	sensitive		
12	optimistic		
13	ambitious		
14	mysterious		
15	affectionate		

2 I need <u>to speak</u>/speaking English for my job.
3 She's got long, wavy <u>hair</u>/hairs.
4 He's always telling us what to do – he's very <u>bossy</u>/shy.
6 I can <u>swim</u>/to swim faster than you.
7 He's got <u>freckles</u>/dimples all over his face.
8 He grew a moustache/<u>beard</u> to cover the scar on his chin.
10 She's got fair <u>hair</u>/eyes.
11 I enjoy <u>watching</u>/to watch sport on TV.
12 He's got pale <u>skin</u>/hair.
14 What does he <u>look like</u>/look?
15 I want being/<u>to be</u> rich.
16 She's wearing false <u>eyelashes</u>/eyebrows!
18 I <u>put on</u>/take off my shoes before I leave the house.
19 She's got the most perfect tooth/<u>teeth</u>.
20 I think I'm going to <u>give up</u>/hang up smoking.
22 He looks tired – he's got bags under his ears/<u>eyes</u>.
23 I'm looking forward to meet/<u>meeting</u> her.
24 She's got a beautiful hair/<u>smile</u>.
26 She feels things very strongly – she's <u>sensitive</u>/sensible.
27 What is she <u>like</u>/look like?
28 When she smiles, small wrists/<u>wrinkles</u> appear next to her eyes.
29 I've decided getting/<u>to get</u> my hair cut.

9 Communication Smile!

Page 179

Activity

Groupwork: board game.

Focus

Vocabulary and word patterns from Unit 9 *New Inside Out* Pre-intermediate Student's Book.

Preparation

Make one copy of the worksheet for each pair of students in the class. Make a copy of the answers (below) for each referee. Each player needs a counter and each team needs a dice.

Procedure

- Put your students into groups of three (two players and one referee) or five (two pairs and one referee) and give each group a copy of the worksheet, two counters and a dice. You will need to give the referee a copy of the answers.

- The students place their counter on the START square and then roll the dice to see who goes first.

- The students take it in turns to roll the dice, move that number of squares forward and then choose the correct alternative. The referee checks the answers. If correct, the student's counter remains on the square. If incorrect, the student has to return his/her counter to its original square.

- If a player lands on a SMILE! square, they should move forward but not try to answer the question. If a player lands on an OOPS! square, they miss a go.

- This continues until a player/pair reaches the final SMILE! square and wins the game.

Follow up

Give a copy of the worksheet to each student in the class and ask them to write out each sentence (with the correct alternative only) for homework.

Review C Money

Page 180

Activity

Pairwork: song.

Focus

Revision of grammar and vocabulary from *New Inside Out* Pre-intermediate Student's Book, Units 7–9.

Preparation

Make one copy of the worksheet for each student in the class. Get the recording ready.

Procedure

- Students read the lyrics of *Money*, a hit for the Beatles in 1963. They choose the most appropriate words to complete the lines. Allow them to compare notes with other pairs, but do not check answers at this stage. Play the recording for students to listen and check their answers.

- Encourage students to quote lines from the song in support of their opinions in 2. You may like to point out that the very opposite of this view of money is presented in other Beatles lyrics such as 'I don't care too much for money; money can't buy me love'.

- Allow students to work in pairs or small groups to discuss what they think the sayings mean in 3 and match them with their meanings. Students then report back to the class with their answers and other money expressions from their own languages.

> **1** 1 free   2 bees   3 thrill   4 bills
>   5 true   6 use
>
> **2** c) Money is the most important thing in life.
>
> **3** a) 3   b) 1   c) 2

Follow up

The following can be used as an opportunity for your students to offer their opinions.

Work with a partner. Discuss these questions:

1 What is your opinion about the singer's attitude to money?

2 Do you know anybody with similar opinions?

3 How would you describe your own feelings about money?

10 **Grammar** Then or now?

Page 181
Activity

Pair or groupwork: discussion about life 100 years ago.

Focus

Used to + infinitive for past habits and states.

Preparation

Make one copy of the worksheet for each student.

Procedure

- Begin by asking students what differences they can think of between their grandparents' lives and their lives now. If you have any old photographs or pictures showing life 100 years ago, you could also show them these.

- Write the first statement from the worksheet on the board with the *I agree/I'm not sure/I disagree* headings.

- Ask students to agree or disagree with the statement and encourage them to give reasons.

- Hand out the worksheets and tell the students to continue by ticking the other statements. Make sure they are working alone. Go round and help with any difficulties.

- Divide the class into pairs or groups. Groups will probably encourage a more lively discussion.

- When students have finished, ask the class to talk about any that they found interesting or that they disagreed strongly about.

Follow up

Note: You may prefer to use this follow up for stronger classes.

1 The students could write a summary of the opinions of their group. For example:

We all felt strongly that…
The majority of us thought that …
Some of us said that …, but others said …
We couldn't agree on …, etc.

2 The ideas that come from the discussion could be used as the basis of an essay about the advantages and disadvantages of life now compared with 70–100 years ago.

3 Photocopy the incomplete statements below and hand out one copy for each student/pair.

Students complete the statements with their own ideas and then discuss them in groups.

> 1 People are more/less interested in _____
> 2 Men are more _____
> 3 People used to have more/less _____
> 4 Governments _____
> 5 Teachers/schools _____
> 6 There is more/less _____

10 **Vocabulary** Features of a car

Page 182
Activity

Group or pairwork: dominoes game.

Focus

Vocabulary of car parts and features of a car from Unit 10 *New Inside Out* Pre-intermediate Student's Book.

Preparation

Make one copy of the worksheet for each group of three students in the class and cut up as indicated.

Procedure

- Explain to the students that they are going to play a game of dominoes by matching two halves of a feature of a car, and that the object of the game is to get rid of all their dominoes.

- Ask the students to work in groups of three and give each group a set of dominoes. Ask them to deal out three dominoes each and to leave the rest in a pile, face down.

- Before they start, explain the instructions:

  1 Player A puts down any one of their dominoes face up.

  2 The player on their left must put down one of their dominoes, making sure that one of their words goes with one on either side of Player A's domino, saying the combination as they put the matching domino down.

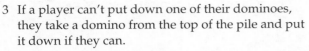

| ts | windscreen | wipers | g(|

3 If a player can't put down one of their dominoes, they take a domino from the top of the pile and put it down if they can.

4 The winner is the first player to get rid of all their dominoes.

• When they have finished the game, students can shuffle the dominoes and play again if they like.

---

windscreen wipers
gear stick
handbrake
headlight
number plate
seatbelt

sunroof
steering wheel
air conditioning
economical to run
leather seats

environmentally friendly
good sound system
satellite navigation system
powerful engine
spacious boot

---

10 **Communication** Food

Page 183

Activity

Groupwork: board game.

Focus

Revision of food-related vocabulary. Fluency practice.

Preparation

Make one copy of the worksheet for each group of four to five students. Each student will need a counter and each group will need a dice.

Procedure

• Hand out the worksheet and dice to each group. Each student will need something small to use as a counter, for example, a coin. Make sure that someone in the group has a watch with a second hand.

• Explain the rules of the game:

1 Students take turns to roll the dice and talk for thirty seconds about whichever topic they land on, without pausing or changing the subject. Tell them that for the purposes of this game, accuracy is not as important as just speaking.

2 If the rest of the group is happy that the student has completed the task, he or she wins a point.

3 The first student to get to the Finish gets an extra three points, the next gets two points and the third gets one. The game ends when the third person finishes.

• The student with the most points is the winner.

---

11 **Grammar** Find the mistake

Page 184

Activity

Pairwork: error correction.

Focus

Revision and consolidation of these language areas from *New Inside Out* Pre-intermediate Student's Book: verb patterns (gerund/infinitive), opinions, present perfect, *for* and *since*, unreal conditionals, *look/look like*.

Preparation

Make one copy of the worksheet for each pair of students in the class and cut up as indicated.

Procedure

• Put the students into pairs and give one the Student A worksheet and the other the Student B worksheet. Tell the students that five of the questions contain a grammar mistake and that five are correct.

• Ask the students to work individually to find and correct the grammar mistakes.

• When they have done this, ask Students A and B to compare the corrections they have made and to identify the correct version of each question.

• Check answers with the whole class.

---

1 What is [it] your favourite song and who wrote it? (Student B)

2 What are you looking forward to <u>doing</u> in the next few days? (Student A)

3 Do you want <u>to continue</u> studying English after this course? (Student A)

4 What <u>do</u> you <u>think</u> of the number one song at the moment? (Student B)

5 Have you lived in your house <u>for</u> a long time? (Student B)

6 <u>Do</u> you <u>look</u> like anyone famous? (Student A)

7 Where in the world would you most like to go <u>on</u> holiday? (Student A)

8 Would you take a year off work if you <u>could</u>? (Student B)

9 How long have you <u>known</u> your best friend? (Student A)

10 How many countries have you <u>been</u> to? (Student B)

Follow up

Ask the students to work in pairs or small groups to ask and answer the questions. Encourage them to ask further questions to find out more information. For example, for question 1: *When did you first hear the song? Why do you like it so much? Does it remind you of a particular time, place or person?*

Ask the students to report back to the class anything interesting from their discussions.

11 Vocabulary Find someone

Page 185

Activity

Class mingle: find someone who …

Focus

Making sentences with adjectives + dependent prepositions.

Preparation

Make one copy of the worksheet for each student in the class.

Procedure

- Give one copy of the worksheet to each student in the class. Explain that they are going to ask each other some general questions. But first they are going to complete the sentences on the worksheet.

- Direct your students' attention to the first sentence on the worksheet and ask what the missing preposition is (*on*) to make the complete sentence *Find someone who is keen on football*. Divide the class into pairs and ask the students to work together to complete the sentences with the missing prepositions (see below).

- When all the students have finished writing the prepositions, check their answers as a class. Then tell them to make questions and ask each other the questions, and that they should write down as many different names as possible. As soon as they've written a 'Yes' answer and name, then they change partners.

- Check the first question *Are you keen on football?* and tell your students that each question will start in the same way.

- Ask them to stand up and mingle. Listen carefully and only stop them when the first student has finished.

- Ask students to tell the class anything interesting they found out.

… keen **on** *football*
… *afraid* **of** *the dark*
… *from a city that's famous* **for** *a particular dish or type of food*
… *fond* **of** *chocolate*
… *worried* **about** *something that's happening this week*
… *proud* **of** *his/her country*
… *allergic* **to** *cats*
… *interested* **in** *classical music*
… *terrified* **of** *spiders*
… *usually late* **for** *work/school*
… *bad* **at** *maths*
… *excited* **about** *something that's going to happen in the near future*

---

11 Communication Homophones

Page 186

Activity

Pair/groupwork: Pelmanism game.

Focus

Identifying two words with the same sound but different spellings.

Preparation

Make one copy of the worksheet for every four students in the class and cut up as indicated.

Procedure

- Read out the following words and ask your students to try to write down two different spellings for each word.

  son (*sun*), bare (*bear*), flour (*flower*), week (*weak*), hair (*hare*), sail (*sale*), eight (*ate*), pair (*pear*), mail (*male*), board (*bored*), meat (*meet*), won (*one*).

- Ask your students to compare what they have written in pairs or small groups.

- Check with the whole class. Go through all the words above, checking meaning and pronunciation.

- Tell your students they are going to play a game in which they have to match two pictures (of the words they have just written) that sound the same (e.g. *sun* and *son*).

  1 Divide the class into pairs and ask one pair to play against another pair. Give each group of four a copy of the worksheet, cut into cards as indicated. Ask them to put all the cards face down on the table.

  2 Each team takes it in turns to turn two cards over. The object of the game is to turn over two cards which have the same sound. If a player does this, they keep the pair of cards. As the player turns over the card, they must say the word, otherwise they cannot claim the pair.

  3 If the cards are not a matching pair, they are turned over again and left for the next pair to try.

  4 The team with the most pairs of cards at the end of the game are the winners.

- The worksheets can also be used for individual classwork or homework (see Follow up stage 1, below).

Follow up

1 Students could follow up the class game by doing the writing and matching activity as homework. Give each student a copy of the worksheet. Ask them to write a word in each box and then match the two words with the same sound by drawing a line connecting them.

2 Ask early finishers to find homophones for these words: way (*weigh*), right (*write*), hear (*here*), red (*read*), wear (*where*), sum (*some*), sew (*so*), there (*their*), for (*four*), by (*bye*).

12 Grammar What happened?

Page 187
Activity

Pairwork: sequencing a story.

Focus

Past perfect (and other narrative tenses).

Preparation

Make one copy of the worksheet for each student in the class.

Procedure

- Ask students if they have ever had an experience they couldn't explain. If the class is quiet or doesn't come up with any ideas, you should be prepared to talk about a strange experience you have had.
- If they can all think of something, ask them to tell the person next to them what happened.
- Divide the class into pairs and ask students to work together to complete Part 1 by writing the missing verb in the past simple, past continuous or the past perfect.
- When they have finished, check answers in open class. Then ask them to work together to put the events in the correct order in Part 2.

1
1 was travelling	6 gave
2 decided	7 knew
3 had never visited	8 had decided
4 asked	9 had spent
5 checked	10 worked

2
1 E   2 D   3 A   4 F   5 C   6 B

Follow up

Ask students to imagine they are George D Bryson. Allow them to make notes, then ask them to take it in turns to tell their partner the story in the first person.

12 Vocabulary Shout it out!

Page 188
Activity

Groupwork: general knowledge game.

Focus

Revision of some vocabulary and topic areas from *New Inside Out* Pre-intermediate Student's Book.

Preparation

Make one copy of the worksheet for each student in the class (to be handed out at the end of the game) and one for the teacher. Cut up the teacher's worksheet and shuffle the cards.

Make sure you have something to time one minute, for example, an egg timer, a stopwatch, or a watch with a second hand.

Procedure

- Divide the class into two teams and explain the rules as follows:

  1 The teacher selects one of the cards and reads out the category for Team A, for example *School subjects*.

  2 The team has one minute to find out the names of the ten items in that category that are on the card. The team members do this by shouting out items, with the teacher telling them *yes* or *no* according to whether or not they are on the card. The items are listed alphabetically to make it easier for the teacher to find them. For example:

  Teacher: *School subjects. Go!*
  Students: *Geography?*
  Teacher: *Yes, one point.*
  Students: *Science?*
  Teacher: *No.*
  Students: *Biology?*
  Teacher: *Yes, two points. etc.*

  3 The team scores one point for each item they give which is on the card. They score no points for items which are in the category, but not on the card. If the team gets all ten items, they get 20 points. Record the score for each round.

  4 Select a different category for Team B and play again. Then it's Team A's turn again and so on.

  5 When all the categories have been used, the team with the most points is the winner.

- Play the game, with a member of the opposing team timing one minute and shouting *Stop!* when the minute is up.

- When the game is over, give each student a copy of the worksheet and go through any unfamiliar language and pronunciation.

Notes

For larger classes, the game can be played with three teams.

For particularly large classes, you could divide the class into several different games with a student in the teacher's role for each game.

The worksheet need not be cut up, and can be used by choosing categories at random and crossing them off as they are used.

The currencies are used in the following countries:

Euro: Ireland, Finland, the Netherlands, Germany, Belgium, Luxembourg, France, Austria, Italy, Spain, Portugal

Dollar: USA, Australia, Canada, Hong Kong, New Zealand, Singapore, Taiwan, Zimbabwe

Franc: Cameroon, Côte d'Ivoire, Switzerland

Peso: Chile, Colombia, Mexico, Philippines

Pound: UK, Egypt

Riyal: Iran, Saudi Arabia, Qatar

Rouble: Russia

Rupee: India, Pakistan

Yen: Japan

Zloty: Poland

12 Communication Let's talk about ...

Page 189

Activity

Groupwork: board game.

Focus

Revision of language and topics from *New Inside Out* Pre-intermediate Student's Book.

Preparation

Make one copy of the worksheet for each group of three or four students in the class. Each student will need one counter and each group will need a dice. Make sure you have something to time one minute, for example, an egg timer, a stopwatch, or a watch with a second hand for each group.

Procedure

- Divide the class into small groups. Give each group a copy of the worksheet, a dice and a counter for each student.

- Explain the rules:

  1 Each player places their counter on the square marked START.

  2 Players take it in turns to throw the dice until someone throws a six.

  3 That player throws the dice again and moves their counter along the board according to the number on the dice.

  4 Players then play in turns moving around the board.

  5 When a player lands on a clear (an unshaded) square, they have to talk about the subject for thirty seconds.

  6 When a player lands on a shaded square, they have to talk about the subject for sixty seconds.

  7 If a player has nothing to say or can't talk for the necessary time, they are allowed to pass and miss a turn.

  8 The game continues until the first player reaches the square marked FINISH.

Review D I Have a Dream

Page 190

Activity

Pairwork: song.

Focus

Revision of grammar and vocabulary from *New Inside Out* Pre-intermediate Student's Book, Units 10–12.

Preparation

Make one copy of the worksheet for each student in the class. Get the recording ready.

Procedure

- Encourage students to read the lines aloud to see which words don't sound right and/or disrupt the rhythm. Do not check answers at this stage, but allow students to compare notes in pairs or groups. Play the recording for students to check their answers.

- Allow your students to discuss what they think are the most appropriate words to complete the statements about the song in 2. Then report back to the class with their ideas.

- Students complete the sentences in 3 with words from the song, and then discuss the sentences in pairs.

1	1 be	2 the	3 no	4 to	5 am	6 for
	7 am	8 free	9 go	10 one	11 do	
	12 does	13 a	14 am	15 for	16 am	
	17 free	18 go	19 go			

3	a) dream	b) sing	c) cope	d) tale
	e) believe	f) something		

Extension

This gives your students an opportunity for an extended speaking activity.

Choose one of the following to talk about. Work with a partner. Use the phrases to help you tell your partner about your (or someone else's) dream.

a) A dream you have for the future.

b) A dream a famous person has/had for the future.

c) A dream someone you know has/had for the future.

> *I hope that one day I'll be able to help other people with my time and money.*

Useful phrases
I want…
I dream of a future when…
I hope that…
I'm going to…
One day I'll…

> *My brother wants to be an astronaut when he grows up.*

> *Martin Luther King dreamt of a future when people of all colours could live together in peace.*

1 Grammar

What's in a name?

 A

Write the first name of ...

1 your best female friend ⟶

2 one of your neighbours ⟶

3 a member of your family ⟶

4 a sports personality ⟶

Names

1 _____

2 _____

3 _____

4 _____

Examples of questions:

- Who / (name)?
- How old?
- Where / live?
- married?
- have children?
- When / birthday?
- speak English?
- What / do?

Tear off this section and give it to your partner when you have written all the names.

B

Write the first name of ...

1 one of your grandparents ⟶

2 one of your colleagues/classmates ⟶

3 your best male friend ⟶

4 a TV or film personality ⟶

Names

1 _____

2 _____

3 _____

4 _____

Examples of questions:

- Who / (name)?
- How old?
- Where / live?
- married?
- have children?
- When / birthday?
- speak English?
- What / do?

1 Vocabulary

Family puzzle

Complete the puzzle with words connected to family or relationships.
Which two family-related words are hidden in the puzzle?

 New Inside Out Pre-intermediate Teacher's Book © Macmillan Publishers Limited 2008

1 Communication

Questions for me

Do you _____ ? _____ asked this question

- FOLD

Have you been to _____ ? _____ asked this question

- FOLD

Are you _____ ? _____ asked this question

- FOLD

Can you _____ ? _____ asked this question

- FOLD

Did you go _____ ? _____ asked this question

- FOLD

What do you _____ ? _____ asked this question

- FOLD

How many _____ ? _____ asked this question

- FOLD

Have you ever met _____ ? _____ asked this question

- FOLD

What's your _____ ? _____ asked this question

- FOLD

Where do you _____ ? _____ asked this question

These questions are for me. My name is _____

2 Grammar

Categorise

1 Put the words below under these headings.

transport	buildings	geography	going out
_____	_____	_____	_____
_____	_____	_____	_____
_____	_____	_____	_____
_____	_____	_____	_____

food	drink	countries
_____	_____	_____
_____	_____	_____
_____	_____	_____
_____	_____	_____
_____	_____	_____
_____	_____	_____

beer	cinema	house	taxi
Brazil	coast	Ireland	tea
bread	coffee	juice	theatre
bus	disco	Malta	traffic
cake	Egypt	meat	Turkey
canal	fruit	mountain	vegetables
car	Greece	nightlife	water
castle	office block	rice	wine
church		sea	

2 Now decide which are countable and which are uncountable.

 New Inside Out Pre-intermediate Teacher's Book © Macmillan Publishers Limited 2008

2 Vocabulary

Places in a city

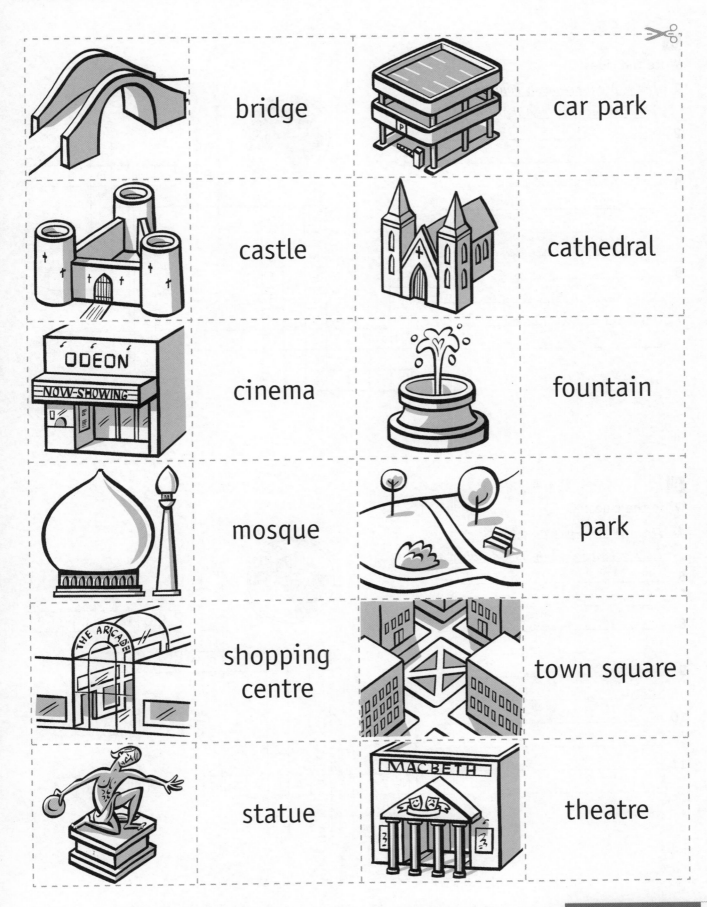

	bridge		car park
	castle		cathedral
	cinema		fountain
	mosque		park
	shopping centre		town square
	statue		theatre

2 Communication

Worldsearch

A

Write the clues:

1 *It's a Mediterranean country.*
   The capital city is Ankara.

2 _____

4 _____

5 _____

6 _____

7 _____

B

Write the clues:

3 *It's a North African country.*
   Its most famous city is Casablanca.

5 _____

8 _____

9 _____

10 _____

11 _____

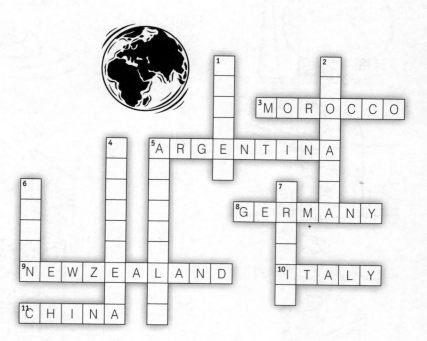

  New Inside Out Pre-intermediate Teacher's Book © Macmillan Publishers Limited 2008

3 Grammar

A love story

A A simple love story

Maria was born in (**1**) _____ in 1867. She was a very clever girl. Maria went to Paris in (**3**) _____ to study maths, physics and chemistry. She was very passionate about science. Maria was studying at (**5**) _____ when she met Pierre. They fell in love and, in 1895, they got married. Maria made France her home. She loved her work, she loved her husband and she loved her adopted country. The French called her (**7**) ' _____ '.

Pierre and Maria lived happily together for many years but, in 1906, Pierre died in a tragic accident. He was (**9**) _____ when a cart hit him. Maria was heartbroken but she continued their important work.

Maria won two Nobel prizes. The first was with Pierre and the second was after his death. Maria died in (**11**) _____ . She was resting in the Alps when she died. At last she was reunited with her love.

Write the questions.

1 Where _____ ?
3 When _____ ?
5 Where _____ ?
7 What _____ ?
9 What _____ ?
11 When _____ ?

- ✂

B A simple love story

Maria was born in Poland in (**2**) _____ . She was a very clever girl. Maria went to Paris in 1891 to study (**4**) _____ . She was very passionate about science. Maria was studying at the Sorbonne when she met Pierre. They fell in love and, in (**6**) _____ , they got married. Maria made France her home. She loved her work, she loved her husband and she loved her adopted country. The French called her 'Marie'.

Pierre and Maria lived happily together for many years but, in (**8**) _____ , Pierre died in a tragic accident. He was crossing the road when a cart hit him. Maria was heartbroken but she continued their important work.

Maria won (**10**) _____ . The first was with Pierre and the second was after his death. Maria died in 1934. She was resting (**12**) _____ when she died. At last she was reunited with her love.

Write the questions.

2 When _____ ?
4 What _____ ?
6 When _____ ?
8 When _____ ?
10 What _____ ?
12 Where _____ ?

3 Vocabulary

Exciting or excited?

What's the most interest ____ book you've ever read?

Find out

When did you last feel frighten ____ ?

Find out

At which time of day do you feel most tir ____ ?

Find out

Which school subject did you find most confus ____ ?

Find out

What's the most excit ____ experience you've had?

Find out

Which sports are you interest ____ in?

Find out

What do you do to feel more relax ____ ?

Find out

What's the most surpris ____ thing about you?

Find out

When was the last time you felt annoy ____ about something?

Find out

What do you do when you feel bor ____ ?

Find out

What's the most bor ____ book you've ever read?

Find out

Describe a time when you felt embarrass ____ .

Find out

3 Communication

A few quick questions

FOLD

_____ | feels _____ today.

_____ | is named after _____ .

_____ | thinks he/she looks like _____ .

_____ | 's friends sometimes call him/her _____ .

_____ | 's favourite country is _____ .

_____ | would really like to visit _____ .

_____ | would love to go on a date with _____ .

_____ | 's favourite celebrity is _____ .

_____ | 's dream holiday is _____ .

_____ | would describe his/her life as _____ .

Review A

Stand By Me

Ben E. King recorded *Stand By Me* in 1961 and 1987. Elvis Presley and John Lennon recorded the song in 1967 and 1975.

1 **Look at the words of the song. On each line 1–12 there is an extra word. Find the word and cross it out.**

1   When the ~~good~~ night has come,
2   And the Disney land is dark,
3   And the moon is the only flashing light we see,
4   No, I probably won't be afraid,
5   Oh, I won't ever be afraid,
6   Just as long as you stand up, stand by me.

So darlin', darlin', stand by me, oh stand by me.
Oh stand, stand by me, stand by me.

7   If the blue sky that we look upon
8   Should tumble and fall over,
9   Or the Rocky mountains should crumble to the sea,
10 I won't cry, I won't cry out,
11 No, I won't shed a big tear,
12 Just as long as you stand up, stand by me.

So darlin', darlin', stand by me, oh stand by me.
Oh stand now, stand by me, stand by me.

And darlin', darlin', stand by me, oh stand by me.
Oh stand now, stand by me, stand by me.
Whenever you're in trouble,
Won't you stand by me, oh stand by me.
Oh stand now, oh stand, stand by me.

🌐 **1.29 Listen and check your answers.**

2 **Tick the best interpretation of the song.**

a) There are going to be a lot of disasters if you stand by me. ☐

b) I won't be able to see very well if you stand by me. ☐

c) If you stand by me, I will feel strong. Nothing will worry me. ☐

3 **Tell your partner about a time when you've really needed a friend to 'stand by you'.**

4 Grammar

Let's talk!

1 START

2 Do you enjoy _____ (speak) English? Give reasons for your answer.

3 Do you spend a lot of time _____ (read) in English? Why / Why not?

4 What kinds of music do you hate _____ (listen) to?

8 Do you need _____ (go) anywhere special this evening?

7 Are there any household jobs you can't stand _____ (do)?

6 What kind of house would you choose _____ (live) in when you're 60?

5 LIKE

9 TRY

10 Are there any sports you hate _____ (play)? Why?

11 What kind of job do you want _____ (have) in five years' time?

12 REFUSE

16 Do you like _____ (go) to the same place on holiday every year?

15 DECIDE

14 What countries do you want _____ (visit) next year?

13 Do you mind other people _____ (smoke) next to you in public places?

17 When did you start _____ (learn) English? Talk about your first teacher.

18 What do you love _____ (do) on Friday evenings?

19 LOVE

20 What sports do you enjoy _____ (watch) but not _____ (do)?

24 HATE

23 When was the last time you agreed _____ (help) someone? What did you do?

22 Do you like _____ (go) out on a rainy day? Why / Why not?

21 Do you mind _____ (go) to the dentist? Why / Why not?

25 What do men waste time _____ (do) in your country? What about women?

26 ENJOY

27 Which shops do you avoid _____ (go) into? Why?

28 FINISH

4 Vocabulary

What's the difference?

A

✂

B

4 Communication

Ten facts

	always	usually	sometimes	hardly ever	never
1 I go to bed early. me					
my partner					
2 I do my homework. me					
my partner					
3 I drive to work. me					
my partner					
4 I read a daily newspaper. me					
my partner					
5 I'm tired at the end of the day. me					
my partner					
6 I eat three meals a day. me					
my partner					
7 I am late for work / school. me					
my partner					
8 I go to the gym. me					
my partner					
9 I have two holidays a year. me					
my partner					
10 I wear jeans at the weekend. me					
my partner					

5 Grammar

As fit as a fiddle

... burn more calories when they exercise than lighter people.	People in the UK are living longer ...	... but getting fatter.	More people join a gym in January ...
... than at any other time of year.	It's important to do thirty minutes of exercise ...	... three times a week.	I play tennis once or twice a week and it helps ...
... me relax and feel less stressed.	Walking is one of the ...	... best forms of exercise.	People should try to do different kinds of physical exercise so that ...
... keeping fit doesn't become boring.	If you're out of condition, don't start with ...	... a very intense physical routine.	Almost 40% of the population ...
... never takes any exercise.	Swimming is an excellent way of ...	... exercising all your muscles.	Activities such as dancing and skiing make our bones ...
... stronger.	He's not ...	... as healthy as he thinks he is.	Healthier living and exercise makes all of ...
... us look and feel better.	Doing sport from an early age ...	... helps establish good exercise habits for life.	I'm much fitter ...
... than I was last year.	Many people prefer to watch sport on TV than ...	... to take part in any physical activity.	Exercising gently every week is better than ...
... exercising very hard but only once a month.	You can start Yoga at any age ...	... and at any level of fitness.	Heavier people ...

New Inside Out Pre-intermediate Teacher's Book © Macmillan Publishers Limited 2008

5 Vocabulary

Sports crossword

A

Write the down clues:

1 *You do it on a track. You need special shoes.*

2 _____

3 _____

4 _____

5 _____

6 _____

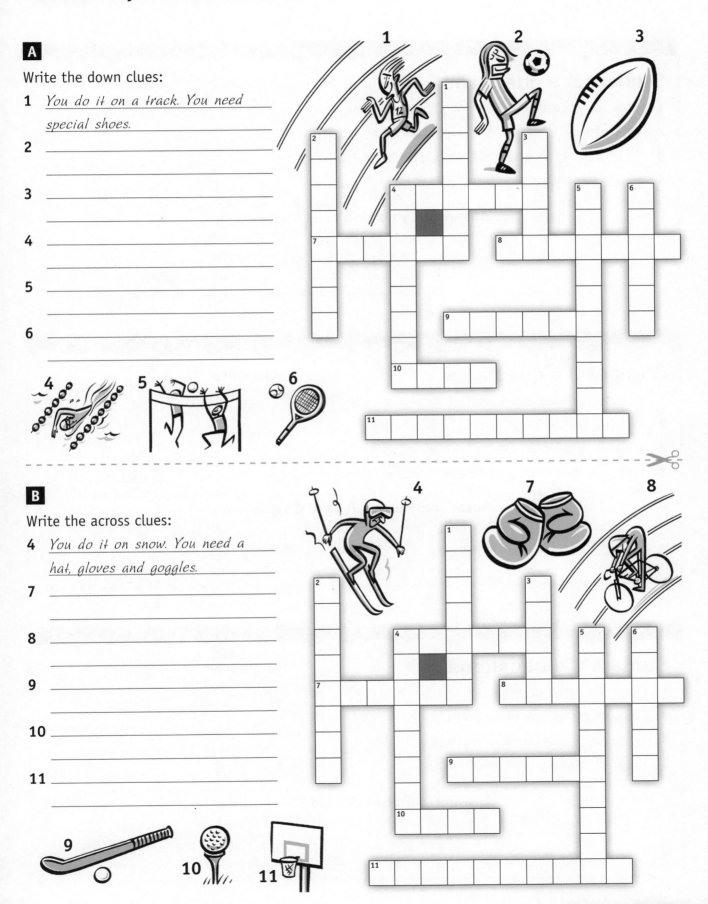

B

Write the across clues:

4 *You do it on snow. You need a hat, gloves and goggles.*

7 _____

8 _____

9 _____

10 _____

11 _____

5 Communication

Numbers, numbers, numbers

Student A's questions   Answers

1 How many bones are there in the human body?   _____

2 What was the biggest crowd ever at a football match?   _____

3 When did Levi Strauss make the first pair of jeans?   _____

4 How tall was the world's tallest human being?   _____

Answers to Student B's and C's questions

900 years ago   100,000 times a day   38 litres   58°C

1948   1,670 kph   250   12,756 km

✂

Student B's questions   Answers

1 How many babies are born per minute in the world?   _____

2 How much water is in the adult human body?   _____

3 When did the McDonald brothers open their first shop?   _____

4 What was the hottest temperature recorded on Earth?   _____

Answers to Student A's and C's questions

200,000   12,756 km   272 centimetres   206   1,670 kph

900 years ago   in the 1850s   100,000 times a day

✂

Student C's questions   Answers

1 How many times does the human heart beat?   _____

2 What is the diameter of the Earth?   _____

3 When did people first wear sunglasses?   _____

4 How fast does the Earth spin?   _____

Answers to Student A's and B's questions

1948   250   58°C   in the 1850s   38 litres

272 centimetres   200,000   206

 New Inside Out Pre-intermediate Teacher's Book © Macmillan Publishers Limited 2008

6 Grammar

Have you ever done it?

Have you ever ...	Name (only if the answer to the question is 'Yes')	Details Complete the questions and then find out the answers.	
		Question	**Answer**
won a prize?	_____	When _did you win it?_ ? _____ Where _did you win it?_ ? _____	
worked in another country?	_____	When _____ ? _____ Where _____ ? _____	
met anyone famous?	_____	When _____ ? _____ Where _____ ? _____	
eaten raw fish?	_____	When _____ ? _____ Where _____ ? _____	
climbed a mountain?	_____	When _____ ? _____ Where _____ ? _____	
been to New York?	_____	When _____ ? _____ Who _____ with? _____	
done a bungee jump?	_____	When _____ ? _____ Where _____ ? _____	
fallen asleep in the bath?	_____	When _____ ? _____ How long _____ for? _____	
driven a sports car?	_____	When _____ ? _____ Where _____ ? _____	
slept in a tent?	_____	When _____ ? _____ Where _____ ? _____	

6 Vocabulary

In an ideal world

A good friend ...

	Very important	Quite important	I'm not sure	Not very important	Not at all important
should be trustworthy					
should live near me					
should be a good listener					
should have the same interests as me					

My ideal job ...

	Very important	Quite important	I'm not sure	Not very important	Not at all important
should be well-paid					
shouldn't be stressful					
should be useful to society					
should have lots of holidays					

My life partner ...

	Very important	Quite important	I'm not sure	Not very important	Not at all important
shouldn't smoke					
should be good-looking					
should have a good job					
should have the same interests as me					

 New Inside Out Pre-intermediate Teacher's Book © Macmillan Publishers Limited 2008

6 Communication

What's my job?

IIIIIIIIIIIIIIIIIIIIIIIIIIIIIIIIIIIIIIIIIIIIIIIIIIIIIIII

Ask questions to find out about your job and write down the answers. Answer questions about other people's jobs, using the key on the right for your answers. Change partners after every couple of questions.

IIIIIIIIIIIIIIIIIIIIIIIIIIIIIIIIIIIIIIIIIIIIIIIIIIIIIIII

▶**Answers**

Yes, all the time
Usually
Very often
Quite often
Sometimes
Not very often
Hardly ever
No, never

▶Questions

1	Do I wear special clothes for my job?	
2	Do I work outdoors?	
3	Do I work with the public?	
4	Do I work at weekends?	
5	Do I have to travel to do my job?	
6	Do I earn much?	
7	Do people admire me?	
8	Do I work with my hands?	
9	Is my job sometimes dangerous?	
10	Do I receive tips?	
11	Is my job creative?	
12	Do I work with animals?	
13	Do I work in a laboratory?	
14	Do I work in a building? Is it an office?	
15	Do I have to be fit for my job?	
16	Do I need a university degree for my job?	
17	Do I have to be good with numbers?	

Think of three questions of your own and add them to the list:

18		
19		
20		

Review B

Suspicious minds

Elvis Presley was one of the most important recording artists of all time. His version of this song was a huge success.

1 **Read the title of the song. Underline the correct alternative.**

A person with a suspicious mind **believes / doesn't believe** what you tell them.

2 🔘 **2.20** **Listen and decide which picture (*A* or *B*) goes with the song.**

1
We're caught in a trap
I can't walk out
Because I love you too much, baby.

2
Why can't you see
What you're doing to me
When you don't believe a word I say?

> *Chorus*
> We can't go on together
> With suspicious minds.
> And we can't build our dreams
> On suspicious minds.

3
So, if an old friend I know
Drops by to say hello,
Would I still see suspicion in your eyes?

4
Here we go again,
Asking where I've been.
You can't see these tears are real I'm crying.

5
Oh, let our love survive,
Or dry the tears from your eyes.
Let's not let a good thing die.
When, honey, you know
I've never lied to you.
Mmm, yeah, yeah.

3 **Read the song again and underline the correct alternative.**

a) The singer **wants / doesn't want** to leave.
b) The singer is **happy / unhappy** with the relationship.
c) The singer **thinks / doesn't think** his/her lover is jealous of his/her friends.
d) The singer **lies / never lies**.

4 **Replace the underlined words with words and expressions from the song.**

a) I don't want to <u>leave</u>. (verse 1)
b) I don't believe <u>anything</u> you say. (verse 2)
c) We can't <u>continue</u> together with suspicious minds. (chorus)
d) Why did your friend <u>come to your house</u> to say hello? (verse 3)
e) Please <u>stop crying</u> and believe me. (verse 5)

Who said these things, the singer or his/her suspicious lover?

5 **Work with a partner. Describe a time in your life when you had a 'suspicious mind'.**

 New Inside Out **Pre-intermediate Teacher's Book** © Macmillan Publishers Limited 2008

7 Grammar

Thirty-second futures

START →

⭐

1 Your next holiday

2 Your best friend's ambitions

3 What you're doing this weekend

FINISH!

4 A happy event in the future

15 Any plans you have to improve your health

5 Your next big purchase

Speak for 30 seconds about...

14 The next clothes you plan to buy

6 Your career plans

13 The next time you're meeting up with anybody from your family

7 Your next important appointment

12 What you are doing after this class

8 Your next meal

11 Something in the future that worries you

10 Your next planned sporting or physical activity

9 Your next journey

7 Vocabulary

How green are you?

1 Do you separate your household waste for recycling?

a) Always

b) Sometimes

c) Never

2 When you're not using it, do you leave your TV or computer on standby?

a) Always

b) Sometimes

c) Never

3 Do you use environmentally-friendly cleaning products in your house?

a) Always

b) Sometimes

c) Never

4 Do you ever leave lights on after you leave a room in your house?

a) Always

b) Sometimes

c) Never

5 Do you try to buy locally produced fruit and vegetables?

a) Always

b) Sometimes

c) Never

6 How much do you cycle or walk compared to driving?

a) A lot

b) I cycle or walk when I can

c) I drive everywhere

7 Do you have low energy lightbulbs in your house?

a) Yes, in every room

b) Yes, in some rooms

c) What's a low energy lightbulb?

8 How many times in a year do you fly?

a) Once or less

b) More than once, less than five times

c) More than five times

9 How many cars do you own?

a) None

b) 1–2

c) More than two

10 Which of the following is true for you?

a) I usually take a bath

b) I usually take a shower

c) I don't usually take a bath or a shower

Commentary

Light green (Between 0 and 10) You just aren't trying. You need to think more about the planet and less about yourself. With some small changes in lifestyle you could be greener and the world could be cleaner!

Green (Between 11 and 28) Well done. You're doing what you can to make a difference. With a bit more effort you could save yourself money and make the planet a better place to live.

Bright green (Between 29 and 40) Fantastic! You're an eco-hero – a perfect example of a world citizen. If everyone was like you, the world would be a safer and healthier place.

 New Inside Out Pre-intermediate Teacher's Book © Macmillan Publishers Limited 2008

MANIFESTO

THE _____ GROUP

Party leader:
_____

FOR

We believe in _____ .

We feel very strongly about _____

_____ because

_____ .

We support _____

because _____ .

AGAINST

We are anti- _____ .

We are strongly against _____

because _____ .

We are not in favour of _____ .

OUR PROPOSALS

We want to ban _____ .

We hope to encourage more _____ .

We want to introduce new laws to _____ .

We promise to _____ .

Please support us!

8 Grammar

Schooldays

1   Make questions for each statement.

	A *Me*	B _____	C _____

1   We had to wear a school uniform.
    Did you have to wear a school uniform?

2   We had to go to school on Saturdays.

3   We couldn't run in the school buildings.

4   We had to switch off our mobiles before class.

5   We had to start classes at 8.30 a.m.

6   We had to do homework every day.

7   We couldn't eat in the classrooms.

8   As a punishment we had to stay an extra hour.

9   We couldn't bring radios to school.

10 We had to give our homework in on time.

11 We couldn't smoke.

12 We had to call our teachers 'Sir' and 'Miss'.

2   Work in groups of three. Ask each other the questions you have written and write the answers in the columns.

3   Report your findings to the class.

   New Inside Out Pre-intermediate Teacher's Book © Macmillan Publishers Limited 2008

8 Vocabulary

Education wordsearch

Find the words →, ↘, ↓ and write them in the correct column below.

I	X	Y	N	T	D	M	E	K	A	P	A	S	O	F	L	M
O	S	–	G	B	G	E	N	P	D	T	R	Y	R	O	G	Z
A	B	J	R	U	G	D	G	M	Z	–	X	I	X	N	–	P
E	L	U	Z	S	H	I	I	R	D	Q	U	V	M	A	G	I
B	A	A	Y	I	M	C	N	H	E	U	P	A	Y	A	R	J
A	N	I	W	N	G	I	E	S	A	E	X	V	O	T	R	C
P	G	X	M	E	T	N	E	E	D	H	I	S	T	O	R	Y
S	U	I	X	S	L	E	R	C	S	I	F	G	S	U	G	J
Z	A	X	T	S	D	S	I	R	E	B	P	G	K	R	O	U
V	G	W	–	E	R	N	N	E	C	V	S	L	E	I	R	N
X	E	C	U	U	A	O	G	T	O	W	–	T	O	S	A	I
G	S	H	Z	O	G	I	V	A	N	W	M	M	Y	M	D	O
B	X	H	Z	E	N	A	L	R	D	R	O	J	U	B	A	R
A	–	L	E	V	E	L	S	I	A	L	B	H	K	N	R	H
W	K	I	N	D	E	R	G	A	R	T	E	N	O	Q	Y	I
Q	M	G	M	B	D	S	N	L	Y	G	K	J	L	A	X	G
C	E	R	T	I	F	I	C	A	T	E	B	E	V	O	L	H

Types of school	Vocational subjects (college/university)	Qualifications	Classic subjects (university)
Primary	*Secretarial*	*Certificate*	*Law*

8 Communication

What's your advice?

Dear Maria

Last week I met someone really nice and we got on really well together. There's just one problem.

_____

_____

_____

_____

What should I do?

✂ -

Dear Maria

I have just left school and now I have to make an important decision.

_____

_____

_____

_____

_____

What should I do?

✂ -

Dear Maria

My partner and I are very much in love, but last night I heard something from a friend and now everything has changed.

_____

_____

_____

_____

_____

What should I do?

 New Inside Out Pre-intermediate Teacher's Book © Macmillan Publishers Limited 2008

9 Grammar

For and *since*

Do you ...	Name (only if the answer to the question is **'Yes'**)	How long have you ... Complete both answers.
live?	_____	for _____ since _____
wear?	_____	for _____ since _____
play?	_____	for _____ since _____
have?	_____	for _____ since _____
play?	_____	for _____ since _____
ride?	_____	for _____ since _____
have?	_____	for _____ since _____
study?	_____	for _____ since _____

9 Vocabulary

Character crossword

Someone who ...

Across

1 ... is ready to support their friends, even in difficult times. (5)

3 ... thinks only about themselves and doesn't care about others. (7)

6 ... is relaxed and doesn't get easily upset. (9)

7 ... (the same meaning as *6 across*) (4)

8 ... (the same meaning as *1 across*) (8)

10 ... keeps telling everyone what to do in a way that annoys them. (5)

11 ... cares about people and doesn't want to offend them. (9)

12 ... is hopeful about the future. (10)

13 ... is determined to be rich, successful or famous. (9)

14 ... keeps secrets or is difficult to work out. (10)

15 ... shows that they love or care about someone or something. (12)

Down

2 ... makes you feel slightly angry or impatient. (8)

3 ... is nervous in the company of others, especially people they don't know. (3)

4 ... (the opposite of *3 down*) (8)

5 ... believes in their own abilities. (9)

9 ... (the opposite of *12 across*) (11)

New Inside Out Pre-intermediate Teacher's Book © Macmillan Publishers Limited 2008

9 Communication

Smile!

1 START	2 I need **to speak/speaking** English for my job.	3 She's got long, wavy **hair/hairs**.	4 He's always telling us what to do – he's very **bossy/shy**.	5 SMILE! Move to Box 7

10 She's got fair **hair/eyes**.	9 OOPS! Miss the next go	8 He grew a **moustache/beard** to cover the scar on his chin.	7 He's got **freckles/dimples** all over his face.	6 I can **swim/to swim** faster than you.

11 I enjoy **watching/ to watch** sport on TV.	12 He's got pale **skin/hair**.	13 SMILE! Move to Box 15	14 What does he **look like/look**?	15 I want **being/to be** rich.

20 I think I'm going to **give up/ hang up** smoking.	19 She's got the most perfect **tooth/teeth**.	18 I **put on/take off** my shoes before I leave the house.	17 OOPS! Miss the next go	16 She's wearing false **eyelashes/ eyebrows**!

21 SMILE! Move to Box 23	22 He looks tired – he's got bags under his **ears/eyes**.	23 I'm looking forward to **meet/meeting** her.	24 She's got a beautiful **hair/smile**.	25 OOPS! Miss the next go

30 SMILE! You're a winner!	29 I've decided **getting/to get** my hair cut.	28 When she smiles small **wrists/ wrinkles** appear next to her eyes.	27 What is she **like/look like**?	26 She feels things very strongly – she's **sensitive/ sensible**.

Review C

Money

The Beatles (1960–70) were the most successful band of all time. They sold over one billion records. Their cover version of *Money* was one of their earliest songs.

1 **Work with a partner. Look at the lines of the song, *Money*. Choose the most appropriate alternative to complete the first two lines of each verse.**
(Note: *it don't = it doesn't*)

The best things in life are
(1) **expensive / free / dangerous**.
But you can keep them for the birds
and (2) **bees / flies / ants**.
Now give me money.
That's what I want.
That's what I want, yeah.
That's what I want.

Your lovin' gives me
a (3) **thrill / headache / lift**.
But your lovin' don't pay
my (4) **rent / bills / taxes**.
Now give me money.
That's what I want.
That's what I want, yeah.
That's what I want.

Money don't get everything,
it's (5) **true / interesting / funny**.
What it don't get, I can't
(6) **believe / use / understand**.
Now give me money.
That's what I want.
That's what I want, yeah.
That's what I want, wah.

Now give me money.
Whole lot of money.
Yeah, I want to be free.
Whole lot of money.
That's what I want.
That's what I want, yeah.

🔊 3.12 **Listen to the song and check your answers.**

2 **Which sentence best describes the singer's attitude to money?**

a) Money can buy love.
b) Love is more important than money.
c) Money is the most important thing in life.

3 **Match the following sayings (*a–c*) to their meanings (*1–3*).**

a) 'Money talks.'
b) 'Money doesn't grow on trees.'
c) 'Time is money.'

1 It isn't easy to earn money, so don't spend it carelessly.
2 If you waste time you waste money as well.
3 You can get what you want if you have enough money.

How many 'money' sayings can you think of in your language?
Which sayings do you like best?

10 Grammar

Then or now?

Think about life 100 years ago. Was it better or worse than it is now?

Look at the statements 1–12 below and decide if you agree with them. Tick (✓) the appropriate box to show how you feel. When you have finished, talk to your partner and compare your answers. Try to give reasons for your choices.

One hundred years ago ...	I agree	I'm not sure	I disagree
1 Children used to be happier.			
2 People used to wear better quality clothes.			
3 People used to be fitter.			
4 Family life used to be better.			
5 People used to have more interesting hobbies.			
6 People used to have a better quality of life.			
7 People used to feel safer.			
Nowadays ...			
8 People work harder than they used to.			
9 It is more difficult to get around than it used to be.			
10 People have a worse diet than they used to.			
11 Women have worse lives than they used to.			
12 People are less intelligent than they used to be.			

10 Vocabulary

Features of a car

seats	windscreen	wipers	gear
stick	hand	brake	head
light	number	plate	seat
belt	sun	roof	steering
wheel	air	conditioning	economical
to run	environmentally	friendly	good sound
system	satellite	navigation system	powerful
engine	spacious	boot	leather

10 Communication

Food

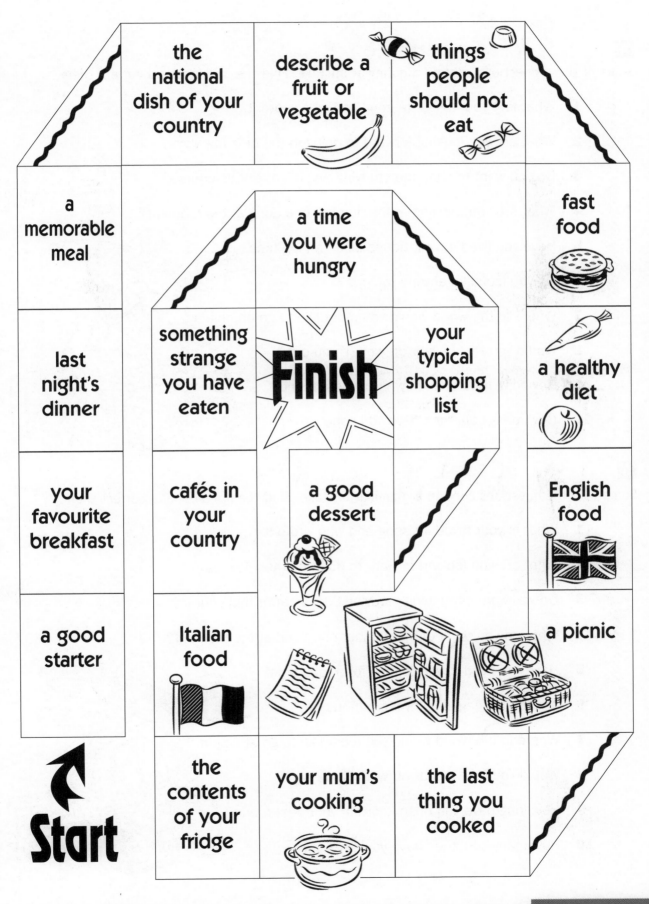

the national dish of your country

describe a fruit or vegetable

things people should not eat

a memorable meal

a time you were hungry

fast food

last night's dinner

something strange you have eaten

Finish

your typical shopping list

a healthy diet

your favourite breakfast

cafés in your country

a good dessert

English food

a good starter

Italian food

a picnic

Start

the contents of your fridge

your mum's cooking

the last thing you cooked

11 Grammar

Find the mistake

A

Some of these questions contain a grammar mistake. Find the mistakes and correct them.

1   What is it your favourite song and who wrote it?

2   What are you looking forward to doing in the next few days?

3   Do you want to continue studying English after this course?

4   What are you thinking of the number one song at the moment?

5   Have you lived in your house since a long time?

6   Do you look like anyone famous?

7   Where in the world would you most like to go on holiday?

8   Would you take a year off work if you can?

9   How long have you known your best friend?

10 How many countries have you gone to?

B

Some of these questions contain a grammar mistake. Find the mistakes and correct them.

1   What is your favourite song and who wrote it?

2   What are you looking forward to do in the next few days?

3   Do you want continuing studying English after this course?

4   What do you think of the number one song at the moment?

5   Have you lived in your house for a long time?

6   Are you looking like anyone famous?

7   Where in the world would you most like to go at holiday?

8   Would you take a year off work if you could?

9   How long have you been knowing your best friend?

10 How many countries have you been to?

   New Inside Out Pre-intermediate Teacher's Book © Macmillan Publishers Limited 2008

11 Vocabulary

Find someone

Find someone who is …	Name

1 keen _____ football. _____

2 afraid _____ the dark. _____

3 from a city that's famous _____ a particular dish or type of food. _____

4 fond _____ chocolate. _____

5 worried _____ something that's happening this week. _____

6 proud _____ his/her country. _____

7 allergic _____ cats. _____

8 interested _____ classical music. _____

9 terrified _____ spiders. _____

10 usually late _____ work/school. _____

11 bad _____ maths. _____

12 excited _____ something that's going to happen in the near future. _____

11 Communication

Homophones

 New Inside Out Pre-intermediate Teacher's Book © Macmillan Publishers Limited 2008

12 Grammar

What happened?

1 Complete the text with the correct form of the verb in brackets.

One day, an American businessman named George D Bryson (1) _____ (travel) from
St Louis to New York when he (2) _____ (decide) to stop and spend the night in a
town called Louisville. He (3) _____ (never visit) the town before. At the station he
(4) _____ (ask) where he could spend the night and was directed to the Brown Hotel.
Here, he (5) _____ (check) into Room 307 and, for no good reason, asked if there were any
messages for him. The receptionist (6) _____ (give) him a letter addressed to Mr George D
Bryson, room 307. Of course, this wasn't possible because nobody (7) _____ (know) that
Bryson (8) _____ (decide) to spend the night in Louisville at the Brown Hotel.
The explanation? The man who (9) _____ (spend) the night before in room 307 was a
different George D Bryson! This one was a businessman who (10) _____ (work) in Canada.

2 Put these events into the correct order.

A At Louisville station George D
Bryson asked for the name of a good
hotel.

B The receptionist gave Bryson a
letter addressed to George D Bryson.

C George D Bryson asked if there
were any messages for him.

D George D Bryson decided to stay
overnight in Louisville.

E George D Bryson, a businessman
who worked in Canada, checked into
the Brown Hotel.

F George D Bryson, an American
businessman, checked into the
Brown Hotel.

12 Vocabulary

Shout it out!

Kinds of music
classical
country and western
dance
heavy metal
jazz
opera
pop
reggae
rock
R'n'B

Shops
bookshop
butcher
chemist
clothes shop
hairdresser
music/CD shop
newsagent
sports shop
supermarket
toy shop

Items of clothing
dress
gloves
hat
shirt
skirt
socks
tie
trousers
T-shirt
underwear

Big countries
Argentina
Australia
Brazil
Canada
China
India
Kazakhstan
Russia
Sudan
United States

Jobs
actor
dentist
doctor
hairdresser
lawyer
police officer
shop assistant
soldier
teacher
vet

Currencies
Euro
Dollar
Franc
Peso
Pound
Riyal
Rouble
Rupee
Yen
Zloty

Animals in a zoo
bear
camel
crocodile
elephant
giraffe
lion
rhinoceros
snake
tiger
zebra

Makes of car
BMW
Cadillac
Fiat
Ford
Mercedes
Nissan
Renault
Toyota
Volkswagen
Volvo

The ten commonest words in English
a
and
in
is
of
it
that
the
to
was

Languages
Arabic
English
French
German
Hindi
Japanese
Latin
Portuguese
Russian
Spanish

Sports
athletics
baseball
basketball
football
golf
motor racing
swimming
skiing
table tennis
tennis

School subjects
Art
Biology
Chemistry
Economics
Foreign language
Geography
History
Maths
Music
Physical education

Character adjectives
ambitious
boring
bossy
confident
friendly
honest
lazy
optimistic
sociable
shy

Vegetables
aubergine
bean
carrot
cauliflower
mushroom
onion
pea
pepper
potato
spinach

Parts of the body
arm
chin
eye
head
knee
leg
nose
shoulder
stomach
wrist

European football teams
Barcelona
Bayern Munich
Celtic
Inter Milan
Juventus
Liverpool
Manchester United
Paris Saint German
PSV Eindhoven
Real Madrid

New Inside Out Pre-intermediate Teacher's Book © Macmillan Publishers Limited 2008

12 Communication

Let's talk about ...

START

1 ... somebody with an unusual name

2 ... your favourite city

3 ... a romantic film

4 ... how you keep fit

5 ... an interesting character in a film

6 ... the best present you've ever received

7 ... the last present you bought someone

8 ... the best or worst job you can imagine

9 ... a retired person you know

10 ... the qualities of your ideal partner

11 ... your favourite subject at school

12 ... things that make you happy or unhappy

13 ... how you relax

14 ... something you feel strongly about

15 ... the last time you went out and had a good time

16 ... a foreign person you know

17 ... the person you speak to most on the phone

18 ... the most helpful person you know

19 ... the healthiest person you know

20 ... a pet you know

21 ... a strange experience

22 ... your dream car

23 ... three good reasons for learning English

FINISH

Review D

I Have a Dream

From Sweden, Abba were the most popular pop band in the world in the late 1970s and early 1980s. *I Have A Dream* was one of their biggest hits.

1 **Read the words of the song. On each of the lines there is an extra word. Find the word and cross it out.**

I have a dream

1 I have a dream, a song to ~~be~~ sing,
2 To help me cope with the anything.
3 If you see the no wonder of a fairy tale
4 You can to take the future even if you fail.
5 I am believe in angels,
6 Something good for in everything I see.
7 I am believe in angels,
8 When I know the free time is right for me.
9 I'll go cross the stream – I have a dream.

10 I have a dream, a one fantasy
11 To do help me through reality.
12 And my destination does makes it worth the while,
13 Pushing through the darkness still another a mile.
14 I am believe in angels,
15 Something good for in everything I see.
16 I am believe in angels,
17 When I know the free time is right for me.
18 I'll go cross the stream – I have a dream.
19 I'll go cross the stream – I have a dream.

 **3.38** **Listen and check your answers.**

2 **Choose the most appropriate word to complete the statements below about the song. Compare your ideas with your partner.**

a) It's a **positive / sad / romantic** song.
b) I think the song is **great / OK / not bad**.
c) I **often / sometimes / hardly ever** listen to songs like this.

3 **Complete these sentences with words from the song.**

a) I had a bad d _____ last night. (line 1)
b) I have a particular song that I s _____ when I'm happy. (line 1)
c) I have to c _____ with a lot of problems in my job. (line 2)
d) When I was a child, I had a favourite fairy t _____ . (line 3)
e) I b _____ in miracles. (line 5)
f) I can see s _____ good in everyone. (line 6)

Which sentences are true for you? Compare with a partner.

Extreme sports

WORKSHEET **A**

James

I've been really into surfing for more than fifteen years. I started learning in England, then I began going on surfing holidays abroad with my mates – we went to Bali in Indonesia, and also South Africa.

After that I started wanting bigger challenges, so five years ago I decided to try the really big waves in Hawaii. Of course they can be dangerous and you have to concentrate one hundred percent, but it's worth it for the thrill you get when you're riding them. It's a magical feeling, like flying above the ocean, and for those few seconds you totally forget everything else in your life.

Susan

Part of me had always wanted to try skydiving, but I was really scared the first time. The worst bit was just before I jumped out of the plane – I wanted to be back on the ground, not 4,000 metres up in the air. Of course, as a beginner you don't do it on your own – you're attached to the instructor who opens the parachute for you. Falling through the air at 180 kilometres per hour is a massive adrenaline rush. That first time was five years ago, and since then I've done more than twenty solo jumps.

Mike

Mountains offer a challenge I find impossible to ignore. I started climbing about twenty years ago, and I've now climbed three of the highest five peaks in Europe. Of course it can be dangerous, and I've had some scary moments, but the sense of achievement when you reach the top is amazing. When you're pulling yourself up that wall of rock it feels like you're in a battle against nature – it's not a feeling you can get from anything in everyday life.

Teresa

I became hooked on snowboarding the very first time I tried it. I soon realized I had a natural talent for it, and it wasn't long before I was winning competitions and getting a bit of prize money. My dream is to be able to make my living just from boarding, so I now take three months off work every winter and concentrate on improving my technique.

I'd recommend boarding to anyone. The exhilaration of going down the mountain, plus the beauty of the scenery – it's just fantastic.

Extreme sports

A

Answer the questions.

1. How long has Mike been climbing mountains?

2. Why did James decide to go surfing in Hawaii?

3. How has Teresa already earned money from snowboarding?

4. Who opened the parachute during Susan's first skydive?

Now decide whether the following statements are true (T), false (F), or if the text doesn't say (D).

5. Teresa doesn't have a job.

6. Susan has done more than ten skydives without an instructor.

7. Mike has climbed more than twenty mountains in Europe.

8. Teresa gives snowboarding lessons.

9. Mike has climbed the highest mountain in Europe.

10. James surfed in Bali before he went to Hawaii.

11. Susan has always felt relaxed before jumping out of the plane.

12. James doesn't think about anything else when he's riding big waves in Hawaii.

13. Mike has sometimes been frightened while mountain climbing.

14. Teresa is trying to get even better at snowboarding.

15. Susan did about ten skydives with an instructor.

Now can you find the words in the text that mean *the opposite* of the following?

16. tiny   17. ugliness   18. failure   19. in your own country   20. learner

Extreme sports

B

Decide whether or not the following statements have been written in correct English. Then bet a minimum of 10 points up to a maximum of 50 on your choice.

		Yes/No	Points bet	Points lost	Points won
1	For the last five years I've been really into snowboarding.				
2	The adrenaline rush you get from surfing is amazing.				
3	Climbing a mountain gives you a fantastic sense of achieve.				
4	My mates love snowboarding, but I've never really enjoyed it.				
5	I could never go skydiving – I'd be too scary.				
6	Have you ever tried surf?				
7	When you're climbing a mountain you have to concentrate one hundred percent on what you're doing.				
8	Surfing can be dangerous, but when you're riding the wave it's a magical feeling.				
9	I know someone who has climbed the highest three peaks in Europe.				
10	My dream is to be able to make my life from surf.				
11	My brother is a skydiving instructor.				
12	He has a natural talent for snowboarding.				
	Total points lost and won				
	Final total (subtract total points lost from total points won)				

Extreme Sports – Glossary

adrenaline noun [uncount]
a chemical produced by your adrenal glands that makes your heart beat faster and gives you more energy when you are frightened, excited, or angry

attached adjective
joined or fixed to something
To take advantage of this offer please complete the attached forms.

battle noun [count]
a situation in which different people or groups compete with each other in order to achieve something or get an advantage
a boardroom battle

challenge noun [count/uncount]
something that needs a lot of skill, energy, and determination to deal with or achieve
I was bored with my job and felt I needed a new challenge.

concentrate verb
to give all your attention to the thing you are doing
Stop talking and concentrate on your work.

exhilaration noun [uncount]
the feeling of being extremely happy, excited, and full of energy

hooked adjective
if you are hooked on something, you find it so attractive or interesting that you want to do it as much as possible

ignore verb
to not consider something, or to not let it influence you
We had ignored the fact that it was getting darker.

into preposition
interested in a subject or activity
Suddenly she's into yoga and things like that.

living noun [singular]
money that you earn to live on
She makes a living as a music teacher.

magical adjective
full of a mysterious quality that is enjoyable or attractive
It was a truly magical evening.

mate noun [count]
a friend
He's over there, talking to his mates.

parachute noun [count]
a large piece of cloth joined to heavy strings, used by someone jumping out of a plane

peak noun [count]
the top of a mountain
snow-covered peaks

prize noun [count]
a reward that you get for being successful in a sport, competition, or game

rock noun [count]
a large piece of stone that rises up from the ground
the Rock of Gibraltar

scared adjective
frightened, or worried

scenery noun [uncount]
natural things such as trees, hills, and lakes that you can see in a particular place
Switzerland has some spectacular scenery.

skydiving noun [uncount]
the sport of jumping out of a plane and falling for as long as possible before opening your parachute

snowboarding noun [uncount]
the activity or sport of riding a snowboard

solo adjective
done by one person alone, without any help
his first solo flight

surfing noun [uncount]
a sport in which people ride over waves on surfboards

talent noun [count/uncount]
a natural ability for being good at a particular activity
She had an obvious talent for music.

thrill noun [count]
a sudden feeling of being very excited and pleased
the thrill of visiting a new city

wave noun [count]
a line of water that rises up on the surface of a sea, lake, or river

worth adjective
used for saying that there is a good enough reason for doing something, because it is important, enjoyable, useful etc
The book is definitely worth reading.

e-lesson   Week starting: 26th November 2007

1. Extreme sports
The subject of this week's lesson is extreme sports. One of the greatest ever feats in surfing was achieved by the American 'big wave' pioneer Greg Noll, who rode what is considered to be the largest wave ever paddled into, in Hawaii on 4th December 1969.

Level
Pre-intermediate and above (equivalent to CEF level A2-B1 and above)

How to use the lesson
1. Brainstorm on the subject of extreme sports, asking students what they understand by the term, and what examples they can think of. What do they think motivates practitioners of extreme sports? Are there any they would like to try?

2. Hand out Worksheet A and give students five to ten minutes to read through the text, encouraging them to look up new vocabulary.

3. When the time is up, divide students into pairs and hand out copies of Worksheet B, in which they have to answer two different types of comprehension question and then find antonyms.

4. Check answers in open class.

5. Keeping the students in their pairs, hand out Worksheet C in which students have to read a list of statements and decide whether or not they have been written in correct English. (The only errors the statements might contain are grammatical or lexical. Note also that a couple of the correct sentences contain examples of informal English.) In the first column, after the statement, they should write Y for Yes if they think the English is entirely satisfactory, or N for No if they think the statement contains one or more mistakes. In the second column they have to write the number of points they are willing to 'bet' on their answer (10 points if they are forced to guess, going up to 50 if they are very confident). As the sentences include vocabulary and grammatical structures from the main text, try to ensure that students attempt it without referring back to Worksheet A.

6. After the pairs have given their answers, it's time to score. Each pair calls out their answer and how many points they have bet. If they have answered correctly, students enter their points in the final column (points won). If they have answered incorrectly they should enter their points in the third column (points lost). In each of the cases where a statement contains a mistake, ask one of the students who answered correctly to explain why the statement is incorrect, and what the necessary corrections would be. At the end, students subtract the total of the third column from the total of the fourth column to give the total number of points they have won. The pair with the most points wins.

Answers

Part A

1. For about twenty years.
2. Because he started wanting bigger challenges.
3. She has received prize money by winning competitions.
4. Her instructor.

5. F   6. T   7. D   8. D   9. D   10. T   11. F   12. T   13. T   14. T   15. D

16. massive
17. beauty
18. achievement
19. abroad
20. instructor

Part B

1. **Yes**
2. **Yes**
3. **No**. Climbing a mountain gives you a fantastic sense of ~~achieve~~ **achievement**.
4. **Yes**
5. **No**. I could never go skydiving – I'd be too ~~scary~~ **scared**.
6. **No.** Have you ever tried ~~surf~~ **surfing**?
7. **Yes**
8. **Yes**
9. **Yes**
10. **No.** My dream is to be able to make my ~~life~~ **living** from ~~surf~~ **surfing**.
11. **Yes**
12. **Yes**

2. Related Websites
Send your students to these websites, or just take a look yourself.

http://news.bbc.co.uk/cbbcnews/hi/newsid_4670000/newsid_4677500/4677520.stm
A short text from BBC *Newsround* in which a British thirteen-year-old explains why she enjoys surfing. Accessible to pre-intermediate level.

http://news.bbc.co.uk/cbbcnews/hi/newsid_6230000/newsid_6234300/6234373.stm
A short text on snowboarding, again from BBC *Newsround*, with links to two other texts. Accessible to pre-intermediate level.

http://www.trymysport.co.uk/extreme_sports_courses_experiences/extreme_sports_experiences.htm#surfing
A commercial site offering brief descriptions of various extreme sports. Challenging for pre-intermediate level.